Explorations with Families

'The institution of the family stands in a peculiarly central, crucial position. It faces inward to the individual, outward toward society, preparing each member to take his place in the wider social group by helping him to internalise its values and traditions as part of himself. From the first cry at birth to the last words at death, the family surrounds us and finds a place for all ages, roles and relationships for both sexes. . . . It has enormous creative potential including that of life itself, and it is not surprising that, when it becomes disordered, it possesses an equal potential for terrible destruction.'

Robin Skynner, *One Flesh, Separate Persons*

Dr Robin Skynner is a pioneer whose challenging methods and ideas have helped to bring group analysis and family therapy to maturity over the last twenty-five years. From his early observations of rapid and startling changes in families interviewed together, a comprehensive theory emerges that brings together current knowledge about individual, group and family therapy to integrate the formerly divided systemic, psychoanalytic and behavioural approaches. *Explorations with Families: Group Analysis and Family Therapy* contains his selected clinical papers and lectures. They stand together alongside his two previous books as a major contribution towards a unified psychotherapy. Edited, abridged and supplemented with current material, these papers are together an original body of work that provides a new landmark for theory and practice.

As the popular success of *Families and How to Survive Them*, written with John Cleese, confirms, his writing is easily accessible to the interested general reader. It has a simplicity and ease of expression that allows the study of change to engage with the reader's own capacities for change. Amongst a professional readership it will be relevant to psychotherapists of all orientations; psychiatrists, general practitioners and other clinicians; social workers, teachers and those who work with children, families, couples and groups; and those with a theoretical interest in social relations and the family.

Explorations
with Families
Group Analysis
and Family Therapy

ROBIN SKYNNER

Edited by John R. Schlapobersky

TAVISTOCK/ROUTLEDGE
London and New York

First published in 1987
by Methuen

Reprinted in paperback in 1990
by Routledge
11 New Fetter Lane, London EC4P 4EE

Simultaneously published in the USA and Canada
by Routledge
a division of Routledge, Chapman and Hall, Inc.
29 West 35th Street, New York, NY 10001

© this collection, 1987 Robin Skynner; editor's introduction and notes, 1987
John R. Schlapobersky
Printed and bound in Great Britain by Mackays of Chatham PLC, Kent

British Library Cataloguing in Publication Data
Skynner, Robin
    Explorations with families: group analysis and family therapy.
    1. Families. Psychiatry
    I. Title   II. Schlapobersky, John R.
    616.89

Library of Congress Cataloging in Publication Data
Skynner, A. C. Robin.
    Explorations with families : group analysis and family therapy/
    Robin Skynner; edited by John R. Schlapobersky.
    p. cm.
    "First published in Great Britain 1987 by Methuen London Ltd" –
    –T.p. verso.
    Includes bibliographical references.
    1. Group psychotherapy. 2. Family psychotherapy.
    I. Schlapobersky, John R.   II. Title.
    RC488.S56   1990   89–49675
    616.89'15—dc20   CIP

ISBN 0-415-04912-1

Contents

116233

Figures

'If one really wishes to be master of an art, technical knowledge of it is not enough. One has to transcend technique so that the art becomes an "artless art" growing out of the Unconscious.

In the case of archery, the hitter and the hit are no longer two opposing objects, but are one reality. The archer ceases to be conscious of himself as the one who is engaged in hitting the bull's-eye which confronts him. This state of unconsciousness is realized only when, completely empty and rid of the self, he becomes one with the perfecting of his technical skill, though there is in it something of a quite different order which cannot be attained by any progressive study of the art.'

D. T. Suzuki, from the foreword to Eugen Herrigel's *Zen and the Art of Archery*

Preface

The papers selected and edited for this collection have been published before and due acknowledgements are made on page xxxvi. Where necessary they have been abridged by the editor to avoid duplication, and the author has re-drafted certain passages in the interests of clarity but without substantive changes.

The author has written an introduction to the book and furnished the editor with historical material and a fresh appraisal of his papers, from which a series of brief introductions has been written to each of the fourteen chapters in the book. These set the context in which the papers were originally published and explain the author's purposes in writing each of them.

The editor's introduction outlines the scope of Skynner's work, the structure of the book, gives a brief step-by-step guide to his practice and ideas, and a brief professional biography. Each of the papers is concluded with footnotes, and the book is concluded with an appendix giving the author's published work in historical sequence; a comprehensive bibliography; and a subject and author index.

J. R. S.

To all my companions on
the journey – patients,
colleagues, family, friends.

Author's Introduction

My work and indeed my whole life have been an exploration, a search for understanding beyond the established frontiers of knowledge, with all the sense of adventure and excitement, and at the same time of uncertainty and fear of wandering too far from known paths, that this word implies. And though the professional nature of the writings that follow is indicated by the subtitle, so as not to mislead those of the public who enjoyed the popular book I co-authored with John Cleese, *Explorations With Families* seemed the most appropriate title to describe my approach to therapy because it conveys best its essential simplicity and directness, its stance of involvement and of sharing in the common human condition, as well as its expectation that both therapist and family will learn from each other. If these features of the work are in some measure reflected in the simplicity and clarity I have sought in the writing itself, the ideas should also be easily accessible to the interested general reader as well as the professional.

No field of study has been as riven with dissension as the study of man himself. In psychology, psychiatry and the social sciences, each new integration of our knowledge has regularly been followed by fresh polarisations either into rivalrous, warring factions or, worse still, into isolated, non-communicating schools which thereby deny themselves all further chance of real change and growth. Yet I have found, in the practical work with actual human problems that has occupied me for over thirty-five years, that almost all the rival theories and schools contribute something valuable towards a fuller understanding.

Underlying most of these divisions and polemics is a more fundamental polarisation. Though I did not at first like to admit it even to myself, the practice of my profession has been at the same time a search for understanding of myself and my own family. For I can now see that I was subject to a contradictory double expectation from the family I grew up in; firstly, that I would somehow rescue us all from our psychological problems; and secondly, that I would do so without obliging us to acknowledge that we actually had any in the first place, or even coming myself so dangerously close to that realisation as to risk inadvertently letting the cat out of the bag.

I have become steadily more convinced that this is in fact a 'Catch-22' from which many, perhaps most, mental health professionals suffer by the nature of their own family dynamics, whereby we enter the mental hospital by the side door marked 'Staff only' in order to eavesdrop and pick up some useful tips towards solving this dilemma as 'patients in disguise', while protecting our families' self-image by outwardly fulfilling the duties of our professional rôles. The real difference underlying our tendency to polarise into opposing camps is the extent to which we have allowed ourselves to know this or not. This theme of the motive for our professional choice, and the fundamental division of mental health professionals into two groups with conflicting attitudes towards the applicability of their studies to themselves, will be the subject of a later volume containing those of my papers concerned with the psychodynamics of mental health professionals and the organisations they work in.

In this book the focus is more upon those self-acknowledged patients who enter through the front door of the clinic, and the way my exploration into their treatment, which required me to go beyond the bounds of existing theories of psychotherapy, made possible a wider perspective and led to the possibility of their integration.

Though in the past I have often felt isolated from or at odds with others in my field, or lost and heading in dangerous directions, it has lately been interesting to see from this broader perspective how I have been not so much 'out of line' with my colleagues as 'out of synch' with broad trends which have since affected the field as a whole.

Thus my search began, when I was twenty and a pilot in the RAF engaged in training others to navigate, by beginning to read seriously on epistemology – how much we can be sure of anything we know – and semantics – how much we can trust the process of communication when we try to pass this information on to others; and in particular the consequences of communicating at different levels of abstraction, which had been addressed by Russell's 'Theory of Types'. Though I have been aware how much these early studies underpinned all my later professional understanding, such subjects appeared to be of little interest to colleagues in my profession until the last ten years or so, when epistemology and the notion of 'paradox' have become central in family therapy. Similarly hypnosis, which I taught myself to use as a student at the Maudsley when it was completely out of fashion (though I soon discarded it) has become fashionable even more recently in family therapy through the work of Milton Erickson.

While training I was also absorbing psychoanalytic ideas and at the same time putting into practice some of the behavioural methods of Wolpe and Eysenck, trying to combine these two forms of knowledge, which appeared to me perfectly compatible, along the lines being developed by Mowrer, Miller and Dollard and others in the US. In the course of this I was sent for a spell to the Department of Neurophysiology at the Insitute of Psychiatry, and was trying to link all these ideas to what I was learning about brain function and hormonal influence.

However, it was encountering S. H. Foulkes at the Maudsley which provided the key integrating factor. His method of 'group analysis' brought psychoanalytic ideas about the inner world, and knowledge of the outer world of society, into relationship with one another. As a psychoanalyst, Foulkes believed that our attitudes are moulded by the social matrix in which we develop – principally the family, but also that we subsequently seek to recreate that early experience, and thereby perpetuate our family relationships, by a reverse process in which we unwittingly seek to influence all subsequent groups of which we become part to behave in the same way. This is no more than an extension of the psycho-analytic ideas of transference and projection, but Foulkes's systematic widening of these ideas to a group context, both theoretically and by the technique of group therapy that resulted, provided new methods of treatment of great power, applicable to education and social learning generally as well as to mental disorder. If psychoanalysis explored inner space but often got lost in the minutiae of what it found there, and learning theory and behavioural methods tended to lose the *person* in their preoccupation with outer space and 'objectivity', Foulkes's group analysis seemed to attend equally to both spheres. It also provided an ideal method of facilitating beneficial change by the way it systematically encouraged the externalisation of the inner worlds of group members into the structure and function of the group, next studying, clarifying and changing it there, so that finally the changed dynamic could be re-internalised. This constant interplay between inner and outer space, which in group analysis involves and affects the therapist also, made possible a chain reaction of new insight and potential freedom from unconscious, outmoded patterns of response.

While I was training at the Maudsley, the first articles were also appearing in American journals about a revolutionary new method of treatment which involved interviewing whole families together, and it was inevitable that I would want to extend Foulkes's methods with 'artificially-constituted-' or 'stranger-' groups to this new field of 'family therapy'. I had begun experimenting with treating mothers and young children together as couples in 1959, finding to my surprise that many of these showed unusually profound and rapid change as compared with the separate treatment of each. This discovery led me, under the pressures of high workload, temporary shortage of staff and my philosophy that a psychiatric service should find ways of helping in some measure everyone referred to it, to begin seeing whole families as groups in 1962. Here too, rapid and dramatic changes were observed even with widely spaced inter-views, while the method appeared, unlike any other I had previously encountered, to work equally well across the whole social spectrum and with people at all levels of intelligence and education. Waiting lists soon disappeared, all who were referred could be offered help and receive it at the moment of greatest need, while results, judged by consumer satisfaction and our own observations, exceeded anything we had previously dared to hope as our understanding and skills grew.

Deprived of contact for ten years (except through the printed word) with American colleagues exploring this new field, my own ideas and methods understandably developed in an independent way, drawing upon a different knowledge-base and integrating a wider range of concepts. In particular, Foulkes's work had already demonstrated the complementarity of individual and group dynamics, so that the polarisation which occurred in the United States between the 'systems' and 'psychodynamic' schools of family therapy appeared meaningless except as yet another polarisation around the question of how necessary it was to examine the therapist's own psychology. The manner in which I found I had to extend Foulkes's ideas to deal with 'natural' groups like families, as well as the way in which group-analytic ideas nevertheless proved the ideal catalyst through which other forms of family therapy could be combined and used in an integrated way, is the story that follows.

The group-analytic approach not only facilitates insight and learning in therapy groups. Its influence can be equally powerful in any group of people working together for a common aim. So another benefit it has brought me came through the many groups of professionals with whom I have collaborated in teaching and practising both group therapy and family and marital therapy, who have shared this basic group-analytic outlook and thereby been able to operate together as powerful 'learning machines' while fulfilling the joint task. The colleagues with whom I collaborated in setting up the Group Analytic Practice, the Institute of Group Analysis and the Institute of Family Therapy have in particular enriched my understanding in this way, but collaborators outside the field have widened it further, especially John Cleese, my co-author of *Families And How To Survive Them*, and the group of bishops and their wives that my wife and I led for some years in a psychological exploration of themselves, their marriages and their work.

Working with the editor of this book, John Schlapobersky, has taken the process a step further. I had anticipated that the editing and publication of these writings would prove to be a somewhat tiresome chore. I could not have been more wrong. When one is exploring uncharted territory one has only a vague idea of where one is heading or what one is hoping to find. One is preoccupied with immediate dangers and problems, has energy only for the day's march, and cannot see till much later just where one has journeyed and how all the landmarks relate. But sharing with me the group-analytic touchstone and coming at the material afresh, my collaborator has revealed to me where I have been, and how what I found on the journey not only fits together in an elegant fashion I had not suspected, but how it connects with, illuminates, and is illuminated by many other areas of knowledge on its periphery. Working on this book with him has been another, this time more reflective, exploration.

Robin Skynner, 1987

Editor's Introduction

Robin Skynner is a pioneer whose challenging methods and ideas have helped to bring group analysis and family therapy to maturity over the last twenty-five years. *Explorations with Families: Group Analysis and Family Therapy* contains his selected clinical papers and lectures. They stand together alongside his two previous books[1] as a major contribution towards a unified psychotherapy for which practitioners identified the need a decade ago.[2] From his early observations of rapid and startling changes in families interviewed together, a comprehensive theory emerges that brings together current knowledge about individual, group and family therapy, to integrate the formerly divided systemic, psychoanalytic and behavioural approaches. This is an original body of work that advances our understanding of the inter-personal field to provide a new landmark for theory and practice.

The essence of Skynner's contribution is his spirit of personal enquiry, and the book is less a statement than a series of explorations and a task still in progress. It is illustrated with many case descriptions and with Skynner's open, reflective examination of himself at work which, as the popular success of *Families And How To Survive Them* suggests, will make it easily accessible to the interested general reader as well as to the professional. For his writing has a simplicity and ease of expression that allows the study of change amongst those described in the text, to engage with the reader's own capacities for change at the intellectual and emotional levels. Psychotherapy and authorship are both communicative arts, and in this book they are conveyed and developed through one another to exemplify many of the therapeutic principles described.

Newcomers to the field, students and those simply curious about themselves and their families will find the book a useful introduction. Amongst a professional readership it will be relevant to psychotherapists of all orientations; psychiatrists, general practitioners and other clinicians; social workers, teachers and those who work with children, families, couples and groups; and those with a theoretical interest in social relations and the family.

The book is organised in three sections. The first contains papers which set out basic ideas and general principles of use to those who seek an introduction. The second section contains those papers describing special applications of the group-analytic approach in child psychiatry, sexual and marital therapy and general medicine. The third section contains Skynner's mature work which is developed through the dialogue between group analysis and family therapy.

The other organising principle for this book is the developmental one. The papers fell naturally into place in a form that illustrates the process they describe. In the first section, group analysis and family therapy are differentiated as separate applications of similar methods and ideas. The second section contains a study of intimacy and its problems. In the third section differentiation and intimacy are called on to integrate group analysis and family therapy in a new unity encapsulated by the title of Skynner's first book, *One Flesh, Separate Persons*.

This introduction traces, step-by-step, the development and application of his methods and ideas; guides the reader to the contents of the major papers in Section Three; reviews the editorial process of working with Skynner to prepare this book; and provides, briefly, his professional biography.

Section One: The New Paradigm: Differentiating Group Analysis and Family Therapy

We are living through a revolution in our understanding of social relations, and in our treatment of psychological problems. The papers in the opening section are of historical importance for they document the first stage of this revolution as family therapy emerged in the work of clinicians practising independently of one another,[3] who arrived at similar solutions to common problems with a new paradigm[4] for making assessments and practising psychotherapy. Freud had introduced the earlier revolution in psychology by locating the source of many problems in early family life. But in neither the creative development of psychoanalysis, nor in the extensive literature on families in social history, sociology and anthropology, was there a conception of the family as an agency through which beneficial changes might be effected in a systematic way on behalf of its individual members. By situating treatment outside the living context of the individual's primary relationships, Freud introduced a kind of disjunction between the developmental origins of many problems, and the therapeutic process which sought to correct them.[5]

Family therapy resolves this disjunction by extending the importance of family process from its previously identified responsibility for 'causing' problems, to its creative power to resolve them within the natural life cycles of the family and community. Whilst many problems continue to require the attention of individual practitioners – psychoanalysts, behaviourists and others – they have been widely influenced by the family approach whose earlier development they had made possible.

Group therapy mobilises the self-help resources of a group of strangers who, in the mediating presence of a therapist, engage with one another in discussion effecting some corrective recapitulation of their earlier experiences. Group analysis is an approach towards both group and family therapy that originates in the work of S. H. Foulkes who described it as 'psychotherapy by the group, of the group, including the conductor'.[6] Through his early work, in papers that were celebrated at the time, Skynner draws on Foulkes's work to formulate the group-analytic approach to family therapy. And he draws on family theory to extend group analysis and provide it with a theoretical basis.

In the papers that follow in Sections Two and Three, he brings to both these applications ideas drawn from attachment and object relations theory, systems theory and cybernetics, all of which have been part of a radical shift in clinical perspective that brings into focus the inter-personal field. Through this focus the fabric of social experience can be viewed, not only as the context for many problems but also, as Skynner shows, containing those agencies for change which, when tapped, release profound self-healing, adaptive and regenerative resources.

Section Two:
Special Applications: Intimacy and its Problems

The papers in the central section explore the theme of intimacy and its problems and belong with *One Flesh, Separate Persons* in the development of Skynner's work. They prepare the ground for what follows in Section Three, and for his other book, *Families And How To Survive Them*, written with John Cleese.

Marriage is a person's primary love-relationship of choice and 'unfinished business' from the past, screened off from conscious awareness, often underlies such choices. This image of the screen is used as a metaphor for the unconscious in *Families And How To Survive Them*, where he shows the powerful influence it can have on sexuality, the nature of inter-personal attraction and the choice of partners.[7] In this section he works out the ideas that are later called on by *deriving the three-stage developmental sequence from psychoanalysis and reframing it in systemic terms*. This synthesis is at the heart of his work and is used to illustrate how the shared unconscious life of a couple can, as they settle, generate *a benign cycle*, an open system which fosters a *philosophy of plenty*,[8] meeting and fulfilling real needs to promote both union and individuality. Or it can generate a vicious cycle, a closed system which maintains itself in the service of illusions to frustrate real needs and preclude both union and individuality. When he extends this account to a study of the family life cycle in Section Three, he shows how such patterns can inform a couple's life and shape the personalities of new family members who may either be enriched by their parents' union, or enlisted in their collusions which are reproduced afterwards in their choice of partners and families of procreation.

The papers in Section Two are primarily concerned with problems that appear more localised like sexual dysfunction, sickness behaviour and other symptoms. Such problems are frequently acting in the service of an underlying collusion in which partners need each other to help avoid the painful consequences of related developmental difficulties. Together they seek false solutions to common problems and the struggle precludes real intimacy whilst the symptom plays some part in sustaining its illusion. Treatment can be brief and focussed but Skynner shows the value of the developmental approach in guiding the therapist to the focal conflict. Accurate interventions, including those drawn from the new techniques in sex therapy, can sometimes do enough to shift the balance towards a benign cycle through which the partnership itself does the rest of the work as it becomes regenerative and enables a couple to recognise their mutual difficulties and transcend them.

In Section Two he explores a range of problems in the relational field seeking a unified therapy in which personal growth and resolution of relationship difficulties can potentiate one another. He includes many illustrations, as he does in Section Three, of conjoint marital and couples group therapy, sometimes undertaken with his wife as co-therapist. The case examples describe the creative interplay in therapy between emphasis now on the pair and now on the person, effecting change in both the psychology of the individuals and the dynamics of their marriages. The Skynners' range of therapeutic interventions shows the emerging integration of behavioural, psychoanalytic and systemic methods. They make their co-therapy relationship available for *modelling*; they sometimes work *transferentially* with individuals' problems and sometimes stand outside the transference to use *systemic techniques* with interactive problems. The partnership between group analysis and family therapy which finally brings this integration about in Section Three has the qualities of a benign cycle at a level above the personal one in the philosophy of plenty in Skynner's work.

Section Three: The New Clinical Method: Integrating Group Analysis and Family Therapy

A: On method

The papers in the concluding section of the book document another more recent stage in the revolution described above, with the emergence of a 'second-generation cybernetics' that situates the therapist in the context of the patterns he describes or seeks to change.[9] Working initially from within the homeostatic model in family therapy, Skynner applies to it principles drawn from both Batesonian and Foulksian literature to arrive at an evolutionary model for psychotherapy.

His contribution is relevant to debate at the forefront of a field in which there is now wide recognition of the relativity of the therapist's position and the subjective nature of his contribution. Group analysis is based on the idea that psychotherapy can be by the group, of the group, *including the conductor*. The five major chapters of this section can be summarised as the systematic application to family therapy of this one concluding phrase above. In the Foulksian approach the conductor of a group is both therapist and group member. He works from both positions to be effective and helpful from either. For engagement without neutrality is potentially dangerous, and neutrality without engagement – what on page 319 Skynner calls the failure to penetrate boundaries – is ineffective. The open-systems group-analytic approach is developed on this principle. Skynner says:

> To use my approach the therapist must simultaneously or in rapidly alternating fashion both maintain a parental 'holding rôle', keeping the situation constant and safe; and provide a model of 'play', to explore, open up, risk and venture out into the unknown . . . the therapist both joins the family and remains outside, oscillating between one and the other positions, in order to pick up the projections and to reflect on and analyse or act from them . . .   [Chapter 13, pp. 360 and 364]

Hoffman calls this a 'bicameral interaction', the jump to a new position or the emergence of new possibilities when a problem is viewed from both of two positions. Working at the same time but at far remove from Foulkes, Bateson arrived at the same understanding and in Skynner's work their respective contributions come together. Writing of the one-way screen Hoffman says: 'One had two places to sit. One could take a position and (from outside the room) have somebody else take a position commenting on or reviewing that position.'[10]

Skynner's method is challenging firstly because it places the requirement for maintaining both points of view on the same person.[11] And secondly because it identifies the therapist's struggle to maintain both points of view as a crucial experience which, when fed back to the family, becomes part of the exploration and a crucial ingredient in the process of change. From the minimum sufficient network at the outset of these explorations, to the philosophy of plenty in Skynner's mature work, these papers describe the progressive development of the method and of the theory that underpins it.

As it is developed through the five papers of this section, the method involves the use of circular questioning which is now well known through the work of the Milan group. But in Skynner's approach there is not the heavy reliance on words that one finds in Palazzoli's. Non-verbal interaction is given great importance and circular questioning is not used for information gathering, nor to direct the interview which is guided but left to some extent 'free-floating'. This sets in motion a process of mutual exploration between therapist and those members of the family who constitute the minimum sufficient network. Both sides are personally engaged in a widening circle of enquiry aimed at pattern recognition, reframing and modelling by the therapist, of new forms of feeling and interaction.

In this section, Chapter 10 opens the dialogue between group analysis and family therapy, Chapter 11 reconciles the behavioural/structural and psychoanalytic approaches. Chapter 12 applies new ideas in the second generation of systems and communications theory to the study of family life and unconscious process. Chapter 13 brings the above together from the viewpoint of clinical method, providing the most complete account of the approach for the practising clinician. And in the concluding chapter Skynner achieves the comprehensive theory he had set out to find, in a paper that is both reflective and provocative, which has the magisterial quality of what is sometimes referred to as late works.

For those who choose to begin with the concluding chapters, the following is a 'retrospective' guide to the book. Basic concepts, general principles and techniques in group-analytic family therapy are contained in Chapter 13. The book describes their evolution and the earlier summary in Chapter 4 is an important milestone. The most lucid comparison of this approach with others, notably Minuchin and the Milan group, is in Chapter 14. Indications and contraindications for its use begin with some early outlines in Chapters 2 and 3, and are thoroughly considered in Chapters 10 and 14. The basic principles are adapted for special applications in all the Chapters of Section Two. And Skynner's approach to the family life cycle and to systems theory is set out in Chapter 12 where it is drawn upon for all his explorations.

B: Beyond method

Concerning method, Skynner cautions that:

Though questions raised about method need to be put and answered, many of them are irrelevant to the practice of my approach, in the sense that a knowledge of knots is irrelevant to the task of cutting the Gordian knot. What is needed is an understanding of how to keep a sharp edge on one's sword – a wide, deep and still attention. [Chapter 13, p. 361.]

To maintain this state of being, he says:

The key requirement in the therapist is a deep awareness of his own identity which he is able to sustain in the face of overwhelming if transient, emotional arousal engendered by encounter with profoundly disturbed family systems. . . . This does not mean clinging to a professional's rôle, to a particular theory or technique or even to one's personality . . . [but] a more intense consciousness [of] reality that is completely distinguishable from fantasy. . . . In this ability to maintain a heightened consciousness of reality . . . the therapist is a landmark or beacon for the family by which they can find and orientate themselves. He need, in fact, do nothing but be with them, in the sense of maintaining his identity and integrity. [Chapter 13, p. 358.]

Simplicity is the hallmark of mastery and a vantage point from which none of us begin. Whilst Skynner's work presents us with a challenge to begin with ourselves, the cook does not have to get into the pot to make soup and, as in other approaches, the therapist must stand with most of himself outside the process that he works with. The comprehensive way in which Skynner guides the clinician on how to stay out and get in at the same time should not, however, be mistaken for a 'recipe-book' approach, and the overriding impression one has on reading his work is that he draws from areas of his own experience that lie outside of method. On how the therapist puts himself into the equation of change, Skynner suggests that:

In working with families and marriages . . . it seems more difficult and less effective to work with a limited professional part of ourselves. We seem to find ourselves in question the whole time, obliged to put ourselves into the therapeutic equation, to change and grow at the same time as those we treat. [Chapter 10, p. 227.]

C: The person and the system

Skynner's contribution is immediately relevant to the field. For example Minuchin, when appraising the Milan group's work, fears their 'systems model could carry the practitioner into new rigidities . . . denying the individual while enthroning the system'. Palazolli, one of the principal authors of the Milan group, replies in a review of Minuchin's work:

> For one who adheres to a systems model it is impossible to deny the individual while enthroning the system, as if dealing with two different things. . . . It is merely a change of level. Indeed the system is not something opposing the individual but including him. Copernicus did not deny the earth when he included it in the solar system.[12]

The revolution through which we are living is, like the Copernican revolution, the outcome of many contributions including the two quoted here. Palazzoli goes on to argue that the 'path for the human sciences', through which they can transcend the crisis posed by the incongruity of their models, is offered by Bateson's vision in 'Steps To An Ecology of Mind'. She concedes that 'there is still a long way to go to reach that ecology of mind' and acknowledges how difficult it is to break out of the old linear paradigm. Bringing the group-analytic contribution to bear on this exchange between Minuchin and Palazzoli, Skynner's contribution is another step in our shared search.

Centred in an open-systems approach which recognises the importance of the internal worlds of therapist and individual family members, it guards against the danger of new rigidities. It helps us to see the system in the person, the person in the system, and the patterns by which these two dynamic levels are related. It illuminates the therapeutic moment at which these two levels are brought into a new, creative relationship and takes us one stage further towards realising Bateson's vision of an ecology of mind.

Demystifying Psychotherapy: The Editorial Process

The preparation of these papers for publication generated a sense of respect – but respect is too ceremonious a word – rather one of joy at discovering a kind of inner logic, an internal coherence in Skynner's practice and thinking. When we discussed this, he said he was beginning to see connections and directions in his work that he was formerly unaware of. It confirmed what he believed but only sometimes allowed himself to experience: there was nothing to fear in not always knowing where you are going. Spontaneity and the undirected journey had their own goals and inner directions.

The editing of these papers has been conducted through this dialogue which began much earlier when things were on a different footing between us. It carries with it a responsibility to Skynner, to the reflective spirit of the papers that make up this book, and to the many others who know something about the deep and lasting benefits that can accrue from the work they describe.

My daughter and I recently watched a television programme in which a group of people including Skynner discussed problems in parenthood. When he talked warmly and openly about his family life and children, she asked whether I tell my clients about our family in the way he talked about his own. 'It would help them,' she said. When the panel discussed how parents tend to replicate the unresolved experiences of their own childhoods, she realised that some of the things I thought she wanted included frustrated wishes from my own past. Since then she has been more able to enjoy these things with a tolerance and humour about my investment in her interests, and I have been more comfortable about doing my own thing.

Psychotherapy is not mysterious. It need not be private and is not so different as is supposed to the ordinary processes of growth and change, like a new insight whilst watching television. Those who offer and those who seek it are largely distinguished by how much farther back the client stands on a path familiar to them both. But why then the costly training, years of experience and thorough supervision necessary to do the job well? Skynner suggests this is to ensure that we are working with our clients' agenda and not our own, as well as to ensure that we can draw freely from our own agenda and use it as one of the resources by which to promote change on theirs.

In psychoanalysis this is known as counter-transference. It sounds mysterious and, legitimately critical of mystery, some family therapists reject the heuristic approach, choosing instead to look to techniques for what they might discover by drawing on personal knowledge from their own life experience. Skynner, equally critical of mystery, has tried instead to demystify the field. Whilst he is not a self-effacing man and has a powerful and commanding presence, he does not rely on leader-centred methods nor on the charisma and personal 'style' of some family therapists. Despite his influence he has not sought to establish a school or following of his own. Rather, as the title *Explorations with Families* indicates, he encourages us to look within ourselves and those closest to us for what we might follow in the search for autonomy and equilibrium. His approach is perhaps best summarised thus: 'When his task is accomplished and his work done, people say, "it happened to us naturally"'.[13]

John R. Schlapobersky, 1987

Notes

1 *One Flesh, Separate Persons: Principles of Family and Marital Psychotherapy.*
Families And How To Survive Them, written with John Cleese.
2 'Many of the therapeutic operations presented are at formal levels, isomorphic, but we do not yet have a generalised conceptual framework for integrating their various approaches. This is the direction of the future'. S. Minuchin, introduction to P. Papp, *Family Therapy: Full Length Case Studies.*
3 See S. Walrond-Skinner's introduction to her edited collection, *Developments in Family Therapy*, where she describes the *leap* from individual casework, counselling and psychotherapy to the treatment of the family system.
4 Kuhn defines paradigms as 'universally recognised achievements . . . that provide model problems and solutions to a community of practitioners for a period of time'. In *The Structure of Scientific Revolutions*, he describes progress not as incremental and accumulative, but more in the nature of a crisis of knowledge and practice that generates challenges for the development of new paradigms. He is referring here to the natural sciences, but his account is generalised to the social sciences including psychology.
5 In his editorials to the early editions of the *Journal of Family Therapy*, Dare poses the interesting question of why some fifty years elapsed before the systematic examination of family life yielded therapeutic principles and processes in family therapy that matched the sophistication of the psychoanalytic corpus.
6 S. H. Foulkes, *Group Analytic Psychotherapy: Methods and Principles*. To avoid confusion all references to Foulkes's publications are identified by their original publication date, where they will be found in the bibliography. There the publication date is given for the new edition issued in Maresfield

Reprints, London, and currently available from Karnacs Booksellers and the Institute of Group Analysis, London.

7 *Families And How To Survive Them, op. cit.*, pp. 15–62.

8 Chapter 13, pp. 330–1.

9 For a relatively recent introduction to what is now a burgeoning literature, see L. Hoffman, *Foundations of Family Therapy*, Prologue and Chs. 15 and 16. See also a more up-to-date account by Hoffman: 'Beyond Power and Control: Toward a "Second Order" Family Systems Therapy', *Family Systems Medicine*, Vol. 3, **4**, 1985; and P. Dell, 'Understanding Bateson and Maturana: Toward a Biological Basis for the Social Sciences', *Journal of Marital and Family Therapy*, Vol. 11, **1**, (1985) 1–20.

10 Hoffman, *Foundations of Family Therapy, op. cit.*, p. 4.

11 The process of working from within and from outside the family system simultaneously, is fostered when co-therapists assume these different rôles. It allows a greater degree of therapeutic involvement by the engaged partner, confident of a 'lifeline' provided by the detached one. A struggle between different points of view can then arise between the two therapists, and partly it is their mutuality, their capacity to share, which is passed on to the family. The 'bicameral' and modelling components of the approach Skynner describes can thus be seen to run together. He discusses co-therapy on pp. 228–9 and 373–4.

12 See Palazzoli's review of Minuchin's *Psychosomatic Families* in *Family Process*, Vol. 18, **1**, March 1979.

13 Lao Tzu, *Tao Te Ching*, Penguin, Harmondsworth, p. 73.

Robin Skynner: Biography

Robin Skynner was born in Charlestown, a sea-port on the south Cornish coast where his father and grandfather maintained a family business mining and shipping china clay. On this side of the family there had been captains in the Royal Navy for several generations and on his mother's side they were also connected with the sea; they lived in a nearby fishing port and his mother was the daughter of a fisherman. Skynner was the oldest of five sons; they attended local schools, he completed his education at Blundell's in 1939 and began training for industrial management.

He volunteered for war service in the RAF at eighteen, was commissioned and qualified as a pilot and in navigation. He spent two and a half years training other pilots in Britain and Canada and then became a pilot in a Mosquito squadron on active service which specialised in low-level attacks. He has written of the trust required between the pilot and navigator who manned these aircraft, and of the total attention and engagement such flying demanded, and attributes to these experiences certain aspects of his therapeutic technique.[1]

After the war he qualified in medicine at University College Hospital and in psychiatry at the Maudsley Hospital. He has written fully of this period himself[2] but there are five associations of note. The earliest was his interest in semantics, epistemology and the philosophy of science stimulated especially by Korzybski's *General Semantics*[3] read whilst he was on war service in Canada. The second, arising out of this early interest, was his membership of the Metalogical Society, a small group initially brought together by A. J. Ayer for dialogue between the philosophers and scientists of whom it was comprised. They met monthly over several years, included Russell, Popper, Medawar and others who were amongst the most advanced and creative thinkers of their time[4] and Skynner attaches great importance to the intellectual confidence fostered by this association. Thirdly, during his psychiatric training, an experience of expanded consciousness under psychedelic drugs led to a lifelong association with others interested in alternative ways towards psychological and spiritual growth described in Christian and Eastern mysticism.[5] Fourthly, he was pupil of Wilfred Barlow who was developing the principles of the Alexander Technique and he was later to apply to psychotherapy this understanding of how posture and movement relate to emotional states.[6]

And finally he was drawn to the work of S. H. Foulkes whom he met at the Maudsley Hospital. Foulkes was a German psychoanalyst who brought with him to Britain the revised understanding of Freudian theory from the Frankfurt Institute that was to also prove influential in the US in the work of Neo-Freudians like Erich Fromm, Adorno and Marcuse.[7] Foulkes first developed his approach to group therapy in Exeter before the war was able to apply it successfully on a large scale to the treatment of war neuroses at Northfield military hospital near Birmingham. He developed ideas and practices there amongst a group of colleagues, that were to have a profound impact on the post-war development of mental health services.[8] Bion and Rickman had attempted an earlier and less successful experiment at Northfield in working therapeutically with groups.[9] Foulkes replaced them and, through the changes he introduced, the first therapeutic community was established. One of his associates there, Tom Main, coined this term to describe their work and later extended these developments at the Cassell Hospital.[10] Maxwell Jones[11] and David Clark[12] were also influenced by these developments, and like Main, they played a prominent part in transforming patterns of practice in mental hospitals and therapeutic communities after the war. Foulkes and de Maré took the Northfield perspectives into the concentrated study of small group work, which Skynner then extended to families.[13]

Based at the Maudsley Hospital after the war, Foulkes gathered about him a small group of clinicians and others who explored the small group implications of these ideas and practices, called it group analysis[14] and established the Group-Analytic Society.[15] Skynner joined them, trained with Foulkes and then established with him and others the Group-Analytic Practice. From this base he designed a course on group work, initially to meet the training requirements of some members of the Association of Psychiatric Social Workers, and brought in another member of the practice, de Maré, to run it with him. This was soon opened to other professionals and expanded, and colleagues in the Practice and others from outside it joined its staff. Together they developed this into the Institute of Group Analysis which offers a clinical training and professional qualifications in psychotherapy, and is the main training centre for group therapists in Britain. The original course Skynner designed in 1964 continues to run and now caters annually for some 150 people.[16] The influence on European psychotherapy has also been considerable and there are now Institutes of Group Analysis in Athens, Copenhagen, Heidelberg and Rome and centres in many cities practice and train for group analysis on both sides of Europe, in Israel, the Americas and Australia. There is a journal, *Group Analysis*, regular European Symposia, and increasing representation of and respect for group analysis at international conferences.

Whilst training at the Maudsley Skynner specialised in child psychiatry and became consultant first in Guildford, then Harlow and finally at Woodberry Down Child Guidance Unit and the Queen Elizabeth Hospital for Children serving north-east London and the East End. These developmens took place at the same time as those described above, and they came together in the mid-1960s when some of the staff at these latter centres attended the early courses on group work. Then in the early 1970s the increasing demand for seminars in family therapy that Skynner was also leading at the institute of Group Analysis increased to the point where another large course was needed, similar to that designed earlier but here concerned with family work.

Skynner now brought together a group of family and marital therapists to staff this new project. Some had worked or trained with him earlier, some had been experimenting independently, and others brought experience of work in the US. This course was soon also catering for 150 participants annually and its staff established the separate Institute of Family Therapy which Skynner served as the first Chairman. Since 1976 this Insticue has offered a range of long and short courses and a clinical training has been developed which offers a recognised professional qualification. A national organisation, the Association for Family Therapy which corresponds in many respects to the Group-Analytic Society, was established in 1976. At the inaugural address to its first meeting, published as chapter 5 below, Skynner outlined the history of some of these events. It is referenced in the appendix where, as in the introductions to many of the chapters in this book, there is further historical material. There is now a Journal of Family Therapy, training programmes at many major teaching centres and a growing number of books on the subject written by members of the Institute and Association.[17]

Bridging these developments in group analysis and family therapy, Skynner and his late wife Prudence worked together in a partnership until her death in 1987. They provided the early leadership of the family courses which led to the Institute of Family Therapy; they helped to establish the credibility in this country of co-therapy with couples and families; and from 1974 they pioneered the development of therapy groups for couples at the Group-Analytic Practice where Robin continues to work. They taught widely abroad and their international standing was affirmed when they were invited, together with Whitaker and Kaslow, to be the main speakers at the 1978 Annual Conference of the American Association of Marriage and Family Therapy, where they were both honoured with Distinguished Affiliate Membership. More recently they worked together leading groups of bishops of the Church of England and their wives, and have been Advisers in the formation of a Pastoral Work Development Scheme in the London Diocese. There are many references to their partnership in this book, and further references to their writing in the appendix. During the course of her illness Prudence continued working, relinquishing her professional commitments as the illness advanced. She was at home until shortly before her death and passed away at the Marie Curie Hospice, Hampstead, in November 1987. The purpose-built family therapy unit at St George's Hospital, named in her honour, is just one indication of the regard in which she was held.

Skynner was made a Member of the Royal College of Psychiatrists on its formation and was later elected a Fellow. He left child guidance work in 1970 and became Senior Tutor in Psychotherapy at the Institute of Psychiatry and the Bethlem Royal and Maudsley Hospitals where he remained until he retired from University and NHS teaching in 1982. His output as an author has been as prolific as his other areas of endeavour, and the appendix to this collection speaks for itself. He was sixty-four when we began working on these papers and his only reluctance was the time it detracted from windsurfing in the summer and from the sequel to *Families and How To Survive Them* that he is writing with John Cleese, to be entitled *Life and How to Survive It*. He remains active in all three of his primary areas of interest – clinical work, teaching and writing – and with his family spends as much time as possible at their cottage in Wales.

John R. Schlapobersky, 1988

Notes

1 In 'An Open Systems, Group-Analytic Approach to Family Therapy' (appendix reference 36), Skynner writes of how 'the experience of low level bombing . . . high alertness, precise timing and accuracy . . . getting in and out as quickly as possible, profoundly influenced my family work . . . night attacks, including dive-bombing in the dark where a navigator watched the altimeter and slapped the pilot's knee to prevent his diving into the ground, may also have been a good preparation for co-therapy.' This material is not available in the edited form of this paper, published as chapter 13 in *Explorations With Families*, but can be found in *The Handbook of Family Therapy*, A. Gurman and N. Kniskern (eds) p. 41.

2 See note 1 above and chapter 7 below.

3 A. Korzybski, *General Semantics*.

4 In his biography, *Russell Remembered*, Rupert Crawshay-Williams, also a former member of the Metalogical Society, names some of the other distinguished figures in this group, including Ayer who established the group, J. Z. Young the zoologist, F. G. Young the biochemist, Penrose the geneticist; and philosophers including Hampshire, Wollheim, Woodger, Hutten and Tarski. Skynner is named in this group amongst the philosophers and though identified as 'a psychiatrist by profession' (p. 60) he was still a medical student at the time.

5 See Psychotherapy and sacred tradition, chapter 11 below.

6 See W. Barlow, *The Alexander Principle*.

7 For references to and studies of the Frankfurt Institute and the new connections established there between psychology and sociology, see for example, M. Jay, *The Dialectical Imagination*. An overview of the Neo-Freudian's perspectives is provided in E. Fromm, *The Crisis of Psychoanalysis* and *Beyond The Chains of Illusion*.

8 See P. de Maré, 'Michael Foulkes and the Northfield Experiment',

and M. Pines, 'The Contribution of S. H. Foulkes to Group
Analysis', both in M. Pines (ed.), *The Evolution of Group Analysis*.
9 See W. Bion, *Experiences in Groups*.
10 See Main's papers, notably 'The Ailment' and 'The Hospital as a
Therapeutic Institution', both in E. Barnes (ed.), *Psychosocial
Nursing*, based on his work at the Cassell Hospital.
11 For an account of the Henderson Hospital which Maxwell Jones
established, see R. N. Rapoport, *Community as Doctor*. For
Maxwell Jones's own more recent writing, see his *Maturation Of
The Therapeutic Community: An Organic Approach to Health and
Mental Health*, and *The Process of Change*. For a recent account of
current practice see D. Kennard, *Therapeutic Communities*, and R.
D. Hinshelwood and N. Manning (eds), *Therapeutic Communities*.
12 See Clark's account of the history of social therapy in psychiatry
and of the relationship between social science and psychiatry in
D. H. Clark, *Social Therapy In Psychiatry*.
13 See M. Pines (ed.), *The Evolution of Group Analysis*, and T. Lear
(ed.), *Spheres of Group Analysis*, notably the account of Elizabeth
Foulkes in the latter, of 'The Origins and Development of Group
Analysis'.
14 Foulkes derived the term 'group analysis' from the work of Trigant
Burrow, an unusual and original figure who was both an associate of
D. H. Lawrence and writers in the Bloomsbury group, and a
research psychiatrist who was a founder and later became President
of the American Psychoanalytic Association. He was later to leave
this organisation over a difference he had in direct dealings with
Freud about the differentiation of group analysis from psychoanalysis. See W. Abse, 'Trigant Burrow and the Inauguration of
Group Analysis in the USA', in *Group Analysis*, 12, **3** (1979) 218–
229; and Abse's book, *Clinical Notes on Group-Analytic
Psychotherapy*. Amongst the most useful of brief accounts that
differentiates group analysis from psychoanalysis is that of M. Pines,
'Psychoanalysis and Group Analysis', *Group Analysis*, 11, **1** (1978)
8–20.
15 See note 13 above.
16 See chapter nine below.
17 See, for example, R. Whiffen and J. Byng-Hall (eds), *Family
Therapy Supervision: Recent Developments in Practice*; A.
Bentovim, G. Gorrell Barnes and A. Cooklin (eds), *Family
Therapy: Complementary Frameworks of Theory and Practice*, Vols
1 and 2; D. Campbell and R. Draper (eds), *Applications of Systemic
Family Therapy: The Milan Approach;* G. Gorrell Barnes, *Working
with Families*; D. Will and M. Wrate, *Integrate Family Therapy: A
Problem-Centred Psychodynamic Approach*; J. Burnham, *Family
Therapy: First Steps Towards a Systemic Approach*; and A. Treacher
and J. Carpenter (eds), *Using Family Therapy*.

'We must pass through the threat of that chaos where thought becomes impossible.'

Gregory Bateson, *Mind and Nature*, p. 143.

'The basic strategy of the new experiential psychotherapy requires that, to achieve the best therapeutic results, both therapist and client suspend as much as possible their conceptual frameworks, anticipations, and expectations during the experimental process. Both should be open and adventurous, ready to follow the flow of experience with a deep trust that the organism will find its own way to heal itself and evolve. Experience has shown that if the therapist is willing to encourage and support such a healing journey without fully understanding it, and the client is open to venture into unknown territory, they will be rewarded by extraordinary thera-peutic achievements.'

Fritjof Capra, *The Turning Point: Science, Society And The Rising Culture*, p. 429.

Acknowledgements

In compiling this book we are indebted to Christopher Falkus of Methuen for his guidance and advice, and to Alex Bennion and Caroline Evans for their thoughtful attention to the manuscript and layout.

We are grateful to Dr Lionel Kreeger for his comments on the editorial introductions to the chapters and to Dr Pat de Maré for historical information about S. H. Foulkes at Northfield, included in the author's biography.

The author has made his personal acknowledgements in his introduction. I should here like to express my appreciation to my family, and to a number of friends and colleagues, who know my gratitude for their assistance, support and understanding during the time-consuming editorial process.

We are also grateful to the following sources for granting permission to re-publish these papers: for Chapter 1, 'The Minimum Sufficient Network', the Editor of *Social Work Today* (The British Association of Social Workers); for Chapter 2, 'Indications and Contraindications for Conjoint Family Therapy', Mrs S. Bierer, *The International Journal of Social Psychiatry*; for Chapter 3, 'Referral for Psychotherapy', the co-author, Dr Dennis Brown, and *The British Medical Journal* (The British Medical Association); for Chapter 4, 'A Group-Analytic Approach to Conjoint Family Therapy', the Editors, Drs Eric Taylor and Michael Berger, *The Journal of Child Psychology and Psychiatry* (Pergamon); for Chapter 5, 'The Physician as Family Therapist', the Editors, Drs Jerry Lewis and Jean Usdin, *Psychiatry in General Medical Practice* (McGraw-Hill); for Chapter 6, 'School Phobia: A Reappraisal', Dr Sidney Crown, the Editor, *The British Journal of Medical Psychology* (The British Psychological Society); for Chapter 7, 'Marital Problems and Their Treatment', the Editor, *The Proceedings of the Royal Society of Medicine* (The Royal Society of Medicine); for Chapter 8, 'Sexual Counselling in General Practice', the Editor, *The British Journal of Sexual Medicine* (The Medical Tribune Group); for Chapter 9, 'Recent Developments in Marital Therapy', and for Chapter 11, 'Reflections on the Family Therapist as Family Scapegoat', Dr Bryan Lask, the Editor, *The Journal of Family Therapy*, (Academic Press); for Chapter 10, 'Group Analysis and Family Therapy', Dr Robert Dias, former Editor, *The International Journal of Group Psychotherapy* (The American Group Psychotherapy Association); for Chapter 12, 'Frameworks for Viewing the Family as a System', Arnon Bentovim, Gill Gorrell Barnes and Alan Cooklin (eds), *Family Therapy*, Vol. 1 (1982) and the abridged edition (1987) (Academic Press); for Chapter 13, 'An Open-Systems, Group-Analytic Approach to Family Therapy', Professors Alan Gurman and David Kniskern (eds), *The Handbook of Family Therapy* (1981) (Brunner/Mazel); for Chapter 14, 'What is Effective in Group and Family Therapy: The Self-Renewing Paradigm', Dr Malcolm Pines, the Editor, *Group Analysis*.

We would like to acknowledge the following sources for permitting the use of extracts from these books: Routledge and Kegan Paul for the extract from D. T. Suzuki's foreword to Eugen Herrigel's *Zen and the Art of Archery* (Arkana, London, 1985); Mrs E. Foulkes and Dr James Anthony for the extracts from S. H. Foulkes and E. J. Anthony's *Group Psychotherapy: The Psychoanalytic Approach* (Penguin, Harmondsworth, 1957); Doubleday for the extract from 'The Archaic Song of Dr Tom the Shaman', from Song 99 in *Songs of the Nootka Indians of Western Vancouver Island: Transactions of the American Philosophical Society*, Vol. 45, Part 3 (Doubleday, New York, 1972); Basic Books for the extract from Irving Yalom's *The Theory and Practice of Group Psychotherapy* (Basic Books, New York, 1970); Gower Publishing Group for the extract from Gregory Bateson's *Mind and Nature* (Wildwood House, London, 1979); International Textbook Co. for the extract from Gregory Bateson's *Steps to an Ecology of Mind* (International Textbook Co., Glasgow and London, 1972); George Braziller Inc. for the extract from Ludwig Von Bertalanffy's *General Systems Theory* (Braziller, New York, 1968); International Universities Press for the extract from Helen Durkin's *The Group in Depth* (International Universities Press, New York, 1964).

J.R.S.

One

EARLY PAPERS AND GENERAL PRINCIPLES

1 The Minimum Sufficient Network

This early paper describes innovations introduced by Skynner and his colleagues to improve child psychiatric services for which they were responsible in the East End of London during the 1960s. It advocates a wide focus on the total social network involved in each referral to define a key combination of people – the minimum sufficient network – with whom intervention is likely to be most economical and effective.

The ideas are simple and once understood appear to be common sense. But they brought about a revolution in practice at the clinics where they were applied and this in turn had extensive influence on the development of family therapy in Britain. In footnote 1 below Skynner makes acknowledgements to his colleagues – some of whom went on to make notable contributions in further developments elsewhere – for their participation in developing and applying these concepts.

A new pattern of practice was set by which previously long waiting lists were reduced to a point where help could be offered at the moment when need and motivation were greatest and treatment was thus quicker and more effective. This in turn freed more time for treatment and for developing new resources and skills, which created an ascending spiral of better and more satisfying work.

In this paper and the one referred to in footnote 2, Skynner extends these principles to the dynamics of referral systems, a subject in which the Milan group has recently rekindled interest. Like many revolutionary developments this early work is still distinguished by its breadth and flexibility.

J.R.S.

Some General Principles

Over the past ten years, my work as a psychiatrist dealing with both adults and children, and as a psychotherapist working with groups as well as individuals, has been carried out in widely different settings. These have included private practice in a large city; a prosperous country town with a high proportion of middle class and professional families; a new town where the population was mainly skilled working class or lower middle class; and a child guidance clinic and a children's hospital serving parts of the East End of London where there are exceptional social problems and the incidence of admission to hospital for psychosis is two or three times the national average.[1]

For a long time it was apparent to us that some types of problem were more suitably treated by individual psychotherapy while others were better placed in selected psychotherapy groups. Some problems proved inaccessible to both approaches, but responded to interviews with the whole family. A few, including families where motivation was low and the concern was mainly in the referring source, seemed to require the participation of the referring agent as well as the family referred.

In studying these differences, especially as we compared the needs of adults and children, and of families with different levels of education and different socio-economic backgrounds, some general principles emerged which have proved helpful in judging what form of treatment is likely to be most appropriate to a given referral. *One of these principles is expressed in the concept of the 'minimum sufficient network'.*[2]

The word 'network', as I shall use it here, refers to a set of psychological structures which need to be connected to one another if the total system is to be autonomous, capable of intelligent response and adaptation.

The simplest instance of this is the situation obtaining in the psychology of a normal, mature person. He will be motivated by certain drives, impulses or instincts such as hunger, self-preservation and sex, common to humans in all cultures. He will also have internalised, from his parents and other important figures influencing his development, a set of acquired motivations, standards or rules designed to modify his basic 'instincts' in such a way that he can fit into the family or wider society. And he will in addition have learned the techniques of self-control whereby satisfactory compromises can be achieved between these two sets of requirements. In terms of the tripartite psychoanalytic model, he can be regarded as having achieved some satisfactory balance between super-ego, ego and id. I think these are simple and widely accepted distinctions. The use of psychoanalytic terminology to describe them does not imply an uncritical acceptance of the psychoanalytic view in general. Those preferring a different frame of reference can substitute other labels for words like conscience, controls and impulses.

Distinguishing Therapeutic Needs

In the kind of neurotic patients with whom psychoanalysis was first practised and developed – mainly middle-class, educated people who had not suffered serious parental or social deprivation – these necessary psychological structures were usually well developed even though distorted or disconnected. The 'network' of psychological functions needed for autonomous operation were all present within the individual. Treatment of that person alone, without involving relatives or other people in contact with him, was more or less adequate.

Nevertheless, even in patients suitable for individual, analytically-orientated psychotherapy or casework, the degree to which the whole personality needs to be involved, understood and changed will vary from case to case. At one end of the scale, a traumatic neurosis resulting from sudden or extreme stress on a formerly well-adapted person may leave a large part of the healthy personality intact. Therapeutic effort can be directed to a limited aspect of the person's functioning and treatment may be relatively swift. In character neurosis, on the other hand, most of the personality may be maintaining a particular set of maladaptive attitudes, and where this is the case we may expect treatment to be more extensive, complex and prolonged.

The addition of the words 'minimum sufficient' indicates that we must include as much of the external network as is essential to achieve our aim, but that we do not wish to make our task more complex than is absolutely necessary. So we wish to exclude from consideration any elements whose influence is sufficiently small to permit them to be safely ignored.

In hospitals, child guidance clinics and other community social services, a certain proportion of cases come to us because the main needs seem to lie in themselves. They knock on the door and complain of depression, of feelings of conflict between conscience and desires, of inability to achieve their aims and find satisfaction in relationships or work. Sometimes parents come in this way for themselves, almost consciously using the child as an admission ticket, seeking help for their own personal distress, their marital difficulties, or their failures as parents. Even when patients of this kind are referred by others, the person referring them may be acting as no more than a signpost and we may not need to consider their rôle or influence. These are the patients for whom psychoanalysis and analytically-orientated psychotherapy or casework, particularly on an individual basis, was designed. As long as this type of treatment for this type of patient is the best main use of our available resources, no particular problems arise.

Using the Minimum Sufficient Network to Define a Problem

Although we may feel more at ease with these 'neurotic' problems, many of the cases referred to child guidance clinics and other public psychiatric services do not fall within this category. With many referrals, particularly among those who are less intelligent, educationally deprived or who come from limited or chaotic backgrounds, there is often confusion over identities and rôles; extensive employment of projection and introjection; use of different family members as externalised good objects or bad objects, and *a splitting and sharing of psychological functions between individuals within a family to a point where it is meaningless to try to consider any one person in isolation.* One child may act out a parent's denied impulses. This parent may then act as a super-ego figure, blaming and punishing the child to control the projection, but their own capacities may be so limited that they use the other parent as a repository of ego strength to achieve this control. Another child, the 'good one', may be used through projection to contain and keep the parents' good qualities safe against their destructive feelings, which are partly projected into, partly directed at, the 'bad' child. *In such a case, no individual is able to make use of the full range of psychological functions that a mature adult requires in order to operate. Only in combination can they operate adequately or be treated. Here, the minimum sufficient network represents the minimum number of individuals in the nuclear or extended family which must be involved in therapy if therapeutic change is to be possible.*

Progress will be much swifter, as a rule, if the network is seen together as a group, since the problem will be in the room and its movement from one family member to another can be pointed out. Assistance and support can be given for them all to share the problem, instead of taking turns to carry the whole burden and blame. The following example is an illustration of the conjoint approach in such a case.

Practical Implications

1. An example of the family group approach

Sandra, then aged twelve, was referred to a child guidance clinic for persistent stealing and jealous, provocative behaviour at home and school. Several months of separate treatment led to symptomatic improvement in the child but complete deadlock in interviews with the mother, who rejected any connection between Sandra's problems and her own personality, despite the fact that she recalled she had been very similar in her own childhood.

Six months later the problem recurred. This time the whole family were seen as a group: Sandra, her sister Susan, one year older, her brother Philip, one year younger, and two younger children, four and five, who played near the father and mother but took no active part.

The first interview

Everyone began by blaming Sandra, who at first appeared to seek acceptance, then became stubborn and defensive and eventually wept. Doing in the group what she was always said to do at home, she excluded herself and drew her brother into mischievous whispering. Mother then spoke of her own closeness to the elder sister Susan. Sandra said, 'But I have got Dad'. Father, looking uncomfortable, denied this. The interview was otherwise unproductive. My co-therapist, a psychiatric social worker, was confirmed in his belief that Sandra's difficulties were not explicable in terms of family dynamics, and I partially agreed. On reflection though, I recalled how hard Sandra had tried to establish a good relationship in the earlier part of the interview, and how she had been driven relentlessly into opposition.

The second interview

At the next family consultation two months later everyone again accused and reproached Sandra, and treated her as the family problem. This time she did not attempt to defend herself and refused to take part even when I invited her to do so. The other children said Sandra was carrying out her threat to keep silent and possibly to leave.

I pointed out how everyone was again focussing on Sandra as the problem and suggested that she was in some way functioning as a scapegoat. I acknowledged that I had colluded in this at the previous session.

At this mother put up a good deal of resistance, pressuring me to alter my assessment, but I reaffirmed it. The parents then began to talk about their own feelings of failure. Father said that Sandra made him feel frustrated, mother that she made her feel helpless and inadequate. Sandra still refused to join in even when I invited her. The other two children said she feared she would be picked on if she spoke, and at this point Sandra said she had been picked on by the whole family after the previous interview. The parents denied this, claiming the children had freedom to speak their minds, and Sandra began to sulk once more.

At this point an unexpected intervention came from the elder sister Susan. (Unexpected in that such interventions are always a surprise, even though in family therapy the siblings often play this crucial rôle.) She hesitated, then plucked up her courage and said: 'It will all have to come out now, it will all come in a rush, and everything will have to be said, even if people get upset.' She then began to attack father, saying he was always picking on the children because he was so grumpy. Father, passive and withdrawn until this point, became animated and defended himself, while Susan's criticisms became more vehement. Sandra entered the discussion again, giving up her rôle of the naughty child and defending her father fiercely against the criticism. From this point on she remained a member of the group and only once fell briefly back into her previous, excluded position. Mother joined Susan in criticising father. Eventually all three children including Sandra were criticising him, saying he was always complaining but never really firm; they said he would keep on at them about doing the washing up, but would eventually do it himself. The three children all agreed that he should be more definite and *make* them do it. As all the children attacked father in this way, mother moved to his defence, though she seemed to agree with their criticisms, saying among other things that the children were not as helpful as they should be.

It was at this point that the attack seemed to move to mother, and it came first from the boy Philip. He complained that even when they tried to help, the parents would not accept it. He instanced an occasion when he had offered to go and make the tea but mother had stopped him, saying that he would only make a mess. The other children began to agree that the mother had no right to grumble, since she would not accept their help when they offered it. A sudden change now occurred in the group pattern. It seemed only a few seconds before the whole family were once again attacking Sandra in the way they had done in the beginning, blaming her for being stubborn and unhelpful.

I interrupted to point out how Sandra had been an active and constructive member of the discussion, accepted by everyone, until everyone had suddenly begun to blame her and drive her outside the family circle. This had followed immediately on some criticism of the mother, the only one who had avoided it till this point. The mother began to argue stubbornly with me, saying that it was Sandra who had been sent to the clinic as the problem; they had all come to have something done about her. I said we had now clearly seen that the problem lay in the family as a whole; they could all be united against Sandra when Sandra was bad but when Sandra was not in this position as scapegoat, other family conflicts immediately began to emerge. Susan said, 'Yes, the real problem might not be Sandra at all, but someone else.' Mother still seemed angry with me. She was determined to keep the problem in the children, and to disagree with my formulation. After a short time the parents and I noticed that the girls were pulling faces and whispering. We asked what this was about. Susan once again took the rôle of family spokesman, this time criticising the mother. Apprehensive but firm and definite, she said that the mother was not the same since the babies had arrived. 'She is different, she has changed completely.' All three older children gradually joined in the unanimous criticism of mother, saying she gave all her love to the two smaller ones and had little left for them. They felt the mother did not realise they still had needs, just as the babies did.

After these criticisms of mother had continued for some time, she began to attack Susan, usually her ally. One of the most interesting and moving moments in the interview came when Sandra then suddenly leapt to Susan's defence, saying, 'Now we are all doing to Susan what everyone was doing to me when we came in.' The time allotted to the interview was nearing its end. I suggested that just as the older children still needed something they had had as babies, mother might have her needs too. The mother said she wanted to give them all the affection she could but that they would have to help her more, so that she could in turn give more time. Susan seemed to be less forgiving and to be dictating terms to mother, while it was

11

Sandra who now defended and supported mother. Strong feelings of affection and need appeared to be released at this point, after the earlier feelings of resentment and rebellion. The older children seemed to be trying to come to terms with the fact that the babies now needed to have what they had had before. Susan said, 'We had all the love before they came. At first I was alone, and I had everything, then Sandra came and she had it, and now the little ones have to have it instead.'

The third interview

At the third family consultation a month later, the situation had changed dramatically. Sandra had been integrated into the family and remained a member throughout the session. She seemed to have little need to speak, she was warm and relaxed and, significantly, looked after the two younger children throughout. Susan, by contrast, was now revealing a full-blown adolescent conflict with the mother, which at times would include all the children and both parents, over the usual adolescent strivings for independence. The father for the first time took a leading rôle and both parents felt that all this was a natural stage they had to pass through. They did not wish for further help but wanted access if necessary.

2. Liaison with the minimum sufficient network in the community

The minimum sufficient network may reach beyond the nuclear or even the extended family to include some part of the wider community. Families which function in a primitive way will often involve others in their psychopathology, projecting personality functions on to community agencies.

One pattern is referred to us in the form of a child who presents a behaviour problem at school but is said to be normal enough at home. Frequently the mother is herself seriously immature and unable to tolerate frustration or rejection. In an attempt to avoid conflict with the child and perpetuate the original close relationship, she projects all controlling functions on to the father, from whom she then shields the child. The parents would then find themselves in conflict but they can avoid this if they both identify with the nurturing rôle (essentially 'motherly') and combine to project all controlling functions (essentially 'fatherly') on to the school. The school then becomes the target of the parents' hostility and the child too is encouraged to displace his own hostility away from the home and on to teachers. The whole procedure has the purpose of maintaining some unity within the family. The situation is not easily changed by work with the parents alone unless the place of school within the network is considered. In such cases I have usually found that facilitating communication between the school and the family, as well as between the two parents (both communications really representing marital interactions), is the most effective approach. In being confronted by, and accepting, the school's authority, the father is supported in fulfilling his paternal rôle within the family, and the mother in turn can accept her authority over the child. But first, of course, the clinic or agency must accept its own authority and responsibility in this situation, which is to confront the various contestants with their true positions in the conflict. This can be done by communicating with the school after the family interview so that the school staff appreciate the nature of the difficulty and try to make a relationship with the parents, particularly the father. Lately, however, we have found it both more effective and time-saving to meet such families with the head or class teacher at the school from the beginning, the school of course being responsible for getting the family to attend.

If we begin to think in this way of a network of functions each time a case is referred to us, several questions occur. Who is disturbed? Who is disturbing? Who has the motivation to alter the situation? Who has the capacity to alter it? Four different people may be involved here, or one. If the former, we are in for trouble and disappointment if we follow our usual individual-centred procedure. Within each network we must locate the main need or motivation, or we will waste our time concentrating on the wrong part of the network or ignoring some crucial aspect of it.

Three categories of motivation

Looking at the problem of intervention from the viewpoint of families' motivation, at least three categories of motivation can be distinguished:

1. To express impulses and gain instinctual satisfaction.

2. To control the impulses because of their actual or supposed harmful consequences.

3. To find a compromise and resolve a conflict between instinctual drives and social controls.

The third category involves, in psychoanalytic terms, the motivation to find a better solution to a conflict between super-ego and id. It includes those cases for which our usual techniques are well suited.

The first category – people who are seeking instinctual satisfaction without personal conflict – never come to us unless we have something they want us to give them or are under pressure from the second category, who are suffering from them and wish to see them controlled. However, if we keep the first two categories in contact (the anti-social family and the socialising forces of society, equivalent to id and super-ego) and help them to communicate by placing ourselves in the conflict as ego-components, we are then dealing with something like the third category, a conflict situation with which existing psychotherapeutic and casework techniques are designed to deal. We can thus hope to facilitate a better compromise.

However, in child guidance clinics we have all too often made the mistake of accepting, explicity or implicitly, the responsibility for changing the people referred to suit the demands of those who refer them. When we do this we automatically become part of the network which carries the motivation. The referring agency sits back relieved of its own anxiety, if it had any in the first place, leaving everything to us, as does the family referred. The anxiety and concern is experienced instead by the clinic staff, who in most cases lack either the facilities to supply what the family needs or the authority or social sanctions required to control them.

Much of the disappointment and frustration that other people experience in their dealings with child guidance clinics and similar psychiatric services controlled by the community stems, I think, from this fundamental mistake. In such situations the clinic's function should always be to act as a communicative link between the people expressing the impulse and those wishing to see it controlled without undertaking responsibility for changing matters themselves. For example, one often finds a situation where a family is in constant conflict with authority, as if seeking to provoke it into some positive action they really need, but where the authority, be it court, school or probation service, hesitates to act because the family are at the same time arousing feelings of concern and sympathy. Where this is the case, the clinic can often bring the two sides to a more fruitful awareness of their relationship, helping the family to see that what they are really demanding, yet resisting, is benevolent control, and helping the authority to provide this without oscillating between attitudes of punitiveness or indulgence.

The Effect of Secrets in the Network

One principle we have discovered is that it is vital not to restrict communication in any way within the minimum sufficient network. To do so is almost by definition a guarantee of failure, for we then disconnect elements of a structure which must remain connected if it is to be capable of intelligent response and change. Our conventional notions about confidentiality often get in the way here. For example, we may find ourselves helpless if, in a dispute within the family, or beween a family and a school, we allow ourselves to receive information from either side with an implicit understanding that this should remain secret. From the beginning we should make it clear that we can only be useful if we are trusted to act as honest brokers who can assist the different sides to communicate better. Dealing with such a network throughout as a group is, of course, the simplest solution, for the communications are automatically shared and the therapist can receive no secrets. But even where people are seen separately, we can avoid the difficulties by *thinking* of them as a group, a network which must remain in contact directly or through our mediation. For example at one clinic there was for a time, after I became the Director, an extensive use of joint marital interviews by several of the staff. Later these were used in a more discriminating way, but the individual work was in some way changed. *One colleague expressed it by saying that the father was always present in her mind, even when she was seeing the mother alone. In speaking of him the therapist or patient would gesture towards his usual chair. The intactness of the network is thus maintained first in the mind of the therapist, and only secondly through actual procedures.*

Responsibility and Agencies in the Network

The foregoing might be an acceptable formulation for the rôle of the psychiatrist and others who staff clinics and voluntary agencies. Integrating and connecting the network so communication produces change is their special task. Can the same be said of those with statutory responsibility who, charged by society with the implementation of its laws, are responsible for actions rather than communication?

Statutory agencies

Social workers enforcing child care legislation, those responsible for special education procedures and probation officers in the courts are linking parts of their respective networks, even in their legal tasks. When a child is taken into care, sent to a special school or brought before a court for breach of probation, the responsible worker is first required to provide a communicative link. Information communicated within an integrated network generates the pressure for change and the worker responsible acts for this change by – for example – admitting a child to care. Such an event will only be experienced as a personal failure by the worker if they had thought it was their responsibility to do more than play this integrative rôle.

Referring agencies

Sometimes we accept more responsibility than we should because pressure is coming indirectly from the patient referred, through a referrer. Insistent demands from referrers that the cases should be seen or treated often arise when the referrer is unconsciously frightened of the rage which threatens if a patient's demands are frustrated. Referrers sometimes avoid this by identifying with the patient and incorporating the demand which is then passed on to the agency. If this is not recognised, the agency becomes wrongly involved in an interminable therapy with the family and behaves as if it feels obliged endlessly to feed an insatiable child, located in both patient and referrer. Discussion with the referrer is of course the right action, so that the demands can be put back in the family where they belong and where they could perhaps provide the basis for more adequate motivation.

16

Inappropriate demands

Networks producing this kind of insistent but inappropriate demand can be quite complex. In one family which functioned in many ways at a psychotic level, treatment enabled the mother to stop accepting the whole family's depressions, which she had done partly to shield the father from an awareness of his own inadequacy. As the mother became more aggressive and faced him with increasing awareness of his own impotence the father, frightened of hitting back at her, wanted to punish the daughter instead. But lacking the capacity even to do this, he repeatedly aroused the anxiety of the child's physician in a hospital where the older sister had died of a kidney infection. This history lay behind the physician's repetitive demand for psychotherapy for the younger sister, despite the fact that treatment was repeatedly offered by the psychotherapist and sabotaged by the family.

I recall a rather similar case referred by a children's department where I was initially unable to understand their insistent demand for psychotherapy. I thought it inappropriate, until it emerged that this was a 'second generation' deprivation case. The children's officer felt doubly responsible because of a belief that the present problem could have been averted through the department's handling of the mother when she was in care during her own childhood.

These are problems which could happen to any referrer lacking sophistication in psychiatric processes. There are other referrals which have more to do with the psychopathology of the referrer, or perhaps of society itself. One school sent us a succession of cases of behaviour problems in children who had suffered deprivation, even where this was clearly being remedied very effectively, if gradually, by the foster home and school, because the headmistress had suffered deprivation herself. Another school showed exceptional intolerance to being made into a 'bad object' as a solution to a family's difficulties, and reacted to this by simultaneously excluding children and referring them to our clinic, which they used as a 'bad object' in turn. A general practitioner referred a large series of patients for private psychotherapy who were often unsuitable because they lacked motivation and came at his persuasion. The referrals ceased when he began his own psychoanalysis, no doubt because he was at last able to refer himself directly instead of vicariously.

17

One can carry this further, of course, and see that many cases are referred because of values in our particular society with which we would not all necessarily agree. Most agencies are familiar with demands from sections of society that children should not be aggressive or sexual, that they should value academic achievement over living experience, or put social conformity above the search for their own identity.

Conclusion: The Agency as Part of the Network

Finally, we must consider ways in which the clinic or agency becomes part of the network. *Since we are always supplying some psychological function that patients cannot provide for themselves, we necessarily become part of the minimum sufficient network until such time as these functions can be internalised.* As far as possible, we try to remain detached from and conscious of these functions, but we will inevitably fall short of this ideal and find ourselves activated by unconscious personal factors such as enjoyment of the protected intimacy of the therapeutic situation, a desire to solve our own problems vicariously, to engage in false reparation and so on.

At least we *may* 'find ourselves' again, and resume a valid therapeutic rôle, if the organisation and atmosphere of our clinics and agencies can contain such difficulties, regarding them as inevitable and natural, and so provide the mechanisms for recovering and indeed learning from them.

Notes

1 I am indebted to my former colleagues at the Woodberry Down Child Guidance Centre, and the Queen Elizabeth Hospital for Children, including Win Roberts and Gill Gorrell Barnes, for their participation in the development and application of these concepts.

2 This paper is developed from some ideas first presented in a lecture at the 23rd Interclinic Conference of the National Association for Mental Health, 1967, entitled, 'Child Guidance From Within'. Here the ideas are used to examine the dynamics of referral systems through a key question: 'If we begin to think of a network of functions each time a case is referred to us, other

questions at once arise: Who is disturbed? Who is disturbing? Who has the motivation to alter the situation? And who has the capacity to alter it? Four people may be involved here, or one.' (See page 13 above.) These ideas were then presented to the second Athenian Symposium on Group Techniques, Athens 1968, and the paper was published in its present form in *Social Work Today*, 2, **9,** 28/7/71. [Ed.].

2 Indications and Contraindications for Conjoint Family Therapy

Clinics which practise a single mode of therapy tend to select only those referrals suited to it, leaving the rejected majority to resume their search for help elsewhere, or to manage without. Skynner believed that in any publicly-funded service, it was the professionals who should do the searching in order to learn and thereby have available a wide variety of methods. A constructive response of some kind could then be made to almost all requests.

Besides his work in child psychiatry within the National Health Service, he and a group of colleagues were developing a private practice which provided group and individual psychotherapy. They were also collaborating as staff of a new course in group work. In NHS and private practice the variety of treatment methods available demanded clarity about the different methods to be used with different cases.

In clinical work with individuals, groups and families, and in the training groups of the new course, he repeatedly observed a three-stage developmental pattern corresponding to three stages in the psychoanalytic theory of child development. He used this pattern to develop a selection procedure in which developmental levels are used to distinguish those referrals particularly suited to family, individual or group psychotherapy.

Today when a larger number of therapists are proficient in more than one approach, the selection procedure remains a valuable contribution towards differentiating between different kinds of problems and the methods likely to help them best. The selection procedure is updated in Chapter 3.

J. R. S.

General Principles in Group and Family Therapy

Many people who have devoted time and study to treatment of the natural family group seen together for joint interviews (family therapy) seem to have reached similar conclusions about general principles. Where these principles differ from those generally employed in groups constituted by the therapist (group therapy), they are dictated to some extent by the different situation and aims.[1]

The artificial group has no significance beyond the therapeutic assistance it can give its members. When its task is performed it is dissolved and vanishes, except in the psyche of each member. Its primary purpose is the promotion of insight, learning and change, rather than the gratification of basic needs. Patients are usually discouraged from meeting outside the planned sessions, making ordinary friendships, eating or sleeping together. Selection is a vital factor, and balances and contrasts are sought as well as similarities.

By contrast, the family group existed before treatment began, derives from previous groups extending into the past, and will continue after therapy finishes. It is there to gratify many fundamental needs of parents and children alike, and it is meeting all the time, the planned sessions forming only a small fraction of the time spent together. It is by definition a 'badly' selected group. The fact that a member has become psychiatrically ill implies that there is collusive use of certain typical defences by the whole family, a shared denial of the same basic problems.

There is a graduation between these two extremes, between the small neurotic group and the natural family group. Such processes as therapeutic communities, social clubs, treatment of an industrial concern or consultation given to an agency as a whole, lie between these extremes.

Foulksian Principles in Family Therapy Technique

Most workers agree that the therapist should relate to the family as a whole, avoid taking sides or concentrating on the needs of any one individual, including the patient so-called. The problems of family interaction are seen to include the father and the siblings. Responsibility for understanding and solving the difficulties should be kept squarely on the family as a whole. The amount of structure provided varies between different workers, as in other forms of group therapy. I am especially influenced by the group-analytic approach, of which Foulkes was the originator. I try to leave the situation as unstructured as possible, at least at first, and seek to facilitate the inherent and unique therapeutic potentialities of the group process on the individuals, rather than to treat the individuals or the group itself (Foulkes, 1948, 1957).

General Advantages of Family Therapy

The indications for and against family therapy derive partly from the advantages and disadvantages inherent in the method itself, relevant to any situation to which it might be applied, and partly from the particular nature of the problem to be treated.

1. Diagnostic advantages

One sees the family in operation, instead of having to construct an image or model from the different accounts of each individual (though one gets these as well). If the interaction is allowed to develop and is skilfully facilitated at the right moments, the problem actually begins to happen in the here and now of the interview, moving from its first locus in the referred patient towards a disturbance of function in the family as a whole. It may quickly be apparent, to take one example, that a scapegoated child is excluded from the family and becomes a problem each time the discussion comes near criticism of the mother.[2] The advantages of this for diagnosis are overwhelming, even if one chooses to halt the process at this point and offers treatment on an individual basis. Further, the balance of motivation for or against change in the family as a whole is often apparent too in the family diagnostic session. Many of the 'interminable' treatments we encounter when only a part of the family is worked with are avoided at the beginning.

2. Shared responsibility with the family

No procedure using interviews with separate individuals can match this, for when the therapist is the only person who has access to all the information provided, it is not unreasonable for the family to look to him to put it all together and tell them what to do, or at least tell them what is wrong. In family therapy, on the other hand, the therapist automatically avoids receiving secrets. He can infer and guess as much as he likes, and will indeed be less inhibited in giving his impressions since no one can misconstrue these are based on a private communication. Responsibility is shared, the therapist having a definite but clearly limited expertise in problems of communication generally, the members of the family being aware of the limited and distorted nature of the knowledge they have given him about their own functioning, which they always know better than he does.

3. Economy of time and effort

Therapy of the artificially constituted group does offer some economies, but in my experience these are more limited than they appear. However, the intensity and rapidity with which family therapy produces its effects, where it is indicated, does make its value outstanding where resources are limited. Not only are major changes in family functioning effected in a few interviews, often indeed in one, but the interviews can be spaced widely without losing this intensive therapeutic character. Partly this is because of the homework the family does between sessions, at discussions often lasting far into the night, so that a meeting once in three weeks is felt as just about right. The enlistment of the overtly healthy members, as well as the more obviously sick one, also increases the therapeutic potential. Time and again it is the non-referred siblings who provide the key information, break a family collusion and generally save the day.

4. Flexible treatment plans

There is also the possibility, in my experience to a greater extent than in other forms of treatment, of a widely variable degree of intervention, from one session to a long series. Each intervention is in some way complete in itself, perhaps because transference phenomena, including dependency problems, are in general kept within the family itself while the therapist remains a more real individual, and also because, if movement occurs, everyone changes and a new equilibrium is reached. All these points, and the suitability of this method to long-term but intermittent contact, may make it especially suitable for the general practitioner and others in a permanent relationship with many family members.

Contraindications

1. Diagnosis

There are hardly any contraindications to this family approach for diagnostic purposes. I have made exceptions where the parents were separated and had a violently hostile relationship, but even here I am not sure that this was a right decision. One can always be quite flexible, terminating the joint interview at any point to see the members in some other fashion, if one is in doubt.

2. Treatment

I have come to see fewer and fewer disadvantages as my experience has grown. People without experience of this method often fear explosive or damaging interactions, but John Bowlby wrote in his early paper on this technique, in 1949, that he had 'no longer come to be alarmed by the hideous scenes which may occasionally ensue'. John Elderkin Bell, in one of the best accounts we have of the technique, remarks that 'there are occasions when the intensity of feeling within a family rises to flood proportions, but in all cases where this has happened, the family itself has been able to control the feelings' (Bell, 1961, 1962). My own experience is similar, and I know of no instance where an interview has had a harmful effect, no matter how alarmed I felt at the time.

3. Limitations

The main limitation of family therapy is that change is naturally restricted to what is acceptable to the family as a whole, rather than adapted to the needs of any one individual. Individual therapy or inclusion in separate groups may be indicated for those who need and want a greater degree of self-knowledge than the more resistant members of the family can accept for themselves.

But even in individual work, the family as a whole will try to impose limits on change which will be effective if the child is still at a dependent stage. In adolescence the natural termination of family sessions occurs when strivings for independence normal to this stage are being expressed and accepted, and here further therapy apart from the family, by individual or group methods, can have its greatest value.

4. Disadvantages for the therapist

Other disadvantages seem to involve the therapist rather than the patients. Family therapy is noisy, confusing and very demanding of one's capacity for attention. It is often a good deal more difficult to keep one's emotional equilibrium than in individual therapy, though less taxing than other types of group work. There is no history to cling to when one feels at sea, not even the obsessional routine of history-taking to fall back on. Nevertheless, it is this exposure of oneself to the family problem, whereby one lives it with them and shares the struggle towards an understanding of what is really happening, that in my view partly accounts for its efficacy. It is fair to add that it can also be very rewarding and enjoyable.

Specific Syndromes

Little has so far been written about the syndromes best treated by family group methods. There seems to be agreement, as one might expect, that it is particularly useful where the children are acting out impulses or expressing feelings which cannot be admitted and coped with in the parents' inner psychology or acknowledged within the family as a whole. Such families need a scapegoat, sick child, delinquent or helpless baby, or an ambitious, successful wonder-boy, to function at all. The joint family sessions are ideally suited to

27

help them include and integrate the child and the problem he represents. Marital problems often provide the key to such family syndromes. It is sometimes possible to trace the disturbance from the symptoms in the referred child to the parents' sexual incompatibility, in one session. Problems of authority and control frequently have their origin in an envious rivalry between the father and mother over each other's sexual rôles. Many writers have commented on the phenomenon of the 'activation of the passive father' which so often occurs in family group work when this conflict is dealt with. The method seems to be especially suited to the treatment of ego-syntonic, acting-out character disorders, and it is worth remarking that the technique seems equally effective at all social levels, from the most intelligent and sophisticated to the most inadequate and primitive. I have not found this to be the case with any other psychotherapeutic technique.

The first level of family development

Families are suitable for, and indeed often only for, family therapy when they are functioning at a basically paranoid-schizoid level, with part object relationships, lack of ego boundaries and extensive use of denial, splitting and projection. In such families, different psychological functions – impulses, controls etc. – are located in different individuals and may move from one to another. *The functioning unit is not the individual but the family, in that only the family as a whole contains the necessary psychological structures by which a mature individual operates, and the individuals are lost without each other, in treatment as in other activities. The family group is not a group, since true individuals do not yet exist.* In such cases the minimum sufficient network for treatment is the family as a whole.[3]

Contraindicated Syndromes

Contraindications have been less well documented. They include families where there is one particularly sick and resistant member, those where the main gratifications come from thinly-veiled sadistic and destructive manoeuvres, with little positive feelings left to provide motivation to face the true state of affairs, and families where there is too little capacity to share.

The second level of family development

While families using mainly paranoid and schizoid mechanisms should for preference be seen together, our experience suggests that families whose members have reached but not securely mastered the depressive position are not suitable. Here the rage and destructiveness resulting from frustration of intense oral hungers is felt as too threatening to vital relationships with others in the family. If these intense, mutually dependent ties are threatened by the arousal of hostility, disagreement or even awareness of separate identity of family members (all of which represent separation or loss in the original mother-child relationship), intolerable depressive anxiety is generated. The technique of family therapy described seems to engender such feelings of separateness without providing a sufficiently personal relationship to 'hold' the individuals and provide sufficient security for them to tolerate and work through the painful affect.[4] We have found that a period of individual psychotherapy is necessary at this stage with at least one family member, though it is still possible to make productive use of family interviews if key members have their own therapists present, maintaining a personal relationship with them as is done in four-way interviews with couples.

Conclusion: The Third Level of Family Development

Later, when individuals can bear some degree of psychological separation, and can face the loss inherent in this, the group becomes possible again. Now it is no longer a fragmented unity – the split-up mother of the primitive levels – but begins to be an assembly of individuals with separate identities, a true group situation.

For families functioning at this third level, it seems that therapy by individual, stranger group and family methods are all available. The most appropriate choice will be determined more by the severity of the problem, the time available, the degree of intervention and involvement desired, and the extent to which the individual problem is personal or conditioned by family reactions.

Where an individual had encountered an identity crisis, and the overt disturbance is related more to the need to master a real stage in development, some family interviews may release constraints to development imposed by family attitudes, but individual therapy may be desirable to help him understand and integrate an essentially personal experience. Again, where family interviews have released straightforward strivings for autonomy, therapy based on the peer group is in accord with normal development.

Notes

1 This paper was presented as part of a symposium on Group Versus Individual Psychotherapy at the British Association of Social Psychiatry in 1967. It was published under this title in the *International Journal of Social Psychiatry*, Vol. XV, **4** (1969).
2 See, for example, chapter 1 above, pp. 8–12.
3 See chapter 1 above, pp. 6–8.
4 See A. Lyons, 'Therapeutic Intervention in Relation to the Institution of Marriage' in B. Gosling (ed.), *Tavistock Clinic Golden Jubilee Papers*, p. 176. There she corroborates the view that when married partners have begun to see and feel sad and worried about what they are doing to each other in the relationship, separate individual help for each of them is indicated. See chapters 9 and 13 below for an account of current practice which includes the use of couples groups. [Ed.].

3 Referral for Psychotherapy
Written with Dennis Brown

Skynner and Brown address this paper mainly to general practitioners and other medical referrers to help them choose amongst
available options when making referrals, but it is relevant to other
disciplines in the helping professions. For it studies the referral
process and choice of treatment in an unusually practical way,
taking account of factors often overlooked like cost-effectiveness,
the amount of time patient and therapist each have available, and
how the principle of the minimum sufficient network – described in
Chapter 1 above – can best be applied.

It thus updates the previous paper on the basis of fourteen years
of experience which refined the selection procedure introduced
above. The psychoanalyst colleague with whom it is written works
with Skynner in the practice referred to above, and in the course on
group work which has become the Institute of Group Analysis.
Brown, working with another colleague, had also co-authored a
popular textbook on psychotherapy.

Here the two authors suggest a sequence of interventions, using
first the most generally applicable and quickest methods, and saving
the more expensive and time-consuming ones for those unlikely to
respond to brief interventions. Brief psychotherapy is an important
new development and the authors' recommendations are well
illustrated with references to the literature.

J.R.S.

Introduction

The referral process is a central part of treatment and can sometimes determine the outcome.[1] Well-considered and appropriate referrals can, when helpfully guided into treatment by the referring clinician or agency, determine the outcome favourably. Whereas problems along the line of referral can do much in a negative direction, leaving both patient and therapist with a burden in addition to the presenting complaint, which will also have to be unravelled if the treatment is to be effective. Sometimes the referrer has a range of therapeutic options to choose from and this brief appraisal of presenting problems and therapeutic methods is designed to help the referrer choose amongst both problems and available helping resources, so need can be matched against what is known to be most effective in meeting it.

A further practical consideration is one of economy in terms of both time and money. In order to provide the best chance of adequate help for the largest number of people, psychotherapy in the public and private services should be guided by this consideration, and the paper suggests ways of identifying problems that can be dealt with more quickly, saving the more expensive and time-consuming methods for those who are unlikely to respond to brief ones.

Assessment Interviews

The assessment interview(s), whether with the individual alone or plus the whole family group, and whether conducted by the general practitioner or specialist, is one of the most important moments in therapy. It allows not only the taking of a history of the patient and his problem, but also permits observation of his behaviour under stress, and provides the basis for the therapeutic alliance. Both parties can see how they enter into the doctor–patient relationship and can see their respective attitudes to the problems presented. In particular the assessing doctor/therapist will want to determine to what extent these problems can be understood in psychological terms, and how much the patient is willing and able to see them in these terms.

Treating the Couple, Family, or Wider Social Systems

In assessing the alternatives, one or more interviews with the patient and his or her family of origin (or, if married, the spouse and then perhaps the family of procreation) should be considered first for the following reasons.

1: A diagnostic session with the family group (or couple) provides important information that would otherwise take a long time to obtain, and some which could not be obtained at all by separate interviews with the designated patient or other family members. One common and important finding is that the designated patient is not the sickest member of the family but is protecting more vulnerable members, or the stability of the marriage, by 'volunteering' to be the symptom carrier, scapegoat, or rescuer.

2: Family interviews have not in our experience been found to do harm, despite careful follow-up of doubtful cases. This is not to say that some members may not get upset or angry, which is often necessary if change is to occur.

3: Family therapy is the 'broadest spectrum' psychotherapy. Though the extent of change may be limited as compared with other approaches (since it must necessarily include a compromise between the different aspirations of all the family members) the range of disorders in which it can bring modest but worthwhile improvement is vastly greater than that of any other approach. Indeed, if the social system beyond the family can when relevant be involved, it is rare for useful changes not to occur, even with 'end-of-line', 'uncooperative' cases with which all other methods have failed. For example, even children showing severe problems at school, whose parents are unconcerned and resistant to attending a clinic, can change if the therapist offers to meet the child, parents, head and class teacher at school. The principle is the simple and obvious one that the person with the complaint – in this case the teacher, not the child or family – must be present if progress is to be possible. This principle is systematically investigated in Chapter 1, where it is called the 'minimum sufficient network'.

4: It can be an extremely potent modality, sometimes effecting enduring change within a single one-hour session, and usually taking under six sessions. It has also been noted independently by workers in different countries that spacing sessions a month apart, instead of at weekly intervals, actually increases the rate of change. This makes such methods highly economic. Though family therapy in Britain developed more in child psychiatry, the approach can be fruitful even when the 'patient' is adult; and bringing the 'well' spouse into the examination and treatment of a disturbed adult can often show the true nature of their disturbance, or increase the therapeutic potential of the marriage, or both. People can help each other in a family or marriage as well as make each other suffer.

We believe it is sensible to consider this approach first and to move on to other methods if:

a: It proves insufficiently effective

b: It is contraindicated by a history of severe depression or early parental deprivation, or current incapacity of the family to meet developmental needs

c: It is impracticable because the person wants treatment in his or her own right or the family live far away, refuse to come, or are mostly dead. Separate therapy has its main value for adults who have left, or established themselves at an appropriate distance from, their families of origin, but have not yet married and begun to establish families of their own.[2]

Therapy Separate from the Family: Advantages of Groups

If separate therapy for the designated patient is indicated by one of the above criteria, when is individual (one-to-one) work preferable, and when is a stranger-group more helpful? Again, the patient's own wishes may decide this irrespective of what the doctor might recommend, but if a choice is possible the group has great advantage with certain types of problem.

1. Ego-syntonic personality disorders

It often facilitates more rapid and deep change than individual therapy in those patients who have little self-understanding or desire for it, and who therefore tend to see their problems as the fault of others. Such 'ego-syntonic' personality disorders are notoriously slow to change in individual therapy, where the therapist faces the dilemma that confrontation sufficiently forceful to penetrate the patient's defensive armour may be experienced as so critical and wounding that rapport and trust are lost. In a well-conducted group other members not only provide far more forceful confrontation than the therapist may dare attempt, but some patients will also simultaneously take a supportive rôle, which enables the criticism to be tolerated without excessive loss of self-esteem. Meanwhile, the therapist can preserve a trusted, neutral 'referee' position.

2. Character neurosis and psychosomatic problems

Patients – many with psychosomatic presentations – who cannot fantasise and are out of touch with their inner worlds, or who excercise a tight control of their emotions so that they give an impression of lack of life and absence of feeling, often 'resonate' to the powerful emotional forces that group interaction generates and begin to experience feelings more vividly themselves, becoming aware spontaneously of previously dissociated aspects of their personalities without any conscious attempt to bring this about.

3. Dependency problems

For similar reasons a group is often more useful for highly dependent patients who seek to put all responsibility for change in their condition on to others, particularly patients who deny any meaning to their symptoms, offer nothing spontaneously, and wait passively to be asked questions or to be given advice.

4. Identity problems

A group is also particularly valuable for those whose sense of identity, including gender identity, is vague and confused, since it not only helps them to find their boundaries by the feedback they receive, but also provides a variety of different behavioural models from both sexes.

5. Early peer problems

Patients with difficulties in coping with groups in life, where the fundamental issues are more to do with those early problems which arise from problems in coping with siblings or peers rather than with parental figures, may also be suitable for this mode of treatment. In such cases a well-constituted group can give a second chance of growing up in a context containing the rich variety of experiences normally provided by a healthy family. This is so whether the group is supportive or analytic.

6. Borderline patients

Some clinicians have found groups to be the ideal setting for *containing* those people with such severe early difficulties that they have chaotic lifestyles and are prone to acting out, drink and drug dependence and recidivism, or to brief psychotic episodes. Even if the motivation arises out of nothing more purposeful than desperation, some of these people can be held in a group situation providing the composition does not contain too many of them, and they can make appreciable gains which would be much more difficult to achieve with individual methods.[3]

7. First recourse to groups

As compared with individual psychotherapy, group therapy has a rather broader spectrum (though there is a wide overlap and each can deal with a range of problems unsuitable for the other). On this ground as well as on the obvious ground of economy (which means wider availability, more intensive provision, shorter waiting lists, or some part of all three) we suggest it should be considered after family therapy, and, when long-term intervention is needed, before individual therapy.

Couples and Multi-Family Groups

Couples groups, where three or four couples meet together weekly to monthly, and multi-family groups, where several families are seen together, combine several therapeutic advantages of both 'stranger' and 'natural' groups. Though the use of such groups is limited at present, they have been found effective by one of us[4] in cases resistant to conventional treatment through individual, group, or even ordinary marital or family therapy. Because these groups combine some advantages of both family and group therapy, patients attending them show more rapid change than in stranger-groups, but they usually need to come for a year or more. This being so, it is best to attempt a short-term intervention first with the couple or family, to make sure that a more economical solution is not possible, and to consider this option later.

When is Individual (One-to-One) Therapy Required?

1. Flexibility

a. Versatility

One-to-one therapy is much more versatile than group therapy, so that the frequency and number of sessions, the level of regression and dependency, the depth and intensity of emotions elicited, the balance struck between reassurance and motivating anxiety, and the degree of focus on a particular task, can all be varied as necessary – that is, it can range from support to exploration at depth. Even when therapy aims at change in the structure of the personality, it can vary between a brief intervention focussed on a clearly defined and limited problem[5] and an open-ended psychoanalysis that may last several years, aiming, like group-analytic psychotherapy, towards the more general maturation of the personality.

b. Specific focus and specific problems

We might need to limit depth or duration of therapy, as well as who is involved. Many patients do not need or want to explore themselves and their relationships, others do not have the necessary capacities, or are likely to be made worse by having their defences challenged and regressive fantasies stirred up. Even when an exploratory approach is sought and not contraindicated, short-term psychotherapy might be necessitated by the limited availability of both patient and therapist – for instance, when the patient has to travel a long distance. One or two consultations can, in some cases, provide a lot of benefit, and this often takes place with only the designated patient, especially when the natural group, such as the family, cannot be mustered together. Similarly, counselling of people who have suffered a bereavement or who are in trouble because of specific problems, such as an unwanted pregnancy or difficulties in studying, may sometimes be best limited to that person and also kept at a relatively superficial level without exploring deeper unconscious conflicts. One-to-one treatment is particularly called for where the individual's needs are for short-term or concentrated work that would conflict with the needs of the group process which takes time to develop; group analytic psychotherapy is rarely considered if the patient cannot commit himself or herself to at least a year of weekly sessions. Patients with unresolved grief reactions may need a lot of individual help to contact and ventilate stifled grief, and to explore related conflicts and defences.

2. Undivided attention
a. Severe deprivation

Though individual therapy can be used valuably in most conditions and situations, if others in the patient's family are not blocking progress, it seems to be most specifically indicated for those severely deprived personalities stunted or distorted by severe failures in the 'facilitating environment' of early months and years.[6] This is particulary so for individuals who lost or never had the experience of 'good enough' parents or parental substitutes. Mild deficiencies of this type may be remedied in groups, where profound regression of one or more members can elicit remarkable care and nurturance. Similarly, in the course of marital or family therapy, family members can be helped to recognise and respond more constructively to regressive needs in day-to-day living at home. Although this may suffice to tip the balance in milder cases, there are clearly limits beyond which it would be unreasonable to expect even the most considerate and patient individual to go on meeting the infantile demands of a spouse or child. Then, the undivided attention of individual therapy, at least as a preliminary or concurrent mode, might offer more realistic hope.

b. Supportive and analytic methods

Such undivided attention may be essentially supportive in aim, as in casework by social workers maintaining severely damaged people over periods of years; sometimes this alone can lead to slow growth in patients' capacities to trust and grow in psychotherapy. This promotes exploration of experiences and fantasies at all levels of development, including the most primitive fusion and separation of the infant self in relation to maternal images.[7] The needs, feelings and fantasies of the individual can be attended to without interference by those of others. This may permit the tentative unfolding of a self that is stunted, distorted and barely held together.

3. Need for prolonged preparation

A third indication for individual work is where patients need prolonged preparation for psychotherapy of a more dynamic and exploratory type. Some patients need a lot of help in beginning to think about relationships and feelings, and to adjust to the idea of becoming more open with others, whether one-to-one or in a group. Ideally such preparation begins with the general practitioner, and the influence of Balint and of Balint groups has done much to alert general practitioners to the possibilities of using even brief medical consultations for this purpose.

Dynamic Versus Behavioural Orientations in Psychotherapy

A further choice has to be made between a more dynamic, exploratory, analytic approach aiming at the development of insight or self-understanding, with the hope that this will lead to conflict-resolution, change in the balance of motivation, and alleviation of the complaint; or alternatively the more behavioural, directive approach. This emphasises the development of skills the patient has not learnt or the changing of previous maladaptive learning through behavioural psychotherapy.

1. Family and marital work

In family and marital work less difficulty arises, since most family therapists, whatever their original training, tend to draw freely on behavioural systems or psychoanalytic concepts and methods and to combine these as necessary. In the treatment of sexual dysfunction, for example, the combination of the behavioural approach with a psychoanalytic exploration of the resistances thereby elicited, appears more powerful than either mode used by itself.[8]

2. Individual and group therapy

In individual and stranger-group work, however, practitioners have tended to remain polarised as adherents of either the psychoanalytic or the behavioural paradigm. The type of treatment that patients receive therefore depends more on the door they happen to enter and the philosophy and personality of those behind it than on what might help them most, so that the choice of the most appropriate door will often lie with the referring practitioner.

3. Training and re-education: the behavioural orientation

In general, patients whose problems stem from simple deficiencies in experience, or whose training has been inappropriate – so that they are aware of their handicap and the need for more education or re-education – are helped most effectively and economically by a behavioural approach, either individually or in groups, for example social skills training for those who have little sexual experience.

4. Resistance and protective layers: the dynamic orientation

If the patient has the wish and capacity, an analytic approach is indicated where a direct approach to re-learning by exposure to new situations is made difficult through the development of complicated defensive systems that obstruct the patient's conscious awareness of the problem and so also limit the therapist's ability to perceive it and to change it directly. For example, forbidden sexual impulses may be disguised as hostility and suffering, as in sadomasochistic behaviour; or complaints of obsessional hostile thoughts may be a way of avoiding taking responsibility for actual, appropriate anger towards others. Where such protective layers have developed to disguise and insulate the original difficulty, the exploratory analytic approach comes into its own. Once the patient is re-connected with the basic problem – becomes conscious of it – he has the possibility of exposing himself to beneficial experience which could help him and which he has hitherto avoided. But if this does not occur spontaneously, a behavioural approach may then be appropriate, as Freud himself noted.

Conclusion: Combinations and Sequences of the Different Modes

We have found that all these different modes can, if necessary, be fruitfully combined, though a different order may be appropriate in different cases. Conjoint family sessions may help parents accept the independence of an adolescent who is expressing their own fears of separation as well as his own, after which separate individual or group therapy for the youngster may provide a 'half-way house' between the family and the outside world. The parents, left alone, may then have to face the marital problem from which their concern over the child distracted them, and this may need therapy as a couple or in a couples group. Specific sexual difficulties that are next disclosed may be resolved most quickly by 'active sex therapy' using a behavioural approach.

While some problems can be equally effectively treated by different methods, benefit may be partial. Then a change of therapy may unblock progress – for example, patients who have undergone psychoanalysis without learning to apply their insights in outside relationships may benefit from group therapy. After one of the briefer forms of individual therapy or family or marital therapy, some patients may benefit from long-term analytic psychotherapy, either in a group or on an individual basis.

A flexible response requires that all psychotherapists should acquire some knowledge of and preferably some basic skill in the individual, stranger-group and family and marital psychotherapies, employing both dynamic and behavioural principles. Though each individual will probably wish to concentrate on one or other of these different approaches, we believe that some acquaintance with them all is an essential part of the training, not only of every psychotherapist but of all psychiatrists.

Notes

1 This paper was first published in *The British Medical Journal*, Vol. 282 (June 1981).
2 F. Martin, 'Some Implications for Individual Psychotherapy from the Theory and Practice of Family Therapy, and Vice Versa', *British Journal of Medical Psychology*, Vol. **50** (1977) 53–64.

3 M. Pines, 'Group Analytic Psychotherapy of the Borderline Patient', *Group Analysis*, 11, **2** (August 1978) and M. Jackson and M. Pines, 'The Borderline Personality: Psychodynamics and Treatment', *Neurologica et Psychiatrica* (1986).

4 See chapters 9 and 13 below for accounts of couples groups.

5 D. H. Malan, *A Study of Brief Psychotherapy*, and *Individual Psychotherapy and the Science of Psychodynamics*; P. E. Sifneos, *Short-Term Psychotherapy and Emotional Crisis*; S. de Shazer, *Keys to Solution in Brief Psychotherapy*; J. P. Gustafson, *The Complex Secret of Brief Psychotherapy*.

6 P. E. Sifneos, *op.cit.*

7 M. S. Mahler, F. Pine and A. Bergman, *The Psychological Birth of the Human Infant*.

8 See chapters 7, 8 and 9 below.

4 A Group-Analytic Approach to Conjoint Family Therapy

This paper played a major part in the early development of family therapy in Britain and remains one of the most lucid accounts of its subject. In 1967 a few people were experimenting with the method in Britain, many of whom attended a day conference at one of the clinics Skynner directed. There the ideas and case study in the paper were first presented, and it was read in its present form at a meeting of the Association of Child Psychology and Psychiatry in 1968. It appeared in their journal in 1969 and in *Social Work Today* in 1970, followed by 'The Minimum Sufficient Network' (Chapter 1 above) and 'Boundaries' (referenced in the Appendix). It was republished some ten years later by Walrond-Skinner in her collection *Developments in Family Therapy* (footnote 1 below). And so, presented on two occasions and published on three, the paper's influence on the social work profession and child guidance movement was extensive and was one of the factors responsible for the strong and early development of family therapy in those fields. It is republished in this collection because, like some of the early papers of Bell, Jackson and Wynne in the US, it is a 'classic' of its kind.

In Britain the prevailing ideas about therapy at the time were that the therapist should be neutral and non-directive. But working with deprived and multi-problem families in the East End of London, Skynner discovered the need for family therapists to take some control and provide a clear structure within which individuals could feel safe to experiment with new rôles and relationships. He had been reassured in this view by Minuchin's early papers, reviewed here, who was then working with an equivalent population in New York and reaching similar conclusions. But Skynner recalls the apprehension he felt at the criticism he expected from his colleagues in London, and his surprise at the warm reception this paper received.

Through his work in individual and group psychotherapy, Skynner maintained his interest in the dynamics of the inner world and was struggling to reconcile his observations there with the dynamics of family systems described here. But in this paper we can see the beginnings of his attempt to integrate the psychoanalytic and systems models, accomplished in the concluding chapters of this book (see especially Chapters 10, 11 and 14). The harmonious relationship between practitioners of these two schools in Britain, who work amicably together to mutual benefit in the Institute of Family Therapy and other centres, owes much to this influence (see the introduction to Chapter 12). There are other 'modern' principles advocated here, like the wide spacing of interviews a month apart to speed up progress (see Chapter 13); the expectation that competent therapy could produce rapid change within a few sessions (see Chapter 3); and the need for modifications of technique to adapt to different levels of education, motivation and insight (see Chapters 12 and 13, especially the tables distinguishing between dysfunctional, mid-range and healthy families).

J.R.S.

A: Introduction

1. A review of the literature

The dynamic interlocking nature of family relationships, where the demands of instinct and society, impulse and control, may be served by different family members, has received increasing study in recent years.[1] Bowlby (1949) reported the bringing together of parents and referred child, during their individual treatments, for occasional joint sessions. Other landmarks include Sperling's (1951) description of the manner in which the child acts out its mother's repressed needs and Henry and Warson's (1951) concept of a 'Family Core Neurosis' which affects all members. Fisher and Mendell (1956) applied various projective tests to two or three generations of several families. They concluded that 'each family tends to be characterised by a special "flavour" or "atmosphere"'. The projective responses of the members of a family manifest certain themes in common, as if there were a key motif that concerned the members of this particular group. In one family all members, at three generation levels, show an unusual preoccupation with themes of exhibitionism and self-display. Their impression that *this transmission process occurs primarily in terms of what is denied, forbidden and concealed is highly relevant, since the focus of family therapy is on facilitating communication in these forbidden areas*.

Amerongen (1954) and Hallowitz (1957) illustrated a growing recognition of the value of including fathers in the therapeutic effort. Ackerman (1958, 1959, 1966, 1967) demonstrated the potential of working with the whole family, including siblings, though his theories are limited by their basis in individual rather than group dynamics and his techniques by a corresponding excessive activity on the part of the therapist. Prince (1961) has described joint treatment of mothers and young children, pointing up particularly the direct information to be gained from physical movements and the highly supportive and reassuring effect, on both mother and child, of witnessing the latent love which lies beneath overt hostility and other defences. Martin and Knight (1962) outlined an intake procedure at the Tavistock Clinic during which both parents met together with the whole clinic 'family'. Howells (1962) treats the designated patient as the family member who may be most obviously handicapped but may also be a scapegoat or an ambassador.

Bell (1961, 1962) views child psychiatric problems as examples of blockage of communication in the family network, as a result of which there is regression from symbolic communication to preverbal signs. A rigid, inflexible pattern of response and rôle-playing develops from which the family can be freed only by an outsider who can translate the stalemate of symptoms and condemnation back into a symbolic form that permits discussion and resolution of the conflict.

A number of authors and teams have developed increasingly group-centred theories of family functioning in association with research into schizophrenia. These enquiries have tended, until recently, to develop rather separately from the research into conjoint family therapy of the broader range of diagnostic categories occurring mainly within the field of child psychiatry, but each is now increasingly shedding light on the other. The concepts of the 'double-bind' and of 'family homeostasis' produced by the Palo Alto group (Bateson *et al.*, 1956) are early examples. Bowen (1960) comments on similar observations of symbiotic pairing of one marital partner with a schizophrenic child, thereby excluding the spouse. Lidz and his colleagues (Lidz, 1963; Lidz *et al.*, 1966) have noted disturbances they describe as marital 'schism' and 'skew', with associated weakness of the normal generation boundaries in families producing schizophrenic members. Satir (1964) has developed a detailed and generally applicable technique from this specialised background.

The Philadelphia team (Friedman *et al.*, 1965), though restricting their study to families of schizophrenic patients, have explored and formulated general problems of family therapeutic technique. They are particularly interesting on issues raised by co-therapy and by the power struggle which they believe must ensue when therapists interact with a pathological family system. The University of Texas Medical Branch team (McGregor *et al.*, 1964), studying a broader range of problems among adolescents, and using an intensive investigatory and therapeutic technique whereby a team and family interact in various combinations for two full days, has produced some of the most interesting concepts regarding family dynamics, particularly in their detailed exposition of the relation between different forms of marital pathology and corresponding levels of developmental arrest in the children. Ferriera (1963) speaks of 'family myths' – fanatasies shared by a family which preserve self-esteem at the cost of self-deception and breakdown of some of its members. Laing and his colleagues (Laing and Esterson, 1964) have made careful studies supporting the notion that schizophrenic disorder can be brought about by pressures to distort the perception of reality.

It appears to be no accident that the best published work is increasingly produced by teams rather than individuals. Sager *et al.* (1968) commented on the way that treatment of the family together has been paralleled by a tendency for teachers to allow their students to learn by being present throughout the treatment process, or to act as co-therapists, rather than by supervision of the students' cases alone or through hearing carefully edited accounts of the teacher's work. This has led to refreshingly frank studies of co-therapy and team-work, and to a more open examination of the therapist's rôle, the effect of his personality and so on. At the same time, growing interest in this field has led to conferences where attempts have been made to integrate existing knowledge (Ackerman *et al.*, 1961, 1967; Cohen *et al.*, 1964).

A number of authors require special mention because of their contribution to specific problems. The University of Texas team (McGregor *et al.*, 1964) has paid particular attention to therapeutic procedures which are based more on example and identification than on insight and intellectual processes. Minuchin and Montalvo (1966, 1967) have carried this type of research even further and have developed special techniques, based on rôle-playing and identification, for treating culturally deprived families. Parsloe (1967) has written on the use of similar methods through home visits and Roberts (1968) has reported on principles we have developed for working with deprived families.

49

Sager (1968) has contributed an excellent paper on selection for, and induction to, family group therapy, while among others Ackerman (1958, 1966), Scherz (1962) and Skynner, in Chapters 2 and 3 here, have attempted to formulate indications and contraindications for the technique.

More recently a number of authors (Leichter and Schulman, 1963; Blinder, 1965; Curry, 1965; Durell, 1969; Powell and Monahan, 1969) have given interesting accounts of multi-family therapy – the simultaneous treatment of several families together. This approach combines many of the advantages of family and of stranger-group therapy and is a particularly promising field.

With the exception of Bell (1961, 1962, 1964), however, little consideration has been given until recently to the theory and technique of therapeutic *group* interaction in this context. General theories of group functioning have tended to develop in association with the therapist-constituted 'small group of strangers', or with 'T' groups or analytically-orientated training groups. In family therapy, much interesting work has been done in studying the typical structure and interaction of families with particular types of pathology, but the therapeutic interventions have tended to be based either on one-to-one techniques or on 'common-sense', spontaneous responses by the therapist.

Recently, some fruitful ideas, with the aim of applying group and systems theory to family interactions, have been put forward by a number of authors, particularly Brodey (1967) and Scheflen (1967). I propose now to outline some possible developments of group-analytic theory in this direction.

2. The group-analytic approach in small group work

The group-analytic method is described by Foulkes (1948, 1964) and Foulkes and Anthony (1957).

1. No programme or directions are given, so that all contributions arise spontaneously from the patients.

2. All communications are treated as the equivalent on the part of the group of the free association of the individual under psychoanalytic conditions.

3. All communications and relationships . . . are seen as part of a total field of interaction, the group matrix.

4. All group members take an active part in the total therapeutic process.

5. The group tends to speak and react to a common theme as if it were a living entity, expressing itself in different ways through different mouths. All contributions are variations on a single theme, even though the group are not consciously aware of that theme and do not know what they are really talking about.

This concept of an unconscious common group preoccupation is a feature of other theories and techniques such as those of Whitaker and Lieberman (1964), Bion (1961), Ezriel (1950) and others. All these have important lessons for us, but the group-analytic approach differs from them, I believe, in the following important respects.

1. There is recognition of the individual and a willingness to focus on his more personal psychopathology when this is indicated.

2. There is recognition of the vital therapeutic functions performed by the group towards the individuals and the emphasis that it is the therapist's primary task to facilitate these.

3. The group as a whole, if its communications are sufficiently understood, stands in a position of authority to the therapist, correcting his own distortions and limitations and including him in the treatment process in so far as this is necessary and he can tolerate it.

In the small group of strangers (usually about seven or eight) which meets with the therapist in the process of group analysis, the therapist or conductor thus functions mainly as a catalyst who facilitates the inherent therapeutic potentialities of a well-selected group. The therapist is a translator who recognises and interprets the group themes as they emerge in the same way as a psychoanalyst links and makes meaningful the apparently disjointed and meaningless associations of the analysand.

3. The group-analytic approach in family work

Modifications and elaborations in these principles appear necessary due to certain vital differences.

Small group technique in stranger groups

1: The issue of authority and control can largely be avoided by selecting patients who have different and conflicting views so that they are likely, despite temporary defensive coalitions, to cancel out each other's extreme attitudes and to represent a reasonable degree of 'normality' as a whole even if they do not do so individually.

2: The members are chosen in such a way that, in the long run, no individual will be so powerful and dominant in relation to others that he can impose his will to prevent change and growth in the whole situation.

3: The patients more commonly chosen tend to have reasonably well developed ego and super-ego functions; they are, in other words, adult enough to ensure that there is sufficient capacity for self-control in the group as a whole to require that the therapist be an authority only in so far as he is an expert with special knowledge.

Group-analytic technique with families

None of these conditions is ensured in family groups.

1: There are usually great differences in the strengths of the family members from the point of view both of their maturity and of the power that society vests in them by virtue of their rôles. In the children at least, self-control may be limited, and if one works with the more inadequate types of families, often referred to child guidance clinics and other community services, the parents may be defective in this regard, too.

2: From the group-analytic point of view the family could hardly be a worse-selected group, since they share a common psychopathology and can be expected to collude to conceal vital information and to oppose changes which will threaten a long-established family equilibrium

3: These facts explain the more active, directive rôle that all family therapists appear to have found necessary in their work, though it has taken some time for theory to catch up with practice and in the literature the conceptual focus was at first on sharing information through the more neutral therapeutic interventions appropriate in the group of strangers in which group analysis was first developed. Active, challenging, stimulating interventions are striking in the protocols of most workers in this field as well as in more recent theoretical contributions (Ackerman, 1958, 1966, 1967; McGregor *et al.*, 1964; Friedman *et al.*, 1965; etc.). Group-analytic theory needs to be clarified and extended to include this dimension. What follows is an attempt to contribute towards this, and to describe the principles by which I have come to operate.

B: Three Principles In Group-Analytic Family Therapy

1. The therapist's central task: facilitating communication

There is a certain correspondence of structure and function between the group and the individual, so that concepts pertaining to the one are, to some extent, applicable to the other. Each is an assembly of parts which, to function effectively, need to be related to one another in a way which will produce a balanced and harmonious whole. Failure to maintain this balance comprises disorder or disease, whether 'physical' or 'psychological', and leads to destruction and conflict rather than creation and growth, or at least to arrest of development or regression to more primitive forms of functioning, in group and individual alike.

Since the system is dynamic and constantly changing, adequate communication must exist between the parts and the whole, whereby harmony and balance are preserved. In the individual, dissociation of an emotion may lead to impoverishment of normal functioning as well as the appearance of seemingly meaningless symptoms which interfere with the effectiveness of the whole organism; for example, fear of negative feelings leading to dissociation of aggressive impulses, which may result in a weakening of the personality in situations requiring assertiveness, as well as head-aches, muscular tensions or other symptoms which operate as handicaps to effective living. In the group we see similar phenomena when one member becomes the chosen (and to some extent self-chosen) container of some aspect of personality which is unacceptable to the others. This individual is then used as a scapegoat to be attacked and rejected and will be seen as, or will become, disruptive; eventually he will be excluded, when another member may become the container in turn. In families, many authors have made us familiar with the rôle often served by the sick or mad child, the delinquent, the child who is said to be always jealous and so on. In the case of the group, as with the individual patient, the task of the therapist is to bridge these dissociations in order to establish communication between the disconnected fragments of the total system. *Most people who have written on family therapy have emphasised this function of facilitating inter-personal communication as the therapist's central task.* To do this, of course, corresponding aspects of the therapist's personality must be adequately integrated already. Persistent scapegoating or harmful subgrouping, like persistence of an undesirable dissociation in the course of individual psychotherapy, must always to some extent reflect a split within the group leader or therapist himself.

2. The therapist's second task: the ordering of authority

The parts of a group, like the parts of an individual, are not all on one level but require arrangement in a certain hierarchical order if they are to function effectively. Groups and families have an optimum type of organisation which must involve a form of dominance hierarchy. While there is again a range of possibilities of varying effectiveness, it appears that breakdown of the authority structure leads to uncoordinated release of tendencies which can be damaging to the whole system, however valuable these may be within proper bounds and in their proper place. On the other hand, excessive restriction of the lower by the higher leads to other forms of disturbance, like the emotional impoverishment of the severe obsessional or the lack of creativity which can occur in a social system where individual initiative is suppressed. *This principle underlies the second main function of the family therapist, as I see it, which is to intervene and take control of the family situation where necessary, handing back responsibility when a more healthy form of interaction and control has been established by the therapist's example.* Among various possibilities, a rigid authoritarian father may be suppressing initiative and denying individuality; a penis-envying mother may be preventing a passive father from taking his proper place in family decisions; or a child may be tyrannising the parents by playing upon their excessive need to avoid frustration or separation anxiety.

54

What constitutes the most effective authority structure is too little explored. The subject arouses strong emotion, such that dispassionate thought about it is not easy. No doubt the requirements are different at different stages in the development of an individual, family or culture. In time of war or great danger a more definite hierarchy may be necessary for the survival of a society, while young children can be made anxious, as we know, by a degree of freedom for which their limited self-control makes them unfitted. At other stages a more flexible pattern, permitting a greater sharing of responsibility, may be required to give freedom to explore new patterns of development. The patterns and cycles seen in therapeutic and training groups or in therapeutic communities suggest that the most effective authority structure is a compromise between that degree of control which gives security but limits change, and that openness and freedom which permits development and growth but contains a danger of chaos and destructive conflict if carried too far. Anthropologists and ethologists can no doubt help us to apply these principles to the family, so that we may see if there are any natural invariant requirements in the relationship of male and female parents despite cultural variations. It seems likely that persistent authority conflicts between the parents, whereby each undermines and denigrates the other, would create disturbances in the children. In our own culture my impression is that families operate best where each parent respects the other and shares responsibility, but where the father is accorded ultimate authority. It may be that a matriarchal pattern works equally well where this is culture-syntonic. Cross-cultural investigation is needed to clarify this.[2]

3. The therapist's third task: facilitating developmental process

I have presented the need for communication between parts of the system, and the need for hierarchy within it as if these two principles were separate. But I think this is only a limitation of my own capacity to understand and formulate the problem, for these two considerations are aspects of the same thing, two ways of viewing the concept of *order*. These two simple principles comprise the theoretical justification for the therapist's rôle in facilitating communication and exercising control.

55

Early Papers and General Principles

The family is a very special kind of group, since it acts as a bridge between the individuals of one generation and those of the next, giving a series of provisions, demands and challenges whereby the dependent infant evolves to an autonomous adult. These successive challenges may be seen, from one point of view, as requirements that the individual should learn to relate to increasingly complex group situations. The first dyadic relationship with the mother requires the recognition of another individual, of boundaries, separateness and responsibility for loving and preserving another. The second challenge, requiring a further relinquishing of omnipotence, involves an encounter with paternal authority, demanding compromises between instinctual drives and the welfare of the family as a whole or of larger social units. (This challenge may be mediated mainly by the mother but it is surmounted or not, in my experience, to the extent that the mother herself accepts the authority of the father, who in turn is more related to the outside world and so the representative of its values in the home.) Awareness of the parents as a pair, and as a sexual couple with a special relationship from which the child is excluded, is a further challenge which requires the child to cope with this exclusion and the jealousy it inevitably arouses, as well as the loss involved in accepting one sexual identity at the price of the other. The need to struggle and share with siblings at home and peers at school entails a further step towards the inter-dependence characteristic of adulthood. Adolescence finally brings pressures, both internal and external, thrusting the individual out of the family to find his main support among his peers, to mate and begin the process again, as leader this time of a new family group.

The family therapist needs to be aware of this developmental sequence in order to see where a given family situation may be depriving its members of the opportunity to meet and master some crucial developmental stage. Development thus involves a series of challenges to master group situations of increasing complexity. It is the therapist's third task to facilitate and support this developmental process.

C: Practising Group-Analytic Family Therapy

1. Including the whole family

As in other approaches, the whole family is expected to attend; both parents are vital and at my clinics the first letter to the family expresses the importance of the father's presence as well as our willingness to try to accommodate his difficulties over obtaining time off. All the siblings are invited; their presence is often the crucial factor in opening up the interview by breaking some family collusion and initiating a vital communication. We find the participation of even very young children is generally helpful, provided the therapist acts as a communicative link by connecting their non-verbal behaviour and play with the more verbal contributions of the other members. For instance, at a point where male potency was being implicitly questioned during a family consultation carried out at a home visit, a young boy ran out and rushed back waving a stick, and the stick then kept changing hands, its possessor at any moment appearing to be the temporarily dominant member of the family grouping. In another interview, at a stage where the parents were speaking of the effect of their child's sleep disturbance on their sexual relationship, the two-year-old concerned began making coital movements against the mother. We find that even the baby can be usefully included, and the way others relate to him and his responses from moment to moment are often illuminating.

Sometimes the family problem is felt to be so intolerable that it is left behind in a member who stays at home. This must often be accepted and the interview can be effective nevertheless if the absent member is 'brought alive' in the interview by asking the family to talk about his behaviour in detail to help the therapist to understand him, since the more the projection is clarified, even without comment, the more its illusory and defensive nature will be recognised and pointed out by another member of the family. The therapist will tend to be cast in the rôle of the absent member and care must be taken not to respond unconsciously to this projection, especially where the therapist is the same sex as an absent parent. Provided one does not make this error one can of course start with those who attend and then work towards including the others. At first a parent may be unable to share the children with the partner until they have had some help themselves.

2. Practical arrangements

As to time, one and a half hours are desirable and most family therapists recommend it. I have come to use one hour in most cases because of shortage of time and have learned to work within it, but even one and a quarter hours are a great advantage. Arrangements can be flexible and I prefer a certain informality. All participants should be able to sit in a rough circle with play equipment, if needed, within the circle so that play activity can be seen by all and included in the discussion. I encourage children to sit and participate verbally. How they respond to such requests from me or the parents gives important information which can be taken up. Whatever they do can be included and used. Seating and change of seating at different sessions can be very informative. One father sat opposite me, then beside me, then away again as he passed through phases of hidden conflict, identification and growing independence. Who takes the lead at any time, who withdraws, the capacity to share the conversation or the need to interrupt or to establish pairing relationships if there is more than one therapist, all give as much information as the things which are said.

3. Focus on group interaction in the here-and-now

Beginners to family therapy often find it difficult to get the consultation started. The essence of the technique I use lies in the personal involvement of the therapist in the family communication difficulties. By having no more preliminary contact or information than is essential to see whether the interview is necessary at all, and to ensure that all the family come, the therapist is automatically exposed to all their difficulties of communication and control from the very beginning as he tries to understand why they are seeking help and what the problem may be. This is inevitably uncomfortable and frustrating but if it is possible to break through this to an awareness of what is happening, in the here-and-now of the interview situation, the understanding is in some way shared with the family in a truly organic way and has an impact on everyone present that is often dramatic. A detailed history enables the therapist to understand only intellectually and in advance, out of time with the true rhythm of the family and out of touch with its living experience. It is certainly more comfortable but I find it takes away my main usefulness. Operating with limited information, the therapist becomes in a sense one of the family, and has to find a solution from that point, not from outside it. It does not seem unreasonable that such a solution found from inside should be of more value to the family itself.

What the therapist has to find is almost always something that is missing. One would expect this, of course, if one starts from the premise, supported by much experimental work, that family difficulties are derived mainly from what is concealed and denied, and so not communicated. This valuable insight, that there are advantages to operating without prior intellectual understanding, I owe partly to Winnicott (1965).[3]

Avoidance of prior information is one factor which, from the beginning, helps to keep the responsibility for solving the problem squarely on the family, with the therapist as a helper who may be more expert in facilitating communication but who can never know as much about them, while seeing them in this fashion, as they do themselves. Most families will try to escape responsibility by going no further than presenting the problem in terms of apparently meaningless symptoms in one child and then waiting for the 'expert' to provide a solution as they might expect a general practitioner to make a diagnosis of some spots and prescribe some medicine. This projection of the 'expert' rôle is at first difficult to avoid, but often the family will expand upon the problem if one resists too quick a response.

There are many ways of meeting this difficulty, but I have found three approaches particularly helpful in moving from the initial presentation of symptoms in one member of a family to the real problem in the family as a whole. In these and other ways the family can be led from the presenting complaint to its meaning as part of a family problem, which can then be explored.

1. One can insist that the symptom is usually hidden communication and ask, 'What is it saying to us?'. By suggesting that the symptom represents some blocked communication, one gives sanction for that communication to be made, and sooner or later a member of the family is likely to make it in a clearer form.

2. It is often fruitful to ask what the 'effect' of the symptom is

on the rest of the family, since this includes everyone in the discussion, and often leads to the 'cause'.

3. One can ask for a detailed, play-by-play account of family interactions centring around a symptom as a substitute for actually seeing them interacting at home. This nearly always leads to the reproduction of the actual conflict in the interview itself, though in different form. An authority conflict in the home will appear, for instance, in the actual way the family describes it, and this can then be commented on.

4. Transference and the therapist's rôle

All therapists I have met who have practised family therapy have noticed that they behave in a much more spontaneous, open and natural fashion than they do when practising individual or other forms of group therapy. While this seems to be demanded by the needs of the situation, it is not clear why this is so. One reason, perhaps, is that one intuitively sees the advantages of keeping primitive transference feelings within the family, and spontaneous, active behaviour by the therapist counteracts the projection of fantasy on to him, just as passive 'blank-screen' behaviour facilitates it. Infantile projections and distortions are clarified as they exist between the family members and the fact that no time is required for such types of transference to develop or be resolved in relation to the therapist is no doubt one reason why such rapid changes are possible, and why each brief intervention is somehow complete in itself.

Transference must exist, of course, but it would seem that the rôle projected on to the therapist is less an idiosyncratic and personal one than a culturally accepted projection of certain universal parental qualities. The easy, relaxed feeling experienced by the therapist in a well-functioning family session suggests that the more uncomfortable projections characteristic of individual or group psychotherapy are not taking place, at least in a large proportion of cases.

Donnelly (1966) has suggested that successful treatment of a family, whatever the method, requires that the therapist be seen as more powerful than the dominant parent, yet able to use this power for the benefit of the family rather than to fulfil personal needs or to protect himself. The therapist needs to intervene and challenge family members only on rare occasions. In my experience these are usually instances where communication was being restricted to avoid discomfort to some members, at the cost of the long-term benefit of the family as a whole. The therapist's use of authority is thus based on his responsibility for representing the demands of reality; it has, in other words, the same basis as the normal authority of the parents. This is conditional, of course, on the therapist's own authority over himself, and this, in turn, is based on his ability to face his own 'inner reality', his ability to take responsibility for himself.

However, the less the therapist takes control in this way the better, for what the family achieves for itself is far more valuable than what is given to them by others. Usually, the therapist can sit back a bit after a crucial intervention, for some previously inhibited family members are thereby emboldened to continue to open up the discussion in a more fruitful way.

Apart from this, it is surprising how little the therapist in fact needs to control the emotional interaction. Bowlby (1949) and Bell (1962) have commented on the safety of the method despite the alarming (to the therapist) intensity of emotional exchange. Beginners commonly fear that the situation may get out of hand and produce harmful effects through continued negative interaction after the family have returned home, if not in the interview itself. I have tried to follow up all cases where I have had fears of this kind, and have not yet encountered one where my anxieties were justified. Indeed, one is often astonished to find how a seemingly disastrous interview in fact had a beneficial effect.[4]

5. Group relationships and individual attention

All forms of group psychotherapy require of the therapist a special form of attention, akin to the wide, unfocussed visual attention we all automatically adopt when we are alert for some expected stimulus but uncertain of the direction from which it will come. Those used to individual psychotherapy often complain that they forget the group, focussing instead on individuals in turn in the way one may focus visually on an object which grips one's attention, neglecting the field in which it occurs.

This needed 'wide' attention comes partly with practice, partly perhaps with a reduction in the therapist's own need to be intimately related in a one-to-one fashion, but it can only be struggled for. Once attained, it automatically relates the therapist to the group as a whole, so that he is never unaware of it even though he may communicate with one person at a time.

I used to believe that I also took a neutral position between members of a family, until tape recordings showed that I frequently took sides. I now believe that an overall fairness is essential, but that siding with children or parents from time to time is not only inevitable but often meaningful and useful, as well as acceptable to the family, provided one acknowledges what one is doing, tries to formulate the reason one has been led to take sides, and remains open to criticism and further dicussion. The therapist then includes himself in the treatment process and may find his reaction has some real justification, subsequently acknowledged by the family, or he may see that it is due to some personal identification. In any case it will be corrected automatically as the interview proceeds. The therapist's ability to be unfair, and to be criticised and corrected for it, can provide an important example for some families where the need to be rigidly fair and reasonable is a problem.

Zuk (1968) has in fact based a whole technique of family therapy on deliberate siding, with the object of breaking down an excessive avoidance of conflict. The tendency to side with the referred patient evidenced by Laing and his colleagues (Laing and Esterson, 1964) seems, on the other hand, based more on an identification with the patient rôle and a simple reversal of values within the schizoid solution, whereby the patient is regarded as normal, the family mad, instead of *vice versa*.

6. Frequency of meetings and duration of treatment

As it is such a fundamental factor in my own technique, I must say something about the frequency of sessions I find most effective. An interval of three weeks seems ideal and several families have said spontaneously that less frequent sessions prevent continuity while more frequent ones prevent their digesting and utilising fully the consequences of each session. I have also found that meeting more often encourages the development of strong transference feelings towards the therapist, including a more dependent and passively receptive expectation that the therapist will do the work and provide the answers. This is a perfectly valid way of working, but it operates through different mechanisms and according to a quite different time scale, similar to individual or 'small-group' psychotherapy. Three-weekly sessions keep responsibility squarely on the family, and exploit to the full the fact that the family continues to work at the problem between the sessions. While the changes may be limited in degree, they are great in total effect, and the intensity of the process even at this frequency has to be seen to be believed.

It has been my experience that this technique either produces striking and satisfactory change within a few interviews – often only one or two, rarely as many as ten – or, on the other hand, it provides early, clear indications that the balance of motivation is against change, without at least a heavy investment of therapeutic time and skill.

The cases dealt with have been those referred to a children's hospital and child guidance clinics in different types of areas. Clearly the same principles would not apply in general to severely disturbed families producing schizophrenic members, though my experience has been that even very severely disturbed families who seem hopeless at first sight can often make limited but worthwhile gains. General principles regarding the suitability of this approach for different types of problem and personality remain to be worked out, though I have tried to summarise our current findings in Chapters 2 and 3 above.

7. Other considerations

I have not dealt with the issues of having two or more therapists conducting family groups, though this is widely practised at my own clinics as elsewhere. It introduces additional complications as well as advantages though it does not alter the fundamental principles set out above. Our experience in combining individual or marital sessions with family therapy is also not dealt with here, though the case illustration which follows contains an example of such a combination. Generally speaking, we have found it possible to be extremely flexible in combining different techniques, provided the therapists have confidence in themselves and each other, and are able to discuss their own reactions to the family and each other frankly.

Little has also been said about the extent to which communication needs to be restricted in family sessions. In fact, it has become clear that probably anything can be discussed, including the parents' and children's sexuality, though the timing is as important as in other therapeutic work. Anxieties about discussing the parental sexual relationship in the family interviews prove to be related more to the therapist's guilt over primal scene fantasies than to real disadvantages.

A more detailed consideration of the ways in which communication takes place in family sessions would require a paper of its own. In psychoanalysis and individual psychotherapy, verbal interpretation of underlying feelings may play the main part, but in groups of all kinds, where people are face to face, expressive posture, action and example become increasingly important.[5]

Our own work in poor districts of east and north-east London confirms the findings of others that with more intelligent and educated families greater reliance can be placed on verbal communication, insight and conscious understanding; while with more limited families good results can still be obtained, provided the focus is more on education by example. In the latter conscious verbalisation of the process is unnecessary and indeed often undesirable, when limited goals need to be set.

For instance, the therapist may meet the needs of the children for attention and communication, for patient firmness and containment of overactivity, demonstrating to the parents that these approaches are more effective than passive indulgence or punitive suppression; or the parents, having their needs met in these ways themselves, are able to internalise the therapist and the skills he demonstrates; or the therapist may tacitly give permission for a more free release of feeling in an inhibited family by behaving in a more spontaneous way himself, showing that he can be childish at times without losing his effectiveness in general. Examples of all these will be evident in the transcript of a session at the end of this paper.

Case Illustration

I shall now outline the course of a series of five family consultations which illustrate several of the points I have made. The interviews were all tape-recorded so that the accounts are reasonably accurate, though the difficulties of condensing five hours of family interaction into such a brief compass will be appreciated. The case is atypical, since the identified patient and the mother had received between them several hundred hours of individual treatment over the previous twelve years, with temporary improvement but without basic change in the family dynamics. The case was therefore better documented than the usual family consultations, and the individual histories were available in a way that is not usually possible or even necessary in this type of family work. This is helpful from the point of view of examining the technique, but I had in fact had no contact myself with this family before the consultations to be described began. I came to them more or less blind, having forgotten by the time I saw them the conference at which they were presented because individual treatment had become blocked. I deliberately avoided reading the case notes until the family sessions were completed, though I have of course done so for the purposes of this presentation.

Case history

I will introduce the family very briefly. Pam, the referred patient, was a girl of fourteen at the time of the first family session, and had a history of repeated separations from the mother, beginning at the age of ten months, which had clearly damaged the relationship between them. The original symptoms twelve years earlier included destructiveness and hostility to the mother, together with depression and separation anxiety which took the central place as she grew older, as well as difficulty in spelling. As she entered adolescence, behaviour problems including stealing, truanting and sexual acting out gained prominence.

The mother was a vulnerable, unstable person, with several admissions to hospital for severe depression; during one of these, lasting almost a year, the children had been taken into care and had not seen her throughout this time. She felt herself to be intellectually and socially superior to the father, an aggressive, forthright 'rough diamond'. Just as Pam, the referred patient, had been used all her life as the container of all the family's unacceptable aspects, Sarah, three years older and seventeen years old at the time I first saw her, was the

65

receptacle into whom all the family's good qualities were projected for safe-keeping. Their appearance was in line with this: Pam sullen, bad-tempered, evasive, poorly controlled, sitting clumsily slumped in her chair; Sarah sitting calm, straight, with a clear level gaze, gentle yet naturally commanding respect.

At the first interview, I invited the family to put me in the picture about the current problems. The mother at once expressed intense anxiety about Pam's stealing and truanting, while the father was more concerned about Pam's failure to return home at the proper time at night, clearly fearing sexual misbehaviour. Pam hung her head, looked miserable and as if about to cry, and angrily refused to contribute. The elder sister, Sarah, opened up the conversation several times: first by saying that father was too strict; then that Pam lost all her friends by being too possessive; and later that she felt Pam was jealous of her and that this was partly caused by the unfair treatment of the parents, who praised her (Sarah) and blamed Pam.

Most of the early part of the session was nevertheless devoted to Pam and her difficult behaviour, and attempts to clarify this led us to focus on the way Pam always felt herself to be deprived and left out. Here it was possible to confront Pam with the fact that she was in fact depriving herself by the way she was refusing to participate in the interview, despite our attempts to include her.

The conversation then moved on to criticism by the children, and later mother, of father for being rigid and restrictive, particularly in his refusal to allow his daughters to have boyfriends. This was then partly explained by the way he expressed unhappiness at losing his former close relationship with Pam as she entered adolescence and made more contacts outside the home. Next, as the girls described their enjoyment at fooling about with father, tickling and teasing him, the first criticism of mother, until then carefully avoided, began to appear as they complained that she would 'moan' and sulk when father and daughters behaved in this way. The mother now becamse increasingly tense and uncomfortable, as if angry yet ashamed and attempting to conceal her annoyance.

The rest of the family, suddenly realising this, became silent and behaved as if paralysed. I pointed this out, and the mother encouraged them to speak freely, but they clearly felt she could not tolerate criticism. I tried to bring the situation more into the open, pointing out how mother had seemed to opt out of a rivalry situation with the two daughters. Father's next statement, that he treated wife and daughters 'just the same', did nothing to improve matters and I questioned whether this was appropriate!

At this point the interview suddenly turned into a discussion of a marital problem, the mother complaining that father was unsympathetic and did not try to understand her disability, the father countering by saying the mother spent all her time talking to doctors and social workers instead of asking for help from him.

One of the functions Pam served in the family was clearly demonstrated when on several occasions they escaped from the marital conflict by uniting to attack Pam again, but this ceased, and the marital conflict resumed, each time I pointed out this defence.

When it was time to stop, the father and daughters appeared involved and interested, and accepted the offer of a further joint interview, but the mother appeared angry and upset that I was proposing no special treatment 'for Pam'.

This account illustrates clearly, I hope, the general patterns of development I expect from a first interview. This begins with the presentation of the problem as the family at first views it – usually as an inexplicable problem located in one individual – and leads naturally, by encouraging exploration of the problem and interaction by the whole family under the stimulus of the therapist's attempt to grasp the difficulty, to the emergence of a coherent and explicable family pattern and to pathology in other members or the marriage itself.

We have become very flexible over combining different methods of treatment and in this case, because of the mother's history and her agitation at the end of the first session, she was offered appointments as she needed them with the PSW who had been treating her for some years (later on the mother gradually gave these up). Seen individually in this way a week later, the mother was still angry that I was 'not going to do anything for Pam'. I had been 'casual', had not seemed worried about the extent of her anxiety. She had felt 'utterly defeated'. Yet she admitted she was pleased, nevertheless, that the focus had not been on Pam, and she was preoccupied with my remark that she (mother) had appeared not to be emotionally involved in the discussion, despite her attempts to appear so. Pam, it seemed, had left the interview 'on top of the world' and had stayed in for two evenings after it.

The interval between the first and second interviews, due to pressure on evening appointments, was two months and this was too long. Nevertheless, the pattern had changed and even though the parents began by accusing and blaming Pam as if nothing had altered, Pam was in fact strikingly more open, cooperative and appreciative. She participated more helpfully in the interview and this greater responsiveness contrasted sharply with the rejecting behaviour of the parents who seemed to refuse to see the improvement demonstrated before them; I felt angered by the way they seemed determined to destroy any progress we made.

Sarah hesitantly supported Pam, and the argument gradually developed from a focus on Pam's behaviour to the familiar quarrel of adolescence with adulthood, especially over symbols of sexual freedom, an important change in the family structuring.

The third interview was arranged after only a month's interval, a spacing which was subsequently adhered to, and progress was more satisfactory. The sessions began with the usual attack by the parents on Pam, but the realignment reached at the previous session had persisted and the girls were now united in criticism of both parents, while the parental coalition, though partly defensive against the marital conflict, was also more secure and healthy as compared with the previous pairing of each parent with one of the children. Indeed, it was Sarah, the 'good' one, who this time received the main attack from father. Nevertheless, movement was blocked by the parents' refusal to acknowledge any share in the difficulty and every approach to understanding would be negated by subtly destructive manoeuvres.

At some point in the interview I realised that I was failing to deal with this straightforwardly in response to my fear that to pursue the truth might risk the mother's sanity, and decided that the danger must be risked and, if necessary, coped with. I then confronted the parents with what I saw as their failure to involve themselves honestly in the transactions, and, as if released by my more active control of the situation, the parents at once began to speak of their feelings of failure and inadequacy. This led, in turn, to a sharing of feelings of concern and responsibility by the children, and painful recollections appeared of the early separations and the mother's illnesses.

At the fourth interview, a dramatic change was evident in the entire family, dating from the previous session, both parents now showing warmth and almost weeping with relief as if they had passed through a depression too deep to risk acknowledging at the time of its greatest intensity. The children both expressed very positive feelings in return and, since the previous interview, all the initial complaints had been in abeyance. Pam was cooperative and helpful, and they were getting on well.

In the rest of this fourth session we focussed on the family problem of envy which, by making them deny their contribution to the solution of the problem as well as my own, led them to feel they had no persisting control of the situation and so to fear a relapse. The fifth session, to which father was obliged to come late, revealed the parents' diffuse ego boundaries and the mutual projection which constantly occurred between them; this was an object lesson in the dangers of treating one parent alone. Also at this session the mother's need to keep Pam ill, or to keep her own illness in Pam, was pointed out by Sarah in relation to the intense separation fears of mother and indeed of both parents.

The sixth session was the last of the treatment series (though follow-ups have continued for two years) and all improvements had persisted in general, though Pam became a problem for a time again in school when mother was admitted to hospital for a hysterectomy early in the year. Pam had a good report from school, had been helpful and friendly about the house, and had become a comfort and support to mother, who almost wept at the warmth of Pam's response and now seemed able to reveal and let the children satisfy her own needs in a way she had not been able to do before. The improvements have since been maintained.

Example of family interaction

It is extremely difficult to convey the experience of a family interview in words, but one can get closer to communicating its intensity, liveliness and impact with an actual transcript. What follows is the second half of the third family interview in the case just described, taken from the tape recording. I have chosen it rather than another excerpt since, although it shows me in a less favourable light than other excerpts might do, it was clearly the crucial episode. Soon after it begins, I confront the parents with my view that they are avoiding the real issue of their own involvement. This is done too violently, due to my having avoided expressing this too long for fear the mother might become mentally ill again (in fact, she went from strength to strength from this point on!), but perhaps my own 'bad' behaviour freed the others to communicate more freely. It will be seen how the children follow by much more direct and open complaints and criticisms of the parents, and how the parents, in turn, react in a more open and fruitful way. Although the situation seems quite unresolved at the end, what followed at home was ultimately constructive and led to the dramatic improvement of the next (fourth) session. My own rôle in this crucial session, it will be apparent, was much more that of an active authority than a neutral, passive interpreter of the communications being made. It is important to emphasise that other sessions did not involve this degree of active intervention, and that I have chosen this extract rather than another not because it is typical but because this aspect of conjoint family therapy is likely to be the most difficult to accept and utilise for those accustomed to an analytic technique.

The transcript begins almost half-way through the third family session.

PAM: Yes, but every time you was ill you always seemed to blame it on me, didn't you? (*Imitates Mother's voice:*) Well, you made me ill, you did that, yes, you did.

MOTHER: Rubbish, that's something of your own making, Pam.

PAM: No, because even when I said it to you, you said 'That's right'.

FEW SECONDS' SILENCE.

DOCTOR (*to Mother*): You did say this last time, if I may remind you, and it was something I didn't pick up, but you did in fact say Pam made you ill.

MOTHER: About Pam's making me ill?

DOCTOR: Yes. Maybe it's not true, but we must face this and see what it is about.

MOTHER: I have been taking Pam to Child Guidance ever since she was two years old, and it's just a coincidence I had three nervous breakdowns during that period, since Pam was two.

DOCTOR: You think there may be no connection?

MOTHER: I think there may be some connection. It is, as you say, a vicious circle.

THE TAPE FADES OUT HERE. TAPE NOT CHANGED OVER, FEW MINUTES LOST.

FATHER (*speaking of his previous close relationship with Pam*): . . . at one time I couldn't pick me cap up without 'Where are you going? Let's come with you.' Then she just changed and she is just the opposite now, and she doesn't want to know anything. Whether or not it's since she has been to this new school.

MOTHER (*interrupting*): You can't blame schools, you can't blame people.

FATHER: Well, it's somewhere, isn't it?

MOTHER: It's no good blaming other people, and it's no good blaming schools.

DOCTOR: Then who are you going to blame?

FATHER: Well, where is it, then? It's got to be somewhere.

MOTHER (*to Doctor*): Well, you know in a roundabout way, you have hinted that it could be him and me.

FATHER: Not necessarily.

MOTHER: It must be.

DOCTOR (*angrily*): I didn't hint. . . . I said I was just always puzzled that it's all *Pam*. That's the story every time you come, it's all Pam. Pam is bad, B-A-D, and there is nothing wrong with you, that's what you tell me every time.

MOTHER: But I know there is something wrong with me.

DOCTOR: You don't. You tell me over and over again how you never put a foot wrong anywhere. I wish I could do as well as that.

MOTHER (*interrupting*): There *is* a lot wrong with me. I'm irritable . . . nasty-tempered. . . .

FATHER: Ah, now, when we say we haven't put a foot wrong, well, as regards the children you might say we done the best for them as we know how.

DOCTOR: That I accept.

FATHER: I am not going to say that we done *everything* for them that we could have done because there's times when we couldn't – when you hadn't got it to do with. I don't know quite how to put it. I mean I know myself I can be quite nasty at times, but regarding having everything they wanted and what they wanted to do, more often than not they done it.

PAM: Sarah has, put it that way.

FATHER (*to Pam*): Well, *you* have, yes you have.

SARAH (*to Pam*): But, Pam, you don't realise when I was your age I had exactly the same restrictions. I had to be in at 9 o'clock and if I wasn't in at 9 o'clock . . .

PAM (*interrupting*): I have to be in at half-past eight.

SARAH: That's when I was fourteen, 9 o'clock.

FATHER (*angrily*): What about Saturday night? What was

going on on Saturday night when I went down and sorted out about twenty yobbos down there?

PAM: Oh, there wasn't!

FATHER: Well, what was they, then?

PAM: About five.

FATHER: Chasing you up and down the stairs, trying to pull your trousers off. Well, that's not right!

PAM: No, they wasn't.

FATHER: Yes, they was. If I hadn't caught you they *would* have done.

PAM: They were trying to chuck me in the bushes.

FATHER: I've got a good pair of eyes, you know.

PAM: Trying to chuck me in the bushes.

FATHER: I've got a good pair of eyes.

PAM: . . . and go and ask if you want to.

FATHER: I asked you which way it was but you wouldn't tell me, would you?

PAM: I don't split, like some people.

SARAH (*to Pam*): Are you referring to me, Pam? How do I split? What have I split on?

FATHER (*interrupting*): Well, I . . .

SARAH (*to Pam*): There is a lot I know about you that I could say, mate.

FATHER (*to Doctor*): The trouble is there is nothing out in the open. They won't bring it out in the open.

DOCTOR: No? Well, I feel it just doesn't come in the open anywhere. I would say the same to you; in some way you don't come out in the open either, as I experience you. You (*to parents*) certainly don't come in the open.

FATHER: Well, I can't say anything more open than what I have said already. Because there is nothing more that I know that I can tell you, other than what I have already told you. As regards coming out in the open, I mean I air my views with the best of people, I don't care who they are or anything else. I mean I have argued with Sarah many a time. But the point is, I mean, I have always been plain straight talking, I don't care who they are or what they are. If I have got something to say I'll say it. I don't care who I offend or who I please. I speak me mind.

DOCTOR: Yes, that's quite true in a sense. . . .

FATHER (*interrupting*): The point is, I have been in trouble over it two or three times with the missus as well over it, she'll tell you that, but the point is this, we can't get to know anything from Pam, because she just won't tell you. Sarah knows a lot more than what she'll say, but she won't say anything. All this business of not splitting and that, I mean it's a load of hogwash to me. I mean if there is something going on like that that shouldn't be, then it should be let out and sorted out, that's my way of thinking. But if you just bang your head against a brick wall, then that's it, you can't do nothing about it. You just don't get anywhere. You can't do anything.

MOTHER (*to Doctor*): Do you think Pam would be better seeing you on her own?

DOCTOR: Who thinks that?

MOTHER: Would Pam be more open on her own with you?

DOCTOR: I don't think it would help because I don't think she is the whole trouble.

PAM: I don't want to keep coming here. . . .

DOCTOR (*interrupting*): I am seeing you as a family because I think the problem is in the family, and I am seeing you together and I don't think seeing Pam on her own is going to make any difference.

MOTHER: But Pam doesn't contribute to this at all, does she? She doesn't say anything.

DOCTOR (*to Mother*): Neither of you contributes, neither you nor Pam contributes. Sarah and her father both (*to Father and Sarah*), you are quite correct, you are pretty direct and you both got at each other, you said what you really think, both got a bit upset and a bit further forward – (*to Mother again*) but both you and Pam somehow sit back, you withdraw and I can't feel your feelings; it is as if you are sitting behind yourself and are not involved in it. Neither of you seems to *feel*, that's all I can say. (*To Father and Sarah*): *You* both feel, certainly.

MOTHER: I don't know what else to do. I have given you and told you everything I feel and I just don't know what to tell you.

DOCTOR (*to Mother*): Well, I rather think the trouble is that you don't feel. *Pam* doesn't *feel*, *you* don't feel. This is what the trouble is about – this lack of feeling. You know, while I have been here with you I can feel you (*to Father*) feeling and I can feel you (*to Sarah*) feeling. I can't feel either (*to Mother and Pam*) of you feeling. You are not *feeling*, you are not *there*, you are not *in yourselves* at the moment, and I feel the lack of it, I feel I don't make any contact with either of you, and there is something important in this; something has gone wrong between you because of it.

MOTHER: You mean Pam and me?

DOCTOR: Yes. That's the best I can say at the moment, though there's more to it than that, between all of you.

MOTHER: What can I do?

FATHER: If Pam would air her views a bit . . .

DOCTOR: (*to Mother*): What are you – what *are* you. . . .

MOTHER: What am I?

DOCTOR: What *are* you? I don't know who you are, I don't know who you *are*.

MOTHER: I'll tell you what I am. I'm irritable, I am nasty-tempered, I feel rotten most of the time, little things upset me. . . .

DOCTOR: Then why did it go wrong between you and Pam when it didn't with you and Sarah? It's gone all right with her, but something has gone wrong between you . . . and why?

SARAH: It's lack of *trust*, that's what I think it is, because Mum trusts me implicitly in whatever I do, but with Pam it's 'Oh, dear what's she doing? Oh, where's me purse? Where's me pay?' She doesn't *trust* her.

DOCTOR: Why? Why is it different?

FATHER: Well, you *can't* trust her. . . .

MOTHER: I can't. . . .

DOCTOR: Well, *now* you can't, but this must have started somewhere.

MOTHER: It started when we first found out that Pam was helping herself, out of my purse and out of her father's wallet!

DOCTOR: Well, I don't believe it, I think it started long before that. These things don't suddenly start, the roots were there long ago. It might be nonsense, but I think it's true (THE TAPE BLURS HERE), there was something wrong from very early on.

FATHER: Well, the only thing that I can see is that it must go back to when the wife was away at the mental hospital, when I had Pam on my own.

DOCTOR: Yes?

FATHER: When they finished up, they went away to a children's home.

SARAH: And it's the worst place I have ever been to, honestly.

MOTHER: So Pam blames me for that; that's something I can't help.

SARAH: But before we were sent away to that place I will say that for Daddy, he did ask us if we wanted to go or not – well, he asked me, anyway.

FATHER (*to children*): The point was, in the finish I couldn't have looked after you if I wanted to because I couldn't even walk, talk, stand or anything else in the finish. That's how I was.

MOTHER (*to Doctor*): I'd like to know a bit more about this feeling you have about Pam and me. I am interested in this because truthfully I come out with everything that I feel, everything that I can think of.

DOCTOR: Well, if you don't feel any more than you said then there is something missing. It doesn't add up. It's too good to be true, it just isn't right, there is something wrong somewhere.

MOTHER: What isn't true?

DOCTOR   (*to parents*): What you describe. There is something wrong, something I don't hear about. I don't hear it from either of you.

MOTHER: Well, Pam doesn't say anything, so you can't hear anything from Pam, can you?

DOCTOR: No.

MOTHER: At least I do make an effort.

DOCTOR: Yes.

SARAH   (*to Mother*): You don't say your *true* feelings, do you?

MOTHER: What do you mean about my true feelings?

SARAH: Well, the impression I get, you only seem to sort of *half* say what you think.

MOTHER: What I think?

SARAH: What you *really* think.

MOTHER: Well, if I say that to the Doctor, what I really think, then where do I stand? I told Doctor exactly what I feel, that I am worried sick about Pam.

DOCTOR   (*to Mother*): And I have said quite honestly to you that this is how I experience you, that you don't seem to *feel*. I feel you are *behind* your feelings, you are not there, being good and bad, black and white, both at the same time. You are somehow standing behind yourself, not really feeling. I can't get hold of you anywhere. I wonder what this feels like to the children?

SARAH   (*to Mother*): All the time you say all the good things you give Pam and you never say anything about the bad things that you give her.

FATHER: Well, what's this about the bad things?

MOTHER: What sort of bad things?

SARAH   (*to parents*): No, not just you, *both* of you. You are explaining about giving everything we want and everything like that – you do, that's true – but you don't say well, you are always moaning, or something like that, or telling her off or having a go at her. I can't really put into words what I feel.

FATHER: Well, I have said that, haven't I? I do go and I give a few wallopings. I give you a few in your time. I mean, that doesn't make any difference.

PAM (*bitterly about Mother*): If I have done anything wrong she moans, she moans, she moans, she moans, there's no stopping her.

SARAH (*to Mother*): It's true, you start on one thing and you never let it drop, all the time.

MOTHER: Because I am worried about it, Sarah, that's why. . . .

BOTH GIRLS TOGETHER: (IT'S NOT POSSIBLE TO HEAR WHAT IS BEING SHOUTED).

SARAH (*to Mother*): Then you start on about pyjamas: 'Oh dear, pyjamas all over the place', another minute and then, 'Oh, dear, these pyjamas all over the place'. You just have to keep on and on . . . and then 'Just look at all the pyjamas over the place this morning' – you keep harping on it.

DOCTOR: What would you prefer to that?

SARAH: Well, you only have to be told once, 'Put your pyjamas away' or 'Oh, these pyjamas', but then you don't have to say anything more than that. It's already in your mind that the pyjamas are on the floor.

FATHER: The point is that they are not shifted, are they?

DOCTOR (*to Sarah*): If they are not moved, what then?

SARAH: They are!

MOTHER: Pam takes her pyjamas off in the morning, irrespective of where they are, they are left there.

PAM: The other day you said 'Put your pyjamas away' and I hadn't even taken mine off!

FATHER: Yes, but that was only this morning; they were put away this morning.

PAM: . . . I hadn't even taken mine off.

FATHER: The whole point is if Pam would turn round and say about these things what's going on and get them here now, then we can clear it all up. We know what we are doing of, we know what's worrying us and there we are.

PAM   (IT ISN'T POSSIBLE TO HEAR ALL SHE IS SAYING BUT SHE
           IS IMITATING HER FATHER SAYING: 'Were you talking
           to him – Yobbo').

FATHER: Well, they are yobbos, aren't they?

SARAH: Every boy is a yobbo unless he is sitting there and,
           you know, being very quiet.

MOTHER: But I went over this with Pam. I have no objections
           to her talking to boys at the gate.

PAM: Yes, but Daddy has.

FATHER: No, I haven't.

MOTHER: Whilst talking at the gate with a crowd of girls and
           boys there's nothing going on. There's nothing
           wrong.

FATHER: As I said to you, I don't mind you talking to them,
           but I am not having you sliding off with them, that's
           what I said to you.

SARAH: Pam thinks she is being unjustly treated because
           she thinks that she is old enough to do as she likes.
           She keeps saying, 'When I'm fourteen I'm not
           coming in at half-past eight, I'm not'.

PAM: I'm not.

SARAH: She seems to think she is (PAM INTERRUPTS HERE BUT
           IT IS NOT POSSIBLE TO HEAR WHAT SHE IS SAYING).
           Well, you do, you think you should be allowed in
           about 12 o'clock every night.

PAM: No, I don't.

FATHER: (*to Pam*): It's very seldom that you are in at half-
           past eight! You come in at half-past eight, I'll grant
           you that, invariably, for about two minutes. Then
           it's 'Oh, can't I go down to the bus stop?' and it's
           about half-past nine time you get back.

           SEVERAL MINUTES OMITTED HERE, WHILE THE ARGU-
           MENT CONTINUES. DOCTOR SUGGESTS SEVERAL TIMES
           THAT FATHER IS RIGID ABOUT THE ISSUE.

FATHER: No, I say it's the same with Pam, now she says she
           has been down there looking at television, now if I
           turn round and say 'Right, you are not to go there
           no more', it wouldn't make much difference.

DOCTOR (*to Father*): Well, you know that you are rather rigid about this. You say, 'Well, that's what I say and you must do as I tell you'. I know that a father must . . .

MOTHER (*interrupting*): Well, you must exercise some control.

DOCTOR: Yes, I was just going to say the father must have authority, and must be respected, but on the other hand it can come to a point where a vicious circle starts and you then say 'No', all the time, and because you say 'No' such a lot, they think, 'Oh, to hell with it, I'm not going to do anything they tell me', and it all gets worse and worse. This seems to be something that has happened. It's a very difficult situation for everybody to get out of. That's why I am hoping you can get out of it by talking in this way. I think you will both have to come half-way to meet each other.

PAM: I know Daddy loves us and everything, but he just doesn't realise that we are growing up. I mean even I'll be fourteen in three weeks' time.

FATHER: So you are, so you are a big girl.

SARAH: But you look on us as eleven-year-olds. He doesn't seem to understand that I am actually seventeen and she is nearly fourteen.

DOCTOR: Well, she thinks she is older than she really is and he thinks she is younger.

SARAH: I know, everybody does. I always thought, seventeen, you know, really getting on, you know.

DOCTOR: Well, you will have to come half-way to meet each other, you know.

PAM: Well, I don't mind coming in at nine, but if I want to go out somewhere and it's 'Be here at half-past nine', you just about get fed up with it then.

DOCTOR (*to Pam*): Well, I think you don't want to accept *any* authority from parents and, if you can feel they are bad and unfair and rotten to you and beastly and, you know, never do anything right, you then feel you don't have to obey them in any way at all

80

and this is the position you have got yourself in, where you can feel free to do anything because you feel they are just rotten parents.

PAM:

SARAH: THEY ARE TALKING ABOUT COMING IN LATE BUT IT IS NOT POSSIBLE TO HEAR WHAT EXACTLY IS BEING SAID.

PAM: As soon as I leave school I'll just get away!

FATHER: Get away where, mate?

PAM: Anywhere.

DOCTOR: Well, we have to stop for today . . . and we'll fix another appointment. . . .

FATHER: We *did* get moving in the finish.

Summary

The literature on conjoint family therapy most relevant to those wishing to practise this technique within the field of child psychiatry is reviewed. It is suggested that the experience already gained calls into question existing theories regarding the nature of the therapeutic factors in group work and indeed in psychotherapy generally, while too little attention has in fact been given by family therapists to the formation of general theories about what constitutes effective therapeutic intervention, as compared with the theoretical constructs already produced through experience with small therapeutic groups and training groups.

An attempt is therefore made to extend group-analytic theory to encompass experience derived from conjoint family therapy. Three principles are seen as fundamental to the technique (and perhaps even to all psychotherapy). The first is the re-establishment of communication between disconnected elements of the system, and this aspect is already well recognised. The second is the establishment of an effective dominance hierarchy to provide a degree of control and consistent structure appropriate to the developmental stage the children have reached; this requires that the therapist should take charge temporarily, and though this aspect is clearly evidenced by the behaviour of family therapists, it is not adequately included in the theories. The third principle views the development of children as the successive mastery of increasingly complex group situations, each requiring a certain type of assistance from the parents, or, where they cannot provide this, from some substitute such as a family therapist.

A technique is then presented which embodies these principles, and which is also characterised by widely spaced interviews, by focus on the therapeutic potentialities of the family itself, and by the therapist's deliberate self-exposure to the family difficulties of communication. The latter is achieved by avoiding reliance on history-taking and intellectual knowledge, in favour of direct involvement in the family interaction and in the here-and-now of the interview.

A case summary, including a transcript of part of an interview, is presented to illustrate some of these points.

Notes

1 This paper was presented to the Association for Child Psychology and Psychiatry, June 1968. It was first published in *The Journal of Child Psychology and Psychiatry*, Vol. 10 (1969) 81–106. It was reprinted in S. Walrond-Skinner (ed.), *Developments in Family Therapy*.

2 This was to be Skynner's first statement on the subject and has to be seen as a provisional view which he revised 'before the ink was dry' as he was to later put it. See Chapter 9, pp. 188–9; Chapter 12, pp. 295 and 297–305; and Chapter 13, pp. 317–18, 322 note 12 and 326. Investigation of gender-rôle issues, both through empirical research findings and clinical material, becomes one of his central preoccupations from Chapter 7 onwards. See editor's introduction to that chapter. [Ed.]

3 When I first attended Winnicott's seminars on his technique of individual therapeutic consultation I found it very hard to understand why he insisted on seeing the child without a preliminary interview with the parents. It seemed to me whatever he could do without a history could be done even better if he had one. Later I came to see that there were similar principles involved in my work with families and found his evident sharing of the child's struggle to reach an understanding of its problem, and his formulation in terms of 'meeting the challenge of the case', very meaningful.

4 My work with training groups, as well as my personal experience, clearly shows that anxieties of this kind, as well as difficulties in taking control, have their origin in fantasies related to the

therapist's own childhood experiences. A personal psychoanalysis or group analysis, or participation in a training group run on group-analytic lines, is therefore of great value. I have described two such training approaches in 'The Large Group in Training' in L. Kreeger (ed.), *The Large Group: Dynamics and Theory* (appendix reference 20) and in 'An Open-Systems Approach to Teaching Family Therapy', *Journal of Marital and Family Therapy,* **2** (1980) 271 (appendix reference 31).

5 The centrality in Skynner's method of the therapist's modelling rôle is already evident in this paper. Other aspects of non-verbal communication, like those referred to here, are systematically developed later. See, for example, the editor's introductions to Chapters 8 and 14. [Ed.]

Two

SPECIAL APPLICATIONS

5 The Physician as Family Therapist

The five following contributions describe the application to particular areas of work, of Skynner's developing integration of psychoanalytic, group-analytic and systems ideas.

The first paper is a good introduction to family work for the general reader. Whilst it is of particular relevance to the general practitioner and other physicians, much of its content applies equally to other fields. Many practitioners find the first steps in a new method particularly difficult and they are often reluctant to take them without close guidance. This paper, written for newcomers to family therapy with little knowledge of the subject, gives a simple and clear introduction to its principles and is illustrated by good case examples. It thus provides encouragement and valuable guidance for those professionals who wish to experiment with the method, but who might be isolated and without access to training facilities and support.

It was commissioned by the leader of the Timberlawn Research Project on healthy families, who had been impressed by the similarity between Skynner's clinical findings and their own research results, and who was co-editing a textbook of psychiatry for American general practitioners. The Timberlawn Project was to become an important source of corroboration for Skynner's later work also, as Chapters 12 and 13 will make clear. Here we see him again using the three-stage developmental model first referred to in Chapter 2, used again in Chapter 10 and indeed throughout his work. Here it is used, along with the simple yet invaluable distinction between two- and three-generational work, to guide the focus of the clinician during interviews.

J.R.S.

Introduction

Family therapy is a relatively new treatment modality, and one that lends itself especially to the practice of the primary physician. Understanding the relatively simple techniques involved and demonstrating an adventurous spirit can help the physician to produce gratifying results with many of the patients seen in everyday practice. Although seeing whole families may seem strange, there are striking parallels between this type of treatment and other forms of medical practice.[1]

Communication is at the core of medical practice. All forms of medical practice involve the gathering of information by a series of questions and answers, according to a set of concepts in the physician's mind about the structure of disease processes and about possible links between symptoms or signs and the underlying disorder that would explain them. Physicians start with the assumption that the patient's complaint is meaningful, and that enquiry about an abdominal pain, an inflamed joint, or the wasting of some muscles will lead, if the questioning is persistent and the physical examination thorough, to a coherent and rational pattern of physical processes. This pattern accounts for all our observations, predicts other consequences that we may search for and find (then or at a later date in the development of the disease), and suggests actions we may take to arrest the pattern or change its course.

This process requires that, in the time interval between hearing the initial complaint and the final reaching of a secure diagnosis, we tolerate a period of uncertainty and puzzlement. We try one hypothesis after another, with each of them failing to fit, and to test them we widen the search into history and bodily signs. The process is like attempting to solve a crossword puzzle: both the process and the puzzle are made possible by our fundamental confidence that each does have an answer – if we are sufficiently persistent and thoughtful – that all the words in the puzzle, or the functioning of all the systems in the body, can be assumed to fit together in a patterned, coherent, meaningful way.

All this is, of course, too obvious to need stating in the case of ordinary medical practice with physical disorders, and the simple but fundamental point is that family counselling applies these basic principles to the family as a system of individuals, just as psychiatry extends such principles from the study of organic systems, as in internal medicine, to the study of the whole person as a social-psychological-physical system.

This is important to realise at the outset, because the practitioner without previous experience in the family approach will at first feel uncertain of its value, much as all medical students need time and practice before they have confidence that the painstaking accumulation of facts through history-taking and physical examination will lead to effective diagnosis and treatment. Just as unsophisticated individual patients may object to examination of their blood pressure or testing of patellar reflexes, and insist that they have come for treatment of a headache and not of their legs or arms, so the non-symptomatic members of families will often make the physician feel that it is quite unreasonable to ask them to attend therapy when the 'problems' so clearly lie in the referred patient, not in themselves. In the same way that the medical student learns to ignore irrelevant objections by becoming convinced through experience that a systematic approach is best, so will the physician discover that regarding the whole family as an interlocking system may produce far more effective understanding and treatment.

Arrangements and Interviewing Techniques

1. Engagement: beginning with the whole family: advantages and problems

Getting the family to attend as a group is not usually a problem, provided one has confidence in the value of family therapy and conveys this confidence in one's voice and manner. It should be a problem least of all for the general practitioner, who has gained the family's confidence and trust through past involvement. In the psychiatric department of the Queen Elizabeth Hospital for Children in London, where most referrals were from paediatricians or family practitioners, it was so rare for a father not to attend that his absence was a source of animated discussion, and usually proved to be the most important fact explaining the presenting problem. Yet this hospital was located in the poorest part of London's East End, where most fathers had to change a shift or lose a half-day's pay to come.

However, if doubts or objections are raised – usually by a parent who says that there are no problems in the family apart from the symptoms of the identified patient – it usually suffices to say that the latter does indeed need help, but that there is more hope of success if other members of the family can be involved. The practitioner is helped both by obtaining information about the problem (parents readily appreciate the fact that siblings may have received confidences or noticed events or coincidences that did not come to their own attention) and by encouraging the collaboration of both parents in a treatment plan that they have worked out and agreed upon together. Few mothers disagree when told that fathers are important too, and that mother will be able to seek the children's welfare and health even more effectively if she has the father's understanding and cooperation through sharing in the discussion.

Once the family is assembled, members are invited to sit in a rough circle, perhaps with some play material in the centre for younger children (these should be such as to avoid too much noise or mess, as well as to give some opportunity for non-verbal communication – crayons and paper, or a doll's house and flexible family figures are ideal). My technique is to indicate that the dicussion is a collaborative effort by sitting in the circle rather than behind a desk, and to direct all activity toward encouraging a 'collaborative' rather than a 'directive' interview in the early stages. I usually shake hands with each member of the family, ask to be introduced to everyone, which not only gives an opportunity to record names, ages and other items of the family structure, but demonstrates my interest in all family members. I indicate my understanding that there is a problem affecting some members of the family, and ask whether the family will tell me something about it. It is important to look with curiosity from one member to another, and to take care not to catch any one person's gaze for too long. In this way the individual who takes the lead will be determined by the family power structure, rather than by a signal from oneself. The pattern of interaction that follows will often say more than the actual words spoken, and is noted attentively. For example, the mother may control the interview and put words into everyone's mouth, while the father looks resignedly out the window or at his watch. The referred child who is alleged to have the 'behaviour disorder' may behave well, though looking depressed, while the allegedly 'good' one behaves abominably and 'gets away with murder'.

2. Identification of problems: using the interview process

In the early stages, attempts will usually be made to get the doctor to change to a more directive form of interviewing by keeping the identified patient in the limelight and by keeping exploration away from more general family relationships: 'Why does she do these things, doctor?' . . . 'We just want some advice' . . . 'Do you think some drugs would help her?' . . . 'Everything's fine at home except for her; couldn't you just arrange some therapy for her?' . . . etc., etc.! All this is best dealt with by explaining patiently that one needs more information from everyone before understanding of the problem is achieved and decisions about diagnosis and treatment are made. *Though there are many approaches, the quickest, easiest, and least anxiety-arousing route into the more general family dynamics, in my experience, is to ask for a recent example of the problem complained of, and then get the family to give a play-by-play account of events preceding and following it by insisting on detail. Asking about the* effects *of the problem on other members of the family and about their* management *of it brings everyone into the discussion in a completely natural, non-threatening way. The family relationships and emotional undercurrents quickly begin to become apparent.* Mother may say that father leaves it all to her, and that she wishes he would take more part. Father may answer that whenever he does, she interferes, so he has given up trying. Mother may reply that this is the whole trouble – he should stand his ground with her and the children and be more of a man. Father may hint darkly that he might play a more active rôle in the daytime if he were encouraged to be more of a man when alone with her at night. And so on.

Once the discussion is underway, the doctor can be less active, making sure that everyone is having a chance to contribute, drawing out feelings people may be too anxious to voice at first, while checking each person's idea about how the others feel against the reality of the actual feelings expressed. The physician chairs the discussion in a relaxed, encouraging, fair and sympathetic way, asking questions to clarify what is being said, and constantly confronting the family with the fundamental principle that *it is their task to make the problem meaningful to the physician if they are to be helped.*

3. Resolution of problems: verbal and non-verbal communication

In a later part of the interview, the non-verbal aspects of the interaction can be made explicit, especially those that contradict the verbal statements. Though the parents may protest that there is never any form of aggression or violence in the family, the children may be enacting scenes of extreme violence in their drawings. Or the parents may both focus on the referred child, and the fact that their eyes never meet may say everything about the unhappy nature of the marital sexual bond.

In a later part of the interview, the siblings too, if tactfully encouraged and supported, will begin to 'spill the beans' and provide the key information that helps explain the mystery and confusion experienced by the doctor when vital facts are being withheld earlier. Indeed, the siblings may do most of the work if they are given firm and fair direction from the physician. They are not only close enough to be aware of the real problem, but are often disengaged enough from the interaction of the parents and referred patient to see this interaction more objectively. *Just to ask the siblings what they think about the problem, and what would be necessary to solve it, leads frequently to answers that are awesome in their appropriateness, wisdom and simplicity.*

However a solution is reached, the element of simplicity is usually striking. All physicians have had the experience of being thanked by patients for helping them to solve problems, when all that was done was to listen patiently and to help them sustain their thought past the point where it usually turned back into the same circle. Once people are helped to clarify their attitudes and aims, they often see

93

contradictions that were invisible to them before, and find more satisfactory compromises. The same process occurs in family counselling as family members become aware, perhaps for the first time in their lives, of agreements and conflicts between their different desires, and then negotiate compromises that are more satisfactory to all. These simple procedures frequently result in profound and rapid positive changes in the functioning of the family, as well as changes in the symptoms that the referred patient had presented. The physician may think that nothing grand or clever enough to account for such improvement has been done, but it often occurs even after interviews that leave both the physician and the family feeling confused and disappointed. The following is a clear example; changes of this extent and rapidity are not uncommon, even with seemingly hopeless cases that have undergone years of conventional treatments.

4. An example of the three stages in one interview

Case A

Ann, aged twenty-seven, was referred to me from a mental hospital in a neighbouring city where she was being compulsorily detained for her own safety because of severe depression and wrist-cutting. The wrist-cutting had occurred repeatedly since the age of eleven, and together with other self-destructive behaviour such as drug overdose and refusal to eat, had led to many admissions. Though she had completed training as a secretary, she was unable to work and was living on welfare. She claimed, and her family agreed, that she had suffered lifelong depression and incapacitating social anxiety, was unable to make and keep friends, spent long periods sitting alone in darkened rooms, and wanted only to die. Besides medication and other routine hospital treatments, she had undergone two-and-a-half years of psychotherapy with a psychologist at the hospital at the time of referral. Change had been very limited. In view of the limited progress, the psychiatrist who had been responsible for the case requested a family consultation, and put strong pressure on the family to accept. His insistence was vital, since the parents, brother (two years younger) and patient lived a long way away, and since the father, a rigid, cold, remote man, was known to be intensely hostile to psychiatrists. He claimed 'if they get their hands on you, they drive you mad', and insisted that there were no problems in the family except those displayed by Ann.

Through the consultant's ultimatum, the whole family was soon assembled for consultation. As expected, the father took over and gave a long and detailed account of Ann's 'illness', assuring me there was nothing wrong with anyone else. I heard him out patiently, nodded and accepted all he said, and then asked for Ann's account. She agreed with her father's description of her as inexplicably disordered from birth, and attributed her self-destructive episodes to despair at her social inadequacy, which resulted from overwhelming feelings of anxiety and fears of further failure.

I next brought in the brother who, to the surprise of both parents, reported that he had always suffered from similar, but less severe, social anxiety. Following this, the mother said that she had always shared this problem too, but had not wanted to divulge this, for fear the children would lose confidence in her. Ann was quite incredulous, protesting that this could not possibly be true. Her amazement was only matched by that of her mother, as the father next reported that he had always felt similar anxiety in social situations as well, and coped only with great difficulty and constant struggle.

This was the essence of the interview. The remainder of the time was used to look at the reasons why Ann had volunteered for the rôle of scapegoat. This was explained partly by her feeling that males were favoured, so that this rôle compensated and gave her an important place in the family. This was really the whole treatment, though the parents and Ann came once more to report subsequent changes a month later.

A few days after the first interview, the father wrote to say that 'Following our recent consultation we had the most relaxed family discussion that we had had for years, and would like to make arrangments for our further meetings.' At the second (and last) session, Ann looked lively and attractive, had changed her drab appearance with a striking 'Afro' hairstyle, played a leading part in the session, and insisted on seeing my secretary afterwards to pay the fee herself, instead of letting her father do so. She confirmed her father's initial statement that 'She hasn't looked back from the moment we left this room. . . .' by saying: 'Everything is just better. I am working, planning for the future, have taken on a three-year course of training. I know it's going to be difficult, but I still want to do it. . . . Before, I had no other aim but the grave . . . but now I want to make a success of it.' The urge to cut her wrists had 'absolutely gone'. Mother confirmed these improvements, saying it was 'just wonderful'.

It was possible to have an unusually detailed follow-up through the assessments of the consultant and of the other professionals who continued to have contact with her. They reported that these improvements had been sustained and increased in the following thirty months, and the consultant confirmed this over six years.

An extract from a letter Ann wrote to me after the second consultation conveys vividly the chain-reaction of improvement even one such discussion can lead to by opening up communication in the family.

It is really quite amazing how things have changed in so short a time. I must say I was terribly sceptical to begin with, and my father was too; we really didn't believe that by just talking to someone, anything could really change at all, but obviously we were wrong, because somehow absolutely everything has changed, and our attitudes now seem to be having a snowballing effect, which is making everything better. . . . I have a picture in mind of each of us ploughing through life up until now, completely enclosed within a brick wall, and although we were a 'family' to the outside world, we were *never* a family at all. It was always a ghastly criss-cross combination of two versus two in some form or other. Now it seems just as though all the brick walls have been broken down, and we can reach each other.

At the end of the letter, Ann enclosed a diagram of the change as she saw it.

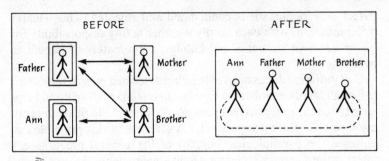

Figure 1

Theoretical Discussion

1. Family rôles and personal differentiation

This example shows with striking clarity the way in which members of a family may assign fixed and limited rôles to each other, thus restricting their ability to grow towards balanced, independent functioning. Instead, members are tied together in a state of partial fusion and are unable to operate autonomously because they need other family members to contain or express some psychological functions for them. This need is most obvious in the case where there is a scapegoat who is assigned the task of containing a particular set of feelings that the family as a whole are excessively fearful of, and so cannot cope with. The rest of the family was enabled to function effectively because Ann carried the burden for everyone. The scapegoat rôle is determined by many factors, not the least of which is a dim awareness on the part of the person filling it that playing this rôle is vital to the psychic balance of the family, and has its rewards and importance as well as its pains and handicaps. The scapegoat is always as much volunteer as victim, and the rôle is fulfilled out of love as well as fear.

Family members who are assigned to carry the 'strong' and seemingly positive rôles are equally bound within the system, because they are threatened with symptoms of disequilibrium unless the 'weak' member carries the fears and failings of all. These weaknesses may in fact be no more than a normal sensitivity or tenderness, which is esssential to a full life and is experienced as a

97

defect only because it is condemned and rejected. Thus clearer differentiation, with each family member taking responsibility for his or her own strengths and failings, is ultimately of benefit to everyone.

Collaborative discussions of the kind described, where the doctor assists all family members to express their feelings clearly and helps each to see the others as real persons, obviously help this differentiation to take place progressively. Awareness of this principle can enhance the psychological benefits of the general practitioner's interventions, even when seeing individual patients alone or seeing a couple without their children. Helping one family member to differentiate and define himself or herself more clearly may lead other family members to clarify their own identities, just as drawing the frontier of the United States draws part of Canada's as well. Bowen (1966) concentrates much of his work on helping a key figure in the family (usually not the referred patient), or the parental couple, to achieve a higher degree of 'differentiation of self'. Bowen's principle is that therapists best help patients to gain clearer identities and boundaries when the therapists define *themselves* as real persons, and are not open to manipulation or willing to control the patients' lives to an inappropriate degree. This forces patients to take responsibility for their lives in increasing measure, and should prove especially fruitful in general practice. Hatfield, a British general practitioner, has attempted to modify Bowen's methods to suit the general-practice setting.

A family whose members have ill-defined boundaries and are low in degree of 'differentiation of self' will be more vulnerable to both internal and external stresses, and disturbances will tend to spread not only through the nuclear family but also through the extended family system, so that a stress initially impinging on one member may lead to dysfunction in several members. Many other individuals in the network may then present to the family physician not only with obviously nervous or psychosomatic symptoms but with injuries, infections and other more obviously 'physical' disorders. Kellner has demonstrated a 'clustering' of different types of illness in members of families at times of stress, illnesses that are seemingly related to emotional contagion (Kellner, 1963). Particularly in rural areas, where the family practitioner is intimately acquainted with large inter-related family networks, knowledge about the spread of such ripples of disturbance not only makes the work more meaning-ful, but allows the physician to concentrate attention at the source of the disturbance, which may greatly reduce the need for pro-longed intervention.

2. Developmental stages

Raising a family can be viewed as a process in which the parents help the children to master a series of developmental challenges by giving the children difficulties they must struggle to overcome, and by giving support and information to help them do so. At the simplest level, for example, the mother no longer ties her children's shoelaces, but patiently helps them to do this for themselves. At the more complex level of learning to form relationships and to fit into society, the response of the parent similarly has to be tailored to the level of social development that the child has reached. During the first year or so, the child is learning to love, trust and internalise a secure and comforting image of the mother; at this stage, the latter must be readily available and must provide consistent care and comfort, while demands for conformity and self-control are at a minimum. Over the next couple of years, the child becomes more active, independent and assertive, so that the parents must provide increasing control and discipline to help the child develop adequate inner controls and find compromises between personal impulses and the demands of society. Later still, at about age four or five, the precursors of what one day will be mature sexuality and marriage make their appearance in a developing curiosity about sexual differences and a romantic attachment to the parent of the opposite sex. Next comes school, and the need to fit into the larger social group in the classroom and in the playground or 'gang'; then adolescence, the first budding of real sexuality as well as social pressures for greater independence from the family; and so on.

The family interview will focus around different types of issue, depending upon the amount of difficulty the family experiences when passing through this developmental sequence. In addition, the interview will have to provide different kinds of 'input', depend-ing upon the developmental challenge with which the parents cannot cope, and which the physician has to help them provide or which he must provide personally when the family cannot do so. With one family, this rôle may be more to act as a model of a nurturing, accepting parent, particularly where the mother has received no adequate model of love and nurturance from her own mother and so cannot meet her child's needs. In another family where no adequate models of firm and kindly control have existed in the parents' early histories, the model for this may have to be provided first by the doctor. If parents are anxious and inhibited about sexuality and any display of physical affection, the doctor may have to provide an example of relaxed acceptance of such matters by the comfortable and open way in which he or she talks about them.

Three examples of the therapist's focus on developmental stages: nurture, authority and sharing

Case B: nurture in a vicious cycle

Jean, who was referred to the Child Guidance Clinic at the age of twelve for soiling, had a long history of disturbance, accidents and physical illness. She had always craved affection, saying that she would not stop soiling until her mother displayed her love. She was showing increasingly violent tempers and outbursts of violence, and would lock herself in the toilet. She had no friends, believed that everyone was against her, and in fact provoked much bullying.

The mother was a thin, withdrawn, apathetic woman who had had a similar history of deprivation and difficult relationships in her own childhood, and wanted to get rid of Jean by placing her in a boarding school. Jean's father had deserted the mother soon after Jean was born.

At the first interview, Jean behaved like a very young child, clinging to her mother and refusing to leave her. I, therefore, saw them for a joint interview where Jean sat close up against her mother, holding her hand and gazing at her silently. She expressed great relief when she was able to reveal, with encouragement and support, that she did indeed feel that her mother did not love her and might leave her, and that she clung to her for this reason. She was then able to admit that she hated her mother, sometimes wished that she were dead, and that her greatest terror was that her mother might find this out, for then she would surely abandon her. Asked what she would choose if she could have 'three magic wishes', her replies were: 'Stop messing my drawers', 'Mother not to be so angry', and 'Not to be so angry myself'.

Following this, it was possible for the mother to express in Jean's presence her feelings of unhappiness and despair over the present situation, especially her own feelings of worthlessness and incompetence as a mother, to a point where she hated Jean for making her feel so inadequate. With encouragment, the mother was then able to speak of her own early deprivation, and to say how difficult she found it to give her child what she had never received herself.

This forty-five minute interview comprised the main treatment needed, and succeeding fifty-minute visits at increasing intervals were primarily for follow-up. Two weeks after the first interview, both looked happier and more relaxed. Jean sat farther away from her mother and no longer needed to touch her. Both agreed that they were less angry with each other and were able to show affection more easily. A month later, Jean was sleeping well, and the temper tantrums had largely ceased. She had lost her fears that accidents would befall her mother or that the house would catch fire (which were present at her first session), and said she now felt sure her mother loved her, and was not worried that her bad feelings would drive mother away. Eighteen months later this improvement had not only been maintained, but Jean had completely lost her paranoid feelings at school, was making friends, and had become able to stand up for herself.

The most striking aspect of this case is the deprivation of maternal love and care perpetuating itself over generations – a vicious circle in which the pain of rejection bred hostility and withdrawal, which in turn heightened the feelings of rejection and inadequacy. *The role of the physician in these interviews was that of a good, nurturing 'mother', providing the affection, acceptance, support and containment that had been lacking in the mother's childhood, and that could not, therefore, be supplied to Jean. Provided there is real acceptance by the doctor of parts of the personality seen as 'bad' and destructive by the family, little is needed sometimes to effect a profound change, since a limited intervention can change a vicious circle of this kind into an ascending spiral of benign relations.*

Special Applications

Case C: therapeutic use of authority

Roger, aged eleven when first seen, had been treated unsuccessfully at two clinics over four years for nocturnal enuresis, anxiety and behaviour problems. Treatment had included a pad and buzzer, various forms of medication, and psychotherapy, while prolonged casework had been done with the mother through separate interviews that did not include other members of the family. A family interview was arranged, and was attended by both parents, Roger and his four-year-old sister.

Detailed exploration of the family interaction and parental management of the problems yielded a picture of parents who grumbled and nagged, but were never really firm. The father acknowledged that he would argue with Roger for up to half an hour to get him to get some coal, but would end by getting it himself 'for the sake of peace'. I pointed out that Roger, who was behaving at the interview like a caricature of passive resistance, doing nothing to contribute to the discussion and leaving everything to the adults, was clearly in control of the family. This was because the parents needed to see themselves as kind, loving, and loved by the children, and always put the latter first and their own needs, including the marriage, last. The parents were encouraged to reverse this order, and to put the marriage first and Roger last.

As the marital relationship was discussed, the mother burst into tears and acknowledged that she felt unsupported by the father, who left all the discipline to her. The father tried to evade the issue, and I deliberately 'stung' him by criticising him sharply, hoping that he would be able to identify with the more active and critical rôle I was playing, and so be provoked into playing a stronger part in the family.

At the second interview, which was arranged three months after the first (note the interval), Roger had improved remarkably in behaviour and was more cheerful, cooperative and confident. The parents also reported that they were getting along better. The bed-wetting, however, was unchanged, and I considered this to be related to the fact that the parental control was still relatively weak and vacillating. I expressed this openly, pointing out how the parents (by appearing so helpless and apathetic) were trying to manipulate me into taking over their responsibility for solving the problem. I pointed out in a blunt, provocative way the resemblance between their behaviour and Roger's, suggesting they were demanding that I should 'wash out the sheets for them', as they felt obliged to wash his. The hope, again, was to stimulate them and strengthen their resolve by making them so angry with me (though within a sufficiently supportive context) that they would be determined not to give me further cause to provoke them.

At the third interview, four months later (seven months after the first), all the improvements in the boy and in the marital situation had continued, and also Roger's enuresis had ceased, except for an occasional wet bed. The whole family appeared happy and satisfied. Asked what had made the change, the mother said: 'Your approach. You brought it out into the open so that we could talk about it, and you were firm with Roger. Other doctors spoke very quietly and made us feel that it was our fault and Roger that it wasn't his fault. In these family interviews there has been talk in which the whole problem has come into the open.'

Note that she does not mention the fact that not only was I firm with Roger, but also placed both parents in the rôle of naughty children, and scolded them too. They had repressed this fact, and remembered only that I scolded the boy, but they seemed to have forgiven me, as I find people usually do when one inflicts pain deliberately in their interests.

In this case, there was adequate maternal affection and care (if anything, over-indulgence), and *the missing function to be supplied was related more to the traditional rôle of the father – to make the demand that the child give up his infantile demands and self-indulgence, and discipline his impulses in a way that would make him a more acceptable member of society*. A certain measure of sternness, abrasiveness and insistent demand for compliance is often required. Psychiatrists who have been trained in analytic techniques often find this very difficult, even repugnant, but the family practitioner who has not moved so far away from the authoritative aspect of the medical rôle may well learn these skills more easily.

Case D: sharing and adjusting to three-person relationships

Alan, aged twelve at the time of his referral for complaints of abdominal pain and loose stools, was seen in the company of his clergyman father, his mother and his elder sister, aged fourteen. Exploration of the problem and the family interaction around it revealed that the boy had considerable anxieties about falling short of the high standards he had set. The father said that he too developed abdominal pain and changes in bowel habits under stress, while the father's mother had recently undergone a colectomy for 'ulcerative colitis'.

Though facts about the family were accumulated, neither my co-therapist nor I felt any real progress was being made towards an understanding of the problem. We seemed stuck with a static picture of two over-conscientious and inhibited parents who were doing all they could to please the children and to avoid arguments, and were also trying to please us by being 'good patients'. In expressing this openly, we saw that this pattern was the essential problem, and pointed out that though the family functioned in a loving and constructive way generally, they seemed over-conscientious, and there did not seem to be much room for 'fun'. This comment was taken up vigorously by the children, who confirmed that this was exactly what was wrong. In particular, Alan obviously missed the company of his father, who tended to withdraw into his study, and gave so much time to his parishioners that there was little left for his family. These exchanges seemed to have considerable meaning for everyone, and they went away thoughtful.

At the second interview a month later, considerable change had occurred. The mother appeared very lively, with her eyes twinkling, and I was struck by a sexual attractiveness not noticed before. Even the father spoke with more lightness and humour, as if he might be beginning to enjoy himself. Both parents reported that the whole family was indeed having more 'fun', and that the children had used the previous interview to insist that the family should go out together every Saturday, which everyone was enjoying.

The parents commented on the improvement in the boy's

symptoms and general confidence, but he still looked glum and wistful. I commented on this facial expression which puzzled me, and my social worker colleague, who was irritated by the father's lack of involvement, suggested that the boy must feel angry with him for his lack of emotional commitment and contact at home, as in the interview.

Supported by this, the children took a more active rôle, complaining that the parents never expressed their real feelings, but instead tried to consider everyone else to a point where there was so much self-sacrifice that the wrong decision was made for everybody, and all felt resentful. At this, the father said: 'This is charity gone mad!' and all agreed they should speak their minds more directly.

Still puzzled by the boy's continuing wistful sadness, I asked whether he had been separated from his mother in babyhood, but it was then reported that the father had been away studying at a university for a whole year when the boy was five, and had seen the family for only a short time each week. The boy's expression now made sense to me, and I suggested that he had never forgiven his father for coming back, or his mother for transferring her affection back to the father. After thinking for a moment, the boy agreed, saying that for some strange reason he could remember the year he had with his mother alone in the clearest detail, and had felt a happy intimacy with her as they went about together. He could not remember his sister during this period, nor could he remember anything about, or after, his father's return.

At this point, the father said that the boy would have an opportunity to make up for this, as the mother and children were going off together for a holiday shortly, while he was obliged to stay at home to continue his work as a minister. We pointed out sharply that this was quite the opposite of what was necessary. It might be more important for the parents to clarify their own marital and sexual relationships, so that Alan would have to face the issue of their attachment to each other, rather than to him. This would give Alan the opportunity to confront and overcome his jealousy. At this point, Alan said how difficult it was to be a vicar's son, and I suggested that, since clergymen were often thought by many people to be above ordinary human vices, including sex, it might be harder to imagine that the parents still had a loving physical relationship, and that he could thereby fantasise more easily that he had the closer tie to his mother. Alan said enthusiastically, 'That really hits the nail on the head!'

Another appointment was arranged for a month later, but shortly before the month was up, the mother phoned to say that the improvements were by then so marked that the family all felt they no longer needed to come (they lived far away from the hospital). It was our impression that this was a consequence of genuine improvement rather than resistance, and it was left for the family to contact us if further problems occurred. Nothing further has been heard.

In this case, there had certainly been no deficiency in nurturance, since the mother had had a warm and enjoyable experience with this boy in his infancy, while the father was very much respected. Control, indeed, was too rigid and restrictive, rather than the reverse.

Though it is true that some of the family problem arose through the father's failure to involve himself actively enough in family affairs, *the main problem seemed to have more to do with the parents' difficulty about feeling comfortable in their relationship as a sexual couple, so that the children had not been confronted with a clear situation in which to face and overcome problems of exclusion, jealousy and sharing.*

3. Structure and hierarchy

Like all groups, families need some decision-making procedure whereby conflict between members can be resolved, and activities can be coordinated for the welfare of all. The Timberlawn Research Project confirmed objectively the impression of most therapists that a *firm parental coalition* is a vital factor in the functioning of healthy families (Lewis, 1976). Ideally, decisions are reached after negotiation in which the children's views are heard and carefully considered, but even a rigid yet definite structure is less harmful than a chaotic, over-permissive situation where no consistent control is provided and self-control, therefore, cannot be learned. The main requirement is collaboration and mutual support between mother and father in the management of the children, so that they form a strong 'government' and are able to make unpopular decisions when these are necessary for the well-being of individuals or of the family as a whole and so that the children are not able to 'divide and conquer'.

Diagrams similar to that spontaneously drawn by Ann (Case A) are often used by family therapists to represent family alliances and hierarchies (see Fig. 2 below). The normal family shows the most important bond lying between the parental couple, with lesser bonds among other members (A). Some examples of potentially pathological patterns include a strong coalition between mother and son with father excluded (B); same-sex pairings between parents and children (C); and excessive preoccupation of the parents with each other, thus excluding the children (D).

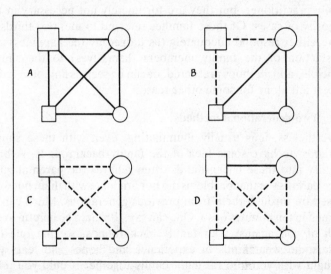

Figure 2

As the above diagram suggests, there is an appropriate measure of parental dominance and agreement. Seeing parents who disagree yet who are able to resolve differences amicably for the welfare of the family is a far more valuable model for learning to cope with the outside world than a rigidly united parental relationship in public, with arguments behind closed doors.

The case histories already given illustrate many of the points clearly, as well as illustrating my impression that, in the course of a child's growth, at first the mother, then the father, and after that the parents as a couple need to take the central place in order for specific developmental issues to be faced. This impression is not necessarily shared by all family therapists.

Technique: Relating Present Problems to the Family History

A variety of family therapy techniques exist. Some focus on present interaction, and others on past history and previous generations. Time-consuming methods are obviously impracticable for the family practitioner, but they are fortunately not necessary in the majority of cases. Of those families referred to me, two-thirds or more either respond adequately (as judged by the happiness and satisfaction of the family members themselves) to the simple principles and methods presented, or can be seen as unmotivated or as best left alone for some other reason.

Two-generational methods

Nevertheless, it is usually illuminating, even with these simple methods, to have some idea of the family backgrounds. A brief enquiry into these backgrounds often relieves the parental guilt, since parents see that problems did not originate with them but were passed on through them from previous generations. Much can be learned in ten minutes or so. One can say, 'It would be helpful to see each of you against your family backgrounds, so that one can understand what kinds of experience and hopes and fears you brought with you into raising a family together. Could you tell – very briefly – what your fathers and mothers were like in their personalities – how you got on with them – your brothers and sisters – that sort of thing?'

Very often, the source of the presenting difficulties soon becomes apparent. The wife may have more difficulty with her sons than her daughters because she resented the fact that her brothers were favoured and given better educational opportunities, while girls were not valued so highly. Or perhaps the husband's own father was away at the war in his early years, and he both lacked a satisfactory masculine model and also resented his father's return. Now he cannot be a satisfactory model for his sons, since not only has he never internalised this rôle, but also fears his own sons' jealousy if he plays it. Or the wife's father may have felt too great an emotional attachment to her as compared with his feelings for her mother, so that the wife reproduces this intense attachment with a son by spoiling him and arousing the jealousy of her husband, who then rejects the son and has an affair because he is angry with his wife, thus driving her and the son even closer.

Such information frequently makes everything more understandable to the doctor and to the family, though in other cases it may be no more than a routine enquiry that yields no additional help. Perhaps the simplest and most common way in which it proves of value is in demonstrating an 'oscillation' of the child-rearing attitudes running through the generations. The children are unmanageable because the parents are over-indulgent, because they are reacting against the fact that the grandparents were strict and punitive, because . . . Parents can change their approach more readily once they see that their attitudes to child-rearing are natural responses to, but over-compensation for, mistakes that were made with them.

Three-generational methods

Some cases, however, prove resistant unless one uses such a 'three-generational' approach in a more systematic way. No doubt these are among the cases the general practitioner will refer to an expert family therapist, after having reached an *impasse* with the simpler 'two-generational' methods described. Nevertheless, the family practitioner needs to know something about these more difficult situations and techniques, just as he or she needs to have some awareness of physical conditions that require the attention of a specialist in order to know when to seek help.

Case E

John, aged fourteen, was referred by the family practitioner because of incessant conflict with parents and teachers, with a vicious circle whereby increasing stubbornness and laziness on the boy's part led to escalating pressure and recriminations from the adults. This in turn stimulated greater resistance and argument. He was seen together with both his parents and his elder sister, June, aged seventeen. The eldest, Richard, aged twenty, was studying at a distant university and was unable to attend.

First session. A picture soon emerged of two likeable and decent parents who were, if anything, over-attached to the children and had too great an investment in their success, making up for the disappointments of their own early lives by trying to give to their children what they wished they had received themselves. To the parents, this felt like loving and caring, but to the children, both of whom shouted angrily at the parents to 'get off their backs and leave them alone', it clearly felt like intrusion into their developing autonomy and interference with their own identities, since the parents were trying to live their lives for them. They later realised that this long-standing conflict had reached a crisis point because John, the youngest, was about to 'leave the nest', and the accusations of his childishness and irresponsibility were in part expressions of the parents' desire to keep him a child. Similarly, his provocative, immature behaviour displayed his wish to remain the idolised baby, despite his complaints of the parents' over-concern. I was struck, also, not only by the way John's behaviour kept his parents' attention focussed on him, but by the way his provocativeness intensified whenever I tried to get them talking to each other, especially when we discussed the marital relationship.

Second session. I pointed all this out again later at a second, similar family session (all interviews were spaced a month apart), but met with much resistance from the parents, particularly from the father. They could see that they were creating the problem and making it worse by all they did, but still wanted advice about how to make John work harder and behave better. In fact, John was improving, they admitted, but the presenting complaint about school work at the first session was replaced by concern at the second that he might be taking drugs, and at the third that he might be stealing.

As this simpler approach was blocked by the parents' resistance to looking at themselves, and particularly at their deprivation and the unfulfilled desires for nurturance that they projected onto the children (and then envied when they gratified them vicariously), the third and fourth sessions were held with the parents alone to study the family backgrounds and marital relationship in the absence of the children's disruptions.

First marital session (third interview). The family histories were explored and summarised in a 'genogram' (see Figure 3), a simple means of portraying a family tree. As this was drawn, the couple became thoughtful when they realised that the youngest siblings in their own families of origin were also a focus of over-protection by their own parents, and were dependent, demanding and irresponsible – 'just like John'. Also, the mother's stepfather (the children's maternal step-grandfather), who was deeply loved by all, had died three months after John's birth. In addition, John's arrival, at a time when the father had returned to college following service in the army and when the mother then had three children to bring up with little financial or emotional support, had been a 'last straw' in the most unhappy period of their marriage. She said, 'Having two was bad enough, but three was awful. If his course had taken five years rather than three, he would have found himself divorced with three children hanging on him . . . I'd have left!' Both agreed that the sexual relationship had been unsatisfactory at this period.

Second marital session. At the second marital session (fourth interview), following this exploration, the parents had begun to accept their own part in John's problems. Mother was aware that, though she had struggled to escape her own mother's clutches, she had been jealous of the attention her youngest sister managed to provoke and felt similarly envious towards John. The father was able for the first time to discuss his own weaknesses – such as lack of ambition, procrastination, day-dreaming – 'many of the things John shows . . . I drove my own mother crazy with it!' Both began to look at

111

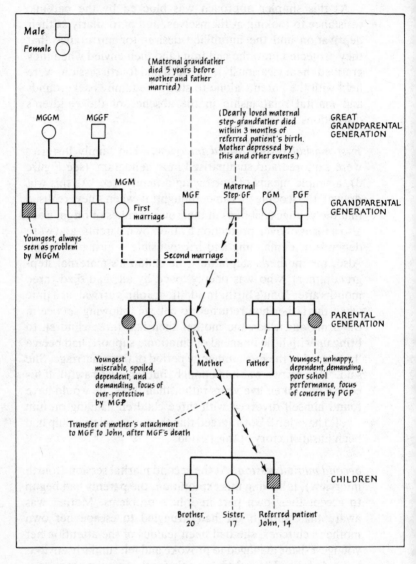

Male □
Female ○

(Maternal grandfather
died 5 years before
mother and father
married)

(Dearly loved maternal
step-grandfather died
within 3 months of
referred patient's birth.
Mother depressed by
this and other events.)

GREAT
GRANDPARENTAL
GENERATION

MGGM   MGGF

MGM   First
marriage

MGF   Maternal
Step-GF   PGM   PGF

GRANDPARENTAL
GENERATION

Youngest, always
seen as problem
by MGGM

Second marriage

PARENTAL
GENERATION

Youngest
miserable, spoiled,
dependent, and
demanding, focus
of over-protection
by MGF

Mother   Father

Youngest, unhappy,
dependent, demanding,
poor school
performance, focus
of concern by PGP

Transfer of mother's attachment
to MGF to John, after MGF's death

CHILDREN

Brother,
20   Sister,
17   Referred patient
John, 14

Figure 3

112

their pain at losing their children as they were growing up, and the need to restructure their lives. Mother said she would like to take a job again, and I ended by prescribing 'more pleasure, several times a day' for the couple, urging them to think more of themselves and less of the children.

Final interview. At the final (fifth) interview, the whole family was seen together, including the eldest, Richard, who was on vacation from the university. The parents sat together on the sofa, looking happy and united as a couple, the mother no longer tense and anxious but relaxed and glowing, both gracefully resisting any effort by John to provoke and involve them. With the parents' permission, I showed the children the genogram, and told them of the painful circumstances and marital difficulties surrounding John's birth; to this they added the interesting fact, which was confirmed by the parents, that the youngest child of the previous generation (mother's youngest uncle) had been regarded as a problem by his mother (the maternal great-grandmother), and the same overprotective/regressive relationship had existed there too.

The session ended on a cheerful and optimistic note, with the father saying: 'As far as problems go, things are a lot better . . . we all seem to be happier . . . the school problems have improved considerably.' They felt they could now cope themselves, and no further appointments were made.

When is Family Therapy Appropriate?

In my experience, this is one of the first questions general practitioners ask when one speaks about the family therapy method, and naturally they hope for a list of conditions or criteria that will enable them to come to a reasonably straightforward and clear-cut decision, as with decisions about other forms of medical treatment. Unfortunately, a satisfactory answer cannot be given in this form. To decide in advance whether family therapy (or indeed any other kind of psychotherapy) is likely to succeed and, if so, whether the problem needs a specialist's help or can be coped with by someone less expert, is unfortunately a judgement that requires the highest levels of expertise. A fair level of competence as a psychotherapist may be attained within five years, in the sense of being able to carry out effective treatment with a wide variety of cases; it is the following ten to twenty years that provide the more difficult knowledge of when to leave well enough alone – how to limit one's intervention to fit the patient's desires and strengths, rather than to fit one's own skills and life values. This leaves us with the impossible situation that only the specialist can safely decide who should not be referred to him!

We have, therefore, to find another approach to the problem, and one possible approach is that already used by the general practitioner for many of the physical ailments that come to his or her attention – that simple remedies be tried before more complicated and time-consuming ones, and that the specialist's help should be requested when one's own efforts have not brought about the hoped-for improvement. However, we need to consider the different uses of the family interview for diagnosis, for counselling or therapy, and for support.

Diagnosis

In child psychiatric or child guidance practice, I made it a routine many years ago to ask the whole family to attend the initial diagnostic interview, and have never encountered any contraindication to this practice. If a private discussion is indicated at some point, the joint interview can be interrupted and others can be asked to wait outside while one talks with the couple or with one or more individuals separately, and then later brings the whole family together for the final summing up and to thank them all for coming

Of course, many problems respond to counselling of the individual alone. Even an obvious family disturbance may be no more than a temporary disequilibrium that is in response to some unusual stress (such as a bereavement, a child's leaving home for college, a promotion to a post of greater responsibility, and so on) for which adequate support systems already exist within the extended family or community, and which will right itself given a little time.

But where the existing psychological forces of healing and growth do not restore the balance, a diagnostic family interview is indicated and may save much time in the long run. This is best proposed along the lines already suggested, as a family conference where everyone will put their heads together to try to see whether some stress or unresolved conflict might be causing disturbance or delaying improvement. By making it clear that this possibility is being eliminated as one might arrange any routine test to make sure that certain diagnoses are eliminated safely, the family interview can be relaxed and unhurried, without any sense of pressure upon the therapist to justify it by producing some dramatic conclusion at the end. If the joint interview is unproductive, that in itself is valuable information, like any other investigation that produces a negative result.

If the joint interview yields some positive result, either directly at the time or indirectly after an interval which affords an opportunity for further interaction and working out of what has emerged in the home situation, then further joint interviews or family counselling is indicated.

Any problems of *relationship* that persist, as well as most *neurotic* symptoms and *habit* or *psychosomatic* disorders are almost always treated more rapidly by further conjoint interviews. Where the problems appear to stem from a mother's difficulty in fulfilling her nurturing function, treatment of the mother and child may suffice. However, even here the father's ability to support the mother in this task may make all the difference and may relieve the physician of the need to perform this supportive rôle personally for more than a brief period. Indeed, one great advantage of family therapy is its focus on mobilising the great supportive and therapeutic potential of the family itself.

In problems centring around control (for example soiling, wetting, stuttering, behaviour problems, tics and other obsessional or compulsive phenomena), the presence of the father is particularly vital, and his failure to participate in discipline and in the setting of limits is most commonly the crucial issue. Problems of jealousy and sharing amongst the children usually have a counterpart in the parents' difficulty in sharing and cooperating with each other. This is demonstrated most readily in a joint family interview, even if its expression in the sexual relationship requires further interviews for the parents as a couple. Psychosomatic disorders also frequently yield more readily to joint family sessions; they so often express, or are triggered by, emotions that are denied and suppressed in the family system as a whole until the physician gives sanction and a sense of safety for them to be discussed openly. Irrational fears of the harmful effect of anger, jealousy or sexual excitement are often prominent in such disorders.

Most problems that are amenable to other forms of psychotherapy are, in general, responsive to conjoint therapy as well, and the greater information provided by direct observation of the family and marital interaction, together with the therapeutic potential of the family itself, usually speeds the process.

Most therapists agree that the discussion of marital problems in general terms with children present is not only harmless, but is often reassuring to the latter, who are relieved to discover that their feelings of responsibility for their parents' unhappiness are unfounded, and that the doctor is going to help. The usual practice, however, is to exclude the children from discussion of the details of the parents' sexual relationship. This explicit exclusion of the children by the doctor is often beneficial in giving insecure parents sanction to 'shut the bedroom door' and to avoid excessive sacrifice of their personal and sexual relationship to the demands of child-rearing.

Such marital therapy may be carried out by joint interviews, but if one of the partners is unwilling, some fruitful work with the more cooperative partner may be worthwhile nevertheless. Individual counselling may also be the only recourse, even when the main problem resides in the family as a whole, if the family cannot be assembled because of the death, geographical separation or resistance of important members.

Also, in adolescence the developmental task of weakening family bonds indicates separate treatment; referring the teenager for therapy in a small 'artificial' group is particularly effective and in accord with the course of normal development. However, a few family sessions may help to reveal and loosen pathological degrees of attachment.

Longer-term support

After· all reasonable efforts to cure or substantially improve a disorder have proved unsuccessful, the task of long-term comfort and amelioration of suffering will often remain with the general practitioner. This is as true for psychological problems as for

physical disease and dysfunction. Less complex psychological problems can be helped by the general practitioner; those of moderate
severity are often responsive to the psychotherapist (whether the
approach is individual or conjoint); but the most severe types of
disturbance may remain intractable to all approaches, and will need
indefinite periodic support together with more active treatments,
such as medication and admission to the hospital, at times of crisis
and decompensation.

In such cases, the conjoint family approach greatly facilitates
supportive work, enabling it to be carried out both more effectively
and with less expenditure of time. Through the physician's support
for the whole family, the family members learn to support one
another. The memory of the last visit to the doctor and of the
emotional warmth and reassurance received can be kept alive by the
family group as a whole far longer than by any one individual. When
one member is in temporary despair, others will remember and
repeat the encouragement and reassurance they all heard together.
Because of this, effective support can be provided, even through
very widely spaced interviews. With many of the deprived,
inadequate, multi-problem families, adequate support can be provided by interviews every three months or more, though even
monthly visits would have been inadequate for the individuals seen
alone. The family visits would be looked forward to eagerly and
recollected as happy; small improvements would be recounted with
pride, and advice and praise would be absorbed attentively.

Similar considerations regarding frequency of interviews also
apply, however, to counselling. Whereas, in individual work, interviews once a week are generally regarded as the minimum
frequency if substantial progress is to be made (and even this, of
course, is very little compared with most analyses), family sessions
are, in my experience, more effective when the interval between
them is longer. When I tried to find the optimum frequency in the
early 1960s, most families said that three weeks seemed about right;
if they came sooner they had not finished working out the implications of the previous sessions and putting those implications into
practice, while a longer interval led them to forget and to lose the
impetus. In practice, I have found an interval of a month usually
equally satisfactory and more convenient administratively. This
possibility, that less frequent intervention is not only as effective but

117

is in fact *more* effective, has been curiously overlooked by most family therapists, though others have more recently reported a similar finding. It is obviously of even greater importance to the pressured general practitioner than to the psychiatrist.

Though conducting sessions every three weeks or monthly is suitable in most cases, it should be emphasised that more frequent interviews are necessary in times of crisis, or when depression is a prominent feature. The same is true when feelings of depression and loss are not apparent at first but are likely to be uncovered through the family discussions. Such families can often be recognised by histories of loss and deprivation (for example, the death of grandparents during the early life of the parents) and by a clinging, 'babes-in-the-wood' quality about the family relationships.

Unlike most conventional forms of psychotherapy, one striking advantage of family therapy is its effectiveness across a wide range of socio-economic, educational and intelligence levels. In my experience, it works as well with the deprived and disadvantaged as with the middle-class. However, a more directive, active, managing approach is often more effective with the former, when the parents have lacked the necessary learning experiences in their families of origin to enable them to be adequate parents themselves. The physician must, therefore, provide some of these experiences through personal example, encouragement and advice. Minuchin and his colleagues (1967) have made a special study of disadvantaged families and have described special techniques suited to their difficulties and limitations. With intelligent, better-educated, less disturbed families, it is often more productive to help them to understand the cause of the problem, but to leave it to them to work out their own solution, as in conventional analytic work.

Research and Training

Research results

Gurman and Kniskern (1979) have recently reviewed over 200 outcome studies of conjoint family and marital work, and those interested in scientific appraisal of the effectiveness of this type of approach should begin with their excellent overview. Two of their conclusions are pertinent:

Family therapy appears to be at least as effective and possibly more effective than individual therapy for a wide variety of problems, both apparent 'individual' difficulties as well as more obvious family conflicts . . . For certain clinical goals and problems, e.g. decreasing hospitalisation rates for some chronic and acute inpatients, treating anorexia, many childhood behaviour problems, juvenile delinquency and sexual dysfunction, systems therapies offer the treatments of choice.

A clinical study of the outcome of referrals to the psychiatric department of a children's hospital throughout one year, after the referrals had been treated by the family techniques described here, reported that about one-fifth improved satisfactorily after one interview, about one-third within two interviews, and almost one-half within five. One-third were clearly demonstrated, within one or two interviews, to be either unwilling to make the changes and effort required for improvement to be possible, or to contain fragile, 'borderline' individuals who needed support rather than exploratory psychotherapy. The accuracy of this rapid screening-out, and the time it saved, can be judged from the fact that almost all of the two-thirds who remained were helped adequately either by the family interviews or by other methods that were based on the diagnostic information provided (*One Flesh, Separate Persons*).

Training

Ideally, some form of training, either through an ongoing seminar or through a few days' full-time experience, whereby expert therapists can be witnessed via videotape or through one-way screens, and where the 'feel' of family interviewing can be obtained through participating as a family member or as a therapist in rôle-plays of simulated families, is desirable. But general practitioners who lack such opportunities can safely, and with benefit, begin looking more closely at the family systems of their patients.[2]

Notes

1 This paper was first published in J. Lewis and G. Usdin (eds.), *Psychiatry in General Medical Practice*.
2 See 'An Open-Systems Approach to Teaching Family Therapy', *Journal of Marital and Family Therapy*, Vol. 5, October 1979 (appendix reference 31).

6 School Phobia: A Reappraisal

Until the 1960s, the child guidance movement focussed primarily on dyadic, mother–child relationships. Psychotherapy for the child, 'casework' for the mother, or sometimes sessions or groups for mothers and children together, were the primary forms of treatment. But school refusal was one of the problems which seemed to benefit from these methods in only limited ways.

With the development of conjoint methods and the benefit of hindsight, it became clear to practitioners that they had been replicating the very pattern in their methods that accounted for some of the problems they were trying to treat. They left the father out of the picture. This exclusion seemed to lie at the heart of the problem in most families of school-refusing children. This paper was written at the point of transition from the traditional child/mother-centred approach to a family-centred one. Rutter had just published *Maternal Deprivation Re-Assessed* and Bowlby was publishing his influential books on attachment. The former brought the father into child psychiatry, the latter brought him into family theory, and in this paper, as in *One Flesh, Separate Persons*, Skynner brings him into the clinic and consulting room of the therapist.

Though this paper was published in *One Flesh, Separate Persons* where it is readily available, it is included in abbreviated form in this collection for two reasons. Firstly, as explained above, it occupies a position of central importance in Skynner's work. It marks his own firm reaffirmation of the father's rôle, and his transition from the mother/child-centred view of the family, with father a peripheral and neglected figure, to one that includes his key contribution. With father included, the relationship of the parental couple now becomes the hub of the family, and in the papers that follow, attention turns naturally towards the marriage and its intimacies.

And secondly, new polarisations are emerging in the field, and many of those working with the problem of school refusal in school psychological services are not orientated towards family therapy. The constructive approach in this paper, and the lively, successful accounts it offers of the conjoint method at work, might encourage those presently dealing with the problem to consider the value of family therapy and to use *One Flesh, Separate Persons* as a useful guide for its treatment. And it might act as an incentive for family therapists who rarely see the problem to look out for it. For 'What Really Happened to School Refusal' is that easy cases are quickly treated without family therapy, and difficult ones turn into something more serious, reaching the family therapist later as an 'intractable' problem with a different label (see note 4 below).

J.R.S.

Introduction

The traditional child guidance approach

It is widely agreed that the essential problem of school refusal lies in an unresolved mutual dependency relationship between mother and child (Johnson *et al.*, 1941). This basic disturbance between mother and child arises from the mother's own immaturity and insecurity in the maternal rôle, and results in an ambivalent and clinging relationship. But the father also has a crucial rôle and the relative failure to involve him as a key figure in the syndrome overlooks the key to its solution.[1] This failure is an inevitable consequence of the child/mother-centred approach in traditional child psychiatry. A family-centred approach as described in this paper demonstrates more clearly the nature of the problem and its remedy.[2] The description of this approach will follow the historical sequence in which the ideas and techniques were developed. There is a literature review; an account of a research case studied intensively by the conjoint family method; a discussion of emerging new perspectives which lead to theoretical formulations; and there are examples of these principles applied to different situations in sufficiently described detail for them to be easily replicated by others.

The rôle of the father

The need to view the child's disorder in the context of the family relationships is certainly emphasised in the earlier literature, but psychotherapy has usually been offered to the mother and child only. Certain clinicians drew attention to the rôle of the father, emphasised the need to include him in the diagnostic and treatment plan and illustrated his involvement in the child's problem through accounts of his participation in conjoint family interviews

(Malmquist, 1965). However, no clear general principles emerged regarding the father's characteristic part in the genesis of the syndrome which were equivalent in clarity to those already established for the mother. This paper puts forward some clinical findings and tentative ideas arising from these findings in order to clarify this question. Emphasis in previous literature on defects in the mother–child relationship neglected a crucial failure of the father to help loosen the originally exclusive mutual attachment between mother and child. In the approach described here conjoint family therapy is used to achieve this aim. Issues of authority and control appear to be central. The crucial event is the confrontation and weakening of the fantasies of omnipotence in the child and its parents.

Literature Review

School phobia occurs in children who have a strongly ambivalent relationship with the mother. When the balance of this ambivalence is disturbed, hostility takes on a dangerous meaning. The anxious clinging can be seen as a form of passive aggression or as a reaction formation against aggressive wishes (Davidson, 1961). Anxiety, depression and guilt distinguish this syndrome from truancy, a condition in which such affects are rarely so prominent (Johnson *et al.*, 1941, Warren, 1948, Hersov, 1960). Differences in symptomatology and outcome have been acccounted for in terms of the child's developmental level and degree of personality integration. Three groups are distinguished: those in which the school phobia is a manifestation of a neurotic problem; of a characterological problem; or a psychotic one (Coolidge *et al.*, 1957, Kahn and Nursten, 1962). Where the fathers of school-phobic children have been investigated, there are consistent findings of their failure to play strong, responsible paternal rôles (Hersov, 1960). Some investigators attribute this to uncertain sexual identification (Waldfogel, 1957) and others attribute it to competition with their wives for the maternal rôle (Lippman, 1957 and Coolidge, 1957). Though exceptions have been reported to this general rule of weak, dependent fathers, even these prove to be more apparent than real. What at first appears like forceful management by a father is often a defensive rigidity in which other members as well as the father collude to deny his inadequacy (Thompson, 1948, Goldberg, 1953, Hersov, 1960).

A Case Studied in Depth

The referral

To investigate the special characteristics of different present-ing syndromes as manifested in the family group situation, a psychiatric social worker and I undertook the treatment of a boy, Richard, referred for typical school-phobic symptoms. The case was chosen because of two special points of interest. First, it was the father who initiated the referral and brought the boy to the clinic, offering to involve himself in any way required because he considered his wife too anxious and unstable to cope with clinic attendance. By studying this apparent exception to the pattern described by most authors up to that time, it was hoped to clarify further the crucial issues of the parental pathology in this syndrome. In addition, a brother two years older had also suffered school-phobic symptoms at the same age (twelve years) so that the family situation had already been thoroughly investigated by more traditional means.

The father was persuaded to allow his wife to attend with him and the referred child but our limited experience at that time led us to yield to the parents' resistance over involving the older brother, almost certainly a grave mistake. My colleague and I met weekly with the referred patient and both parents for a total of thirty sessions of conjoint family psychotherapy, each lasting one hour.

Main themes

The theme of authority and control appeared central throughout the discussions. The boy had fears of vomiting which formed a central anxiety during the school-phobic episode, but which had always been present during his school life *except* when his brother had been school-phobic and under treatment. This symptom was clearly linked with fears of being immature and childish, including losing control of 'bad'

125

regressive impulses and harming loved ones, perhaps causing the death of needed figures. The main anxieties appeared to stem less from a fear of being controlled and frustrated than from an expectation that those in authority or in a parental rôle would be defeated and destroyed. Hostility and aggression were dealt with by projection or displacement so that all dangers were seen as lying in the outside world safely excluded from the family, except in the case of sibling rivalry which was intense and clearly encouraged as a solution to the dreaded conflict between parent and child.

In later sessions the theme of genital sexuality emerged with fears of being a baby and lacking something, together with equal anxieties over becoming dangerously potent. It was revealed that pains in the testicles had been a prodromal symptom of the phobic episode. Fears of 'madness' were linked with anxieties over being excluded and made to feel jealous and rivalrous towards the parental couple – 'mad with rage and jealousy'.

Changes in family relationships

As these themes developed, the family relationships changed considerably. The mother showed the most remarkable progress. At first she appeared completely identified with Richard, living in and through him. As she gradually became able to express hostility towards him and to work through her fears of damaging him, she became a separate person, developing considerable strength and independence and beginning to lead a life of her own. Richard also showed a steady improvement in confidence, with loss of his initial depression and anxiety. As the mother became stronger he was able to separate from her after experiencing anger and pain at her possessiveness, which he saw as one primary cause of his problem. He was soon going to school with his father. Later he went alone, but although he began to mix with his friends, joined in football at the sports field and appeared perfectly normal in all other ways, he was unable to manage the last few yards through the school gates until the critical confrontation, to be described. Even by the sixth session Richard was clearly demanding a firm line over school attendance from his father –

described by the boy as a 'push' – which the father felt totally unable to provide. The latter spoke repeatedly of fears of damaging the boy and making him into a 'broken animal'. By the eighth session, my colleague was demanding from me the firm control the father felt unable to give but my response – I first mentioned the possibility of boarding school about this time – was half-hearted and aroused such anger and reproach in the family that I hesitated to persist. Both Richard and the father avoided any real confrontation over authority, either with each other or with us, by placatory subservient attitudes which concealed rigid resistances, rebellion, and the threat of withdrawal. Although active criticism by us aroused stubborn resistance which was always denied, the anger they felt in response would usually be admitted the following week when they would have 'swallowed' the criticism and would appear both stronger and less resistant. Richard was able to attack the school, next the therapists, then the mother, but could never bring himself to confront the father. The father revealed an increasingly panic-stricken, almost psychotic core lying beneath the strong façade the whole family helped him to maintain, and acknowledged that he had suffered periods of phobic anxiety himself, sometimes preventing him from going to work.

The concluding confrontation

Towards the end of the treatment, the unresolved authority conflict between Richard and the father had moved into the relationship between the father and myself. He was clearly determined to defeat me in the same way that Richard was defeating everyone else, and he was terrified that this would be discovered and avenged in some harsh way. Interpretations to this effect were denied and were clearly regarded as further manifestations of my weakness and inability to act. Finally, after experimenting with a few separate interviews for Richard and the parents, which were even less fruitful, I informed both Richard and his father that I saw no medical reason for further failure to attend. I said that medical cover would be withdrawn at once, and that if he did not return to school immediately I would see to it that he was brought before the court and that residential placement was arranged. *It so happened, because of the changed arrangements, that this ultimatum was delivered first to Richard and then to the father two days later. It is of particular interest and relevance that Richard returned, not when I told* him *this, but the day after I confronted the* father. The family refused further appointments but the boy returned to school, and indirect information indicated that he was settled and happy.

The rôle of co-therapists

The general impression gained for the family dynamics was reinforced by the way in which the co-therapists were used in the transference. My female PSW colleague was described several times as 'soothing', and seen more as an indulgent mother who would intercede with me. I was cast more in the rôle of a harsh father and punitive authority, and was spoken of as 'probing'. In fact, this distinction was based much more on transference expectations than on reality, for we both tended to alternate between rôles of firmness and attempts to understand. There were occasions when one or other of us was obliged to be away and the family found it easier to speak when one therapist only was present. Mention of genital sexuality and the prodromal symptom of pains in the testicles first emerged in an all-male session when both mother and female co-therapist were absent. This led the parents to suggest that the co-therapy situation might be more difficult for Richard, but although he agreed that this was so, he was quite insistent that he made more progress when both therapists were there.

Although my colleague and I were cast in different and mutually incompatible rôles, the family seemed to keep us abnormally free of conflict in the co-therapy situation by the pre-oedipal, dependent position they adopted. Their needs to deny jealousy in the family, or difficulties in the marriage, appeared to be mirrored in their need to see the co-therapists as always in agreement and to avoid provoking any conflict between us. However, in the twenty-fourth session, in a context where the father was being actively confronted and had threatened to leave treatment, I criticised my colleague openly for trying to identify with me rather than being herself. This had a profound and dramatic effect on the members of the family. They all attacked us and were able to express real ambivalence for the first time, as if reassured by our own 'marital quarrel', and perhaps by the firm position I was taking towards my colleague, that it was possible for spouses and families to argue and fight without inevitable destruction and loss.

Towards a New Model

Looking at development as the mastery of a series of challenges presented by the social environment (Erikson, 1950, Skynner, Chapter 4 above), it appeared from the case described (later supported by the more recent papers in the literature already reviewed), that the essential problem in families producing seriously school-phobic children lay in the parents' failure to help their children relinquish omnipotent demands for exclusive possession of the mother. From this arose the persisting difficulties over separation from the mother and home as well as the subsequent need to establish similar exclusive and controlling relationships with teachers. Thus a child able to cope in the 'one-parent' situation of the junior school could not do so in the 'multi–parent' environment of the senior school nor with friends, so the child felt exceedingly vulnerable to the loss of its one exclusive peer attachment.

This crucial challenge appears to be avoided by the parents. Typically the mothers maintain exclusive and possessive relationships with their own mothers until these are transferred, in turn, to their own children. Bonds between individuals are, as it were, 'vertical', running from parent to child, the emotional forces being essentially the same whether a given individual is in a subordinate or superior position. There is a corresponding failure to establish 'horizontal' peer-group or genital-level bonds, i.e. mutual attachments between individuals functioning on an equal level. In such families, therefore, the primary attachments always remain between parents and children rather than between spouses.

In a normal family the primary attachment is between the spouses, expressed partly by the sexual relationship but also by all the other mutual, complementary interactions which accompany

129

this. When a child is born, the mother needs temporarily to enter into an intense and exclusive relationship with it, regressing to a state of what Winnicott (1956) has termed 'primary maternal preoccupation' in order to perceive the infant's needs directly through re-experiencing that stage herself. The father, if sufficiently mature, is prepared to forgo his previous unfettered enjoyment of his spouse to allow her to carry out the maternal function while he fulfils his responsibility by 'holding the life line' and supporting the mother in her biological task.

An adequately mature father will, nevertheless, be prepared to forgo his normal demands on his spouse only as long as necessary and in the child's interest. All being well, as soon as the child no longer needs the mother's exclusive attention, and when indeed the attachment needs to be weakened, he will automatically begin to intervene and disrupt the exclusive mother– child dyad by demanding that the mother resume her relationship with him and make the marital relationship primary again. There are two ends to any piece of elastic, and by cutting the attachment at the mother's end, the father puts the child in the position where it has to cope only with its own attachment, rather than the mother's as well, in order to escape and gain the next developmental stage.[3]

In school-phobic families, by contrast, genital primacy is not achieved by the parents; the marital relationship is weak; the father is either a peripheral figure or a dependent child, rather than a supportive and protective figure during the child's infancy; the mother–child bond remains intense throughout life and is only swung from the grandmother to the child rather than being out-grown; and the father is typically unable to disrupt or weaken this primary attachment.

Having reached this conclusion, the next step was to find ways of presenting this challenge to the school-phobic children referred to us and to support them in mastering it. Since we were more interested in facilitating maturation than in relieving particular difficulties, and also because we were driven, through limited resources, never to do anything for a family we could teach them to do for themselves, a number of techniques were developed for dealing with school-phobic children and their families, depending upon their maturity, ego strength and motivation.

Techniques of Intervention

A summary of the group-analytic approach

A group-analytic approach to conjoint family therapy is described in Chapter 4 above. Briefly, the main principles are as follows:

1. At least the whole nuclear family, including the father and siblings, is included in the interview, as well as any other figures who appear to have a crucial influence.

2. The focus is on the family interaction, the 'here and now' of the interview, although past history is included when it emerges, as it tends to do at appropriate moments.

3. As will be evident, there is a particular focus on non-verbal communication. Making this explicit, and thereby confronting the family with its hidden system or rules and attitudes, constitute the main interventions. Interpreting the intra-psychic dynamics is largely unnecessary because, as Beels and Ferber (1969) have pointed out, the non-verbal system is a direct expression of much that is signified, in another frame of reference, by the term 'unconscious'.

4. Exploration is directed towards discovering the developmental stage the parents have been unable to help the child transcend, and towards both presenting and giving help in mastering this developmental challenge.

5. There are clear advantages in using a very few widely spaced interviews – often only one (excluding follow-up) – since this increases the sense of responsibility felt by the family for tackling the problem themselves. This limits the displacement of transference attitudes from family members on to the therapists and ensures that most of the working through will be carried out in the home situation. What is thus emphasised is therapeutic interaction amongst family members, rather than that between family and therapist.

6. Where possible, change is achieved by increasing insight and understanding through interpretation, enabling the family itself to supply the skills and resources it lacks. Where this does not

appear possible, however, the therapist either supplies the missing parental functions through his own responses, or arranges for them to be provided by some other agency outside the family (social worker, club leader, court etc.). Some examples follow illustrating these different types of approach.

Type 1: Cases where the parents can, given interpretation and support, present the crucial challenge to the child

Case A

Jacqueline, aged ten, was referred with the complaint of nausea and occasional vomiting over about three months, fear of which was greatest in the morning assembly. She had been away from school for several weeks. There was a variety of the usual precipitating factors noted in school-phobic children. I interviewed the child with both parents in the company of a student social worker and the supervising PSW, both of whom had seen the family for their initial interview. For teaching purposes, the student was encouraged to take the lead but neither he, nor later the PSW or myself, could get a fruitful discussion going. The child saw the problem as lying entirely in some unwholesome tomato sandwiches she had eaten before the onset of her symptoms. The parents saw the problem as lying entirely in the child and avoided all possibility of a connection with their own attitudes or relationship. There were some complaints of an interfering and possessive maternal grandmother, but the mother denied any resentment or jealousy and this line of enquiry also proved fruitless.

After three-quarters of an hour, with no progress and fifteen minutes left, *I focussed on the non-verbal interaction and commented on the doting look the mother showed towards the child, as if Jacqueline were a great treasure with everything valuable the mother possessed locked up inside her. The mother confirmed my comment by her response. Her face crumpled, she appeared on the verge of weeping, shut her eyes and kept her fist tightly against her mouth, being unable to speak for a time. When I asked what effect this intense attachment had on the family as a whole, the father commented that the mother had experienced an insecure and miserable child-*

132

hood; her father had been brutal, her mother had rejected her, and it was therefore terribly important to her to make a success of bringing up this child and to give her a different sort of life. To confirm my point, I said to the mother, 'Who are you married to?' Immediately, the mother looked at the child, not the father, and this further non-verbal communication, which summarised the underlying problem, was pointed out. This led on to a discussion of the sleeping arrangements, in which it proved that the girl still slept in the parents' bedroom. When I asked what effect this had on the sexual relationship, the mother said that it did not matter because she was 'not bothered' and said on enquiry that she was frigid. At this the father interrupted angrily to say that he was highly dissatisfied with the present relationship, although he had not complained before for fear of upsetting his wife. The mother countered by complaining that she had always wanted to lean on her husband, but that he did not support her emotionally and it was always she who had to take the decisions. *The interview ended at this point and I suggested that if the husband could satisfy some of his wife's needs that her father had failed to meet, she might not need to re-live her childhood through this intense identification with her daughter.*

The family was not seen again as they lived far from the hospital and requested referral to a local clinic. Four months later the child and mother were seen by the psychiatrist there, who reported that Jacqueline had returned to school after the interview described. She was more able to stand up for herself and cope with stress that previously had been too much for her. Further treatment was not judged necessary. Follow-up two years later showed no further problems over attendance.

Case B

Lindy, aged eight, had been out of school altogether for thirteen months, having been given a bad prognosis at the Child Guidance Clinic serving the area in which they had been living. Psychotherapy had been recommended there for Lindy, but she was still on the waiting list. A family interview was attended by both parents and Lindy, who was the youngest child, together with a sister of twelve and a brother of fourteen. A fifteen-year-old brother had just started a job and was not pressed to come. After getting to know the family, I enquired of Lindy about the onset of her symptoms. She immediately looked at mother several times but when I pressed mother not to answer for her, Lindy cried weakly, refused father's offer to take her on his lap, and clung to mother like a passive baby for the rest of the interview. The father appeared rather tense and nervous, but was insightful, straightforward, and more objective than the mother about the needs of the children. He had wanted to return Lindy to school soon after her refusal began even if it upset her, but had been advised by the psychiatrist not to do so. Father said that he had put pressure on the fourteen-year-old boy when he had suffered a school-phobic episode at the same age as Lindy, and in the interview this boy acknowledged that, although he had been angry with his father at the time, he was now grateful for his firmness.

Both parents described how they tended to focus their love and attention on the youngest child, finding it almost impossible to perceive that it was getting older until a new baby came along, when they would suddenly see it more objectively. The brother's resistance to attending school had ceased the day Lindy was born, as if some projection had been withdrawn. The father described how he enjoyed babying and cuddling them until the age of eight, the typical age of onset, when his feelings would suddenly change and cause him to push them away. The other children thought the parents were much too soft with Lindy, saying that she was spoilt and got away with things. Lindy appeared to accept all this discussion without distress.

We agreed with the siblings that Lindy was fit to return to school. *We emphasised as the crucial problem the difficulty both parents had already described about allowing the youngest child to grow up, and encouraged them to pay more attention to each other and their own relationship, and less to Lindy.* The main responsibility for this was put upon the father who was much the more insightful parent. As Lindy had seemed quite upset during part of the interview, we were reassured to learn from a psychologist who later saw Lindy at our request in order to decide which local school would be best for her, that Lindy had appeared 'quite positive about returning to school' and did not give any impression of being simply coerced. Lindy returned to school without difficulty but mother, whose motivation appeared uncertain, joined a mothers' group for further support. Follow-up three years later showed normal attendance.

These cases illustrate clearly the way in which these children receive a projection of a split-off, denied, infantile aspect of the parents' personality and the way in which this ties the parent to the child in a regressive way (and vice versa), with a corresponding weakening of the marital bonds.

Type 2: Cases where the therapist needs to share the task of presenting the challenge with the parents

In this category the parents are adequately motivated to gain control of the situation and separate from the child, but are unable to bring themselves to do this even with support. Usually the mothers are more rigid and ambivalent, and the fathers are more passive than the parents in the first category and unable to take a firmer line. The task of confronting the child with the challenge of relinquishing its omnipotent demand for a total attachment to the mother has to be carried out by the therapist, although this has the parents' support and they are allies in the task. This may be done by making it clear that residential placement will be arranged if a return to school does not take place. This technique fulfils the function the father has failed to perform of intervening between the child and the mother and disrupting the original attachment as part of his family and marital rôle. The therapist thus engages with the underlying problem and assumes real authority and power using the medical and educational systems.

Case C

Susan, aged eleven, had been refusing school for thirteen months at the time of her referral to the hospital for a second opinion. She lived in a distant area and had previously received psychotherapy from the psychiatrist at the local clinic, but had refused to attend again after he had been

135

critical of the mother in a joint interview. The mother was continuing to attend the local clinic for interviews with the PSW. There were many features of the usual school-phobic pattern.

At the initial family interview with us, the mother presented as a rather rigid, ungiving and critical woman, who was nevertheless unable to be really firm. The father was passive, placatory and had himself been school-phobic as a child; he was clearly unable to take a more active rôle himself. While the marital relationship was a limited one, it was clearly satisfactory to both parents and unlikely to change. They described Susan as being anxious and depressed, but she showed no striking sign of this and in fact looked wilful and manipulative, failing to answer some of my questions, looking out of the window, and behaving in a generally unhelpful and uncooperative fashion. *When I focussed on this non-verbal communication, rather than the family's description of her, she looked furious and became even more stubborn and resistant, evidence which was also used to confront Susan and her parents with her wish to control the situation.* Her elder brother, who also attended, said that he believed Susan was manipulative and that she usually succeeded in dominating the parents.

I stated that Susan was clearly not suffering from any illness and that medical cover would be withdrawn immediately. I said I was sure she would be able to return to school, prescribed some medication (to be described later) in order to reassure the parents that any residual anxiety would be removed, but said that I would be very pleased to help by recommending a residential school if there should be any undue difficulty. *Despite Susan's fury when confronted with firm authority she appeared friendly, open and relaxed towards the end of the interview, smiling warmly at me over her shoulder as she left.*

Seen for the second time two weeks later, the parents reported that she was 'completely changed', a 'different person'. She had returned to school, she was happy and showed no problems over attendance. She did indeed look very different, appearing cheerful, lively, bright-eyed, confident and considerably more mature. Her parents reported that she had shown increasing open aggressiveness, saying 'no' to everything during the week following the first family session, culminating in a furious row with her mother over wearing her anorak. The mother finally lost her temper and had been able to use her anger constructively. The following day Susan had appeared cheerful and relaxed and had asked her mother to take her to school. The mother said that it had been the 'worst week of her life' and felt she would not have been able to maintain a firm position throughout had she not been clearly warned that such a reaction was likely and supported in advance in standing her ground.

Follow-up revealed that Susan's attendance remained secure for over a year, when the mother telephoned the hospital as Susan was refusing school again. An appointment was offered but was cancelled a week later by the mother, who reported that Susan had resumed regular attendance. Fifteen months after this (twenty-seven months after the interview described above), she was again referred by the GP for school refusal. Susan refused to attend for interview, but the parents were seen. They both described their fear of Susan, who got in such terrible tempers if she was opposed by the parents, that mother felt helpless and ill.

After arranging further family interviews including the brother (whose departure for a distant university had deprived the parents of support in handling Susan), residential placement was recommended as Susan still declined the appointments offered. This was not acted upon by the local authority, which allowed itself to be manipulated into offering changes of day school, without result. Eventually, Susan was referred back to the local psychiatrist from whom she continued to receive certificates of her unfitness to attend school, despite her refusal to attend for interview.

This is a good example of the difficulty in dealing with such cases if one is not able to influence the relevant professional network through trust built up by regular collaboration.

Type 3: Cases where the parents are colluding fully with the child

A more difficult problem is presented by those cases where the parents see no problem in themselves or the child, but seek to prevent conflict in the family by siding with the child against the school or external authority. In such cases, the therapist needs to challenge the parents' own omnipotent fantasies. The power to do this is available through the fact that only medical sanction prevents the implementation of the law regarding school attendance.

Case D

Pamela, aged twelve, had shown school refusal at two secondary schools and the parents were demanding yet another change. She appeared sulky, angry and manipulative at the initial family interview, but there was also more depressive symptomatology than in most of the other cases and the mother was also particularly anxious and inadequate, trembling with fear throughout the interview. An anti-depressant was prescribed for the child and she was encouraged to return. After the interview the PSW who had acted as co-therapist asked me why I had not taken the usual firm line and I found myself unable to explain adequately why I had been so permissive.

Pamela did return gradually and claimed the tablets helped her, but seen a month later she was still only partially involved in school activities and appeared to be making limited efforts to overcome her difficulties. The PSW once again remarked on my gentleness with the family and queried my motives.

Three months later the housemaster complained that Pamela was still manipulative and that the mother was repeatedly coming into the school, criticising, interfering and creating problems. At the next family interview, both parents openly colluded with Pamela in criticising the school, the teacher, and indirectly the hospital and myself. I then challenged the manipulative and resistant attitude of the parents as well as Pamela, 'read the riot act', and said that if Pamela did not return to school on a normal basis at once, I would see that they were all taken to court. At first there was violent protest and denial of their non-cooperation, which gave way to cooperation as soon as they perceived that we were not to be manipulated. A month later, Pamela was attending normally and appeared well. A month after this she was attending regularly and fully, said she was enjoying school, and both she and her mother reported that there were no further complaints or symptoms. She was cheerful and friendly, looked tougher instead of immature and soft, and said that she could hold her own better with other children. They said they had forgiven me for the painful confrontation and felt that this had helped in the long run. Nothing further was heard from them.

Type 4: Truants referred as school phobics

This group is composed of truants as defined by Hersov (1960*a*), but they either show some admixture of school-phobic symptomatology or are referred by schools or agencies which prefer to avoid a disciplinary challenge by using a diagnosis which will transfer the child to medical responsibility. Unlike true school refusers there is little evidence of depression, anxiety or guilt, and the parents often openly encourage the child to remain at home for their own advantage. The parents are usually uncooperative with psychiatric services and the father often fails to attend at all.

Theoretical Discussion

Therapy and authority

The approach described here requires the therapeutic use of real authority in relation to these families, over parents as well as children. Even in cases of the first type, where the therapist does not actually play a parental rôle, he is nevertheless introducing a clear value system about what that rôle should be. Many who work in the medical or social work fields might find this type of action difficult to undertake and some might even object strongly in principle to its use. It certainly went against the inclinations and ideas I favoured when I first entered the field of child psychiatry. It took several years to feel comfortable in the rôle I now adopt. This change has come about through using conjoint family techniques generally, which obliged me, like many others, to perceive the vital but neglected place of authority, hierarchy and issues of power and control in families and social systems. These issues have been discussed in Chapters 1 and 4.

Not only does the therapist need to accept an authoritative rôle

139

and a position of personal responsibility within the social hierarchy, he is also dependent upon corresponding views in related parts of the social network – the education welfare officer, the court and so on, all playing their rôle. Unfortunately, the pendulum governing this issue seems to be swinging to its extreme point at the present time and it becomes increasingly difficult to persuade many teachers, magistrates and members of social service departments that appropriate cases need an intelligent use of authority and limits as much as others require permissiveness and encouragement. Recent legislation changing the function of the juvenile court has made the position still more difficult.

The family therapist is particularly dependent on the support and common understanding of any colleagues who may have become involved with separate members of the family containing a school-phobic member, since any conflict among the professionals concerned is skilfully exploited. *In particular, the psychiatric team needs to guard against the danger, well known in co-therapy situations, that the family pathology may be reproduced in their own relationships. Inter-professional conflicts over the timing of a return to school can be a warning sign of this.*

Moreover, to treat school-phobic cases adequately, the therapist must himself be in an appropriate position in the social system, i.e. employed by, and ultimately responsible to, the wider community even though the therapeutic aim is to meet the needs of its 'deviant' members. I have not found it possible to apply the above principles successfully in private practice, for there the therapist is paid by, and so under the control of, the family who fail to return and often fail to pay their fees if their manipulative demands are not met. Clearly, school phobia is best understood as a psychosocial problem rather than as a purely medical, intra-psychic or even intra-familial disorder.

Control or coercion?

It may be objected that the techniques described simply put the clock back to the time when coercion, force and fear obliged the child to return to school, no matter how terrified and disturbed he might be. Short of providing an opportunity for those who possess such doubts to see with their own eyes the increased health and happiness of the children and parents concerned, or to hear the families' own positive comments at follow-up, it is difficult to refute this. Perhaps the other main argument lies in the fact that coercion and fear were never in fact very successful and most people are familiar with examples of children against whom the full legal sanctions were applied without success.

The fact that the techniques described here are usually both successful and psychologically beneficial rests on the psychological meaning *of the action taken which is designed to assist the family to cope with a developmental challenge they have previously failed to transcend.* It is not the threat of the court or of residential placement which produces the essential modification, but the fact that someone in a position of parental authority is both concerned and friendly, yet prepared to use sanctions that will arouse hate and rejection but are in the family's interest to bring about a certain change in their functioning. *That change is an increased tolerance for the experience of separation, through an ability to contain and cope with the rage that the threat of separation provokes.*

Medication

Medication was routinely prescribed to cover the period of return to school in many of these children. Even a placebo effect has some value in reassuring child and parents, and giving practical evidence of support and interest, in these families which function so much at primitive, near-psychotic levels including magical thinking. Any method which eases the transition back to school and reduces unnecessary distress should be considered. Frommer (1967) found a combination of an anti-depressant (Phenelzine) and chlordiazepoxide (Librium) helpful in such cases. I have mainly used the latter, finding it effective where there is excessive fear and inhibition of aggressive and hostile feelings, which are especially prominent in this condition. One typical effect, seen clearly in Case C, is for hostility towards the parents which has been displaced on to teachers to return to its real object and to cause increased, overt conflict in the home. Parents need support in coping with this, and usually there is a change in the level of tolerance of aggressiveness within the whole family which persists after the drug is stopped. It is often helpful to prescribe the drug for the mother, or for both parents in addition if they are also frightened of aggression. For children, the dose of chlordiazepoxide required is larger than that

141

normally recommended and I usually give 5 mg t.d.s. for children under seven and 10 mg t.d.s. for those of seven and over, continued for a month after return to school. This medication by itself greatly improves the chance of return and often averts development of school refusal in early cases; while there is as yet no scientifically acceptable support for this view, the placebo or other effect should obviously be taken account of in any attempt to replicate this method.[5]

Other therapeutic measures

In addition to medication, other forms of help were arranged whenever this was judged necessary. Although it was taken for granted that the first step was to return the children immediately to school, excessively timid children were sometimes helped by inclusion in psychotherapy groups and some mothers were helped to become more independent of their children by attending psychotherapy groups for mothers. School change or other special education arrangements were rare, since demands for these seemed usually manipulative and part of the symptomatology. Another promising technique, preferably combined with therapy groups for mothers and for children, is multi-family therapy. This has the merit of combining some of the advantages of both family and 'stranger' group techniqes. The understanding gained in the interviews continues to be worked out by the families at home, but the members of each family are able to be more objective about other families than about their own. The therapeutic task and the issue of authority and control can, for this reason, be left more to the group as a whole. One particular advantage is the way in which the parents of one family can understand and help a child in another, because they are able to be more detached and neutral than the child's own parents. Another advantage is the possibility for the children in all the families to support each other and so enable each to speak more freely. Mothers and fathers also benefit from this kind of mutual support, as in the following example:

> In a multi-family group centred on the symptom of school phobia there was a striking fear of aggression and conflict, while the fathers were passive and allowed the mothers to dominate. The fathers gained in confidence by recounting

their war and other stress experiences, where they agreed that even the bravest men experience fear in battle. They then combined to criticise the (male) psychiatrist, something they had never dared to do without this mutual support, and subsequently they became more involved and assertive with their own families in a beneficial way. A description by one mother of having finally struck her daughter across the face after mounting conflict, following which the girl returned to school and the family relationships improved, at first aroused gasps of horror in the other families but led eventually to an increased acceptance that such anger and conflict could sometimes be beneficial and indeed evidence of caring.

This particular multi-family situation was combined with a weekly group for the children and another for the mothers, with the fathers joining in the multi-family sessions which were held every six weeks.

Conclusion

Both the normal developmental model offered here, and the account of school phobia as a consequence of distortions in such family norms, is simplistic and schematic. But simplicity is no disadvantage in a preliminary hypothesis as the model can be tested and its deficiencies can be recognised.[4]

Notes

1 This paper was first published in *The British Journal of Medical Psychology* 47, **1** (1974).
2 I would like to thank those colleagues, education officers and education welfare officers who made the referrals here; and to acknowledge the help of my psychiatric social worker co-therapists, both in the treatment process and in discussions of the issues involved, particularly Mrs P. Goldblatt, my co-therapist with 'the exception that proved the rule', and the late Miss P. A. Brierly, with whom most of the work with school-phobics was done.
3 Although it may look at first sight as if the crucial challenge presented by the parents is the oedipal confrontation, I do not believe that this is the case, nor even that the father's rôle here is that of representative of the wider society characteristic of the 'anal' stage. I see the challenge as being concerned with

something much more primitive, the first disruption of the exclusive attachment characteristic of the oral stage, the first weakening of omnipotent possession. However, secure mastery of this earlier stage underpins later achievements, so that failure at this level does also create difficulties in the resolution of oedipal and other subsequent conflicts. Thus the symptomatology is often complex, with derivatives from various levels occurring simultaneously.

4 For a discussion of current practice in treating school refusal, in which the conjoint method has become a routine approach, see 'School Refusal' in M. Rutter and L. Hersov (eds.), *Child and Adolescent Psychiatry*, and L. Hersov and I. Berg, *Out of School*, and the discussions in the *Newsletter of the Association of Child Psychology and Psychiatry* **7,** summer 1981; **8,** autumn 1981; and **15,** summer 1985. [Ed.]

5 Although Skynner's recommendation for the use of medication appears to contradict his caution about its use later in the book (p. 372), he confirms that, if necessary, he would continue to use anxiolitics in the treatment of school phobia. These vulnerable families are in many cases still functioning at primitive levels and, as he says, the reduction of unnecessary distress during the period of returning to school is an important consideration. [Ed.]

7 Marital Problems and Their Treatment

Many family problems can be solved by a small improvement in the parenting skills of the parents, and less serious marital conflicts can sometimes be reconciled indirectly through discussion focussed on the child's management, without directing attention to other aspects of the couple's relationship.

This is not always possible though, and Skynner came to believe that an anxiety typically experienced by all beginners learning family therapy had its roots in the possibility that the subject of discussion would shift from events in the life of the family as a whole into the parental bedroom and its confidential intimacies. Since the family therapist needed to identify to some degree with the feelings of both children and parents, this could arouse echoes of their own childhood embarrassment at the thought of crossing the parent/child boundary.

Encountering and gradually understanding these anxieties himself as his interest moved increasingly from the family to marriage, and to the sexual relationship at its centre, much of his work has been directed towards helping professionals to feel more at ease in these confusing transitions across family boundaries.

In this paper he provides a concise and readable account of intimacy, marriage and the central significance of sexuality, to introduce the more detailed papers that follow in which he sees marriage as the main determinant of the healthy functioning of the whole family, identifies the key rôle of sexuality within the marriage and evaluates the available evidence on gender rôles. These are the concerns also of *One Flesh, Separate Persons*, one of those rare texts that deals with sexuality and family life in an integrated, holistic way.

J.R.S.

Introduction

Much can be done to improve marital relationships using very simple methods, especially in cases that present for the first time rather than as a result of repeated failures of previous therapy. I shall begin with these, leaving the more difficult (and fortunately less numerous) cases for later discussion.[1]

Improving Communication

All cases of marital difficulty deserve an unhurried, careful and thorough exploration of the problem as the partners present it, setting the couple the task of making it understandable to the therapist. Curiously enough this is often therapeutic, even curative in itself, especially if it is carried out with both partners present. Misinformation about sexual functioning, and taboos over talking with others about it, have led in a vast number of couples to misconceptions that not only produce disappointment and frustration instead of affection and happiness, but which have no hope of correction unless the process of communication is initiated by an outsider and more correct information is supplied. Once communication is opened up, many difficulties disappear of themselves, often in one or two sessions. I have found that good results are often achieved swiftly with sexual problems by insisting on a very detailed description of the couples's actual sexual activity, but treating this in a matter-of-fact, light way, even with the careful use of a little humour. A model is thereby provided which gives them permission to be frank, direct and 'comfortably naked' with each other.

Case 1

A late adolescent with schizoid traits, after some years of

successful individual psychotherapy by a colleague to whom I had referred him, married a lively and attractive girl. I was asked to see him again because of difficulty in the marriage, and the joint interview revealed that neither could take the initiative sexually and that they both, because of their backgrounds, were too shy to speak about the problem to each other. A 'play-by-play' account of their interaction and sexual relationship revealed among other things that the wife's clitoral sensation was too intense and sensitive to permit direct pleasurable stimulation, though she could be excited by the stroking of her pubis and other areas near the genitals.

At the second joint interview they were enjoying sex more frequently and fully, and by the third session were able to discontinue treatment. The wife said that she had felt 'dreadfully embarrassed' at the first interview by my insistence on such detailed descriptions, but had begun to feel relaxed by the end of the first session and since then had been able to talk and act with her husband sexually with a freedom she had never thought she could attain.

The real problem in such work is, of course, the fact that we have all been subject to the same cultural taboos and evasions as our patients, even if in lesser degree, so that it is not easy for us to make them feel completely at ease when discussing intimate sexual matters, or to know how to advise them even when we have understood the problem. Few professionals, I find, have received systematic help in overcoming such anxieties and acquiring needed information, as part of their training. We are usually left to muddle along as best we can, or to pick up ideas and techniques haphazardly from students and colleagues, or we are told to read a book! It is, when you think about it, simply a reproduction of the inadequate sexual instruction so many of us received as children, and this issue is often avoided by us in turn when we become medical educators, just as it was by our parents. In the United States systematic courses have recently been developed to cope specifically with this problem, and it is to be hoped that we will have similar provision here before too long. (Rosenberg, P. and Chilgren, R., 1973)

Clarification of Contract

During this process of communication, the behaviourists have emphasised the importance of clarifying the covert contract between the couple. Each has needs the partner can supply, as well as others that must be satisfied in other ways, if at all. Once a vicious circle of frustration and mutual rejection has begun, the mutual rewards and satisfactions diminish as each withdraws from an increasingly painful interaction, leading perhaps to a chronic 'cat-and-dog' existence if not to breakdown and divorce. Each fears to take a step towards reconciliation, for this will expose him or her to the risk of further humiliation if the attempt is made when the partner happens to be in an unforgiving, bitter mood. But at least in the early stages of a deterioration of this kind, intervention by a professional who can avoid taking sides and can act as an honest broker permits the negotiation of a ceasefire, provides a temporary peace-keeping force while negotiations are resumed, and then helps the couple to work out a more explicit contract whereby mutual rewards are maximised and frustrations are diminished. This is not in itself a difficult procedure. Often all that is needed is a referee, but as with all refereeing absolute impartiality and extreme firmness are vital.

Such negotiation is vastly easier if the couple are seen together and helped to communicate their feelings, hopes and fears to each other directly. When one sees members of a couple separately, it is much more difficult to avoid being manipulated and placed in the rôle of judge, supporter or persecutor. This is partly because it is far more difficult to get at the truth about the real relationship, which is often blatantly obvious after fifteen minutes of watching a couple interact before one's eyes rather than listening to their prepared and carefully edited accounts. No doubt this is one reason why Crowe has found, in his controlled experimental study of different marital therapies at the Maudsley Hospital (Crowe, 1973), that the theoretical model used – whether analytic, formal behavioural or simple support and encouragement to talk – seems less important than the use of the conjoint method itself.

Developmental Levels: Separateness and Responsibility

I have personally found a developmental model the most useful in understanding marital interaction. The category Dominian (1974) has labelled 'Personality Disorder – Psychopathy' is composed of individuals who are really functioning at an *infantile* level. Like toddlers, they are unable to perceive the needs of others, have not learnt to give and take and still possess a limited capacity to tolerate frustration or delay, so that they are apt to lose their temper and become violent when demands are not met. One does not hope to deal with infants by reason alone, and similarly explanations and interpretive, analytic methods are wasted on this group. The professional must take a firm managerial rôle, like a parent of a difficult child, if he is to achieve anything at all. He may need to scold and bang the table, though this will only be effective, as with children, if the firmness is provided within a context of support and friendliness.

The category Dominian has labelled 'Personality Disorder – Crisis of Identity' I would be inclined to label '*Childish* Functioning'. These individuals are immature, unready for an independent existence, often anxious and over-needy of approval from the partner, but they are more responsive to an attempt to help them understand their problems, and more able to help themselves if they are given information enabling them to do so, in a sufficiently supportive context. Many of the marital problems we see arise from the over-demanding, over-dependent relationships that stem from such immaturity. They may take the form of over-dependency and clinging, as in agoraphobia, separation anxiety and some depressive states. Or a compulsive attempt to avoid such denied dependency may be more prominent, with rows, obsessional stubbornness, separations, infidelities or constant work away from home which all have their roots in a fear of engulfment, and attempts to overcome this tendency to excessive attachment which was not surmounted in the family of origin. Though both of these are manifestations of an essential childish dependency, one needs to remember that conflict and seeming deterioration in a relationship may be a necessary step on the road to independence, just as tantrums in a toddler or adolescent rebellion may be signs of moves towards autonomy.

Unfortunately, many cultural influences idealise and encourage immature relationships, so that it is often regarded as a virtue and a sign of true love to be so possessive as to be unable to share the partner, to be unable to live without him or to maintain and continue within marriage some independent growth and life. In the married couples groups my wife and I conduct together, this healthy separation, or rather individuation, of the couples from an original suffocating childish attachment is a striking development in all couples who have done well. As they achieve it, it would often look at times to outsiders as if we are providing an arena for facilitating marital breakdown rather than marital therapy, for the maturational process is often at first marked by false attempts at independence. Increased ability to fight often precedes a real ability to be honestly involved and to love and consider the partner. Temporary trial separations, which are usually revolts against feelings of being trapped and coerced, sometimes lie on the path to a more real and permanent commitment. Because of this, we have found it counter-productive to be too concerned about the marriage as such, and more valuable to be interested in the increasing growth and maturity of each partner as an individual.

Most couples do choose to remain together in a happier marriage and, being deeply grateful for the happiness my own marriage and family have brought me, I will not deny that I derive greater personal enjoyment from this result. But the couples that separate (and some in fact come specifically to be enabled to do this with the minimum of pain to each other and while retaining a good parental rôle with their children) have often demonstrated a capacity for affection and concern towards each other and in relation to the care of their children never possible until after they have separated, so that even these results are less unhappy than they might appear.

This fundamental requirement for any real relationship to exist – that each partner should be sufficiently differentiated to take responsibility for himself rather than looking to his partner to make him happy – is expressed in the second part of the title of my textbook, *One Flesh, Separate Persons*.

Internalised Models

The first part of the title, *One Flesh*, is taken of course from

151

Genesis, which anticipated the object relations school of psychoanalysis by several thousand years: 'Therefore shall a man leave his father and his mother, and shall cleave unto his wife; and they shall be one flesh.' Genesis gives us the broad guiding principle, and it is left to us to work out the details as Dicks (1967) has done superbly in his book *Marital Tensions*. But the essential idea is nevertheless there: manifestations of transference in the psychoanalytic sense underlie much marital pathology; we must outgrow our parental attachments, and see our partners as they are, instead of projecting our internalised parental images onto them, if a true marriage is to be possible. In a recent paper contrasting adjusted and maladjusted couples using the double-dyad-grid, Ryle and Breen (1972) have provided interesting confirmation of this fact:

> The finding of greatest interest is the demonstration that patient couples differed from controls in that they were more likely to see the relationship with the partner as resembling their relationship with their parents, and that when the relationship was going badly they perceived their own rôle as more child-like while that of their partner became less parent-like.

I have been impressed, like Dicks and his collaborator Teruel (1966), with the constant finding that disturbed marriages are haunted by disturbing internalised parental figures, and that many less viable marriages – perhaps those most likely to break up – have occurred in an attempt to render more manageable hateful parental introjects which show similar features in both the partners, and which each partner previously found it even more difficult to cope with on his own. Sometimes each partner will keep his or her own ghostly persecutor safely contained in the spouse, with inevitable mutual rejection and attack as well as equally inevitable inability to separate. Other couples form a tight alliance in order to keep the dreaded shared internal figure projected into a scapegoated child, or outside the family altogether into a generally persecuting world.

In dealing with such marriages we as therapists must of course not only recognise the manifestations of these internalised, undigested parental figures, but we must expect that at moments they will be projected on to us and that we will be treated as if we have become them. Some measure of correction is then possible not only by the more conventional analytic method of interpretation, pointing out the misperception, but also by providing a different model to that expected. But whichever method is used, the experience of receiving such transferences is often extremely disturbing and one may feel almost as if one is possessed by some alien force and in danger of losing one's senses. At such times collaboration with a co-therapist has its greatest value, for one partner in the therapeutic team will be less affected by the projection and can not only rescue his companion but observe the interaction objectively and use it in a therapeutic way to understand and explain the related marital disturbance.

For some reason no one has yet satisfactorily explained, therapeutic work with marriages and families seems to demand more natural, human and spontaneous behaviour in the therapist than is called out from us in other kinds of therapy. In co-therapy the provision of a model of a relationship characterised by enjoyment, affection and a capacity for constructive argument seems of quite astonishing influence in producing improvement in marital rôles and relationship. This 'modelling' factor, which now seems to me one essential element explaining the puzzlingly rapid changes that characterise conjoint therapy, whoever uses it and whatever theoretical orientation is employed, is even more in evidence in couples groups. Here constant learning takes place not only through the therapist's example, but also through a variety of models provided by the couples themselves. Couples groups thus combine the advantages of conjoint therapy (i.e. continued 'homework' between the formal sessions, which is of course not possible in a therapy group composed of people who are strangers to each other) with the advantages of the artificially-constituted therapy group (which include a variety of rôles, social skills, attitudes and values which complement or interact with and alter each other, rather than the collusive defensive system and shared rigid values which inevitably characterise disturbed couples and families). My wife and I have been working with such groups since 1972, and there is still much to be learnt, but this mode of therapy at present seems particularly promising in the way it offers the best of both worlds and maximises the effects of limited therapeutic time.

The second example is taken from such a group, and illustrates simultaneously the way in which parental projections interfere with marital harmony, the way these are projected on to, and absorbed by, other couples and by the therapist couple at times, and also the therapeutic use that can be made of such situations if the underlying dynamics can be understood. The example also has the virtue of being quite amusing, and having a happy ending.

Case 2

A couple who showed a particularly profound over-protective/destructive relationship, based on the experience in both spouses of extreme ambivalence at the hands of essentially psychotic mothers, were placed for therapy in a married couples group. Here their endless ambivalent bickering and mutual provocation seemed unresponsive to any intervention, though the other couples, who all showed less severe mutually destructive relationships (we called it our 'Who's Afraid of Virginia Woolf' group) were improving. At one session another couple, who had made good progress and were planning to leave, complained that they had returned home after the previous group to find themselves 'having this couple's row'; they said that this couple 'should have their own rows instead of getting others to do their dirty work for them'. Like the rest of the group, my wife and I were amused by this event, but during a meal together after we got home, usually a pleasant relaxation at the end of the day, found ourselves also having a blazing, unexpected row. I accused her of not appreciating me, while she countered that if I really appreciated her she would have an automatic dishwashing machine. We slept back to back at opposite sides of the bed, but as soon as I awakened I realised that we had ourselves 'had the row' for this couple. It at once became clear that the conflict was based on our both taking positions of jealous siblings, placing the partner simultaneously in the position of a parent from whom approval was desired, and also of a sibling competing for that approval.

The group were even more amused when we reported these events to them, but the understanding gained from our internalising and working out this conflict based on their relationship-model enabled them to understand the basis of their arguments also. The incessant quarrelling of this couple now yielded to continued therapy, while our automatic dishwasher was delivered two weeks later!

1 This paper was originally published in the *Proceedings of the Royal Society of Medicine*, Vol. 68 (July 1975).

8 Sexual Counselling in General Practice

Skynner and his wife shared the leadership of a course set up in 1973 to train mental health professionals in family therapy, out of which the Institute of Family Therapy developed. They became aware of the discomfort professionals reveal, sometimes only in their non-verbal reactions, when pursuing the detail of sexual problems, and advising on their management. They decided to get some more advanced training in the new American methods of improving sexual interviewing techniques, including the 'active sex therapy' recently developed by Masters and Johnson.

These are essentially based on 'modelling', a mode of influence already central to Skynner's approach, in which he describes it as the largely unconscious internalisation of the attitudes and emotional states of others. When used in the active sex therapies, this mode of influence equips therapists to help their patients towards a less inhibited, less anxiety-prone attitude towards their own sexuality, by modelling a frankness and ease as the problems are explored. Whilst non-verbal cues are thus an essential part of the process, Skynner believed it was also possible to use this 'mechanism' by conveying attitudes 'between the lines' in written communication, an approach which other professionals – similarly influenced by Masters and Johnson – were also beginning to put to good use in sex manuals.

This chapter, written to give simple guidance on sexual interviewing to general practitioners and other physicians, and which is equally relevant to other professionals, puts this principle into practice. In passages that merit attention in their own right for their affirmative quality, he informs the technical, scientific language of the field with a humanity not often encountered in professional literature.

J.R.S.

Introduction

In this chapter I shall set out and illustrate by examples some basic principles helpful to general practitioners and other medical staff who are consulted about sexual problems and who deal with at least the less complicated cases themselves.[1]

The first part of the chapter outlines techniques for exploring the complaint, where any investigation must obviously start; the second part deals with exploration of the patient's background, the third with the understanding and use of projective mechanisms and 'transference', and the fourth with indications, selection, degree of involvement or depth, and a number of other relevant considerations.

The Interview Process

Many sexual problems can be helped satisfactorily by careful, detailed exploration of the presenting problems, by facilitating communication between the partners, negotiating more mutually satisfying sexual practices and, where necessary, by adding advice and 'homework' in order to remedy ignorance and to correct inappropriate expectations.

1. The value of conjoint interviews

Though much of what I will say is applicable to the interviewing of individuals on their own, I shall be writing (unless otherwise stated) about *conjoint* interviewing: that is, seeing couples (or families) together. I am now so convinced of the greater efficacy and speed of conjoint work that I never now use separate interviews unless practical considerations make it unavoidable, or when there are specific indications for using it (to be described below). *My first and most emphatic advice to all professionals would, therefore, be to learn to work with couples or families as well as individuals.* To develop the necessary skills, there are a number of courses now available in family and marital therapy.[2] Failing this, the best way to begin is to add a conjoint interview to one's existing way of working, with the aim at first only of getting a picture of the interaction and without any other expectation whatever.

This avoidance of any aim other than observation of what happens is important, because the main obstacle to learning these techniques in general, or to perceiving the nature of the fundamental problem in any particular joint interview, is usually an excessive anxiety to 'do' something, to justify one's professional rôle.

This impulse is natural, but such urgency to achieve results makes it difficult to tolerate the disagreements, circular arguments and fruitless exchanges of blame and recrimination with which such interviews so frequently begin, and which produce feelings of chaos and confusion.

If one waits, however, at least a clear perception of what is actually happening between the couple will emerge, and this will frequently bring with it, towards the end of the interview, some perception of the pattern of the essential difficulty and also a prescription for action.

The latter may involve little more than feeding back, in more condensed and coherent form, what the patients themselves have said and agreed upon, but not really heard.

2. Examining the detail of the complaint

The second requirement is to study the detail of the complaint and all the interaction centring around it, including the nature of the symptom, its beginnings and development over time; its effect on the partner, how both partners feel about it and react to it; what they have each done (or not done) to try to communicate about it and to solve it, and so on.

The more such detail is insisted on, the more one moves quite automatically from the realm of imagination, conflict, argument and blame to the realm of fact and agreement. In addition, the fundamental problem, which is always contained in what is left out in the patients' presentation (whether a deliberate, conscious suppression, or based on unconscious avoidance) will begin to take shape in the therapist's mind if there is space for the pattern to be registered – through an open, relaxed and receptive attitude rather than anxiety about, or over-activity towards, achieving results.

There is, of course, a particular difficulty here in the case of interviewing about sexual problems. Professionals have grown up subject to the same cultural taboos as their patients and have developed similar, if less intense, inhibitions over sexual matters. Unless special efforts are made to overcome this, the professional will convey embarrassment and awkwardness in his voice and manner, which will further inhibit the patients, even though he is making an effort to appear at ease and is unaware of the discomfort he is radiating. Also, he will avoid crucial issues without recognising it, hurrying along to other aspects.

Thus, it is just those areas of sexuality about which the patient is least likely to confide, and needs encouragement and routine questioning to help him to do so, that the professional is most likely to leave unexplored. This might include such matters as promiscuity and adultery, wife-swapping, oral sex, anal intercourse, homosexuality and so on. To counteract such avoidance I believe it is essential to write out a carefully formulated series of questions on sexual matters, and then to rehearse these until asking them becomes second nature, without hesitation or awkwardness.

3. The requirement of neutrality

Thirdly, the professional should be neutral, or at least fair. He should try to listen to both points of view and to see both sides, keeping the interests of both patients equally at heart. This is not to say that temporary siding is not appropriate, once a trusting relationship is firmly established. At any given point, one partner will be in a stage of stronger resistance than the other. This will provoke the therapist to stronger criticism of the resistant partner, which usually leads to a 'leap-frog' in this partner's progress, and the next time the other is likely to be the laggard and to receive the greater pressure.

4. Formulation of the problem is a kind of resolution

If the professional begins to make use of such exploratory interviews for the purpose of observation, he will soon be surprised to find how many problems are resolved in a manner that satisfies the patients without any attempt at change or formal 'treatment'.

One often receives gratitude from patients for helping them to

161

solve problems they have set before us, when we have in fact done no more than listen without comment. A great proportion of psychological problems are a consequence of the fact that we are not clearly aware of what we want until we try to make it explicit.

Once we begin to do so, we often see contradictions invisible to us before, and then automatically find more satisfactory compromises. This applies in conjoint as in individual interviewing, but one also finds that even people married for twenty years have never actually communicated to each other what they like and dislike in sexual activities, and as the first exploratory interview is often the first time that such communication has taken place, it is not surprising that profound changes frequently occur afterwards in their relationship.

Thus, for many cases, indeed the majority, one or a few interviews in which the couple are helped to persist in a clear and explicit formulation of the problem is all the treatment needed. By his attitude of relaxed acceptance and frankness, and friendly but firm, persistent exploration, the professional behaves in the opposite fashion to influential figures in the patient's early life – parents, relatives, teachers etc. – from whom they have learnt habits of embarrassment, concealment and avoidance over sexual matters.

This good effect of the doctor's relaxed mode of response may be reinforced by explicit encouragement and support. Information and advice are added as necessary in the light of the specific problems, or of general ignorance over sexual matters, which may have been revealed during the interview.

5. Directive help and other practical guidance

Improved techniques of stimulation to overcome retarded ejaculation or frigidity, or measures of dealing with premature ejaculation and so on are explained in detail, and 'homework' is planned to be reported at the next session. For those with high anxiety over further failure, advice to avoid penetration temporarily and to enjoy instead relaxed mutual pleasuring may be appropriate.

For others with strong inhibitions on sexual pleasure based on cultural taboos, 'doctor's orders' to have sexual intercourse at some agreed frequency may counteract early negative parental attitudes.

The details of such specific methods cannot be given here for reasons of space. Many are dealt with in the literature, and often common sense or personal experience suffice. A number of books and papers can be referred to by those requiring more detailed guidance regarding the treatment of specific sexual problems.

For patients, too, books have their place. Alex Comfort's *The Joy of Sex* is the book I most generally recommend and a copy is useful in the consulting room, too, for explaining sexual techniques by means of the illustrations. The fact that the doctor shares such explicit visual material with the couple also provides a further beneficial model of relaxed acceptance of sexuality.

Among other books, many patients have particularly praised two by Robert Chartham, *Advice to Women* and *Sex Manners for Men*, as being especially helpful to them. Suitable erotic films perhaps have a place here, and a number of patients have spontaneously reported greater sexual freedom and enjoyment after seeing the film *Emmanuelle*, a highly erotic but very beautiful film which lacks the distasteful elements that often characterise pornography.

6. A clinical example

In the example that follows, a couple were successfully treated in three interviews over four months. The case illustrates the interview process and the four technical principles described here. Conjoint interviews are held in which neutrality is maintained between partners, and the couple are primarily helped by the formulation – with them – of their problem for which a certain amount of directive help and practical guidance are offered.

Mr and Mrs S, a middle-class couple of Indian origin and roughly fifty and forty respectively and married for sixteen years, were referred by the social worker at a Child Guidance Clinic. They had been involved with this clinic for ten years because one of their children was autistic. They were referred for a consultation regarding sexual problems over which divorce was being considered by the wife.

The nature of the sexual problem was not clear from the referral letter, but more background information than one usually receives was included. Much of this was highly significant. For example, the husband had lost his idolised mother from a snake-bite at the age of ten and was subsequently brought up by an uncle and aunt who had rejected him and deprived him of physical affection. Also, the wife's mother had been unable to show physical affection to her, resulting in feelings of rejection and depression throughout her childhood. All this and much else had no doubt been discussed in great detail during previous psychiatric involvement, but I mention it here only to emphasise that I ignored it all, except to recognise that I should relate to them in a particularly gentle, warm and sympathetic, but undemanding way, to offer the sort of relationship they had lacked in their childhood and so to have a greater influence with them.

The referral letter reported that they had recently seen their general practitioner, who had told the husband that, because of his age, it was too late to do anything about the sexual problem.

At the first joint interview with me, the wife was fiercely critical and attacking, the husband passive and withdrawn. The impression of shared deprivation and depression was intense, and the obvious expectation of the patients that doctors should be brisk, brief, authoritative and emotionally distant, rapidly giving advice or medication, obliged me to struggle with a feeling that I should 'do something'. It was not easy to remain relaxed, open and attentive, and to wait for them to amplify the difficulty.

Gradually they acknowledged that they were both sexually shy, inhibited and unadventurous, partly because of the rather constricted attitude of the class of Indian society in which they had grown up, but also because of their own restricted family backgrounds.

They had never been able to discuss their sexual relationship in any detail, and indeed discovered for the first time during this interview what forms of pleasure the partner best liked in order to be awakened and stimulated before intercourse. The wedding night had been a disaster, and he had dreaded each new experience with an increased fear of failure.

It had taken six months to consummate the marriage, and his lack of pleasure and increasing sense of effort and duty had made it unpleasant for his wife as well. Intercourse had become an event to be avoided, taking place once a month or less throughout the marriage, leading to deep frustration on her part and emotional withdrawal by both.

164

I helped them to see how each was equally terrified of being rejected, how each hesistated to make advances in case they failed, and instead blamed the other and failed to see that they both suffered from the same difficulty. Neither dared initiate sexual activity, leading to a vicious circle of rejection, frustration and blame.

So much was this the case, that the wife dealt with my efforts at reconciliation by insisting it was all too late, and that divorce was the only answer. I respected her defences and did not dispute this, but said that whether they stayed together, or sought new partners, they clearly needed more accurate sexual information and could perhaps learn from their mistakes with each other in order to benefit in their possible new lives.

I continued to discuss in a detailed way, using pictures in *The Joy of Sex* which was open on the table, how his difficulty in retaining an erection might have been helped by techniques she could use.

Her interest and excitement showed clearly, despite her superficial attitude of critical, harsh rejection. I said that in other cases I would recommend a regular frank discussion of sexual desires, using such a book to help them, and gentle, undemanding experimentation in pleasuring each other, stopping short of intercourse. What a pity, I added, that it was too late!

At the second interview, six weeks later (the summer holiday had intervened) she was still fearful of rejection and her defensive and critical attitude was still present, but she had decided to 'live for the day' and had stopped considering divorce. He was far more supportive and tender, and also less fearful and passive towards her attacks.

They had, in fact, followed my prescription and were beginning to court each other once again. Sex had been resumed fairly frequently, but penetration had not been attempted and she had not achieved orgasm.

Further encouragement and advice were given, the main ingredients being that she should stimulate him manually, up to, and after penetration; that he should be more generally attentive and kind to her on evenings where sexual activity

165

was intended; and that he should make more use of clitoral stimulation.

But I emphasised that there should be no concern over 'success' and that they should simply continue to practise sexual enjoyment, by whatever means were necessary.

At the third and final interview, ten weeks later, they were regularly attempting intercourse, which was usually successful and gave pleasure to both. His erection was still not very firm, but she was often attaining orgasm, nevertheless.

Though still a quiet, emotionally inhibited couple, there was now a definite sense of warmth and affection between them. He said he now felt supported and encouraged by her, which enabled him to feel confident and to respond.

Both reported that the improvement was steadily increasing, that they felt confident of a happy relationship, both sexually and otherwise. They said they felt satisfied that they could continue on their own, and no further appointments were made. Several years have passed and they have not been referred again.

Exploring Family History

Where tensions, hostilities, inhibitions and anxieties are more profound and interfere with the simple forms of treatment described already, exploration of the family history is necessary to uncover and understand the early experiences which have led to these attitudes. A systematic exploration of the past is best left to a later part of the first interview, leaving the early part relatively unstructured and devoted to an exploration of the problem as the patients present it. During this time the early background may be mentioned spontaneously and some marital therapists believe that the first parent mentioned in this way is often a dominant figure with crucial influence, whose attitudes have played a particular part in the marital dynamics (Teruel, 1966, Dicks, 1967).

What is omitted in the early stages is even more important than what is actually said. The family patterns for which one is searching are complex and varied, and cannot be more than hinted at here; for details the reader is referred to such books as those by Dicks (1967),

Pincus (1970), Paul (1975) and myself (*One Flesh, Separate Persons*), the last being a more general introduction to the subject.

A few simple principles can be suggested. *The first is that all emotional disorder (in my experience at least) becomes* understandable *when enough information is obtained, so that 'meaningless' emotional symptoms always indicate either that the patient has withheld vital information – whether deliberately or through self-deception – or that the doctor has missed the point, even though the clues have been presented.*

The more one becomes convinced of this by experience, the more often will the truth of it be demonstrated, since uncovering the vital facts which render the whole pattern meaningful and treatable depends ultimately on confidence and persistence as well as knowledge.

A second principle is that emotional problems, including those producing sexual dysfunctions, are related to what one might call unfinished business, *some process of growth and development which has not gone to completion.* For example, inadequate love and care in infancy due to death or separation from a parent, or birth of an ailing sibling while the patient's needs for nurture were still intense, may leave a degree of emotional hunger too painful to expose readily, leading to a withholding attitude and excessive control in the sexual act.

By bringing such 'unfinished business' to light, the resulting inhibitions of emotional expression and sexual exploration can be rendered meaningful, so that the patient can understand the need to risk facing and opposing them and, with encouragement and support, can begin to struggle to overcome the fears. Here the therapist's approval and support, once the issue is recognised, can provide a half-way house, enabling this vital step towards independence to be taken as well as providing a counterweight to the jealousy and envy that would have been aroused in the original family if the patient had outgrown his parents' immaturities. This fear of having more happiness than the parents is nowhere more evident than in the sexual sphere, where the greatest potential pleasure arouses envy of equivalent strength.

A third general principle of great assistance is that of assortative mating, *that couples choose each other with uncanny accuracy; presumably by non-verbal, unconscious cues, on the basis of shared*

167

early experience and developmental arrests. However, similarities at deeper levels may be hidden by marked superficial differences.

For example, in the case of a woman seen recently because of depression and frigidity extending over a year or so, her problems proved to be related to the inadequately mourned loss of her father at the age of six, feelings which had until then been held tightly in check but which were aroused again by fears of losing her husband, an older man with a fatherly relationship towards her. Seeing them together for a joint interview later, he could scarcely have seemed more different superficially, but his bland complacency and denial of problems proved to conceal a similar loss of his father, also at the age of six. The fact that his wife was almost certainly carrying the pain for both, so that her fear and depression was compensated by her ability to rely on his outward strength, made the treatment of either problematic.

It is this underlying similarity in the dynamics of couples which accounts for the frequently observed phenomenon of the 'strong' husband collapsing when the previously 'neurotic' wife improves during psychotherapy, or other cases where the husband who protests his sexual normality becomes impotent when his wife is cured of her frigidity.

This is also one reason why conjoint therapy is so much more effective with couples, since the interlocking personality structures are easier to understand and to change if looked at as a whole.

The following example, of a couple still in treatment, illustrates some of these points. Mr Y, suffering from depression over about three months, had been hospitalised and treated with anti-depressants and other drugs whose variety and limited effects suggested that psychological factors had been insufficiently explored.

No sex had taken place since his discharge, worsening the already strained relationship, and he would lie in bed and demand that his wife hold his hand and commiserate with him as if she were a mother rather than a spouse. Exploring the problem in detail, the depression was at first said to have begun following his father's death, but later it became clear that he had been mildly depressed and irritable since he and his wife ceased to live near his parents, five years earlier.

In the first interview, the husband behaved like a resentful, passive baby, attacking his wife's family for their snobbish rejection of him as a suitor when he had been courting her, attributing his depression to this and in particular to the fact that her family had persuaded her to terminate a pregnancy resulting from pre-marital intercourse without consulting him about the decision.

I suggested that he was really angry with his wife for dividing her loyalty and attention, but that he was also fearful of alienating her and so was displacing his anger with her on to her parents. This led to a dramatic change in his whole behaviour half-way through the first interview. His collapsed, apathetic, depressed manner disappeared, and the acknowledgement of his own anger temporarily brought him to life and adult activity. Both agreed that they could not cope with feelings of hostility towards each other, and therefore withdrew emotionally, bringing about a sexual alienation also.

I next explored the family backgrounds, remembering that patients who attack the family of their spouse are often really deflecting anger which belongs within their own family of origin. It soon became clear that this was in fact occurring. The husband had been overshadowed by a brilliant elder brother and made to feel inadequate by his parents. He had reacted to this by becoming a 'drop-out', had left school prematurely and taken labouring jobs until he met his present spouse and, to win her, had used his good intelligence to take a professional qualification. His resentment of his own family's rejection of him in favour of his brother had clearly been displaced to his wife's family whose demanding and rejecting attitude fitted the pattern well.

In the second interview both partners reported a dramatic change in him, so that he had returned to work. This change was evident from his lively and responsive behaviour during the interview. By contrast, the wife looked disgruntled and miserable, to the same degree that he seemed more cheerful, as if they were at opposite ends of a see-saw. As the interview proceeded he spoke of his demand for total commitment and sexual fidelity from her, returning to a previous theme of resentment of two love-affairs she had had before she met him.

At this point he said she was 'like her mother' and suddenly changed to his previous depressed, apathetic and frozen manner of the first interview. He was unable to explain this change, saying how good things had been for both of them up to that moment since the previous session, including their sexual interaction. He gave the impression of punishing her remorselessly for some crime he could not explain, and the associations which followed indicated that he was identifying her with his mother and his mother's ambivalence towards him in childhood. I said so, and at the third interview there was a further improvement in the husband, while the wife was still depressed but with some underlying warmth and trust beginning to appear. She acknowledged that the sessions were raising profoundly painful and disturbing issues for her and 'making everything well up inside emotionally'.

At this session the focus came more upon her and her family. She said she believed his mother had in some ways spoilt as well as rejected him, and agreed that she had continued to indulge him too. Enquiring about her reasons for giving so much to him, it emerged that she, like him, had been overshadowed by a cleverer elder brother, and was in addition displaced by bright, younger twin siblings, so that she felt like Cinderella. She had clearly reproduced this pattern in the marriage. She had sacrificed herself to give him the attention she had seen her sisters receiving and had always desired herself. But at the same time she resented it deeply and spoilt what she offered him. She thus repeated her mother's combination of rejection and unhelpful, infantilising 'spoiling'.

He reported that the discussions had led to a more mutually giving, relaxed relating on both sides, with a steadily improving sexual relationship. But their shared interlocking pattern of rejection by their parents, and ambivalence towards favoured siblings – conflicts somehow safely 'bound' within the marriage despite the problems this solution also caused – are still to be escaped from. As clarification of these powerful forces of jealousy also 'unbinds' them and brings them into the open, stormy passages may be expected before more fundamental change occurs.

Understanding and Using Transference

The meaning of transference and counter-transference

We need next to look at those situations where, despite his efforts to remain a neutral and sympathetic observer, the professional finds himself personally embroiled in the problem and cast by the patient in some rôle related to the patient's early history.

Where the development of an individual is relatively normal and there is not, in the phrase used before, too much 'unfinished business' in it, he will have learned a variety of rôles which enable him to deal with the world in an effective and satisfying way. His parents, and later, members of the extended family, teachers, friends at school and their parents, will have met his needs for relationships at appropriate stages and provided a variety of models of behaviour which can be called upon to deal with the wider world in later life. Where this is the case, the doctor, therapist or counsellor is seen in a relatively objective way, and complications in the doctor/patient relationship are limited.

But if something has gone wrong with this developmental process, the doctor/patient relationship itself may be affected, sometimes to a degree which interferes completely with the professional aim. Thus, a patient who has suffered maternal deprivation in childhood may cast the doctor in the rôle of a parent. This is expected to make up for all the earlier disappointments, leads to frequent visits for trivial complaints which never reach a satisfying conclusion and which usually extend past the time allotted for the appointment, and leave the doctor feeling exhausted, drained and dissatisfied with his efforts.

In addition to learning distorted or inadequate models of relationship, children are also often cast into rôles by parents, based on the parents' early experience with the grandparents. A person who was made excessively ashamed of feelings of jealousy or nervousness in his childhood may, when he becomes a parent, deny such feelings in himself and project them into one of his children, who

171

then becomes a scapegoat, labelled 'the jealous one' or 'the nervous one'. Acceptance by a child of such a scapegoat rôle is brought about not only by parental pressure or victimisation, but even more through an intuitive awareness by the child that this scapegoating plays an essential part in maintaining the family system, as well as giving him an important and vital place or part to play within the family.

The school-phobic daughter who needs to hold her mother's hand away from home knows at some level that mother needs support and may go to pieces if she lets go of her, and that acceptance of this rôle of the 'nervous child' is the price she has to pay for having an effective mother at all. Because the daughter cannot let herself 'know' this truth in a conscious way, she may repeat such clinging behaviour in all future relationships where she seeks support, including those with her husband and her doctor.

Freud's most important contribution to our understanding perhaps lay in his discovery that the transfer of such early patterns of relationship into the therapeutic situation itself could be a valuable source of information, rather than just a tiresome interference with the doctor/patient relationship.

In recent years, there has developed increasing awareness that important clues to the nature of this 'transference' of early relationships can be gained by the professional noting unusual features in his own emotional response during an interview, since the 'counter-transference' feelings evoked in him by the patient's behaviour will often be understandable in terms of attitudes towards the patient, held by the parent or other family member in whose rôle the doctor is being cast by the patient.

M. and E. Balint (1961) have focussed particularly on the way in which this kind of knowledge can be utilised by the general practitioner in his daily work, and I have tried to show how similar information can be utilised in the treatment of couples and families.

However, it is where transference/counter-transference manifestations are so pronounced as to block effective treatment altogether, that the patient should be referred to a specialist psychotherapist for treatment, or at least for consultation and advice, for it is in this most difficult area that the psychotherapist's special skills reside.

But, even an awareness of the possibility that a transference pattern may be interfering with an interview will enable the doctor to step back periodically, to take a quizzical look at his interaction with his patient, and enable him often to see things not visible when his attention is completely absorbed in his customary professional rôle. And a brief exploration of the family history, along the lines outlined above, will often provide a simple explanation of what is happening.

Applications to psycho-sexual problems

In the treatment of sexual difficulties, the most troubling example of such transference/counter-transference problems is that of the female patient who 'falls in love' with her male doctor and whose advances are not discouraged by his insistence that his relationship is wholly professional.

This leads at best to embarrassment and rumour, at worst to false accusations of impropriety or even to a real embroilment with medico-legal consequences. Such women have usually grown up in a family where the father's sexual feelings have been directed more towards them than towards the mother, though in an emotional rather than a physical sense, and without this state of affairs being consciously acknowledged. She then tends to repeat this unresolved situation with males who are in a parental, authoritative position, particularly a male physician whose rôle is, in many ways, similar to that of a father, including the taboo on physical sexuality with those in his care.

The physician will find himself anxious and confused to the degree that, like the patient's father, he is uncomfortable and out of conscious touch with the erotic feelings her behaviour engenders in him through her projection on to him of her father's intense but denied sexual feelings for her.

But if the physician recognises the true situation, if he can feel quite comfortable with any real sexual attraction for the patient while keeping a firm boundary between such normal, human feelings and the maintenance of his professional rôle, he will then be able to distinguish, and to be unaffected by, the sexual provocation coming from the patient's projections. Instead of being under her power through fear and confusion, he will be providing exactly the experience she needs, and in which her father failed her. This is the experience that her sexual attractiveness can be enjoyed by her and

173

by others, without boundaries being improperly transgressed and important relationships thereby destroyed. The basic requirement, then, is for the doctor to be completely at ease with his own sexuality.

The other most common difficulty in the treatment of sexual problems is the manipulation of the doctor into feelings of impotence, rather than sexual excitement. For example, a man aged twenty-six was referred with the complaint of complete inability to ejaculate during intercourse with his wife, or even when she was present in his imagination, let alone in reality. He had never attempted intercourse prior to the marriage two years earlier, giving strong religious prohibitions as an explanation. But he had been able to masturbate alone, or to ejaculate into his pants during petting with her. On her side, she had expressed desire for pre-marital intercourse, though she also acknowledged that despite successful orgasms with other men previous to meeting him, she had been 'switched off' sexually from the beginning of their relationship.

Attempts over the previous year to help him by marriage guidance counselling, and then by the referring psychiatrist utilising exploratory psychotherapy and behavioural methods, including Masters and Johnson techniques, had not led to improvement, but had disclosed fears that he might urinate into his wife or that his penis might snap off. His main concern was less about missing the pleasures of sex than about feelings of inferiority that their friends were raising families, while they were unable to conceive, and so were not 'keeping up with the Joneses'.

It emerged that his mother was powerful and over-controlling, and though ambivalent to her, he felt closer than to his father, a less dominant figure, towards whom he felt obvious strong competitive-ness (based on oedipal rivalry) which had never been openly expressed and worked through, and indeed of which he was not at first conscious.

This competitiveness and inability to risk any kind of failure or defeat showed itself in my first interview with him (when he was seen alone) by, first, an impression that he had somehow provoked the first psychiatrist into increasingly heroic efforts to cure him, while the patient felt less and less responsibility for his problem; and second, by my awareness that I was following the same pattern and becoming inexplicably anxious that I would fail to help him, as if the whole responsibility lay with me.

Realising that I was cast in his father's rôle, and that I was somehow falling into the same position of taking responsibility for his inadequacy, when the true cause of that lay in his subtle avoidance of confrontation and acceptance of the authority of a more potent male, I told him of these feelings I was experiencing. I also gave my explanation of them, saying that inability to ejaculate was fortunately not one of my problems and that, while I would certainly do my best as a therapist to help him, ejaculation into his wife was his problem and responsibility, not mine. Following this statement, my own discomfort and anxiety immediately disappeared, while he began to show some proper concern and motivation for the first time.

After a joint interview with his wife, it was agreed that they should be treated together and that success was more likely in a couples group where my wife and I, acting as co-therapists, could provide not only advice and understanding, but also different models of interaction from those provided by their parents. In the group his pattern of passive manipulation of others to take responsibility for him, covering an intense competitiveness and superiority, showed itself repeatedly as he demanded advice from everyone, but then said it was all useless.

His defence was that he had 'nothing useful to say'. This was removed by instructing him to 'ejaculate some sounds into the group' at each session, even barking or squeaking (following which, he began to sit up and look uncomfortable, and to make some effort instead of lying back passively in his chair), and by the subsequent forceful confrontations by other group members. He was successfully encouraged first to talk about masturbation before his wife in the group, and then at home to masturbate in his wife's presence, next to let her masturbate him, and finally to ejaculate within her.

As he became more potent, his wife, as expected, went through periods of frigidity and neither of them could avoid perceiving her intense resistance to allowing him to be potent. It was over two years before fully satisfactory sexual performance was achieved by both partners, while their personalities changed in ways that made both of them more likeable.

Despite temporary setbacks, progress was maintained and

indeed extended after completion of therapy, and the birth of their first child, conceived towards the end of therapy, was a rich experience for them.

Normal Sexuality and Its Problems

In this final part of the chapter, various points are raised relative to the indications and contraindications for different forms of counselling. Many family arguments, temporary separations and extra-marital affairs are signs of immaturity. Indeed, many of these incidents are attempts to grow up and thus escape from previous smothering factors. These in turn spring from parental upbringing.

It is possible to define what good sexuality should be. Sexual relationships can reach their highest meaning and fulfilment only within the context of a stable relationship.

Since I first advocated conjoint interviews, my personal impression has received very strong support from the most comprehensive review of research on family and marital therapy[3] so far produced, covering over 200 research or follow-up studies of varying quality. Some of the conclusions have profound implications for all work in this field:

1. Individual therapy for marital problems is a very ineffective treatment strategy and one which appears to produce more negative effects than alternative approaches . . .

2. Couples benefit most from treatment when both partners are involved in the therapy, especially when they are seen conjointly . . .

3. Family therapy appears to be at least as effective and possibly more effective than individual therapy for a wide variety of problems, both apparent individual difficulties as well as more obvious family conflicts . . .

4. Short-term and time-limited therapies appear to be at least as effective as treatment of longer duration; moreover, most of the positive results of open-ended therapy were achieved in less than five months. (Gurman and Kniskern, 1979)

Therapeutic methods

The authors emphasise that for certain clinical goals and problems, including *sexual dysfunction*, conjoint therapies offer the treatments of choice. However, though the general advantages of conjoint counselling are fully confirmed in the above study, it is acknowledged that individual interviews still have their place. They are obviously indicated if one wishes to exclude organic disease or to make a careful examination of a psychiatric condition. Separate treatment of members of a couple may also be indicated when divorce or separation has become inevitable, to support each partner through the painful experience of loss and to aid them in starting new lives apart, even though conjoint sessions may still be desirable to negotiate amicable cooperation over the vital issue of care and custody of any children.

Also, though conjoint interviews are in my experience the only way of dealing with couples so enmeshed that there is no clear boundary between them, and where each projects their unaccepted aspects into their partner, separate individual or group therapy is often preferable at a more mature stage where clearer differentiation and identity formation has begun, but is still precarious. It is in the latter situation that individual sessions with separate therapists, combined with four-way 'round-table conferences', which include both partners and both therapists, perhaps have the greatest value. Each therapist can maintain his or her primary relationship to the spouse they are seeing individually, but act as a kind of advocate for their point of view in the joint discussions. The model provided by the ability of the two co-therapists to take sides and disagree, but in a cooperative and constructive way, as well as the rôle models available from two therapists of different sex, are additional advantages.

Some general practitioners, nurses, health visitors and social workers are already working together in this cooperative fashion, but some supervision, or at least the opportunity for peer-group discussion with a team of colleagues, is desirable since co-therapists often automatically begin to mirror the problems of the patient couple if these are not clearly understood.

For example, co-therapists working with a sexually inhibited couple may find themselves inexplicably unable to get together to

177

discuss their plans for future sessions, or inhibited in their discussion when they do. If opportunities are available to discuss the difficulties that have become reflected in the professional relationship, the difficulties themselves can of course become a vital source of information, since the therapists will have experienced at first hand, and, with help, will have understood and resolved precisely what is really troubling the patient couple at a deeper level.

Two other methods should be mentioned, though they are best left to the specialist in this field. In some disturbed marital situations where progress was quite impossible because of incessant argument or completely incompatible accounts, even with the help of a co-therapist, I have arranged some sessions to include the children as well, if these are adolescents or young people. The good sense of these youngsters, and their supportive and sensitive awareness of the essence of their parents' difficulties, including sexual incompatibilities, has often been profoundly helpful and sometimes deeply moving. An account of a series of such family interviews, carried out by my wife and myself and arranged as a last resort with one such 'impossible' couple, has been published.[4]

Another treatment modality is the couples group, where about four selected couples meet regularly to undergo psychotherapy together. Though not yet widely used, perhaps because leadership of such groups requires a high level of experience both in marital therapy and in the understanding of group dynamics, the additional learning and change produced by the stimulus of mutual support and encouragement, by powerful but objective criticism and by sharing of understanding, has for me made this the treatment of choice whenever possible, where longer-term work is required.

Co-therapy by two professionals of opposite sex is particularly desirable in such work, and, like some American and European colleagues, I find it a great advantage to share the leadership of these groups with my own spouse.

Types of problem

Provided one is realistic in one's assessment and sets limited goals, a large proportion of cases can be helped to a worthwhile extent. One is constantly impressed by the way in which small changes in personality and function have a big effect on the quality of a relationship and the happiness of a couple or family.

Often small and simple interventions suffice to change a 'vicious circle' into an 'ascending spiral'. The fact that successful sexuality is so pleasurable, and that the pleasure automatically enhances other aspects of life and relationships, makes such work particularly rewarding.

The general practitioner is in an especially good position to work with such limited goals through the fact that ongoing contact with couples or families over long periods gives opportunities for limited and short but repeated interventions at moments of high motivation.

Effective work can be done in this flexible way with a wide range of psychiatric diagnoses, or of severity of pathology. Generally speaking, far-reaching and long-term work is more appropriate with the moderately disturbed, while short-term, limited intervention is paradoxically more suited not only to milder problems, but also to the sickest individuals or most chronic difficulties in relationships (where a mainly supportive, symptomatic focus in times of crisis may be all that is realistically possible, or where it is better to 'let sleeping dogs lie').

Those attempting counselling of couples need, however, to be aware of some situations where intervention, at least by the beginner, should be cautious or minimal. Some couples, for example, appear to maintain their sanity only by projecting their own unaccepted, 'psychotic' aspects into the partner (each being ideally suited to the part) and then attacking and blaming them. These paranoid couples (who often achieve very pleasurable sexuality between fights) readily induce the medical and legal professions to take sides in their antagonisms, but one needs to remember that the incessant conflict and criticism is part of a vital mutual defensive system, and to restrict one's intervention to whatever control of violence is possible, or to 'first aid' where it is not. Many rows, temporary separations or extra-marital affairs are merely signs of immaturity and attempts to grow and escape from a primitive, smothering fusion, so that a supporting, 'holding' operation, keeping lines of communication open and not taking it all too seriously, is often more helpful than heroic attempts at psychodynamic exploration, or joining in the drama.

Also, much marital conflict is, of course, a consequence of simple selfishness, greed and envy, where sometimes a fierce and stern rebuke by a doctor who is respected and valued for past medical services and who can express his criticism forcefully, but against a background of concern and affection, may sometimes achieve more than years of psychoanalysis. Nevertheless, some patients continue to want something for nothing, to blame the world for their difficulties or to pass their misery onto others, whatever one does, so that one has to accept one's professional limitations and preserve one's time for more responsive cases.

I have, of course, been speaking here of the treatment of sexual *dysfunctions*, where the sexual object-choice and aim are normal but some disorder interferes with satisfactory performance. In sexual deviations (also called perversions and variations) it is not so much the sexual function but rather the choice of sexual object or sexual aim that is abnormal. Examples of abnormal object choice include homosexuality and bestiality; sadomasochism is an example of abnormal sexual aim. Treatment for these problems requires specialist knowledge but much relief of anxiety and suffering is possible through the support that contact with the general practitioner can provide.

What is 'normal' or 'optimal'

This chapter so far contains no definition of what I believe good sexuality to be. I shall conclude with a quotation from my book on family and marital therapy, *One Flesh, Separate Persons*, which declares my own belief, derived from both personal and professional experience.

> Though, like all things that are fully formed and perfected, it is not easily won and demands effort and work before it can become effortless and spontaneous, sexuality should reach an expression where it can be a model for, and illuminate and transform, all other aspects of the family relationship.
>
> In a fulfilling sexual act, the two opposite genders, at their most different and separate, simultaneously become one totality, merging with one another in an experience going beyond the capacity of either.
>
> Each is most centred in, and aware of, himself or herself, yet also wholly open and responsive to the other. Each

temporarily loses his boundary and surrenders to a greater unity. Both are as spontaneous as they could ever be, yet this spontaneity is possible because of a fundamental self-discipline, an ability to deny oneself, to wait, to adapt and adjust to the other as in the unfolding of a dance.

It is non-manipulative, non-controlling; the self is offered freely, from generosity and trust, and, since there is no demand, the return comes equally freely and fully, each emotionally responding and keeping time with the other. Each gives most generously, yet takes most uninhibitedly too, without hedging or bargaining. For a moment, both partners are fully in the present, letting the process unfold in its own form and pace, no longer lost in the concerns of the future or memories of the past.

And the climax, when it 'comes' in its own time, is productive, creative, sometimes through the beginning of a separate new life, but always in a renewal of the separate lives of the partners and the joint life of their relationship, so that the wild, tender, simple act of affirmation is never tired of, never loses its fulness of the refreshing quality of a draught of spring water or mountain air.

Sex is not everything, of course, but it is a catalyst for many other things, and since so many other things must be right for it to function well, it is also a touchstone for the quality of the total relationship. When it is good, people look different. The emotional atmosphere one senses in a house where it is right is one of calm and peace, yet also of lightness, fun and humour, and everything moves easily. Above all, the children sense it and are happy for it, though they do not necessarily know what they sense, any more than they know or care about the cost of the good food that nourishes them (p. 129).

Although I believe that the more relaxed and liberal attitude towards sexuality characteristic of our present time is generally beneficial, and welcome it, it will be clear that I see the sexual relationship as something that can reach its highest meaning and fulfilment only within the context of a stable marriage and family. But I am sure that no physician is in a better position to be convinced of the truth of this than the general practitioner, who has

Special Applications

the greatest opportunity to see the symptom in the context of the whole person, and to see the individual in the context of the family.

Notes

1 This paper was originally published in four parts in *The British Journal of Sexual Medicine*, Vol. 3, **6** (December 1976); Vol. 4, **1** (January 1977); Vol. 4, **2** (February 1977); and Vol. 4, **3** (March 1977).
2 See 'An Open-Systems Approach to Teaching Family Therapy' (appendix reference 31).
3 See A. S. Gurman and D. P. Kniskern, 'Research on Marital and Family Therapy', in S. L. Garfield and A. E. Bergen (eds.), *Handbook of Psychotherapy and Behaviour Change: An Empirical Analysis* (2nd edition), 1979.
4 A. C. R. Skynner, 'Family Therapy Techniques', *Proceedings of the Association for the Psychiatric Study of Adolescents: Tenth Annual Conference* (ed. D. O. Biddles, A.P.S.A.) (appendix reference 17).

9 Recent Developments in Marital Therapy

This major review of the field of marital therapy introduces Skynner's mature work but is included here, rather than in the next section, because it completes the sequence on intimacy. It was written to counter an increasing neglect of the marital side of family work, and also served the further integration of the systems, psychoanalytic and behavioural approaches to marital therapy. These were becoming increasingly split and polarised for, as he saw it, the same defensive reasons as the separation of marriage from the family and of sex from the marriage.

In the paper he is clearly less enthusiastic about the behavioural paradigm than the two other approaches, though he allows some of its most articulate practitioners to speak for themselves. But he is more open to certain ideas from the 'systems' schools he had formerly rejected. He had been deeply distrustful of 'systems' ideas as practised by the 'strategic' schools such as those of Haley and the Mental Research Institute at Palo Alto. He acknowledged their results in changing people but believed, like Bateson, that their methods were faulted and based on power rather than understanding. He thought that, as with the behaviourists, this was in order to exclude the therapist's own problems from the system under consideration, and so to avoid the requirement of personal insight and change. In other words, he rejected such 'systems' methods because they were not systemic enough!

But we see here the first attempt to include the ideas of the 'Milan group' whose work he had now observed when two of its members, Boscolo and Cecchin, had demonstrated it in London at the Institute of Family Therapy and the Tavistock Clinic. He was rapidly convinced that their methods were based on understanding, not manipulative power or 'overstanding', and would be effective whether or not the intervention was explained to those to whom it was directed.

Special Applications

At the time he recalls describing what he saw as philosophy, pure mathematics. He accepted that any comprehensive theory would have to embrace these ideas, and for the next few years set about learning to make them his own and relate them to his other work. We will see this process developing in the next section.

J.R.S.

Introduction

In the first part of this paper some general considerations are offered about health, marriage and the family.[1] In the second part the main ideas of the different theoretical schools are set out and some contribution is made towards an integration of the psychoanalytic and systems perspectives whose proponents have usually presented them as polarised, incompatible paradigms. In the last, more clinically orientated part of the paper, the focus is narrowed to concentrate on the simplest and most general principles of interviewing. This section draws on the most widely accepted areas from all perspectives to help those with limited experience of couples therapy to begin exploring this rewarding and fascinating field. It is intended that enough information should be provided here to guide those who wish to go further, towards the literature most relevant to their needs.

On the Development of Couples or Marital Therapy

Family therapy had its principal origins as late as the 1950s and 'Couples therapy,' as Ables and Brandsma (1977) point out, a stepsister to family therapy, has remained a poor relation. Lacking leadership and shadowed by family therapy, it partakes of family therapy knowledge but has developed less clearly as a discipline in its own right. Gurman (1975) found that the marital therapy literature experienced its major growth spurt as late as 1960, with about half of the marital therapy publications appearing after 1967. This developing trend is evidenced by the fact that between 1972 and 1978 the number of papers describing the outcome of couples therapy has increased from 30 to over 150 (Gurman, 1978).'

Perhaps the history of the field parallels the professional development of many of its therapists. To understand the psychology of patients as individuals is for many years difficult enough. The additional task of grasping the complex dynamic interaction of two or more persons is daunting indeed. Only after it is finally attempted do we discover that the structure and function of individuals, couples and families (as well as larger social systems) have common features whereby the study of each facilitates understanding of the others: indeed it is much more difficult to understand and treat the individual in isolation. Just as suturing a wound in a detached limb is less successful than doing so to a limb still part of the living body, we discover that, despite its greater initial complexity, we are nevertheless dealing with a unit large enough to possess adaptive and self-corrective therapeutic powers of its own which, if facilitated by the therapist, will ultimately simplify his task and do much of the healing work for him.

The difficulty about developing a discipline was compounded by the prevailing influence of the classical psychoanalytic model, whereby repressed emotional conflicts originating in the family of origin had – it was thought – first to re-emerge in relation to the therapist as fantasies and feelings within the *transference*. Whatever the advantage of this technique in providing access to, and influence upon, the emotional life of *individuals*, it was unnecessary when the *original* family members were actually in the room (as with parents and children in family therapy) or where the transferences were already fully established between the two spouses, who could be witnessed interacting together and where it was precisely these transferential projections of early family difficulties which were the source of the problem. Widely accepted paradigms are hard to escape from, but psychoanalysts such as Grunebaum and Christ (1978) and Sager (1966) in the US, and Main (1966) and Dicks (1967) in Britain eventually demonstrated that, when families or couples were seen together, therapy could be quicker, more effective and more widely applicable if the disturbing emotional relationships were clarified and changed where they already existed in a troublesome way, rather than through encouraging their repetition in relation to the therapist.

The fact that the prevailing psychoanalytic paradigm was thrown into question by the development of other theories and techniques, such as learning theory/behaviour modification and systems/communication theories, both claiming equal or greater effectiveness, provided new perspectives from which existing ideas could be viewed afresh. (This was more the case in the US – in Britain the fact that psychoanalysis has had much influence but little real power has made criticism and innovation easier.) Though early proponents of the different pardigms have tended to present them as mutually exclusive, these partisan attitudes have appeared increasingly as 'territorial' struggles for power (patients, students, research grants) as well as problems of identity and boundaries characteristic of professional 'adolescence' (Gurman, 1978). An important and hopeful feature of the current scene is the attempt by many representatives of the different methods to be open to each other's ideas and to seek to integrate them. One fruit of this new spirit is the appearance of the first comprehensive textbook on the subject of marriage and marital therapy (Paolino and McCrady, 1978), differentiating the concepts and methods of the main schools and providing an overview, critique and comparative analysis. The reader seeking to explore this field further is strongly recommended to begin with this book, starting with the final overview (Gurman, 1978).

Health, Marriage and the Family

The needs of the individual, and the purposes of society as a whole, which the marital relationship is expected to fulfil, vary across different cultures and different periods of history, but there are common features despite this. A detailed account is not possible here and the reader is referred for concise accounts to the first five chapters in another book (Grunebaum and Christ, 1976) concisely outlining current knowledge, while Dominian (1980) has recently provided an outline of marital breakdown. Major recent changes include greater equality for women and the effects of this on men, whose rôle as fathers had already become more peripheral in the course of industrialisation and separation of home and workplace. There is also greater freedom and higher expectations regarding the sexual relationship; a rising divorce rate with a high proportion of re-marriage; and the increasing prevalence of non-marital cohabitation (Macklin, 1978), often in relationships as committed as marriage itself.

Special Applications

More important for the therapist, perhaps, is the definition of health in such a relationship, and on this there now exist good research data. In the Timberlawn Research, Lewis *et al.* (1976) differentiated a spectrum of health, ranging from 'optimal' families at the most healthy end, through 'adequate' to 'mid-range' and finally to 'chaotic' families at the extreme of family dysfunction. Like 'optimal' families, 'adequate' families produce healthy children but only with great effort and struggle and despite substantial marital dissatisfaction. Mid-range families produce a proportion of neurotic, anti-social and reactive psychotic children. Chaotic families produce chronic psychotic or psychopathic children.

These categories could be reliably differentiated from each other on a number of factors, using a variety of research measures. At the least healthy extreme, reality was denied with escape into fantasy satisfactions, while in the most healthy the images of self and family were congruent with reality. Communication in the most unhealthy was vague, evasive, contradictory and mystifying. In the most healthy it was open, clear, direct and spontaneous. The most unhealthy families showed the poorest differentiation, with blurred boundaries, unclear identities, much invasiveness and creation of scapegoats; the most healthy families showed high respect for individuality and demonstrated clear, secure, identities, permitting high levels of both separateness at some times, and of intimacy at others. The production of unhealthy children was associated with distrustful, paranoid, negative attitudes, and contrasted with trust, warmth, reaching out to others and acceptance of normal ambivalence in those families who had healthy children.

A particularly interesting finding was the seemingly crucial ability, necessary for maximum health, to deal straightforwardly with change and growth, including the pain of separation and death. To the surprise of the researchers, this was clearly linked with physical as well as emotional health. Mid-range families achieved this only with great difficulty, while severely dysfunctional families showed high levels of *denial* of separation, loss and death.

In the least healthy families the marriage was usually unsatisfactory, with a strong coalition beween index patient and a parent (usually the mother, with the father excluded). This gave way in the mid-range to spouses either competing for dominance (which tended to be associated with *behaviour disorders* in the children) or with a rigid dominant submissive relationship (associated more with *neurosis* in the children). The most healthy families showed a strong, equal-powered parental coalition, both spouses being highly responsive to, and appreciative of, each other, and both experiencing a mutually rewarding and pleasurable relationship, both generally and in their sexual life (though the spouses also had separate lives of their own and much involvement outside the home).

The Main Paradigms

The development of the main prevailing theoretical models, and the therapeutic techniques deriving from them, antedated these research data on optimally healthy families and the characteristics which differentiated them from the statistically normal, as well as from those showing psycho-social disorder. Nevertheless, the main theories each appear to have recognised correctly *some* aspects of the differences between healthy and dysfunctional families, often emphasising some and neglecting others in a way which at first makes them appear conflicting and incompatible (an impression increased by some of their more partisan proponents). The present time is characterised by increasing cross-fertilisation and integration of the different views, perhaps because each has developed a clear enough identity for theoretical 'sharing' or 'marriage' to be possible and profitable.

The psychoanalytic perspective

A: The broad base of the psychoanalytic perspective

It is easiest to begin with the psychoanalytic perspective because, whether or not one accepts its basic concepts, they can claim the broadest base since they 'offer a model that substantially bridges the gap between private, inner experience and public, outer behaviour' (Gurman, 1978, p. 479). The extent of the increasing flexibility even in this traditionally conservative approach may be judged from a comment by Nadelson and Paolino (1978, p. 113), both psychoanalysts:

Methods of diagnosis and classification, as well as treatment rationales, are based on the utilisation of psychoanalytic,

189

systems and learning theories. Since these theoretical positions are increasingly more often combined and tailored to the needs of each couple, the therapist should have an understanding of the principles of each orientation and its therapeutic application.[3]

B: Marital and object relations

The following outline incorporates that set of concepts, usually referred to as 'object relations theory', developed from both classical psychoanalysis and from Kleinian theory. This is the psychoanalytic perspective that has the most useful application to marriage and marital therapy and also – in part at least – underpins the group-analytic approach. It has the advantage that it can easily be related to systemic concepts which might be unacceptable to many psychoanalysts but which have been advanced by practitioners like Bowen and Minuchin who, deriving originally from a psychoanalytic tradition, have moved away from this perspective and now see themselves in a separate school of family therapy.

Essentially, the following fundamental concepts underlie the application of psychoanalytic concepts to marriage and marital therapy:

1. The idea of conflict between parts of the psyche.

2. These conflicts, though natural during development, become crystallised into relatively permanent form where strong anxiety is associated with the struggle between the desires of the individual and social pressures.

3. The crystallisation is associated with diminished awareness either of one or other side of the conflict, or of both sides, which prevents some integrative function of the psyche from resolving it.

4. Restoring the conflict to conscious awareness establishes some re-connection which enables this integrative function to work upon it, thus resolving the conflict in some new solution.

5. Such conflicts originate in early childhood, and arise from parental mishandling of a sequence of developmental stages

concerned with such matters as nurturance/dependency, control/autonomy, genital sexuality/sharing etc.

6. An early conflict over sexual attraction to one parent, and fear of rivalry by the other (oedipal situation) is associated with a special anxiety and is of particular significance in this perspective.

7. Various typical mental mechanisms (defences) are employed to limit the anxiety, which give rise to avoidance behaviour or 'resistance' when the conflict is stimulated or approached in therapy.

8. Some particularly important inter-related mechanisms are 'denial', 'splitting' and 'projection', whereby an individual copes with conflict by experiencing one side of it *as if* it is not in fact contained within the self, but seen in another person. The anxiety associated with the intra-psychic conflict is then diminished, at the price of conflict between the two individuals concerned.

9. When such a projection is made on to another person, the behaviour of the second individual may actually be affected, in such a way that the expectation the projection leads to ('You don't like me', 'You want to persecute me') is confirmed.

10. *Marital partners tend to choose each other on the basis of some 'fit' between their projective systems, recognised without conscious awareness (with quite uncanny accuracy, as some training rôle-plays show – presumably by non-verbal information of some kind) so that each partner is especially well suited to collaborate with the other in this mutual projective and introjective process, as well as in avoidance of its recognition. This is held to account for unions which are deeply troubled and painful yet enduring.*

11. *Children, when they arrive, may be pressed into service as 'containers' for the parts of the psyche which have to be projected. By accepting them, the children alleviate conflict in the marriage, at the cost of disturbed parent/child*

191

relationships and problems in the child's development, similar to those suffered by the parents in their childhood.

12. *Similarly, the conflict may be seen as passed on to the parents by the grandparents, and so on through the generations.*

13. Therapy involves getting the projections back somehow into the individual selves, and afterwards (or at the same time) helping the individuals to experience them with full consciousness so that the integrative function of the psyche can reconcile the contradictions, as in individual psychoanalysis or psychotherapy.

C: Implications for technique

The word 'somehow' is used advisedly above for, at this point, the powerful explanatory model seems to lose its way. Analytically-oriented practitioners, in Gurman's words (1978, p. 466), become 'technical eclectics' when it comes to technique. In Britain one observes a similar situation: psychoanalytic concepts are used to *understand* the dynamics, followed by a motley of different inter-ventions – rôle-plays, sculpting, genograms, modelling, altering the seating arrangements etc. – which are all valuable methods within their own different conceptual frames but are unrelated and not systematically derived from the preceding principles.

This is mainly due, in my view, to the inappropriate focus on the concept of 'transference' – the reproduction of the unresolved conflict(s) in relation to the *therapist* (usually cast in a parental rôle) – and reliance on *interpretation* to bring it to awareness. Several authors have recognised that the unconscious conflicts are already fully developed in the mutual projective system between the couple, and could be better dealt with directly rather than by the indirect methods of 'transference'. But a mode of intervention specific to the natural group (couples, families), deriving from the concepts above, is so far missing.

D: Towards a single paradigm: the group-analytic perspective

In the third section of this book, the group-analytic contribution towards a single paradigm is developed through the five chapters of which it is comprised. The crucial issue in this approach, of which only brief mention will be made at this stage, is that the therapist 'absorbs' some important aspects of the family's projective system, particularly the part or rôle usually occupied by the identified patient. He identifies with the problems inherent in this rôle and speaks from a position closely associated with them.

E: Psychoanalytic family therapists

Bowen (1978) employs many of the ideas set out above, even if in a different nomenclature. His 'degree of differentiation of self' has a similar meaning to the idea of level of developmental arrest, or of permeability to projection by the spouse, in psychoanalytic writers. Minuchin (1974) is another family therapist who has nevertheless had experience of psychoanalytic ideas, and is also especially concerned with *boundaries*, change which would have a similar effect to change in Bowen's 'differentiation of self' or to alteration in the tendency towards 'denial, splitting and projection/introjection' described by the object-relations schools.

At this point great divergence occurs in therapeutic technique among those who no longer rely on the classical psychoanalytic model of interpretation of transference, but the aim does not seem very different. Bowen now supervises or 'coaches' individuals while they explore the reality of their family history, and thereby necessarily also experience the continued action of family patterns in the present by contact with their actual families, rather than through reproduction of such patterns in the transference. In this approach Bowen has developed a new, self-consistent form of intervention with a similar rationale to the psychoanalytic focus on transference and its interpretation.

Systems approaches

A: Basic concepts of systems theory

Bowen is one systemic family therapist who denies that his approach derives from general systems theory. As we have seen, his work seems to have been a natural development from psychoanalytic ideas. But systems theory, developed by Von Bertalanffy (1968) and others from 1928 onwards, has had a profound influence on the field. It was developed as a reaction to the scientific world view based on reductionism and a linear concept of cause and effect, of which the original focus of psychoanalysis on the individual, excluding other family members, was one natural consequence. Basic concepts of general systems theory have been elaborated with great clarity and conciseness as they apply to living systems by Miller (1965). They include:

1. The whole is greater than the part, and cannot be explained solely by the operation of the parts. New or 'emergent' events develop at certain levels of organisation, not explicable by a reductionist study.

2. The universe is most accurately viewed as a *hierarchy of systems*, each (e.g. a family) contained within a greater one – its *suprasystem* (e.g. a community), and containing *subsystems* (e.g. individual family members).

3. *Boundaries* define the limits of a system and protect its integrity, permitting some exchange (e.g. communication with others) but also limiting it (e.g. protecting privacy).

4. The parts of the system are coordinated by a 'decider subsystem' (e.g. brain of an animal, chairman of a committee, government of a nation) which regulates the exchange with the environment across the boundary and preserves a balance in the dynamic relationships of the subsystems, as a thermostat controls the temperature of a heating system.

5. Causality is seen as *circular* and may be *negative*, as with the thermostat which gives information to the boiler about room temperature which opposes the tendency to depart from the temperature setting, and so keeps it within a small oscillatory cycle; or it may be *positive* (as with the screaming of a panicking crowd), which magnifies change and would lead eventually to a 'runaway' effect.

6. Some applications of these concepts to clinical examples are as follows: a symptomatic child may be seen in systems terms as providing negative feedback to a marital disturbance. Quarrelling between a couple may be reduced when a child is ill, leading to learning whereby the child's symptom increases when the couple quarrel, whereupon the parents cease quarrelling because they cooperate in their concern

over the child's care. The symptom then subsides, so that the parents are no longer distracted, and so become aware of, and attack, each other again . . . etc. Similar reverberating patterns occur between spouses independently of the children and are seen as a fundamental aspect of enduring relationships. A husband may become anxious, and in danger of becoming less adequate as a breadwinner. If the wife develops an anxiety state at this point, he is distracted and loses his own anxiety temporarily, so that he regains his confidence, whereupon she calms down, whereupon he becomes self-preoccupied again and loses confidence once more, etc.

B: Systems theory, marital and family relations

A 'systems' way of thinking sees marriages and families as whole structures where there is constant movement or interchange, but where the parts are being held in a dynamic equilibrium by a multitude of repetitive, oscillating, regulatory feedback circuits. If this is so the possibility arises that a therapist can employ the energy regulating the system (and so resisting the changes the therapist is trying to bring about) by *interfering in these feedback circuits*, using a minimal energy to effect a large change – as in judo, for example, or as in altering the thermostat setting of the heating system – interfering in the system's own control mechanisms and using the system's own energy to change it, rather than, as it were, 'pushing it from outside' by the application of external forces.

In the early stages of its development, systems theorists emphasised negative feedback and 'homeostasis', more character-istic in extreme forms of unhealthy families. 'Morphogenesis' – facilitating change in the system – is now seen as the other end of the same stick. Steinglass (1978) in an excellent review of such concepts and their different applications, has emphasised the link between this and developmental stages. In marriage, morphogenesis or change is induced when the marital system is stressed by the new demands – the birth of a child or a financial crisis, for example – requiring changes in the system to adapt to new conditions. Between these 'developmental crises' homeostatic mechanisms prevail in quiescent periods; the system thus alternates between periods of growth and stability. This schema could be related to the ideas of psychoanalysts like Bowlby, who describes alternation between 'attachment behaviour' under stress and 'exploration', and to those of Winnicott, who describes the need for the security of 'holding' if the exploration of 'play' is to be possible. Heard (1978) has attempted to relate the ideas above to family systems. 'Family identity' describes an enduring set of characteristics of the family over time, which is perpetuated from one generation to another partly by 'family myths' (Ferriera, 1967; Byng Hall, 1973; Steinglass, 1978).

C: Implications for technique

There exist a number of clinical applications of general systems theory, each emphasising a different aspect of the whole set of concepts. Bowen's (1978) ideas give the appearance of a natural evolution from psychoanalytic concepts, and he has stated that general systems theory did not influence him, but he employs a thorough-going approach to the family as a system extending and developing over generations, and succeeds in doing so without losing the importance of the individual and his inner world. The Mental Research Institute at Palo Alto is best known for its 'pure' systems approach, where man is regarded as a 'black box' whose contents can be ignored because sufficient can be discovered by studying its 'inputs' and 'outputs' and finding regularities in the relationships between these, to enable the therapist to make communications (inputs) which will produce a predictable change in behaviour (outputs), such as symptom relief or alteration in marital interaction. Communication is seen as having two functions: 'Report' (neutral information, e.g. 'I have a headache') and 'command' (an attempt to control the partner's behaviour, e.g. an intonation, non-verbal posture and facial expression conveying subtly 'If you had behaved differently I would not have this headache').

Their concept of the double-bind (Bateson *et al.*, 1956) which has entered popular language, describes a situation where an individual receives messages containing conflicting 'commands', and where he is also forbidden to recognise the contradiction openly – such 'paradoxical' communication is claimed to be characteristic of severely disturbed family and marital systems. However, 'paradox' can also be used therapeutically, 'setting a thief to catch a thief', as it were. This method is difficult to describe briefly, but the reader is referred to Sluzki (1978) for a very clear, concise and eminently practical presentation of such interventions as they may be applied to marital work.

Some of the 'systems purists' give the impression of choosing the 'black box' approach in reaction against the abuse of psychoanalytic concepts to explain everything, and thus nothing. The price they have paid is the neglect of the inner world of the individual, and it may be a lack of inclusion of this which, despite the brilliance and effectiveness of the interventions, makes the ideas so much less rich at a more abstract level and difficult to integrate with other schools of thought, as well as making them hard for beginners to understand (or easier for beginners to *mis*understand).

The Milan group (Selvini-Palazzoli *et al.*, 1978), working in a very 'pure' systems fashion, but all with a thorough psychoanalytic training, have moved towards linking the contents of the human 'black box' with the communicational 'inputs' and 'outputs'. They see *hubris* or pride motivating a relentless yet concealed struggle for control, as a central factor in severe family disturbances like those producing schizophrenic members. And although they do not complete the link in their book, *hubris*, the challenge to God, implies a desire to be 'everything', to be omnipotent, to have no limits, etc. It is not far from this idea to the psychoanalytic concept of a level of infantile undifferentiation and omnipotence before boundaries and limits are recognised, which describes the accompanying difficulty of tolerating the fact that one cannot control the universe, especially mother. *A glance into the 'black box' might reveal the very simple fact that* all *paradoxes of this kind are attempts to maintain a fantasy world different from reality, by expressing both fantasy and reality at the same time in a form which conceals the discrepancy between the two, and by also conveying a 'command' to others to collude with the self-deception and so preserve the speaker's fantasy world (or the joint fantasy of the marriage or family)*. Paradoxical *therapeutic* interventions can then be seen as subtly breaking the rule that fantasy and reality must be kept apart, relating the two in a disguised, seemingly innocent fashion. Once the couple or family accept the bait, they cannot avoid seeing more than appeared to be implied in the original paradoxical intervention.

197

Special Applications

Minuchin (1974) also employs many systems concepts, concentrating particularly on establishing *boundaries* to maintain the integrity and adequate separateness and privacy of subsystems like the marital dyad, as well as ensuring adequate communication across them. These goals are achieved through clearly defined interventions which restructure communication and relative power. The mainly two-generational frame of his work is directed (at least in published writings) at families rather than couples, and this 'structural' school at present is of limited usefulness to the marital therapist.

All the above tend to exclude consideration of the *person* of the therapist from the therapeutic interaction. With Minuchin's techniques certain acceptable parts of the self (warmth, empathy etc.) are deliberately used in a professional way, but Bowen, the Palo Alto group and the Milan group operate from a position of emotional disengagement. As with behaviour modification, there is no *explicit* use of counter-transference, nor do such personal reactions figure in the theories of intervention. *To make good this lack, I have attempted to develop a theory which explicitly employs the therapist's personal reactions as part of the therapeutic system, whereby he or she accepts and operates from the 'scapegoat' rôle.* This appears below as Chapter 11. Whitaker (Napier and Whitaker, 1978) has always made use of this type of intervention even if he has not elaborated it into a coherent theory.

The behavioural perspective

A: Behavioural principles

Most efforts towards behavioural *systems* approaches have taken place from the 1970s, and the more general concepts and theories regarding marriage, its dysfunction and possible change still appear very naïve and simplistic to those with experience and understanding of the other, more developed perspectives. In 1973, I brought together a multi-disciplinary staff group comprising behaviourists, psychoanalysts, group analysts and American 'systems' experts for the task of training students in Britain, and developed thereby a much clearer idea of the inter-relationships of these methods. Moreover my textbook (1976) also makes an attempt to integrate psychoanalytic concepts with the behavioural social learning

198

approach of Bandura (1969), among others, using the bridging concept of 'model' (example; internal object). However, I lean more towards the psychoanalytic and systems ideas because they appear to account better for the complexity of the clinical observations, and it is perhaps best to quote authorities in the behavioural field from recent reviews.

Two reviews which offer clear and systematic expositions of behavioural principles are provided by Weiss (1978) and by O'Leary and Turkewitz (1978). The former describes the growing rapprochement between cognitive and behavioural work; the latter describes the application of such principles to marital problems. A less detailed overview is provided by Crowe (1978a) which is amongst the most helpful introductions. He describes the behavioural methods as 'distinguished from other forms of psychotherapy by a close observation of behaviour, a concentration on problems complained of as the goal of therapy, a general reliance on principles of learning, an empirical approach to innovation, a general tendency to use directive interventions and a commitment to objective evaluation of efficacy'.

B: Implications for technique

The principles underlying treatment are not difficult to understand. In an approach used by O'Leary and Turkewitz (1978), for example, the aims are '(1) to improve communication and (2) to increase mutual satisfaction by promoting clear communication about desired changes, and, where those changes appear reasonable, prompting their occurrence through therapist suggestion and the encouragement of social reinforcement between the spouses' (p. 289). Once one has mastered the jargon used by behaviourists – which does not make concessions to attract those outside the field – and provided one perceives that the daunting complexity of its more general attempts to explain marital interaction are the result of stretching simple ideas further than they will fit, the ideas are straightforward enough and will, at least in outline, appear 'common sense' to anyone who has owned a dog or brought up a child. The main difference from such 'common sense' knowledge is the way in which processes have been studied in great detail experimentally, so that learning may be brought about as swiftly and efficiently as possible.

199

Special Applications

C: The detail of interview procedures

The behavioural approach has unique value in the way in which it has developed the detail *of interviewing or treatment procedures in a way that beginners can easily learn, a task that the other perspectives in general neglect and leave students to learn all over again for themselves.* The following outline of teaching problem-solving skills is from O'Leary and Turkewitz (1978):

> One method of shaping such skills is to clearly state rules for problem-solving discussions and to provide feedback on the application of these rules. Some examples of these rules are:
>
> 1. Be specific.
> 2. Phrase requests in terms of positive changes, as opposed to attacks on negative behaviour.
> 3. Respond directly to a complaint or criticism, rather than responding with a cross-complaint of your own.
> 4. Keep the topic of conversation confined to the present or future.
> 5. Wait for your spouse to complete a thought before giving your reactions or comments.
> 6. Confine your comments to observable behaviour, rather than making remarks about motives or character analyses.
>
> The therapist reminds the couple of these rules through both positive and negative feedback. The negative feedback typically takes the form of specifically pointing out a non-productive behaviour and explaining the negative consequence that ensued.
> Training in empathic skills is also used to increase close communication . . . the spouses are taught to reflect what they hear their partner saying. Initially, this skill is taught in the context of very structured discussions of non-problematic issues. One spouse is designated as the speaker and limits his/her speech to a couple of sentences. The therapist then summarises what has been said, to provide a model of empathic listening. After the therapist models, the spouses speak to each other, alternating speaker and listener rôles, with the listener reflecting both the content and feelings in the message. The speaker is always given the opportunity to comment on the accuracy of the reflection and make corrections when needed.

Of course, trainees studying the other perspectives acquire much knowledge of this kind through apprenticeship, modelling their behaviour on that of their teachers, but such detailed, systematic exposition of valuable technique is unique to the behavioural perspective.

Gurman (1978) has noted other advantages of the behavioural approach. These are:

1. It has a highly focussed approach to the problem complained of, avoiding more work than necessary.

2. It attempts to develop specific treatments for specific problems and has greater appeal to the less sophisticated or insight-oriented patients (with its corresponding disadvantage that its rather narrow and simplistic approach is often rejected by the more sophisticated).

3. A behavioural approach has value in revealing *resistance*. This concept is not emphasised by behaviourists, but many psychoanalysts and 'systems' therapists have found that task-setting throws the defensive system into prominence, thereby facilitating its treatment.

4. It is particularly useful in active therapy of sexual dysfunction, where a behavioural approach (Masters and Johnson, 1970) has transformed the outlook for disorders which were difficult to treat with existing methods. The combination of such behavioural approaches with analytic understanding and methods (Kaplan, 1974) seems more effective still.

D: Limitations of behavioural marital therapy

The main limitations of behavioural marital therapy appear to follow from its very recent development and the consequent inability of the theories at this stage to match the complexity of the processes involved. Gurman (1978) has demonstrated that the theoretical structure is not as watertight as it looks, and is based on some assumptions which have long been abandoned in psychoanalytic and systems perspectives. For example, a major problem is the fundamental assumption in behavioural theory that the cognitions of a spouse will change as the behaviour of the partner changes – an idea which some behaviourists acknowledge is contradicted by the facts, and which is well explained in psychoanalytic theory by the fact that the perceptions of spouses are deeply influenced by early learning in their families of origin, whereby they perceive their spouses, and manipulate them to behave, as if they resemble important influential persons in their childhood.

Special Applications

Gurman and Kniskern (1978) point out that the behaviourist seeks to replace one form of manipulative control by another. Even though the resulting relationship may be an improvement on the first, it may be questioned whether an optimum marriage is really a 'business' relationship of this sort at all. The ideal to which the behaviourists aspire (understandably from their base in the 'statistical' concept of 'normality') in many ways resembles the mid-range or at best the 'adequate' family in the Timberlawn scheme (Lewis *et al.*, 1976). 'Optimal' families do not seem to exist in the behaviourist world and the Timberlawn Research is curiously neglected in its literature.

Behavioural approaches require an alliance with reasonably mature and adult aspects of the spouses' personalities, and are difficult to implement when there are primitive, psychotic or borderline aspects in the functioning of the couple that produce unrealistic expectations which are hard to modify; an incapacity for understanding the need for reciprocity; a lack of commitment or an extreme vulnerability. By contrast, the psychoanalytic approach addresses itself to the irrational, infantile aspects of the personality and embodies ways of working with these, while many 'systems' approaches were developed in response to the problems encountered with families producing schizophrenic and other severe forms of disturbance and are highly suited to their treatment. In particular, the behavioural approach does not offer a means of understanding, or techniques of coping with, the pressure upon the therapist to 'join the system' through the influence of the 'countertransference' beyond giving a very clear format to hold on to like a lifeline.[4]

Interviewing Methods

Conjoint and individual methods

It is helpful first to look at the *interviewing arrangements* which are likely to be most effective. As research findings on the results of marital and family therapy, such as they are, bear heavily on this issue, it is helpful to restate some of the conclusions arrived at by Gurman and Kniskern (1979) in their comprehensive review quoted in Chapter 8, 'Sexual Counselling in General Practice'. They show evidence that couples benefit most when both partners are involved in the therapy, especially when they are seen conjointly.

My own experience has led, in line with research findings, towards an increasing use of conjoint or conjoint-group approaches because of their generally greater efficacy and speed as compared with those forms of therapy where the spouses are seen separately, but there are nevertheless exceptions. Separate interviews may be desirable in order to exclude organic disease or to make careful examination of a psychiatric condition. Separate treatment of members of a couple may also be indicated when divorce or separation has become inevitable, to support each partner through the painful experience of loss and to aid them in starting new lives apart, even though conjoint sessions may still be desirable to negotiate amicable cooperation over the vital issue of care and custody of any children.

Also, though conjoint interviews are far more effective in dealing with couples so enmeshed that there is no clear boundary between them, and where each spouse projects unaccepted aspects of the self into the partner, separate individual or group therapy is often desirable at a somewhat more mature stage where clear differentiation and identity formation has begun but is still precarious.

Where such differentiation is less precarious, individual sessions with separate therapists, combined with four-way, round-table conferences which include both partners and both therapists, have their greatest value. When less individual support is needed, four-way joint interviews of this kind, where the therapists act as 'advocates' who each side with one of the patients, speaking for them and helping them to speak, may provide adequate individual support without parallel individual sessions being necessary (Bannister and Pincus, 1965; Lyons, 1973). Otherwise, conjoint therapy appears preferable.

Couples groups

If the family histories of the spouses are more positive or if the early marital experience was satisfying, but the couple have been unable to cope with the challenge of some developmental change in the marriage (e.g. when a child is born, becomes adolescent, or leaves home) therapy can often be more focussed and short-term, ranging from one to ten or more sessions, provided the therapist sees the couple together and works towards a limited and definite goal. More chronic difficulties, particularly where there is much use of denial and projection, or where the partners are unwilling to share responsibility for the problem and so blame each other, can also be treated by interviews as a couple but are often more effectively dealt with in a couples group. In such groups the combination of strong mutual support and criticism from other couples, together with the 'mirror effect' (Foulkes, 1965) whereby individuals can see their own faults in each other and can also perceive and copy more healthy modes of functioning from other members, are powerful forces aiding the therapist(s). Such chronic, highly defended disorders, where the problems are ego-syntonic and where the marriage actually helps each member to avoid facing his or her own difficulties, usually require a long duration of treatment varying in our experience from a minimum of about one year of weekly attendance, to two years or more. However, the power and efficacy of such groups is so impressive that they are also used for preference where couples wish, and can afford the time and expense, to go beyond the immediate problems and grow both as individuals and in their capacity for relationship.

Combinations of method

We have found no difficulty in combining individual, conventional-group, conjoint and conjoint-group methods, if any one mode appears insufficient. Within the general principles set out above, less time-consuming or expensive methods should obviously be given a trial first, adding other modes if progress is blocked.

Grunebaum et al. (1975) have reached similar conclusions, except that they lean rather more towards the use of individual transference-based interviews rather than conjoint sessions in those intermediate cases where either individual or couples-group therapy is not strongly indicated. They also note that the prognosis for all forms of marital or separate therapy is particularly poor for couples with chronic difficulties which become acute when the children leave home, or where alcoholism, gambling and eating problems are prominent features. We have reached similar conclusions. By definition such spouses are extremely primitive in their personality development, are often unable to take responsibility for themselves or each other and instead use their children to contain, and vicariously to punish *and* gratify, their own infantile needs. The departure of the children from home therefore confronts them with both their own and their partner's inadequacy, in a way they can avoid while the family is together. However, we have found that some joint interviews with the children present can be helpful at least in clarifying the situation, and sometimes also in facilitating small but worthwhile changes. The children know their parents well and can in fact nurture them, provided the parents are given permission to be receptive.

Interviewing Techniques: Eleven Principles

1. The requirements of effective therapy

The three main theoretical 'schools' described above can be seen in terms of difference of emphasis rather than incompatible positions. If we return to the Timberlawn Research as a foundation, we might anticipate that to be effective, therapy should involve:

(a) Helping the couple to communicate more clearly and directly.

(b) Clarifying and if necessary changing the structure of the marriage and family. This will include encouraging a clear parental coalition and proper inter-generational boundaries if there are children, and ensuring that spouses respect each other's rights and negotiate decisions aimed at mutual satisfaction, rather than each fighting to have his or her own way through coercion or manipulation.

(c) Facilitating change from attitudes of fear, distrust and self-protective withdrawal, towards attitudes of trust, openness and generosity.

(d) Facilitating the growth and differentiation of each spouse, so that they need each other less and so can enjoy each other more (a mutual independence which requires that each also becomes more separate from, and independent of, their families of origin).

These principles fit very well with what clinical experience teaches us is necessary. Though the different schools of therapy emphasise different aspects among these four, almost all include the first three

205

in some measure, and many include the fourth as well. The four aspects above have been set out, and will then be outlined, in an order beginning from the simplest and potentially briefest type of intervention, useable by any clinician, and ending with aspects of change requiring intervention which will usually be more complex, prolonged and so best carried out by clinicians with more training and experience.

2. Working in the present

The first three types of intervention set out above all mainly involve the *present:* they involve the observation and change of behaviour as witnessed by the therapist during a joint interview. The history of the marital relationship needs to be explored to some extent, to be sure, but changes can be brought about in many cases without any detailed exploration of the pre-marital history of each spouse. For improving communication, setting up a more effective decision-making structure, and facilitating affiliative attitudes, the knowledge and understanding required of the therapist draw more on everyday 'common sense' experience and wisdom than on expertise in in-depth psychology. Indeed, the latter can even be a handicap in enthusiastic, newly-trained hands, eager to try out knowledge to the limit in every case, unable to accept the inevitable limitations of marriage and insufficiently experienced to know when to 'let sleeping dogs lie'.

3. Keeping the responsibility with the couple

Work on these aspects of the marital relationship does not need to wait until 'treatment' following a period of extensive 'diagnosis'. It can begin as soon as the couple are invited to report their problems. All the therapist has to do is to show interest and concern, ask the couple to describe the complaint, and then attempt to understand what they are saying, asking for clarification as necessary. It is however absolutely vital that the therapist should feel, and should make clear to the patients, that it is *their responsibility to help him to understand the problem*.

This avoidance of any aim other than observation of what happens is important, because the main obstacle to learning such techniques in general, or to perceiving the nature of the fundamental problem in any particular joint interview, is usually an excessive anxiety to 'do' something prematurely in order to justify one's professional rôle. This impulse is natural enough, but such urgency to achieve results makes it difficult to tolerate the disagreements, circular arguments and fruitless exchanges of blame and recrimination with which such interviews frequently begin, and which inevitably produce feelings of chaos and confusion in the therapist. Too much activity on the part of the therapist also leads automatically to a decrease of feeling of responsibility and activity in the couple, so that they soon become silent and look to the therapist to provide a solution, or at least to ask them questions.

If one can be patient, quietly attentive and expectant, at least a clear perception of what is actually happening between the couple will emerge, and this will frequently bring with it, towards the end of the interview, some perception of the pattern of the essential difficulty and a recognition of some of the changes necessary to solve it.

4. The content of the complaint and the form in which it is presented

The most effective route to this understanding is to study the *detail of the complaint* and all the *interaction centring around it*, the nature of the symptom, its beginnings and development over time, its effect on the partner, how both partners feel about it and react towards it, what they have each done (or not done) to try to communicate about it, to solve it or at least to manage it, and so on. The more such detail is insisted upon, the more the couple must necessarily move from the realm of imagination, disagreement, argument and mutual blaming to the realm of fact and agreement, since the demand for increasing *detail* and specific *examples* makes this inevitable.

As this occurs, the fundamental problem (which is always contained in what is *omitted* in the patients' presentation, whether by deliberate, conscious suppression, or through unconscious avoidance) will begin to take shape in the therapist's mind if he or she is sufficiently open, relaxed and receptive so that there is space for the pattern to be registered.

5. The requirement of neutrality

As well as seeking to *understand*, the professional should be *neutral*,

207

or at least fair; that is, he should try to listen to both points of view and try to see both sides, keeping the interests of both patients equally at heart. This is not to say that temporary siding is not appropriate, once a trusting relationship is firmly established. At any given point, one partner will be more in a state of resistance than the other, but the stronger criticism this draws on to the resistant partner usually leads to a 'leap-frog' in this partner's progress and the next time the other is likely to be the laggard and to receive the greater pressure. Provided the therapist is understood by both members of the couple to be essentially fair, such temporary siding is usually accepted, particularly if the therapist takes care to look at some issues from both points of view within each session.

6. Clarifying the covert contract between the couple

By seeking clarification of what the spouses are saying, the therapist will simultaneously be *clarifying the covert contract* between the couple, as I have described in Chapter 7 above (p. 149). Once a vicious circle of frustration and mutual rejection has begun, the mutual rewards and satisfactions diminish as each withdraws from an increasingly painful interaction, leading perhaps to a chronic cat-and-dog existence, if not to breakdown and divorce. Each spouse fears to take a step toward reconciliation, for this will expose him or her to the risk of further humiliation if the attempt is made when the partner happens to be in an unforgiving, bitter mood. Intervention by a professional who avoids taking sides and acts as an honest broker permits the negotiation of a ceasefire, can provide a temporary peace-keeping force while negotiations are resumed, and he then helps the couple to work out a more explicit contract.

7. The therapist as referee

Many less severe problems resolve very quickly when the therapist does no more than act as a firm and impartial *referee* in this way, looking for points of agreement or inconsistency in an effort to understand the problem. A high proportion of psychological problems are a consequence of the fact that we are not clearly aware of what we want until we try to make it explicit, by talking to another person. Once we begin to do so, we often see contradictions invisible to us before, and then automatically seek more satisfactory compromises. Most therapists have received thanks from patients for helping them to solve problems, when all they have in fact done is to listen without comment. Similarly, a therapist who meets with *couples* and tries to understand their complaints not only finds that each spouse will become aware of inconsistencies in his or her own desires, and adjust them, but that both spouses will become aware how little they really know the needs, fears and hopes of the partner, and how little they are understood themselves unless they make their feelings more plain. The attentive interest of the therapist thus leads towards a process of negotiation and adjustment even without any specific attempts to bring this about, though skill and experience enable this process to be facilitated.

8. Slowing down the process

The therapist's questions and other interventions, indeed even the therapist's silent presence, not only make the spouses more aware of their interaction (which at home may have become habitual 'gramophone records' to which neither listens attentively) but also introduce a *time delay* into the exchanges. 'Catastrophe Theory' (Zeeman, 1978), the study of sudden, discontinuous changes, explains how some chain-reactions of marital conflict cease if the interaction is slowed down sufficiently. For example, a wife may at first be able to be warm and understanding towards a husband who arrives home irritable following a bad day at the office, but her patience has a limit, and, if it snaps and she loses her temper before he gets over his, an escalating fight may follow with consequences lasting for days. But if she maintains her cool until he simmers down, the explosion may be avoided. Much marital therapy probably works because the time relations of the emotional exchanges between the partners are altered in this very simple way, even though the therapist may not realise this, believing that the improvement is due to the 'insight', rather than the delay, brought about by his attempt to understand the problem.

9. Modelling affiliative attitudes

Effective intervention is also likely to be based on the therapist's personal preference for affiliative rather than oppositional social attitudes. By convening the interview and helping the couple to communicate, listening to both respectfully and negotiating mutually acceptable solutions, a preference for open communication,

Special Applications

respect, trust, generosity and sharing, as compared with manipulative power struggles, is automatically conveyed. Over a period of time, not only is the model of the therapist likely to influence the couple towards similar affiliative values, but they will also learn for themselves the greater satisfactions that these bring.

10. The aim of systemic change

Therapy focussed on *present* interaction aims to improve the marital relationship rather than to change the individual partners in any fundamental way. In many cases quite small changes in *system* functioning (e.g. replacement of competitiveness by greater cooperation, improvement in negotiating skills, increase in satisfaction or frequency of sexual intercourse), which can often be achieved in a short time, bring about very great increases in the personal happiness of the partners.

11. Historical material

Where these simple approaches (which are more characteristic of the behavioural and systems perspectives) are ineffective, it may be necessary to pay more attention to the past, to the way in which the spouses are still embedded emotionally in their families or origin, and the manner in which they are manipulating, and colluding with, each other to reproduce their original family dynamics.[5] Here the psychoanalytic perspective, as well as developments from it such as . those of Bowen (1978), Framo (1976), Sager (1976) and myself (1976, 1981) become more relevant, while therapy can be expected to be more complex and prolonged.

However, the distinction between treatment based on present interaction, and that based on past experience, is to some extent arbitrary and concerned more with degree of involvement and treatment duration. Even the most brief, behavioural, systems-oriented therapy usually has some effect on defining boundaries, clarifying personal identities, and so facilitating some measure of differentiation; while even the briefest treatment is often made easier by some awareness of the family history and development of the spouses.

A systematic exploration of the past is best left to a later part of the first interview, leaving the early part relatively unstructured and devoted to an exploration of the problem as the patients present it.

Some schemes for marital history-taking involve hours or days of detailed enquiry (Martin, 1976) but a great deal can be learnt in five or ten minutes. About two-thirds of the way through the first interview, one can say: 'It would be helpful to be able to see each of you against your backgrounds. Could you tell me – very briefly – something about your families, what your fathers and mothers were like, your brothers and sisters, how you got on with them, that sort of thing?'

What is omitted is even more important than what is actually said (this is the main reason for limiting one's questions and leaving the structure of the interview to the patients, as far as possible). If the mother is not mentioned at all, or the family history is provided in the way many of us learnt history at school, with a series of dates and events with no feeling, or if the informant arrives at his boarding school within two sentences, such information is given a special significance and explored by more detailed questioning later.

Conclusion: The Principles of Change

The family patterns for which one is searching are complex and varied, and the reader is recommended to the literature. Four simple principles can be suggested, the first two of which are set out on p. 167 in more detail.

Firstly, emotional disorder becomes understandable when enough information is obtained for pattern recognition. Secondly, marital problems, like many other emotional problems, arise out of unfinished business in the partners' related developmental difficulties. Seeing the pattern enables the therapist to identify and facilitate those processes of growth and change that have been arrested. Thirdly, the therapist should be alert to stress or deprivation in the partners' past experience which has interrupted or distorted normal developmental processes. Fourthly, meaningful patterns and connections in the total story are frequently available through attention to what is missing in the material, as it is presented. What is worked with is the process as it unfolds. The greater one's experience the more readily one is inclined to seek sense in precisely those aspects of it which are puzzling or uncomfortable.

For example, impairment of maternal care in infancy through puerperal depression, or illness and hospitalisation of mother and

211

child, may limit the growth of love and trust and show later in life during marriage as fear of emotional and sexual intimacy. Lack of kindly firmness at the toddler stage, when self-will and tempers are normal, may result later in fears that violence may become uncontrollable and damage the partner, so the legitimate expression of frustration and anger is avoided leading perhaps to chronic tension, depressive states and failure to resolve important conflicts.

Death, illness or other powerful events occurring at developmental stages when sexual awareness and conflicts are prominent, for example around puberty, or in the earlier oedipal period between four and six when sexually tinged feelings towards the parents are strong, may be misinterpreted and, by association, lead later to a nameless dread that sexual impulses always lead to some kind of disaster. By bringing such 'unfinished business' to light, the resulting inhibitions of emotional expression and sexual exploration can be rendered meaningful, so that the spouses can understand the need to risk facing and opposing the fears and, with encouragement and support, can begin to struggle to overcome them.

Often the 'unfinished business' lies not just in the developmental task the patient has avoided and so is repeatedly presented with again, but in inhibitions and immaturities that have limited his parents' maturation and capacity for sexual enjoyment, and which have perhaps affected the whole family over generations. *No obstacle to treatment is more powerful than the taboo on accepting happiness denied to (or rejected by) one's parents, perhaps because to be happy then feels like leaving the family, finally separating and standing alone, even enduring rejection and envy from less fortunate family members.*

Here the therapist's approval and support, once the issue is recognised, can provide a half-way house enabling this vital step towards independence to be taken, as well as proving a counterweight to the jealousy and envy that would have been aroused in the original family if the patient had outgrown his parents' immaturities. This fear of having more happiness than the parents is nowhere more evident than in the sexual sphere, where the greatest potential pleasure arouses envy of equivalent strength.

Notes

1 This paper was originally published in *The Journal of Family Therapy*, **2** (1980) 271–296.

2 'Couple therapy' is a preferable term nowadays to 'marital therapy', since the important issue for choice of treatment method is the stability and commitment of a relationship rather than its legal status. For simplicity the words 'marriage' and 'marital' will continue to be used here to refer to both forms of relatively stable commitment.

3 In this paper the main principles applicable must be grossly over-simplified, as must be the case with the presentation of the other perspectives too, and the account can only hope to provide the reader with an outline sketch of the field which may perhaps assist those less familiar with it to get their bearings. The task is made more difficult still by the fact that '. . . there is considerable disagreement about criteria for marital success, the goal of therapy, the indications and contraindications of therapy, and the techniques to be used', though this is partly compensated by the fact that '. . . most experienced and competent therapists do not differ as much in their techniques as they do in their theory, their use of language, or their focus' (Nadelson and Paolino, 1978, pp. 152–153).

4 For those wishing to explore these methods, two texts have recently been published, by Liberman *et al.* (1979), and by Jacobson and Margolin (1979).

5 An excellent and readable introduction to this developmental process, as it affects later functioning, may be found in Pincus and Dare (1978), which is supplemented by the summary and outline by Dare (1979).

Three

GROUP-ANALYTIC FAMILY THERAPY

10 Group Analysis and Family Therapy

S. H. Foulkes was Skynner's analyst and teacher. The first paper in this final section was written just before, and delivered as a lecture to the Group-Analytic Society just after, Foulkes's death. The event aroused strong expression of the affection and warmth Foulkes's humanity evoked in so many of his pupils. This is conveyed by the paper, but as the debt is acknowledged a sense of the lively intellectual struggle between the two men, their enjoyment of friendly challenge and debate, comes across clearly as well.

1976 was an eventful year in other ways. Skynner had developed family therapy training programmes within the Institute of Group Analysis and in order to staff them well had been obliged to recruit many teachers from outside the Institute, including those from behavioural and other non-analytic schools of thought. Foulkes had fully supported this, despite the disquiet amongst some members of the Institute. Earlier in the year the two groups had been brought together in the London Workshop to explore the relationship between family and group therapy, but the year ended with the family therapy teachers setting up the separate Institute of Family Therapy.

Family therapy and group analysis subsequently developed strongly and independently, the former coming more under first the American and then the Italian influence and moving away from the psychoanalytic model, the latter returning to a closer identification with it. Skynner accepted the first chairmanship of the Institute of Family Therapy but maintained his allegiance to both groups and describes some of the events referred to above in the paper 'Institutes And How To Survive Them', which he delivered as the eighth S. H. Foulkes Annual Lecture in 1984 (Appendix reference 43).

Moving back and forth several times a day between the two types of therapy, each of which seemed to him to complement and illuminate the other, he now set himself the task of finding a comprehensive theory which would explain them both. In order to do this it would have to find common ground between the systemic, behavioural and psychoanalytic approaches to family therapy. In what follows he begins his task, clearing and marking out the territory.

J.R.S.

'Offer a donkey a salad and he will ask you what kind of a thistle it is'
Ancient Sufi proverb, quoted by Idries Shah in *The Way of the Sufi*

Introduction

It is a matter of very great sorrow that my need to postpone this lecture on the relationship between 'conventional' small-group work and conjoint family techniques has prevented me from putting forward the ideas that follow in the presence of S. H. Foulkes, whose death casts a shadow upon us all corresponding to the illumination he provided to our understanding.[1] My own work owes so much to him, in a far more fundamental way than just the reception of facts and skills from a teacher, that I would have liked him to see what I had made from some of the materials he gave me.

Those who have read my book on family and marital psychotherapy (1976) will have noticed that though I started from, and am still most firmly rooted in, the group-analytic approach to both stranger and natural groups, I was obliged to expand my field of view, embracing ideas and techniques I had previously seen as conflicting rather than compatible with group analysis, in order to make sense of the phenomena I was observing in studies of families and marriages. I would like to widen the field of view and try to see if there is some simple and meaningful developmental relationship between the psychotherapies as a whole, of the kind I have hope-fully discovered through studies of the family. If we look at psychoanalysis and its derivative individual psychotherapies; at psychotherapy based on behaviour modification; at family therapies as a whole; and at the range of stranger-group therapies (whether these group therapies are based more on analytic or on behavioural concepts and techniques), can we find some order and

meaning in their relationship, even some deep meaning and consequent order in the very fact that they are often presented by their
exponents as in conflict and incompatible? I believe we can, if we
are open to the possibility that we are involved here in a *developmental* process, involving an increase in complexity over time, and if
we search for the vital clue within the structure of the family itself.

Order of Complexity and Order of Appearance

I begin here with individual psychoanalysis, move next to behaviour
modification approaches (which also began as an individual
psychotherapy, and still finds great difficulty in moving out of the
dyadic mould), thirdly to family therapies, leaving stranger-groups
till last. This conflicts with the order in which these approaches have
developed, but it was not until I rearranged the order in this way
that I found my ideas began to crystallise into a clear and simple
pattern. Beforehand, I had tended to assume, because professionals had actually tried systematically to work with stranger-
groups many years in advance of serious attempts with natural
groups, that adequate theories regarding the treatment of stranger-
groups (what we generally call 'group psychotherapy' or here call
'group analysis') had been developed before adequate theories
about the treatment of natural groups (generally called 'family
therapy'). I now see that this is not the case.

Attempts to treat families and couples together have indeed been
more delayed, but since such work began, progress in construction
of theory and refinement of technique has been astonishingly swift
and successful, engaging its practitioners, despite the wide range of
orientations and concepts with which they began, in a constructive
and fundamentally cooperative joint activity that has been lacking
in all other fields of psychotherapy. By contrast, I have begun to see
that the field of stranger-group psychotherapy, despite the fact that
experimentation began much earlier, is still in a much more primitive and ill-defined state even where attempts have been made to
map some of the territory involved. It contains, moreover, much
disagreement and contention between its different practitioners. *I
believe now that this is the case because the theory and practice
required for really effective stranger-group psychotherapy, of a level
we can attain with natural-group psychotherapy, is* most complex of

all, *and that the rearrangement of the order of the psychotherapies I have already mentioned, placing stranger-group psychotherapy as the last item, correctly reflects this difficulty and complexity*. Though discouraging at first sight, I personally found this realisation a great relief. It explained, in a way that is stimulating rather than a cause for despondency, why I am able to give what seems to me quite a clear, logical account of the work I do with families and couples, while I find myself unable to give a similarly coherent and intellectually satisfactory description of what I do with stranger-groups, although I have been working with them twice as long, spend three times as much time on them even today, and believe that I am quite skilful at working with them.

Now this is not to detract from the excellent work that has been done in the study of stranger-groups, nor to suggest that there is not already information sufficient to enable one to *use psychoanalytic techniques in groups*, to *employ behavioural techniques in a group situation*, and so on. All these are useful, rewarding and will contribute towards an eventual adequate understanding, but they do not constitute a systematic theory of stranger-group psychotherapy.

Let us move on to consider how my rearrangement of the sequence in terms of *order of complexity*, rather than simple *order of appearance over time*, at once suggests a simple and elegant understanding of the situation. As is always the case, many years of struggle to reconcile apparent contradictions and discrepancies, seemingly requiring a theory of ever-increasing complexity, led suddenly and unexpectedly to a perception of a simple pattern. Though it made sense of all the problems to me, the pattern was too simple to see as long as one was standing too close to it. It was necessary to step back and take a wider view before it could be registered. *There is a similarity here to my description of a family interview. An increasing mass of unrelated data leads to growing confusion and fear that it is incomprehensible, resolving suddenly to perception of a simple pattern that unifies the whole* (p. 340 below). Here perhaps is another simple 'systems' principle, which may be applicable to all levels of function.[2]

Development as a Three-Stage Sequence

Here I shall put forward the unifying idea first, and then apply it to the facts, although of course things actually happen the other way around.

The basic integrating principle is well known to you all, forming as it does the essence of Freud's developmental scheme: that of oral, anal and genital phases. Of course he employed it in a particular way, elaborating this central three-stage process in terms of the physics of his day and producing his ideas about a libidinal energy being attached successively to different bodily zones. These details are today rejected by many, and certainly I do not find them a useful way of thinking myself, but the central concept seems to have astonishingly wide relevance on many levels. I am indebted to Helen Durkin, whose book *The Group in Depth* is still to my mind the best introduction and overview to the stranger-group field. In Chapter 4 she relates this three-phase developmental sequence of Freud's to a similar three-phase pattern in the theories of other workers: Shutz's 'inclusion, control and affection', for example, or Bion's 'dependency, fight-flight and pairing', and Bennis's 'submissiveness, rebellion and independence' and related 'identification, self-identity and inter-dependence'. I have tried to work out some clinical applications of this phasic sequence of challenge and response in my book, *One Flesh, Separate Persons*, though I realise that I did not give sufficient credit to her influence.

My own modest contribution to these concepts, for good or ill, is the further idea that certain social situations form challenges *to which the phases are* responses, *in the sequence* mother, father *and* couple. *Of course, this is in many ways stating the obvious. I imagine there will be little disagreement that in the first, oral phase, the mother is the central figure (or perhaps one should say today that the functions traditionally associated with mothering are essential to the child's requirements). Nor would those influenced by Freudian concepts, I imagine, disagree that the third, genital or oedipal phase is concerned with the relationship of the parents as* a couple, *particularly a sexual couple, rather than with their separate personalities as individuals. If I have made any contribution, it is only to emphasise that the second or anal stage is concerned particularly with the issue of social control and the development of self-control, with independence and auto-*

nomy, with achieving compromises between the demands of society and of the instincts, and that this phase centres particularly on the father (or rather the functions that are traditionally associated with the fathering rôle). This seems so obvious, once stated, that I feel rather foolish at mentioning it again. At the same time, it does seem to me that this obvious fact has somehow been subject to a curious neglect, or even avoidance, in recent years, perhaps because we have been passing through an era in which there has been great emphasis on mothering. It has been a time too when the female rôle has been making up much lost ground as it ceases to be subordinate and devalued and comes to be appreciated as complementary and of equal importance to that of the male.

A Developmental Sequence for Therapeutic Modalities

If we now look again at our series of psychotherapeutic modalities in the light of this phasic developmental sequence, I hope you may share some of my excitement at the correspondences which at once appear. Though all the psychotherapies are concerned with facilitating maturation towards more responsible adulthood, there do seem to be rather different emphases in concept and method.

1. Psychoanalysis and maternal functions

It seems to me that psychoanalysis has certain traditionally *maternal* virtues as part of its core of philosophy and technique, such ideas as complete acceptance, of understanding both cognitively and in the sense of sympathy and capacity to identify with another. It provides a protective environment with secure boundaries within which it is believed that spontaneous growth will occur if harmful influences restricting it are removed. The patient is confronted with reality, to be sure, but in a graded fashion at the pace he can manage, where the very nature of the analytic sessions shields him from many pressures. Beyond this, the analyst does not make demands upon him for achievement and seeks to avoid as far as possible imposing his own values. Much of this corresponds to the relationship of a mother with a young baby in the oral phase of development, when patient care and nurturance provide a situation where growth occurs spontaneously, in a period before demands for socialisation and self-control are appropriate. Here, also, we see the gulf between the patient and therapist at its most extreme. In theory, at least, attention is directed entirely to the patient's needs, not those of the analyst, just as a mother in the earlier stages expects to give without return (though perhaps psychoanalysts, like mothers, can make hidden demands they do not recognise?). In no form of psychotherapy is the psychological distance greater, further from mutuality. Even the relative postures emphasise this, the patient prone upon a couch, the analyst upright, attentive but relatively passive. It is scarcely surprising that psychoanalysis, and the individual psychotherapies based upon it, are indispensable in the treatment of profound disturbances originating in the first year of a child's life.

2. Behavioural therapies and paternal functions

If we move to behavioural types of psychotherapy, based upon learning theory, we see a very striking difference. We see less concern with understanding in the sense of total acceptance and empathy. The therapist's values are more openly involved, and he is much more likely to function as an educator seeking to change the patient so that he may learn to adapt more effectively to society's values. He sets standards, makes aims for the patient and exerts pressure of one kind or another to help him attain them, whether by painful punishment or through support, encouragement and rewards.

The gap between patient and therapist is also less, though this is at first perhaps not so apparent. There is a clear hierarchy, it is true. The behavioural therapist functions as an expert who knows best what will benefit the patient, but they are in the relationship of teacher and pupil, and the gap is less than in the analytic situation where, theoretically at least, there is no possibility of ordinary human contact or showing of the therapist's needs at all. Maslow and Días Guerrero (1973) give the following clear if extreme account of maternal and paternal functions:

> We postulate that the major task of the mother, *qua* mother, is to love unconditionally, to gratify, to heal and comfort and smooth over; and that the major task of a father, *qua* father, is to support and protect, to mediate between the family and reality (the world), and to prepare his children to live in the extra-familial world by discipline, toughening, instruction, reward and punishment, judging, differen-

tial valuing, reason and logic (rather than by unconditioned love), and by being able to say 'No' when necessary.

If there is any truth in this, it would certainly seem that behavioural psychotherapy is based on traditional paternal (rather than maternal) functioning, and that it is perhaps particularly appropriate where this influence has been lacking.

Perhaps this begins to explain the curious, implacable hostility between psychoanalysis and behaviour modification psychotherapists. 'Hostility' is perhaps the wrong word, for it does at least imply sufficient relationship for disagreement and conflict to exist, while what one observes is almost complete non-comprehension, non-communication, based on a strange inability of each to see things from the other's point of view. This has always mystified me, but if one's choice between the different types of approach is in fact based on a predominantly paternal or maternal identification, or perhaps a defence against the opposite one, the intensity of the resistance each type of psychotherapist shows to the theories of the other, and the resulting incapacity of each to look at things from the other's point of view, begins to make sense.

3. Family therapy and the sexual union

It makes sense if one supposes one further condition: an inherent difficulty in the two sexes getting together in a mutual, complementary way, in which each respects and acknowledges the special qualities and advantages of the other, without giving up their own, and recognises that the very differences and difficulties of communication which cause the problems are a source of rich potentialities. In other words, there needs to be a perception, on both sides, that the whole purpose of the differences is the creative act of sexual intercourse, not a battle of the sexes.

It seems to me that this extraordinary phenomenon begins to be understandable, and indeed to fit meaningfully into the developmental sequence I am proposing, if we remember a central tenet of Freudian theory, that of the oedipal conflict and the jealousies and inhibitions regarding parental sexual intercourse associated with it. If we assume that this dynamic can be reflected in systems at different levels – in this case in the system of the 'helping professions' as a whole – we might then anticipate that the development of conjoint family and marital therapy would have to involve a very remarkable leap forward, not only in concepts and techniques but also in the demands it would make upon its practitioners for personal growth and for change in their relationship to colleagues; and we might anticipate too that it would take some time for the jump to be made.

When we look at the development of family therapy, we see a number of striking features which do begin to seem meaningful, at least to me, in this context. Conjoint work has indeed been slow to develop, and the early approaches to it have manifested continued splitting, schismatic processes, even if these have gradually become less extreme. Thus treatment facilities for adults and for children have in general been kept separate and it has continued to be the custom for professionals to learn to work with one or the other, rather than both. Even in Child Guidance Clinics, where the family has been viewed more as a unit, adults and children have usually been seen separately, and provided with separate therapists. These clinics in turn have not usually been very interested in, or have not developed adequate skills at, the therapy of marriages, particularly sexual problems; while the latter problems have similarly been split off and dealt with in Institutes of Marital Studies or by Marriage Guidance Counselling, where the associated family and children's problems are not usually studied or treated simultaneously. If one wanted to keep the parental sexuality as far as possible from that of the children, and to deny the vital rôle of sexuality in the family, one could hardly conceive more effective arrangements for doing so.

The Development of Family Therapy

1. Family therapy as a meeting ground for different approaches

With the development of conjoint family therapy, we see a kind of quantum jump in which we have at last begun to 'get it together'. Of course, family therapy has and will continue to have, like every other profession, its 'lunatic fringe' – extremists who need to polarise the world so that everything they cannot cope with in their own psyche is projected into an opposite camp and then attacked, to keep it from getting back inside themselves. But what is striking –

indeed quite startling to anyone who has watched the development of psychological and therapeutic theory – is the astonishing degree of openness and willingness to share and integrate knowledge within this field between hitherto competing doctrines. Not only do different schools of dynamic psychotherapy find a common meeting-ground within it, but even dynamic and behavioural orientations are becoming integrated, as my book demonstrates and – I hope – takes a little further. Ethology, communication theory, genetics, social studies and other disciplines have found it a uniquely productive meeting-ground.

At the same time, such work demands not only a greater openness to different concepts and theoretical frameworks, but also presents a more forthright challenge to the therapist as a person, both from patients and colleagues. Working with families and marriages, it seems more difficult and less effective to work with a limited, professional part of oneself. We seem to find ourselves in question the whole time, obliged to put ourselves into the therapeutic equation, to change and grow at the same time as those we treat if the full capacities of the process are to be exploited; our own needs and values cannot be hidden if we are to be effective. The overall 'distance' between patient and therapist is also here further diminished, with control, challenge and stimulation operating in both directions, though at the same time the *range* of psychological distance is in many ways greater as the therapist seeks to identify with the mother, the father, an adolescent, a baby, a teacher, a policeman, by turns.

2. Family therapy and the family of the therapist

This change to a more open-systems orientation has not only removed some barriers maintaining the dualisms of intellect and emotion, of verbal and non-verbal, of conscious and unconscious, and of 'self' and 'other'. It seems also to help the therapist towards a different relationship to his own family. Although so much of our work in individual dynamic psychotherapy and psychoanalysis seems directed towards family dynamics, one often has the impression that therapists seem to view the family as rather like a prison camp from which an escape is being organised, so that the family dynamics remain a shameful secret, still hidden from the world, even though the analysand gains some measure of freedom from it. By contrast, the move towards conjoint work has encouraged a reconciliation with the real family and its internalised representation, and indeed, in the work of Bowen (1978) and Paul (1975), a physical, geographical return to the family of origin to explore it more deeply. Though I was at first doubtful what the value of such direct exploration of one's family might be, experience during a visit of the Nathan Ackerman Institute team from New York in 1973 was a great liberation. Revealing my family pathology openly, I began to discover that all the other professionals had very similar families; then I began to see that there was only one family, the human family, within which variations of certain parameters – failures to present and cope with certain challenges – provided all the variety we encounter. Now, seeing that I need not flee from my family, they are allies in the therapeutic task.

3. Co-therapy and the capacity to share

Another corresponding change has been the tendency to work in pairs, as co-therapists, and in teams. Whether or not one believes that this is more effective therapeutically, it is surely a very big move away from the possessiveness so characteristic of physicians and psychotherapists, and the tendency to talk of 'my' patient. There are of course theoretical indications for making use of co-therapy. For example, where patients have not been provided with satisfactory gender rôle-models by their own parents, or where psychotic confusion and destructiveness is so intense that two therapists, 'roped together', as it were, can undertake a perilous descent not possible for one therapist alone. But I think the tendency to work in pairs and teams is as much influenced by the realisation of therapists that, if the capacity to *share* underlies all satisfactory marriage and family life, they may need more practice at it themselves if they are to become more effective teachers. For example, in the Family and Marital Course I set up within the Institute of Group Analysis (which later became the basis of the Institute of Family Therapy),[3] a joint exercise was held each week with two of the small groups and their leaders, joined by my wife and me in which the express object was to oblige us, and the small group leaders, and the two groups, to face and struggle with our problems of sharing. Everyone found it immensely difficult, and the worst arguments that my wife and I ever had took place on the way home after these sessions.

Psychoanalysis then seems to make central some of those qualities that are most important in a mother as she succours her infant. Behaviour modification techniques base themselves upon activities which are more the responsibility of the father towards the older child. *It seems as if the whole pattern and purpose of conjoint treatment of the marriage and family group makes central those issues and problems which are involved in satisfactory sexual intercourse, in the sharing and reciprocity of the marital relationship in general, and of the whole range of activities involved in bringing up the family that results from the liaison.* From this point of view, the very striking differences in theory, practice, professional relationship and personal development within the family therapy movement, though at first rather surprising and puzzling, fall naturally into place.

Stranger-Group Psychotherapy

A review of the field

If we now turn to the field of stranger-group psychotherapy as a whole, in the same way as we have just looked at the field of family therapies, we encounter a very different situation. I find myself at sea, with no firm ground to stand on and with no clear and agreed landmarks. I find I do not know how to begin to organise the subject, or where to start in trying to make order and sense of it, for myself and my students. And I feel personally relieved to find from the literature, or from discussions with colleagues, that everyone else is in the same case and unable to help me, since I see that the whole field is still at a far more primitive stage of development than that of family therapy. It is characterised by competing schools which ignore each other's work or conflict with each other when they are forced to take notice at all, each striving to make sense and order of the field by oversimplifying, and ignoring or attacking those aspects of reality which fail to fit the preferred theory, rather than attempting the much more complex but infinitely more promising task of trying to see how the whole thing fits together. The theories range from extensions of individual analysis, with the 'psychoanalysis-in-groups' of Alexander Wolff (1949) at one

229

extreme; through Slavson (1950), still based on individual analysis while also rejecting group-process ideas, though at least acknowledging the educational value of the group; through Bion (1961) who at least attempts to look at the group as a whole, even if he reduces it in the process to an essentially dyadic situation again; to Foulkes and Durkin who come closer than any others to recognising the full potentialities of the *group*, though still (until recently in the case of Durkin) within an essentially psychoanalytic framework. Then we have the explicit use of learning theory and behavioural approaches, by therapists utilising much more fully and systematically the educational possibilities of the group. The encounter movement, psychodrama and EST are also much more open to the educational aspects of groups, the transmission of experience by *modelling*, giving much more importance to non-verbal communication. Then we have different types of groups for children, for adolescents and for adults. And we have small groups, large groups and therapeutic communities where there is ongoing contact between the sessions and the situation is somewhere between the stranger-group and the natural-group dynamic.

All these might be useful, yet we see a strange separation between them, and a failure to examine actively the possibilities of integration. In the United States there has been a split between those who saw value in the psychodramatic approaches of Moreno (1959) and others who preferred, like Slavson, to stay close to the psychoanalytic model. Similarly, one sees articles on Bion's work, both in this country and in the US, from which one would never learn that Foulkes existed, though I think the acknowledgement is a little fairer the other way round. There has also been a fierce opposition between the analytic group therapists and the encounter group leaders in the United States, and though I have personally found patients undergoing group analysis to make more rapid progress if they attend occasional encounter marathons, I am puzzled that I have not made a more systematic attempt to bring these two modes together rather than leave the possibility of the combination to chance and the patients' initiative.[4]

Similarly, though the fact that patients learn from each other is recognised in most theories, analytic as well as behavioural, somehow it seems to be 'something extra', something left to chance, something not fully developed and integrated within the theory of

230

group management. Moreover, the importance of the therapist's input (other than the provision of insight and analysis of resistance), while recognised in encounter methods and in family approaches, seems neglected in analytic theories. It is likely that the learning and modelling that goes on between therapist and patient, and between patient and patient, may be producing far more beneficial change than the accompanying analytic interventions, vital though the latter may be in periods of resistance and blockage of learning through projective processes. I realise that there are exceptions to these rather sweeping statements. For example, Helen Durkin (1964) says of the therapist's task:

> (1) He must be vigilant in bringing such misplaced and maladaptive resistances to attention. Yet (2) he is reminded that analysis of resistance is not an end in itself but merely an essential prerequisite to restoring normal input and optimal spontaneity. To accomplish this dual goal his own boundaries must be firm and flexible. *He can then exert his realistic authority in exercising his control function and employ his own creativity in stimulating spontaneous exchanges which lead to growth* [my italics].

2. Therapeutic factors in stranger-groups

The more we survey the situation, the more we see that this apparent backwardness of the subject is more apparent than real, and is due to the fact that the problems and possibilities involved in this kind of therapy are very much greater than in the others. In other words, stranger-group psychotherapy has potentially far more power and possibility than the forms we have considered already and it is not surprising, therefore, that we should find it a far more difficult continent to conquer. Let us just look at some of the factors involved. First of all, group psychotherapy (at least in the form Foulkes taught us to use) can have many of the advantages of individual psychoanalysis – indeed we do a brisk trade in, and are relatively successful with, some patients who have had ten or fifteen years' psychoanalysis without much movement. In a stranger-group, the individual is not limited in his progress by the family defences and the common family goals. He can regress profoundly, especially in large groups, to a degree often avoided in individual analysis, and can work out many problems at very primitive levels, if the group is run properly. He has a wide range of objects to work with in examining his transference responses. Indeed the group is

231

ideal for studying projective processes, since the anxieties which inevitably arise in the individual situation from the fact that the therapist is not only victim but also prosecutor, judge and jury, are reduced in a situation where any projective process can be scrutinised by people who are not involved in it, whether it takes place onto the therapist or onto another patient.

Similarly, as far as learning processes are concerned, the group offers unrivalled opportunities. Much of this takes place by direct interaction, but as Foulkes has pointed out, a great deal also occurs through vicarious learning by 'mirror reaction'. My own experience suggests that this is enhanced in large groups, where people can learn through watching the interaction of others, remaining safely concealed themselves until they feel more ready to venture out into the fray. The group also can reproduce the family, giving a second chance to re-examine and re-learn patterns first acquired in an unhealthy early situation. It also goes further than this since it is not an actual family, but more a microcosm of social life. *As Foulkes has emphasised, provided selection is reasonably careful the group as a whole is far more normal than the individuals contained within it, forming a consensus which is a reliable guide to the outside world and thus permitting constant re-socialisation and re-education in more healthy and helpful values and forms of interaction. Moreover, the stranger-group does not share (again given careful selection) the coherent defensive system that is such a feature of the individual or of the family group and marital couple. Both the analytic and re-educative work are carried on much more by the group itself, in contrast to the natural group or individual situation where the therapist has to take the main responsibility for change.*

Most important of all, and most fully utilised in the group-analytic technique, the stranger-group has one further invaluable advantage. If the therapist can learn to listen to the group-as-a-whole, and to understand and decode and express in ordinary language the communications he receives, a vast additional potential is tapped for the therapeutic work. The group becomes a computer, producing answers to the questions being fed into it in the form of the individual patients' problems, going far beyond anything that the individuals themselves, or the therapist – no matter what his skill – could achieve alone. In this the large group has special possibilities quite apart from the profound regression which it encourages and supports.

Moreover, the large group, if it is managed by a group of leaders who share the task and interact in an open and non-defensive way, takes the advantages of co-therapy, employed so usefully with families, a stage further. The rate and depth of change in group functioning, and in the personal growth of those participants one had information about, in the course of the six to eight weekly sessions of the large-group experience on our General Course[5] (where these principles are operative even though the focus is more on training than therapy) was startling every time I saw it.

Now, if psychotherapy by stranger-group methods has potentially at its disposal all these different modes of change and technique, many of which will be operating no matter what method is made central, and if the ideal technique would take account of them all, the task of producing an adequate and comprehensive theory is obviously very difficult indeed. To put all this together within a unified set of concepts and principles requires a degree of effort, and a conceptual leap beyond what has already been achieved in the field of family and marital therapy, to the same extent that the systems ideas developed to cope with the treatment of families have required a leap in our thinking far beyond the individual-centred dyadic theories which sufficed for individual psychoanalysis and for behaviour modification based on learning theory. Once this was borne in upon me, in the course of preparing this talk, I found myself beginning to feel much easier about the difficulty I have experienced in clearly explaining even to myself what it is I do in stranger-group psychotherapy. At the same time a certain feeling of frustration and inadequacy was replaced by a more positive feeling of challenge, even a certain excitement, which I hope others may share with me.

Why has it taken me twenty years of practice and thought to come to this conclusion – that I don't really understand very clearly what I am doing in this chosen work which occupies the greater part of my time? Partly, perhaps, it is due to the fortunate fact that the forces of repair and healing, and the motivation towards growth and change in our patients, are very strong, so that good results occur despite our own limitations and mistakes. The 'good enough' therapist, like Winnicott's 'good enough mother', does not have to be very good, luckily for the patients as for babies. But I believe there was another, more harmful cause: an 'Emperor's clothes' phenomenon whereby we have all somehow believed that an adequate theory of group psychotherapy existed, even if we ourselves had never quite been able to grasp it clearly. There is no point in going shopping if one thinks the larder is full, and we have therefore had no motivation to look at the whole matter afresh and try to remedy the deficiency. *Instead, when pressed to be more specific about what we actually do in groups we tend, like the donkey with the salad, to retreat to simpler concepts which have been more clearly worked out and with which we are familiar.* Very often I find that those colleagues whose training has been through individual psychoanalysis tend, when pressed, to retreat to psychoanalytic explanations; while I, happier with the concepts of the family system, tend to lay more emphasis on the recapitulation and correction in stranger-groups of disturbed family patterns. All this is certainly an enormous burden on our students, who in my experience tend to feel their lack of clarity about group functioning, and about the way to intervene therapeutically, is due to some deficiency in themselves. Often it is not. *It is due to the fact that, in addition to not having a clear and comprehensive theory to teach them, we are behaving as if we have.*

This is not to say, of course, that we do not have the *beginning*s of a theory, fragments which, like pieces of a jigsaw in the early stages of its assembly, form isolated parts of a picture of which we cannot yet see the whole. In particular, Foulkes in this country has directed our attention towards the whole, has made us aware of it, interested in it, often able to use it even if only in an intuitive way we cannot explain. In the United States Helen Durkin did much, in *The Group in Depth* and her subsequent papers, towards the integrated theory we all need, and she and James Durkin (1981) have gone far to develop the concepts of systems theory, so vital in the family field, in relation to the stranger-group where the idea of the 'system' so obviously corresponds to Foulkes's 'group matrix'.[6]

Since I was a student I always enjoyed teasing Foulkes a bit, and though he would get rather ruffled and on his dignity, he seemed in a curious way to enjoy it too, so that it became for me an important feature of a very warm and rewarding relationship I had with him, which I greatly valued. At this point in this lecture I was quite looking forward to the probability that he would have become a little pink and upset, having realised that I was saying that *he* was the Emperor in the imaginary finery everyone was applauding, and that I was saying that he really had nothing on at all, or at least that his apparel was rather threadbare. All great men have their weaknesses, and he was no exception. He prided himself on an ability for conceptualisation which in fact was not one of his strong points, not only in my opinion but according to the reaction of practically every audience of which I was a member, or in which I chaired his presentation. I can say that now he is not here, and I think it should be said, if only for the sake of the future of his own work.

What I was looking forward to even more, however, was the prospect of turning to him at this point, and saying that an Emperor, surely, was not an Emperor by virtue of his *clothes*. Anyone can wear fine clothes. An Emperor is a particular person; he is an Emperor by virtue of who and what he *is*.

Recognising this, I am able to see why I feel so rich in knowledge and confident in skills in relation to my stranger-group work, even though I still find myself so hopelessly inadequate when I try to formulate it.

Conclusion: The Legacy of S. H. Foulkes

From the beginning I was attracted to what Foulkes *was* rather than to his ideas alone and I see that, without putting it into words, or perhaps without even recognising it in theoretical terms, he demonstrated in his own person and way of relating an actual integration of a variety of the fundamental modes of influence I have already spoken about, combining many of those now recognised and utilised explicitly in family therapy, as well as in psychoanalysis and other theories. His openness, his ability to be completely human and natural without losing his objectivity and therapeutic stance, his absence of defensiveness and easy communication about his personal experience – including his past life and the family with which he had such a good relationship, his ability to learn from others at the same time as he taught, and to listen with equal respect to the most senior colleague and a new student, his ability in particular to learn from the group itself and to see psychotherapy as in some measure a shared exploration – all these things developed later as striking features of the family therapy movement. Even though he may not have succeeded in conceptualising it adequately, he *was* to a very considerable degree a living actualisation of the integration we are speaking about. And of course the ability to be, and to do, is the aim of therapy, to which the theories and techniques are only incidental. As those who have read my book on family therapy will know, I find the concept of 'modelling' of very great and central importance, and think it plays more part than we realise in all forms of treatment. Those of us who have had contact with Foulkes, like myself, have received vast amounts of knowledge through this modelling process, absorbing information by a kind of osmosis, without recognising it. This I think is the explanation of the profound change which often occurred in anyone who had personal contact with him even for a short time, and why his writings have not given him the degree of recognition he deserves.

It is our task, then, to take this knowledge he has given us, which we have absorbed and made part of us as food becomes part of our bodies, and together try to conceptualise it, to put it into a form which can be communicated more adequately across space and time, through the written word. It is our task to fashion for the Emperor the clothes that he deserves.

Notes

1 This paper was presented to a Scientific Meeting of the Group Analytic Society in 1976. It was first published in M. Pines (ed.), *The Evolution of Group Analysis.*

2 This process of pattern recognition was to become a central part of Skynner's clinical method. See the editor's introduction, page xxii above. The sudden and illuminating perception of patterns is an important feature of gestalt psychology (as distinct from gestalt therapy) and was brought into group analysis by Foulkes from the work of Kurt Goldstein and others. For this history see M. Pines, 'The Contribution of S. H. Foulkes to Group Therapy' in M. Pines (ed.), *The Evolution of Group Analysis, op. cit.* For the use Skynner makes of this process in family work see for example chapters 13 and 14 below, pp. 340 and 393. [Ed.]

3 See 'An Open-Systems Approach to Teaching Family Therapy' (appendix reference 31).

4 It is true we have tried to combine these methods in the family and marital training, and that many do so in their family practice as well. My colleague Malcolm Pines has also been notably open

in this respect, and while maintaining his basic position as a psychoanalyst and group analyst he has spent much time obtaining a thorough training in psycho-dramatic principles too.

5 See 'The Large Group in Training' (appendix reference 20).

6 See S. H. Foulkes, *Therapeutic Group Analysis*, and J. E. Durkin, *Living Groups: Group Psychotherapy and General Systems Theory*. For an account of the Foulksian concept of the matrix in psychotherapy and social relations, see J. P. Roberts, 'Foulkes' Concept of the Matrix', *Group Analysis*, 15, 2 (August 1982); G. Van Der Kleij, 'The Group and its Matrix', and G. Ahlin, 'Reflections on the Group Matrix', both in *Group Analysis*, 18, 2 (August 1985). [Ed.]

11 Reflections on the Family Therapist as Family Scapegoat

A major step towards integration of the family therapy schools is described next, as the behavioural/structural and psychoanalytic approaches are brought together. Until this point Skynner had seen the 'modelling' component in his work as akin to Minuchin's 'structural family therapy'. In the latter's work, interventions to change family hierarchies or boundaries are consciously planned on the basis of known general principles of family structure. These appeared different from analytic interventions based on insight.

It now became clearer to Skynner that his own behavioural interventions aimed at changing family structure were usually informed by feelings the family aroused in him when he opened himself to them and temporarily allowed himself to 'join the family system'. In other words, guidance for the 'structural' intervention was being provided by counter-transference information. This reduced the need for time-consuming history-taking or rational deliberation, as well as for recording or remembering previous interviews, so that therapy could be quicker and more effective.

This new understanding seems to have become available to Skynner through his readiness to open himself to painful issues in his own family background, with the support of other family therapists then exploring their own histories. The paper below explains how the therapist, in using this method, takes on a rôle similar to that of the patient or scapegoat in the family, though for a more constructive purpose. The therapist allows himself to become 'part of the problem' and speaks from a position closely identified with it in order to integrate, at first in his own person, previously disconnected elements of the family system.

Discussing this with Skynner, he was well aware that presenting the ideas in the personal way he chose to here could put him in a similar rôle with his audience and the profession generally, bearing the same dangers yet also possibilities for facilitating change. But

Group-Analytic Family Therapy

Skynner explained that the lecture which this paper describes was designed to enact the emotions he is describing in the presentation, as if the audience are the family and he is the therapist, containing and expressing in his own person some unsolved problem of the professional 'family'. Skynner regards *Families And How To Survive Them* as a book in which the same technique was used to maximum effect. And he attributes to this the profound life-changing experiences which members of the public often report to him after reading it.

J.R.S.

Introduction

In 'A Group-Analytic Approach to Conjoint Family Therapy' (Chapter 4 above) I gave an account of the family as a system. I presented the need for communication between parts of the system, and the need for some form of hierarchy within it, as if these two principles were separate.[1] I could see that these two considerations were merely two aspects of the same thing, two ways of viewing the concept of order. But I felt strangely unable to see how they connected with each other until I realised that these two aspects relate to the traditional rôles of male and female parent. Both parents are concerned with the maintenance of order and harmony in the family, but in their *traditional* rôles it is the mother who holds the family together and encourages communication and expression of feelings by all members, while the father is more concerned with issues of authority and control, and therefore with the maintenance of the parent/child hierarchy and with order and family structure generally. It would be surprising if the family therapist did not feel called upon to play both these parts when helping troubled families, and my earlier difficulty in integrating the two principles may reflect the difficulty such parents typically experience in cooperating over these two aspects of child management.

In what follows, I shall examine different forms of therapeutic intervention and advocate the use of an approach which combines psychoanalytic with behavioural principles. The resonance of the therapist's own emotions to the nuclear conflict in the family clarifies the underlying problem in the therapist's mind and indicates the most effective point of intervention. This 'counter-transference' reaction will mirror the family conflict between the denied emotion on the one hand, and the feared consequence which has led to its exclusion from consciousness on the other. The therapist now functions as a 'connecting apparatus' to restore the dissociated emotions to consciousness, or to enable the scapegoat to be reaccepted by the rest of the family (which are equivalent integrations at individual and group levels).

However, at this point the therapist also stands in the same dynamic relationship to the family as the scapegoat, since he now contains, and will feel both an urge to express and a fear of expressing, precisely those emotions or actions the family as a whole cannot cope with. If the therapist has gained the family's trust sufficiently, and can find a way to express or enact the feared emotion despite the family's disapproval, and at the same time can acknowledge and explain their fear and support them through it, the intervention can have immense impact. This accounts for the dramatic changes that seem to take place during or following sessions at which there is some strong confrontation between the therapist and some powerful person or subgroup within the family, such that the therapist affirms, in a forceful way, some values contrary to the family ethos and wins a battle as much in himself as with the family by doing so.

This active use of what psychoanalysts call 'counter-transference', as a guide to intervention in family therapy, is part of what characterises the group-analytic approach. I shall derive some principles for its application from an examination of my own emotions in the course of such work. And I shall consider the relevance of these considerations to questions about professional motivation amongst therapists, and to questions about their choices of therapeutic orientation.

Forms of Intervention

Interpretations

An *interpretation*,[2] as I understand it (unless it is carrying other hidden messages), is an attempt to point out certain possible connections among the patient's associations or actions which the therapist has noted, but of which the patient is seemingly unaware. It may be a comment connecting the material the patient brings about his outside life with the behaviour he is currently manifesting towards the psychotherapist. Or it may connect the patient's current behaviour, whether that described in his life outside the session or his reactions within it, with past events previously described, usually those involving interactions with important figures in his family of origin. Or the therapist may point out a recurrent pattern he has noticed in the patient's contributions over several sessions, whether they concern relationships outside, those with the therapist, or both. If the intervention is a true 'interpretation' without overtones carrying other hidden messages (such as 'No doubt your failure to pay your fees once again is yet another manifestation of your intractable hostility towards your father'), it is emotionally neutral, non-judgemental, provided for the patient to do with it what he pleases and without any pressure for him to take any particular action about it. The truth expressed may be painful, of course, and resisted on that account, but the analyst does not take any particular side or express any of his personal values, other than the value judgement that facing the truth, or reality, will lead to less pain in the long run whatever discomfort it may cause initially.

Interpretations are made, it seems to me, very much from the *mind*. They are *intellectual* constructions, and even though the therapist may use information derived from his feelings in constructing them, the absence of strong emotion or of the analyst's involvement as a person are seen as desirable features.

There are two particular advantages attached to the interpretive mode, seen in its truest form in psychoanalysis. The analyst seeks to make available to the patient additional information about the motivations underlying his behaviour, and about its consequences, which if accepted, understood and applied will give the patient more control of his behaviour and at the same time increase his awareness and responsibility for its effects. Whether the patient accepts this greater responsibility is left up to him – he is free to reject the greater freedom available if the anxiety at stepping off the safe and known ground of his neurosis is too great. Also, since interpretations are conveyed through the conscious recognition of linguistic symbols, the patient is aware that the analyst is proposing some change to him, and is thus sufficiently on his guard for rejection of the new information to be possible.

But there are corresponding disadvantages. The fact that communications take place at an intellectual level, from the *mind* of the analyst to the mind of the patient through symbolic abstractions, requires a long subsequent process of experimentation, trial and error, before this verbal information can make a systematic difference to behaviour. It is rather like the difference between being given an instruction manual for playing the guitar and actually producing music. This process of translation, whereby the concepts conveyed in the interpretation are ultimately transformed into new behaviour, is dealt with rather sketchily in the analytic literature: the term 'working through' being used liberally as a kind of conceptual putty or 'polyfilla' to fill the enormous gap between the changes originally expected to follow the interpretations, and the fact that these often occur only after long delay, if they occur at all, with a timing the theories do not explain.

The fact that the interpretive mode avoids taking over the patient's responsibility for his own life, though an advantage with patients who do not have very much wrong with them, who are capable of trusting relationships and who have some adequate sources of self-esteem, has serious disadvantages when used with the more seriously disturbed who are unable to carry this responsibility. In a recent paper Lieberman, Haffner and Crisp (1978) found this a central problem. They say, for example, that 'interpretations were a particularly troublesome problem in that many trainees felt that the essence of successful psychotherapy was to make authoritative interpretations as soon as possible. These frequently produced unexpected or undesirable reactions in patients unprepared for them' and '. . . requesting a patient to form a treatment alliance and to adopt an active and self-exploratory rôle within it often simply exposed the massive and perhaps insoluble personal and interpersonal problems which had led to the patient's admission to a mental hospital'. In their work with severely deprived, multiproblem families in slum areas of New York and Philadelphia, Minuchin and his colleagues (1967) came to similar conclusions, recognising that interpretations which might be appropriate and acceptable for healthy families were experienced by the very sick as destructive attacks, undermining their limited self-esteem, making unbearable the already severe state of pain in which they existed, and offering nothing for them to put in the place of their present mode of functioning.

Much of my own work has been carried out in the most severely deprived areas of the East End of London, with unusually high rates of delinquency, psychosis, multi-problem families etc., and there our findings were exactly the same.[3] Moreover it became clear to us that the neutral, analytic position from which we tried to operate, which was positively experienced by our middle-class patients as a form of respect for their freedom and independence, was experienced quite differently by the deprived and disadvantaged. The more severely deprived and disturbed seemed to feel this as a lack of caring on our part, a lack of interest in their welfare, a refusal to offer them some more effective mode of functioning which our higher economic status suggested to them we possessed, in place of the inadequate one they were utilising already, which our interpretations seemed only to shatter and leave in greater ruin than before.

Modelling

In our work with severely deprived families we found, like many other workers had done before in similar situations, that the therapist has to go beyond recognising and describing what he perceives as missing or distorted. He actually has to provide what is missing in the individual or family, or to correct what is distorted through his intervention. He must be actively involved, and seen to be involved and concerned, providing an input designed to change the family's functioning in a direction he believes, to the best of his judgement, to be in their interests. I have used the term 'modelling' to cover these types of intervention, partly because Bowlby (1967) had just proposed it as a preferable concept to substitute for the 'internal object' of psychoanalysis, partly because the word was already accepted for this type of intervention in the language of learning theory and behaviour modification, so that it offered the beginning of a common language for these two fields. But whether or not that word is used, others who have studied and been successful with the psychotherapy of the more inadequate and disturbed have found it necessary to base their work on an educative rather than an interpretive model, utilising identification processes, rôle-playing and active control rather than an intellectual, analytic, explanatory and verbal approach alone.

The great advantage of interventions based on 'modelling' is that the effects, when they are successful, are often immediate, or at least exceedingly rapid. If one provides an input of forceful control

245

to a family where the problems are all stemming from absence of clear structure and hierarchy, changes in the family functioning can be noticed during the interview itself. Subsequent increasingly heated exchanges show mounting anger inhibited by mounting anxiety culminating in an explosion where a parent 'reads the riot act' and a clear hierarchy is finally established and conflict and anxiety suddenly drop. This is very characteristic of school-phobics, who return happily enough to school after this final crisis. Parents often say such things as 'It was the worst week of my life', 'I would never have been able to bear it if you hadn't warned us what it would be like'. Among many similar communications, I had a Christmas card from the mother of a school-phobic child long under treatment at a Child Guidance Clinic, but sent for a second opinion to me by the general practitioner, and seen only once. It reads 'Thanks for the hell; but it worked. Have a happy and restful Christmas from the W – family. P.S. Jessica W – ex-patient; school phobia cured; thanks.' Needless to say, someone will have to validate these impressions of rapid change by controlled experiment, but everyone who has tried this approach will have experienced it as an unmistakable fact.

Though this approach was developed in the treatment of family groups, I have found it possible to employ it in group and individual therapy as well. There were two striking examples recently in a group of couples.

The first time he attended the group, a man who had been referred for tinnitus (after exclusion of physical causes and skilful but unsuccessful individual therapy) mentioned that this was worse when dealing with groups of students he taught at college. He was obviously frightened of their covert hostility, but instead of just interpreting this I described in an amusing way a situation parallel to his where I was supervising a staff group in which there was great resistance to discussing their work as group therapists. I explained how I was provoking them, putting them in double-binds, using paradoxical injunctions and systematically making them angry – which also had the effect of getting them to talk about the resisted subject by provoking them. At his second attendance at the group a week later he was quite remarkably changed, much more confident, assured, firm and relaxed. He said: 'I felt greatly relieved after last week's session. I found it very helpful. This week has been remarkably clear. I found myself listening to you (here he looked at me) last week and later adopting a rather different line as regards my students, taking the line that they would only get out of it what they put into it, and the rest of the week really went quite well.' At the same session a man who suffered severe depressions, and who until then had been unable to stand up to his persecuting wife, also seemed remarkably changed. From this point on, he stood his ground with her and was more confident, active and involved, instead of sinking back into lethargy. The husband in the recently-arrived couple, who began by describing the changes he had noticed in the week since he started, commented on the change which had occurred in this second husband, saying 'Well, it's just that when we first came two weeks ago you gave the impression that you were being dragged into this unwillingly and you were adopting a sort of submissive rôle; and now you are talking very positively in clear-cut terms which to me are very different from the way you were talking before!' The second husband replied: 'For myself I think I have seen a fair amount, I've personally benefited an enormous amount here, I don't know how, it's rather an odd process that goes on in this room – it's very strange. I can't put my finger on it – it's very simple but there is some sort of underlying thing which I haven't been really able to see.'

In these cases, the patients were aware of the model which had affected them, but this is in no way necessary. Indeed, the absorption of a model is more effective when it occurs unconsciously, and making the process conscious by commenting on it more often interferes with the process, partly by putting the person on guard by alerting him to something the therapist is trying to do to him, and perhaps also because the rapid learning which takes place through modelling seems to involve parts of the brain other than those concerned with intellectual thought, where awakening the intellectual faculty has a similar disrupting effect to trying to think about one's movements as one runs down stairs.

The disadvantage of this is that the therapist has to take over responsibility for the patient's life to a certain extent, and is in a sense imposing his values, which may of course be unhealthy or prejudiced. People who make modelling interventions exclusively tend to develop theories and techniques which are applied rigidly and uncritically, limiting the further development of the theories. And since criticism is not two-way, the personality and behaviour of the therapist do not come under scrutiny, so while inputs are received by the patients to improve their functioning, the therapists do not receive inputs from the patients which would improve theirs. I think this criticism applies for example to the 'structural family therapy' practised by Minuchin and his colleagues, and it is the main criticism I would make of conventional behaviour modification approaches.

The Therapist as Scapegoat: Using Counter-Transference

The therapist's anxiety as a response to the family's emotions

I have found it difficult to understand the anxiety I first experienced when I directly challenged the value system of the patient or family group and struggled to win the day. In Chapter 4 I gave an account of a session with a family which contained a scapegoated adolescent girl first referred for therapy twelve years earlier at the age of two. After trying to use a more interpretive mode in earlier sessions, I lost my patience in the fourth session, stopped stuttering and mumbling and confronted the parental couple with their dishonesty and manipulation, particularly the mother, who controlled the whole family with her psychotic depressions and suicidal intentions. The response was dramatic and immediate, as if for the first time they felt safely held and able to face the truth. From then onwards the scapegoat returned to the fold and no serious problems recurred over several years of follow-up (see pp. 65–81).

Despite this success I suffered intense anxiety when I presented this case to colleagues and at conferences. I genuinely expected strong criticism from my colleagues for stepping out of the netural, non-judgemental, supportive rôle my training had taught me to adopt. Yet on each occasion my presentation was received with seeming pleasure and approval, almost as if I were saying something everyone knew to be true but that no one had dared to voice. Why, then, had I been so apprehensive? I was certainly breaking with the traditional analytic stance by using a modelling approach here. But if I was simply providing a model which later events confirmed the need for, the degree of anxiety I felt about the possible adverse judgement of colleagues was quite inappropriate. The explanation, I now understand, is that in this method of family therapy the therapist stands in the same dynamic relationship to the family as a family scapegoat.

The scapegoat represents or contains those emotions or actions the family as a whole cannot cope with, and so deal with by denial, repression and exclusion. The inability to integrate the emotions represented by the scapegoat – anger, jealousy, sexuality, dependency or whatever it may be – in the family as a whole is the essential problem underlying all the more superficial dysfunctions and complaints. Reintegrating the scapegoat with the family, or reintegrating the emotions the scapegoat represents as normal and accepted parts of the consciousness of each individual, is precisely what the therapist has to bring about.

The essence of my technique is that I, as therapist, voluntarily and actively undertake the scapegoat rôle. I do not distance myself from the family emotions, but at first allow myself to be open and receptive to them. Gradually I become part of the family system and begin to feel, without being able to explain it, strong impulses of one sort or another. I may feel pain at their emotional isolation, anger at the chaos and disruption or irritated by their prudishness and impelled to make some provocative sexual remark. Of course, whether, when and how much I release this is a skill based on experience, like the timing of an interpretation. But I am now coming to believe that the dramatic increase in the speed of change I mentioned earlier is connected with the fact that instead of making *interpretations about* the repressed or denied emotions in families or individuals, from a detached and uncommitted position, I begin to *manifest* these emotions and actions in my actual behaviour. Instead of describing what is missing I actually *become* what is missing. The emotions the family cannot deal with begin to happen in their midst, in the actual person to whom they have come to save them from this dreaded experience, and short of escaping through the door they

249

have to cope with them somehow. Seen in this way the situation is so horrifying, so shocking that one might be surprised if something dramatic didn't happen!

At this point, of course, one is in the position of having struck with a very large salmon on very light tackle. Real skill, which can come only from long experience, lies in knowing when to strike and how to land the fish without breaking the tackle – to know whether, when and in what measure to release the denied feelings one is containing for the family as voluntary scapegoat, and how to provide the support, warmth and empathy which will enable them to retain the therapeutic alliance despite the fact that one has become, by definition, something they are programmed to reject. But the metaphor is not quite satisfactory. The therapist is the salmon and has to hope that the patient or family will not see too clearly that they only have to throw away the rod to escape.

All this begins to explain, at least for me, why I felt great anxiety at making this forceful intervention with the family concerned, but it still does not explain why I anticipated and feared the reaction of my colleagues when I described it to them.

The therapist's anxiety as a product of his personal history

It gradually became clear to me that these feelings I had experienced bore some relationship to the structure of my family of origin. In order to release the scapegoated child in the case described from her excluded position, or rather to release the whole family from the collusive need to maintain it (a collusion, in my experience, in which the scapegoat voluntarily shares, a fact which the Laingians do not seem to recognise adequately), I had first to enter the family system and to participate in their shared fear that a direct challenge to the mother's controlling rôle, particularly her maintenance of this scapegoating pattern, would threaten her sanity. The past history strongly supported a fear of this kind, for the mother had spent periods of as long as a year in mental hospitals with psychotic depressions and had been regarded as a serious suicidal risk. I recall very plainly what I felt during the crucial intervention when my voice changed and I began to take control of the situation. At that moment I decided I was going to drive the mother mad, if that was necessary, to take responsibility for her and try to see her through it. In fact, she did not go mad, and indeed the severe depressions did not recur at least during quite a long follow-up period. Instead, it quickly became apparent that she was locked into her depressed rôle by her fears of loss of attachment due to intense unsatisfied infantile needs. She defended herself against these by avoiding any form of dependency and maintaining the dominant position, but thereby deprived herself of what she needed. My disruption of the system led to a general recognition of this situation and an ability on the part of the mother to let the family repair her deprivation, this nurturing coming particularly, it is interesting to note, from the former scapegoat. Before I took hold of the system in an active way which combined control and support, this rearrangement had not been possible. Father, himself needy and deprived, was unable on his own to reverse the hierarchy his wife had established, and the two acting collusively blocked the children from playing a nurturing rôle to both, even though they were old enough by then to do so.

It then gradually became apparent to me how similar this situation was to that in my family of origin: my mother, who had lost her own mother at the age of four and subsequently defended herself against her own unmet needs by mothering everyone else; my father, who, needing mothering too much himself, colluded with this pattern and never really challenged it; my siblings and I, taking on the dependent, infantile projections to preserve them both, yet always resenting and rebelling against it. I saw that the family interview described had provoked such anxiety partly because I had challenged the collusive defensive pattern of my own family, no doubt re-evoking early anxieties that my own parents would turn into helpless children, or even go mad (which is what I think madness meant in my family) if they had to face the truth about themselves.

However, the apprehension I felt on presenting this particular case, and others similar to it, to professional audiences still did not seem sufficiently explained. At the same time, an increasing interest in the family dynamics of other mental health professionals, which I was obliged to study through my work in training group analysts and family therapists, led me to suspect that this family pattern might not be as personal to me as I first thought. The most convincing demonstration came in the course of the first Tavistock/Ackerman Family Therapy Conference in London. Various members of the

Conference, including myself, portrayed their families of origin through descriptions or through the physical technique of 'family sculpting', some of them publicly on stage. Over and over again, a pattern emerged similar to the family I described in Chapter 4, page 65, and similar to my own.

This has brought with it the marvellous realisation that, instead of having a secret and shameful family pathology from which I must escape, or which I must at least conceal (even if I suspect that other people have different but equally shameful and secret pathologies) there is actually only one family, the *human* family, showing different patterns because certain inputs or developmental challenges have been lacking and where we can all help each other to recognise and supply those missing experiences, in our professional family, if only we can acknowledge them.

Parental Identification Amongst Therapists

Perhaps this changed perspective about our relationship to our families of origin has something to do with a fundamental difference I have noticed between the colleagues I work with who have mainly been trained through psychoanalytic techniques alone, and those who have worked with families or undergone family therapy training. The family therapists seem more able to make constructive use of the disturbed earlier relationships in their families, and feel at ease at revealing these to colleagues. By contrast, despite real collaboration and friendship, I know little more now than I did twenty years ago about the early history or the families of origin of those colleagues whose main therapeutic experience has been individual psychoanalytic training, despite the fact that I have encountered them daily for up to twenty years. I have begun to wonder whether their therapy has been more of an escape from their early family history, rather than an attempt to understand, accept, be reconciled and find a new place within it.

This new perspective on one's family of origin brought into a different focus and relationship some observations about which I had become more and more certain during twenty years of experience of working with therapy and training groups containing almost every discipline of mental health professionals. In 'An Open-Systems Approach To Teaching Family Therapy' (appendix

252

reference 31) and in 'Make Sure To Feed The Goose That Lays The Golden Eggs: A Discussion On The Myth of Altruism' (appendix reference 42), I have pointed out how each discipline seemed attracted to their work, and to be potentially especially skilled at it, by the fact that they had shared a similar developmental problem to the clients or patients their agency served, or for which their particular form of therapy was most appropriate. I now began to see the transition from individual to group, and from group to family therapy, which I had undergone myself, as perhaps understandable in these developmental terms.

I had noticed that psychoanalysts attending our group or family courses had a strong inclination towards intimate, exclusive, one-to-one relationships, finding any threesome, let alone a group, contrary to their most comfortable mode of functioning. The behaviourists also did not find groups easy, but they were very different. While the analysts were most comfortable with a passive, accepting, understanding rôle, and were at ease in silence (though less able to confront, to challenge, or to move), the behaviourists were intensely uncomfortable with passivity, regression and silence, finding their particular skills more in activity, teaching, training, controlling, judging, valuing and generally hastening others towards mature socialisation.

The analysts therefore showed characteristics suggesting a strong *maternal* identification, the behaviourists a corresponding *paternal* identification. But the great difficulty each group showed at learning the skills of the other suggested a predominantly paternal or maternal identification which *also rejected the opposite rôle*, a dynamic which for the first time began to explain for me the implacable hostility of behaviourists or analysts towards each other. Indeed, there is more than hostility (since hate implies at least some kind of relationship), rather the curious inability of each group to hear what the other was saying, even to recognise them as existing in the world at all. My long work with families suggested that such one-sided choices of analytic or behavioural methods might be explained quite simply by identification with one parent in a marriage which was not a true union, in which indeed the budding therapist had been a substitute for one of the marital partners.

Given this possibility, the fact that family therapists had brought together behavioural and analytic concepts, and also tended to work together in male/female pairs, became understandable, even obvious. *To be a family therapist one surely has to bring one's parental identifications together, to have both possibilities available. Put most simply, one has to let one's parents be a couple, to accept, perhaps, that they have in fact always been a couple – to let them have intercourse. Analysis and behaviourism, like men and women, can be bitter adversaries; they can also unite to form something new and richer than either. One and one can make three or more, rather than two.*

Seen in this way, the fact that each mode of psychotherapy existed for quite a long period before the next one appeared, and the great difficulty we all experience at the transition points where we have to move from one to another, began to be understandable in a rather exciting way. It held the promise that we might structure our training programmes deliberately in a way that would systematically help people through the challenges or transitions presented, in the same way that the family helps its children from dependency to autonomy and self-control, then to peer-group participation and finally to sexual involvement, coupling and marriage.

It now also became obvious why I had personally found such difficulty in moving from the passive, analytic, one-to-one mode to a group, which already confronts one with the issue of authority, control and challenge which is absent in the former. There is a need for some measure of involvement in terms of the traditional paternal stereotype as well as that of the maternal one. *I also see why I over-reacted at first, taking the father's side against the mother (a fault often criticised by others) before I realised this error and recognised that the main issue was one of* sharing, *of bringing these two aspects together in oneself, and bringing the two parents together in a true partnership, before I could move on to think in terms of* couples.

The family and marital trainings I was setting up at the Institute of Group Analysis, which later came together as the Institute of Family Therapy, therefore came to be built explicitly on these principles.[4] I have suggested how the simple three-stage pattern seems to run through so many developmental processes, mother, father, couple; nurturance, control, sharing; passive absorption, argument, dialogue or group discussion; attachment, hatred, love –

though I did not fully understand the implications at the time I wrote it (*One Flesh, Separate Persons*).

Of course, I realise that I am not really saying anything that has not been said before. Many psychoanalysts, and family therapists coming from a psychoanalytic tradition, have helped us to understand these events in terms of transference/counter-transference, and more generally in terms of projective systems and the effect of projective identification on its recipient. Jung (1954) in particular, has spoken very clearly about the possibility of the analyst taking the patient's illness into himself, working upon it and returning it after some measure of constructive change. Recently Fordham (1969) has explored this issue in greater detail. I have already acknowledged the similarity of the type of intervention I am describing to the individual 'Therapeutic Consultations' with children described by Winnicott (1971) and to the cases described in Malan's (1963) research into the effects of psychotherapy where striking changes followed upon one session.[5] If my own experience has done something to take our understanding of the *process* by which such changes occur a little further, I will be fully satisfied.

Conclusion

By way of conclusion I provide an account of an interview that gives an unusually clear demonstration of the principles set out above, and which demonstrates the rich personal benefits which can accrue from this way of working. This was a demonstration interview on closed-circuit television in Nova Scotia, Canada, where my wife and I gave two workshops for mental health professionals.

> The family comprised four children between the ages of eleven and three, two adopted and two 'natural', together with the parents who both attended. The mother, who appeared a pleasant, effective and competent person, did most of the talking and described the problem: stealing in the second eldest – one of the natural children. The father was courteous and cooperative, but had little to say; indeed, there seemed little opportunity for him to add anything to his wife's very effective account.
>
> My wife, who shared the co-therapy task with me, conducted her part of the interview with striking confidence and

effectiveness, which I greatly admired. I found it difficult to think of anything to add, and found myself playing with the baby, whose sex I kept mistaking, and receiving presents of pictures from the other children where I repeatedly became confused as to which were the natural children, and which were adopted.

After about twenty minutes of this, I commented that there seemed to be no place for me in the interview because my wife was being so effective, and I related this to the difficulty the father seemed to be experiencing in contributing when his wife was so competent. The father identified with this comment, and obviously felt supported; although he had been somewhat resistant in earlier interviews at the clinic, it was reported later that he had left the session 'walking on air'.

My wife commented on the feeling of deprivation in the family, saying that her impulse was to pick up the referred patient and cuddle her. I said that I had felt a similar feeling towards the mother, as if her competent exterior covered strong needs for support and affection that she could not reveal to her husband for fear of disappointment. The mother confirmed that this was true, and was able to reveal that she had resembled the referred patient as a child.

The interview seemed to be effective in opening up dynamic patterns which had not previously been apparent to the professionals dealing with the case. But the interest in the present context lies in the way in which my wife and I quickly began to mirror the family dynamics in our co-therapy relationship. My ability to sustain an excluded, incompetent rôle (which extended even to letting the interview overrun the videotape, a mistake I had never made before) and my wife's ability to be over-competent and exclude me, provided the vital information which gave the key to the underlying parental dynamics. This quickly reached the mother's feelings of deprivation, and enabled me to support the father in perhaps the only way possible without diminishing him.

Following the interview, my wife was quite withdrawn and depressed, and this mood continued well into the next day. I am usually intolerant and attacking when this occurs, feeling that she has deserted me at a time when I most need her support, but the family interview had given me a new understanding of our own relationship, which changed my behaviour and enabled me to perceive her need for me to be supportive and accepting. This enabled her, in turn, to go through the depression and to face, constructively, a feeling of inadequacy which underlay it. Later in the visit, when she had recovered and I was beginning to experience the anxiety I always feel as endings and departures approach, I was able to reveal this to her more easily, and her ability to know this and keep me company in it, rather than to withdraw or to support me, was a good experience.

The incident, which put us both in touch more deeply with early deprivation experiences, demonstrated unusually clearly how the resonance of the therapists' emotions to those of the family not only provides the most effective point of intervention therapeutically, but often enables the therapists to gain better understanding and resolution of their personal problems.

Notes

1 This paper was first published in an earlier form in *The Journal of Family Therapy*, **1** (1979) 7–22.

2 'Interpretation' is being used here to represent one end of a continuum of therapeutic intervention, the other end being represented by the word 'modelling'. I am presenting these two techniques in a rather polarised way in an attempt to clarify these two extreme positions as they occur in my own work. I mention this because many analysts may use the term 'interpretation' to apply to a range of interventions along this continuum which may sometimes include strong emotional participation on the part of the analyst or even some degree of what I have called 'modelling', though these interventions in general would lie towards the 'interpretive' end of the scale rather than the other.

3 When this paper was reviewed in *The Journal of Family Therapy*, **1** (1980) 1–23, Treacher and Street's criticisms included an erroneous one that Skynner overlooks the important contributions made by Minuchin and his school to 'the problem of working with disadvantaged families'. As the chapter introductions and references to the early papers in the first section of this book make clear, Minuchin and Skynner were working with equivalent populations in New York and London

respectively, and their early papers supported one another's approaches. In his reply to Treacher and Street in the same edition of the *Journal*, Skynner writes: 'I followed Minuchin's work with great interest from 1965 because we were both working in poor areas of large cities, and I was excited to find someone who . . . had reached similar conclusions'. [Ed.]

4 See the section on training in chapter 13 below, page 372 and Skynner's 'Open-Systems Approach To Teaching Family Therapy' (appendix reference 31). [Ed.]

5 See Chapter 4, p. 61 and note 3. See also C. J. Groesbeck and B. Taylor, 'The Psychiatrist as Wounded Physician', *American Journal of Psychoanalysis*, **37** (1977) 131–139; and more recently, for the use to which Skynner's work is being put in the US, to establish the position of the therapist inside the equation of change, see J. P. Gustafson, *The Complex Secret of Brief Psychotherapy*, chapter 23, footnote 8. [Ed.]

12 Frameworks for Viewing the Family as a System

By 1982 when this chapter was written, the Institute of Family Therapy had become a flourishing independent organisation. Three of its staff, Gorrell Barnes who had worked with Skynner at Woodberry Down (see Chapter 1), Cooklin and Bentovim co-edited a textbook of contributions, largely by Institute staff, describing the further development of the open-systems approach they had begun with at the Institute of Group Analysis seven years earlier.

Skynner was given the task of setting out current views on healthy family functioning from three perspectives – systems, psychoanalytic and experiential – to set a framework for his colleagues' clinical contributions that followed. The editors' decision to begin by asking what is optimally normal or healthy, before other contributors went on to look at how to deal with the 'abnormal', was rather unusual at the time. What 'pathology' was being measured against was often based on a clinician's personal experience, sometimes of an idiosyncratic kind. If this was examined or at least made known it could free clinicians to view their clients more objectively. (Skynner's contribution to this literature on training and professional motivation awaits re-publication.) He had begun his career with such personal questioning, so here when he locates his enquiry not in the internal world of the therapist but in the empirical one of family studies and research, he is well-suited to his task.

His account of the systems and psychoanalytic perspectives provide good introductions to these ideas. But his account of the third, experiential perspective breaks altogether new ground as it reconciles modern with traditional views about health, growth and change, relates the new systemic techniques to analytic ideas about resistance and insight, and sets this in a broad context. As his contribution in the first section of this collection captures a point in history at which paradigm change occurred to introduce family therapy, this paper, along with its companions in this section, captures another point, the emergence of a 'second-generation cybernetics' as the homeostatic model in family therapy gives way to an evolutionary one.

The last part, an outline of the results of the Timberlawn studies first referred to in Chapter 5, provides research material corroborating Skynner's clinical findings. Problems of method were being found in the Timberlawn studies, notably by Gurman in the US. But the fact that he commissioned Skynner to produce the following Chapter 13, which also refers to the Timberlawn work, indicates that shortcomings in those studies do not invalidate the use Skynner makes of them. The complex information drawn from family studies which Skynner has condensed in tabular form enables the reader to gain valid and reliable information about family development and is a valuable resource for those with a theoretical interest in social relations and the family.

J.R.S.

Introduction: Systems Theory and the Concept of Homeostasis

Imagine the situation of primitive man, familiar with fire and able to build a crude hut, who comes upon a modern house, deserted by its occupants, which possesses an efficient central heating system.[1] After exploring the house, the man chooses a room to live in, but finds it a little too cool for his liking. The room is fitted with a fireplace and, recognising the ashes from previous fires, he gathers sticks, creates a flame by friction between pieces of wood, and lights a fire.

As the flames take hold and throw out heat, he experiences a pleasant warmth. But soon the room is as cool as before. He throws on more wood. Again there is a transient increase in temperature, but away from the direct heat of the fire itself, the room soon feels no warmer. Finally, when the wood is exhausted, the fire dies out. Having found it difficult to generate any warmth in the room even with a large fire, he expects the temperature to drop rapidly now that the fire is no longer providing heat. But even more mysterious, it hardly changes at all!

We know something that he is unaware of: the thermostat in the hall is designed to switch on the central heating boiler at a temperature set on its dial, and to switch off again when the temperature is a few degrees higher. The temperature of the air, at least in the vicinity of the thermostat, will move up and down between those two limits as the boiler is repeatedly switched on and off by the device.

Though the doors and windows to the exterior were shut, the rooms were connected with one another. This being the case, when the visitor lit his fire the warm air in the room gradually passed out into the hallway so that the thermostat exceeded its upper limit and switched the boiler off. Eventually, the more the fire warmed the room, the more the radiators cooled to compensate, keeping the temperature more or less constant. The reverse principle applied when the fire went out.

Here we have a simple, commonly used example of a *system* (in this case a heating system) maintaining *homeostasis* (keeping the temperature more or less constant) through the principle of *negative feedback* (the thermostat informs the boiler about the effects of its performance in achieving this task, in such a way that it *resists* change: i.e. it stops the boiler when the air gets too hot, and starts it when it gets too cold, rather than the reverse). It is able to achieve this throughout the house because the house is an *open system* (the doors are open or partly open, so that temperature changes in individual rooms are communicated through the house over a period of time). Had the *boundaries* defining the parts (rooms) of the whole system (house) been more rigid and closed (i.e. if the doors of the rooms had been shut), it would have been possible to change the temperature of separate rooms without affecting the whole house, and without producing the 'negative feedback' effect described.

Though this type of analogy has been used often enough before, we begin with it here because it emphasises the essential simplicity of the concepts of systems theory, provided they are properly understood rather than employed as a new jargon substituting for thought. The situation of the therapist who attempts to change one individual, without taking into consideration the effects of any success he may have upon the whole family system, is very similar to that of the man who lights the fire in one room of the centrally heated house. Changes may be achieved, to be sure, but they last a short time only, and are mysteriously reversed by influences invisible to all but the trained eye. The patient improves in hospital (subsystem boundary closed = door to rooms shut), but relapses as soon as he is well enough to go home, or perhaps even deteriorates during the visit of a parent (open boundary = doors to rooms open). Not only is it difficult to change him for the 'better', while he remains connected with his family; it is also puzzlingly difficult to make him 'worse' while he is part of this system. In short, the widening of our perspective from its earlier focus on the individual to an awareness of family and community systems has shown us some clear reasons for the extraordinary difficulty everyone has found in changing individuals separately from their family systems; or in changing families separately from the influence of their neighbourhood communities, as long as they remain in close psychological contact with, and so are deeply affected by, these larger structures in which their lives are led.

But the other side of the coin is as encouraging as the first is depressing. If the man who had tried to warm the room with his fire had understood the function of the central heating system, a slight movement of his fingers, taking less than a second and using scarely any energy at all, would not only have led to a change in temperature of exactly the order he was seeking through his laborious fire-making efforts, but would have maintained temperature at that level until he chose to change it. Similarly, once we begin to understand the feedback systems which govern the behaviour of families by the way they maintain homeostasis in the repetitive patterns of interaction between the members, we have the possibility of finding crucial points of intervention (like the dial on the thermostat in the heating system) where a small intervention can have a maximum effect of the kind we aim for upon the total functioning. Moreover, once achieved, this is likely to be maintained within a new equilibrium without further efforts on our part. The implications of this understanding for psychotherapy are radical and far-reaching. Some of these implications are described in Chapters 10 and 11. They describe a method of family therapy derived from this understanding and whilst they make reference to and draw upon theory, they do not discuss theory in any detail. I shall here be concerned with the theory itself in so far as it helps us to an understanding of normality in family life. It is this understanding, derived from group-analytic and systems theory, that directs us towards such crucial points of intervention as the one described above.

In the first section of this chapter, I will be looking at the functions of the family and its individual members. I will consider the family as an interacting system in the present and will study its cyclic operations without much reference to its past history. In the second section I will consider the family as a system developing over time in which newer members are being assisted by older ones to transcend a series of developmental stages. These two sections examine objectively described processes. In the third section I shall be describing the subjective aspects of family processes and will be concerned with consciousness and experience. In the fourth section I shall survey some of the research findings available at the time of writing to assess whether the theoretical views I offer are borne out by empirical investigation.

Family Interaction in the Present

Here I shall consider how the idea of *feedback* in understanding change, and the idea of *circular causation* in accounting for it, both point towards the need for a *general systems theory*. The constituent elements of human systems are *boundaries, subsystems* of various kinds, and a *hierarchy* which demarcates subordinate and super-ordinate subsystems.

1. Change and feedback

The example of the central heating system does not help us to explain the idea of *positive* feedback, for though this could be provided by changing the designs of the thermostat so that it turned the boiler on just above the temperature setting, and off just below the setting (that is, the *reverse* of the negative feedback condition), this arrangement would quickly lead to the air in the house rapidly reaching either its maximum or its minimum temperature and remaining there, an arrangement which could serve no useful purpose. But even this makes the point that positive feedback produces *change* rather than stability. An example may be seen in a business enterprise, where some proportion of the profits is fed back into the business itself. Then, the more successful the company, the greater the capital investment and the greater the productive capacity. Given an initial success and stable external conditions, the business will steadily grow with time. Similarly, if the business begins to fail, less money is put into capital investment, output diminishes, and the business shrinks at an increasing rate, leading ultimately to bankruptcy. The principle of positive feedback is thus at the root of *changes* in a system, whether in the form of growth or decay, just as negative feedback is concerned with keeping the system steady.

Biological systems will usually contain a combination of both negative and positive feedback loops of this kind, which together determine the 'balance of nature' at a given moment. Positive feedback alone leads to an exponential increase in whatever the positive feedback loop applies to, such as the screaming of a panicking crowd, where the *expression* of the panic through the screaming constantly magnifies the panic; or in the failure of the negative feedback or control mechanisms at the Three Mile Island nuclear reactor.

2. Circular causality

It will be seen that, in moving towards the systems approach, *causality* becomes *circular* rather than simply *linear*.[2] The model of linear causality with which we grew up no longer suffices as an accurate way of construing the world. This may be typified by the image of the movements of balls on a billiards or snooker table, where once we know the speed and direction of the intial shock, we can in theory predict the movements of all the balls according to the principles of Newtonian mechanics, and can accurately assess the transmission of energy from one ball to the next as they bounce against each other. Once we introduce the ideas of feedback and of circular causality, the individual billiard balls become equipped with self-steering gear or pre-programmed automatic pilots as it were, which ensure that they all fall into the pockets no matter what motion the player gives to the first ball, or alternatively, that they all avoid ever falling into the pockets; yet again, that they sometimes do and sometimes don't depending upon the state of the game, etc. If these billiard balls are already beginning to resemble living organisms, that is because, as Bateson (1972) constantly points out, such feedback loops are among the most fundamental character-istics of 'life'.

3. The need for a general systems theory

So far we have presented some of the concepts of systems theory in a manner which is in some ways more typical of a pre-systems, reductionist approach to science. That is, we have given examples of 'chunks' of the world, and though we have looked at the relationships within their boundaries, we have treated them as if they can be studied in isolation from the rest of the universe. To some extent we can do this, of course, and all science must be based on approximations of this sort if we are to simplify things sufficiently to be able to think about them at all. As Von Bertalanffy (1968) expressed it:

> The system problem is essentially the problem of limitations of analytical procedures in science. . . . 'Analytical procedure' means that an entity investigated be resolved into and hence can be constituted or reconstituted from, the parts put together, these procedures being understood both in their material and conceptual sense. This is the basic principle of 'classical' science, which can be circumscribed in different ways: a resolution into isolable causal trains, seeking for 'atomic' units in the various fields of science, etc. The progress of science has shown that these principles of classical science – first enunciated by Galileo and Descartes – are highly successful in a wide realm of phenomena.
>
> Application of the analytical procedure depends on two conditions. The first is that interactions between 'parts' be non-existent or weak enough to be neglected for certain research purposes. . . . The second condition is that the relations describing the behaviour of parts be linear; only then is the condition of summativity given, i.e., an equation describing the behaviour of the total is of the same form as the equations describing the behaviour of the parts; partial processes can be superimposed to obtain the total process, etc.
>
> These conditions are not fulfilled in the entities called systems, i.e., consisting of parts 'in interaction'. The prototype of their description is a set of simultaneous differential equations . . . which are non-linear in the general case.

If we take these ideas seriously, we see that we cannot stop at considering discrete parts of the world one at a time, but that, if these 'systems' principles are accepted as applying to any one scale or level of organisation, they must apply at all others and indeed to the whole. In the words of Von Bertalanffy (1968) again:

> There appear to exist general system laws which apply to any system of a certain type, irrespective of the particular properties of the system and of the elements involved.
>
> These considerations lead to the postulate of a new scientific discipline which we call general systems theory. Its subject matter is formulation of principles that are valid for 'systems' in general whatever the nature of their component elements and the relations or forces between them.

Thus, not only can the world be seen as made up of systems, but the systems at any level are parts of larger systems still, in the way that a number of fields are part of a farm, a number of farms in turn may be part of a district, the district a part of a county, and so on. To quote Von Bertalanffy (1968) again:

> The above considerations pertain particularly to a concept or complex of concepts which indubitably is fundamental in the general theory of systems: that of *hierarchic order*. We presently 'see' the universe as a tremendous hierarchy, from elementary particles to atomic nuclei, to atoms, molecules, high-molecular compounds, to the wealth of structures, electron and light-microscopic between molecules and cells . . . to cells, organisms and beyond to supra-individual organisations.

If we look at human life from this point of view, we may consider any level of organisation as a system. If we are focussing particularly on an individual, and regard that person as the 'system', then the larger system of which he is a part (the family) is termed the *suprasystem* and the *parts* of the individual are called *subsystems* (e.g. the nervous system, the circulatory system, the 'unconscious'). However, if we are focussing on the *family* as the system, then the individual is the subsystem (one of its parts), and some higher level of social organisation such as the extended family or community is then the suprasystem of which the family is a part. The whole of mankind can then be viewed as a series of concentric circles or 'chinese boxes', each circle containing smaller ones contained within larger ones. We hope that readers familiar with these ideas will bear with us while they are presented. A good grasp of them is essential for understanding modern developments in family therapy, and the difficulty in presenting them is somehow to combine an expression of both their profound simplicity and their profound generality. Emphasis on the generality alone tends to make readers shrink before the vast scale to which the ideas are applied, which suggests a daunting complexity; emphasising the simplicity alone, however, often has the contrary effect of causing the reader to brush the ideas aside as too trivial and obvious to need emphasis.

4. Boundaries

In our image of concentric circles, the circles themselves would represent the *boundaries* of the system (space) they surround, and in human systems, the boundary can be seen as the dividing line between one system and another on the same level, all marking off the system from its suprasystem and defining the subsystems within itself. Nevertheless, the boundary may be easier to define when it is spatial, like the membrane of a living cell, or the skin of a man. The boundary of a family has more to do with distinctions between the special degree of experience and information, shared among family members as compared with outsiders, and also a certain centring of movement or communication in space, in a dynamic rather than a static sense. Similarly, the boundary of a family subsystem such as the parental couple is recognised by the special degrees of physical intimacy, privacy and depth of information exchanged, and the degree and duration of commitment in their relationship, which is greater in the relationships of the spouses than other family members. 'Boundary' denotes a point of transition where *differences* can be observed in structure, function, behaviour etc. on either side. Seen from another viewpoint, the boundary is defined by the rules as to who may particpate in certain kinds of interaction and information sharing, and who may not. In technical terms applicable to all systems, Miller (1965) defines the boundary as that region round the exterior of the system 'over which there is less transmission of matter/energy and information than there is within the system or within its environment.'

5. Decider subsystems

The other vital part of the system is the *decider subsystem:*

> . . . the essential critical subsystem which controls the entire system, causing its subsystems and components to co-act, without which there is no system. . . . Of (the systems) only the decider is essential, in a sense that a system cannot be parasitic or symbiotic with another system for its deciding. A living system does not exist if the decider is displaced upwardly (to the suprasystem), downwardly (to the subsystem) or outwardly (to another system, i.e. parasitic or symbiotic). [Miller, 1965]

On different levels, the 'decider' may be the chromosomes in a fertilised egg, the nervous system of an animal, the brain of the nervous system, the queen of a colony of bees, the parents of a family, or the government of a country. The decider has the task of coordinating the activities of all the parts of the system in the light of what is required of it by events in the outside environment. The coordination must concern the welfare of the whole system, since the decider's fate is bound up with it. The decider is *responsible* for the whole system, in the original sense that it must be able to *respond* appropriately to the situation. And for this to be accomplished, it must receive information about the functioning of all the parts of the system, and of events in the environment.

The decider thus ensures the *integrity* of the system, and its continued *differentiation* from the environment. It has a similar function to the boundary, over which it has a varying degree of control, but they each protect the system's integrity in a different way, which, as we shall see, has great relevance to the functioning of families and their treatment. In the case of a nation, for example, a looser structure with more freedom to the subsystems may be possible if its boundary is relatively impermeable. Such is the case of Britain's tradition of democratic institutions, which owe much to its sea boundary and past naval power; or the similar case of the United States, divided by oceans from comparable power of potentially predatory neighbours. The democratic traditions of Iceland, even more protected by its inhospitable northern waters, are even older. But a powerful unity and identity may also be maintained despite a lack of protective boundaries of this kind, through shared values, information exchange and clear rules regulating insider/outsider status, as in the case of the Jewish diaspora.

6. Hierarchy

In addition to pointing out that a system cannot exist without its decider, Miller (1965) notes that: 'If there are multiple parallel deciders, without a hierarchy that has subordinate and superordinate deciders, there is not one system but multiple ones.' This is obviously of crucial importance to us in considering the division or sharing of power between father and mother in a family. Unless there is a hierarchy with either mother or father dominant, or some satisfactory system to ensure collaboration between the two parents, with either shared decisions, clearly defined separate rôles or even alternating dominance, there will not be one family, but two.

The Family as a System over a Period of Time

Our discussion of systems ideas has used mechanical/electrical examples to illustrate the principles; or, where living organisms

269

were discussed, it has focussed more often on short time-spans than on the lifetime of an individual. But the one certain fact of 'life' is the fact of death. Living organisms are not only vulnerable to irreversible damage from forces in their environment, including other organisms, but are actually programmed to self-destruct after a variable but limited period of time. Life involves continuance only for the group, not for the separate individual member, and to maintain it, new members must repeatedly be created, to replace those who die. In the transmission of human structure and function, the life cycle of the family is crucial. This section applies the concepts and ideas so far discussed to the different stages in the life cycle of the family and to the developmental processes responsible for growth and change.

1. The family as the unit of reproduction

If the continuation even of the group is to have any meaning, some *pattern* regarding the structure and function of the members, both as individuals and as a group, must be transmitted from the existing members to the newly created ones. Much of this process takes place in, and is the *raison d'être* of, the family, the smallest unit within which this process can be fulfilled. As dysfunction is dealt with in Chapters 11, 13 and 14, the focus here will be on *healthy*, 'optimal' functioning, the 'ideal' rather than the statistically 'normal', average or mid-range.

Transmission of the pattern is achieved through a number of routes. The act of sexual intercourse between the parental couple initiates the union of sperm and egg, resulting in a genetic programme different from each parent yet with characteristics of both. Protected at first within the mother's body, and later within the safety of the family boundary, matter/energy is at first absorbed from the mother's blood, then from her milk, later at the high chair and finally the family table. The basic shaping of this material by the chromosomal instructions is further modified by information absorbed by the sense organs from the environment, particularly from other family members. At first the very fact that things exist as they do and where they do; the fact that mother exists, has a certain shape, and gratifies; while at other times seems not to exist, does not gratify, but yet appears again repeatedly; all these begin to form within the infant's inner commuicational network 'a model' or 'map' of the outside world. During this early period in particular (say about the first year or so) a certain stability and regularity must obtain in the immediate environment to avoid such a bombardment of new impressions that the infant has no hope of bringing order out of seeming chaos, and is driven to 'blinker' itself from the overload. The mother's nurture, both in terms of feeding and of comforting presence, must also be reliable enough to keep *internal* stimulation within manageable limits, avoiding extremes of rage or frustration so that emotional responses may gradually be integrated and mastered. In the early stages, this requires the provision of a protective boundary by the mother while these delicate processes are proceeding, and the mother in turn will need to be looked after herself and to have the family boundary guarded by others, particularly the father or the grandparents, while she gives attention to her immediate task.

2. The child's discovery of some of its own boundaries

During this period, the infant will be discovering that *not everything is itself*, that it has an *edge* (boundary), beyond which its wishes and fantasies have less effect than they do within that edge (a task not helped by the fact that it discovers it does not have very much greater control even *within* that edge). It is not so much that the infant *thinks* he *is* the world, that he desires to be omnipotent and omnipresent, but rather that there is no reason to be aware that there *is* anything else, anything other than self, until the 'not-self' makes its presence felt. The infant is necessarily 'all', 'everything', indeed 'God', until it discovers otherwise. If its needs could be anticipated and met in every detail, it would perhaps have no reason to suspect that it was in any way separate from the rest of the universe. It is the *failure* of the environment to behave as if it is part of the infant's self that shows where the edge or boundary is, thereby providing the beginning sense of identity of self and of difference from others (though as already suggested, this failure must be carefully graded to what the infant can tolerate if it is to endure the painful realisation that it is *not* God, that indeed it is almost helpless and dependent on another being with a life of her own). Winnicott (1958) has developed this issue particularly clearly.

271

3. Learning about the insides and outsides of the system

Klein (1932) and her followers have emphasised how one aspect of this increasing discrimination between inside and outside, self and other, is an increasing ability to experience feeling-states as contained within that boundary, rather than as if pervading its view of the external world and distorting the infant's perception of it. And this process is accompanied by a similar integration of perceptions, both internal and external, whereby love and hate, and the gratifying or frustrating behaviour of the care-giving person to which these two states are related, are integrated instead of being kept separate. 'Good mother' and 'bad mother' become one mother, who is sometimes there and sometimes not. Pure love and pure hate, both overwhelming, become fused to form manageable ambivalence, sufficiently variable through the balance of its positive or negative components to permit management of attachment and rejecting behaviour. The infant is then capable of functioning in what Klein calls the *depressive position*. But poor handling of this developmental process, with excessive frustration in comparison to gratification, does not permit the infant to move beyond the *paranoid-schizoid position*, with consequent failure of integration and discrimination demonstrated by *part-object* relationships (failure to perceive others as separate whole persons), *splitting* (inability to integrate positive and negative aspects of external reality or of internal responses to them) and *projection* (the attribution to persons or events, outside the self, of unacceptable aspects too painful to contain within it). Even where depressive-position functioning has been to some extent achieved but is only precariously established, stressful situations, leading to frustration too painful to bear, may cause a regression to paranoid-schizoid position functioning (as with a badly handled hospitalisation).

4. The need for adequate parental boundaries

If these tasks characteristic of the first year of the infant's life are to be accomplished, one requirement which is perhaps not always sufficiently emphasised is that the parental figures should be clear about their own boundaries. If the primary care-giving figure (usually the mother) is not clear and secure about her own personal boundary, she will be unable to help the infant to find its own. If we mark the border defining the northern boundary of England, we automatically define the southern edge of Scotland as well. In similar fashion, parents who are clear about their own boundaries and secure in their identities will automatically provide relationships through which the child can define itself, even without any conscious attempt to address this problem. Parents who are unclear in this matter tend to attribute feelings to the child which belong to themselves and vice versa, making the infant's task of self-definition more difficult. Moreover, even in the earliest stages of nurture of the infant, when some degree of fusion between mother and child is appropriate through the mother making her boundaries more permeable, empathising with the infant's experiences, Winnicott's state of 'Primary Maternal Preoccupation' (1958) may be rendered impossible if the mother's fragile sense of identity makes her fearful of entering into this kind of relationship, with all its vulnerability. Nevertheless, if all goes well, mother and infant are able at first to enter this symbiotic state, with father and perhaps other relatives protecting them.

As the child grows, the mother is able to re-establish her own boundaries once again, 'failing' the child's expectations sufficiently to enable it progressively to define itself. In this she will usually be aided by the father, who at first protects the *family* boundary and 'holds the life line', permitting the mother to enter safely into this degree of regressive interaction with the infant, then 'hauling her back' by stages towards a primary investment in the marital relationship, rather than in the child. It is perhaps this crucial function of the father in assisting the mother and child to grow apart progressively, thereby facilitating self-definition and independence, which makes the presence and active involvement of the father so important in the next stage, comprising roughly the second and third years of life. He needs not only to restore close affectionate and sexual bonds with the mother as the child needs her less, but also to form a close and trusting relationship with the child. By nature of the fact that he is inevitably a different person in some respects, he provides another dimension through which the child can find out who he is, just as a ship, by taking two bearings on different landmarks, can establish its position. The first year of the infant's life is concerned more with the taking in of matter/energy and information, with the establishment of a *base*; in the second

273

period the infant ventures out and explores the environment. Increasing maturation of the nervous system brings with it increasing control of movement, freedom of action and the possibility of impinging actively on the surroundings. The child begins to walk, talk and gain control of its sphincters, and with these new powers comes the possibility of collaborating with, or resisting, the parents.

5. Parenting and social information

During this phase therefore, the foundations are laid for self-control and initiative, the achievement of some compromise between the demands for social conformity and the satisfaction of personal needs, together with the development of a sense of identity, differences and separateness from others.

If the child is to accomplish this, the parents and other adult figures must achieve a satisfactory compromise between on the one hand providing freedom and space to try out these new powers, in order to test out the developing will and initiative and to explore the world, while on the other hand also providing sufficient firmness, limits and requirements that social demands be heeded, in order to enable the child to feel safe in his explorations, and to internalise those social values needed to make satisfactory relationships with others. The prominence of the issue of toilet-training during this period led Freud to call it the 'anal' phase, though it seems likely that the importance of this issue is due to the fact that it is the first battleground on which the conflict between the desires of the individual and the demands of the society are fought out.

During this second stage, problems may arise if the parents are uncertain about their own identity or have unresolved conflicts over accepting authority or social demands, as well as where the father is absent or ineffective, or the parents are unable to collaborate over discipline and setting of limits.

6. Parenting and sexuality in childhood

A third phase, reaching its height around four to five years of age, is characterised by childhood precursors of adult sexual feeling, by interest in its own and others' genitals and in the origin of babies. Something like a love affair with the parent of the opposite sex develops, together with jealousy of the parent of the same sex.

If the parents are at ease with their own sexuality, have a

satisyfing sexual relationship themselves, and treat these manifestations with respect and naturalness, the foundations are laid for
sexual confidence in later life. The son discovers that mother finds
his sexuality pleasurable, but that she belongs to father and is not
available; the daughter likewise with her father. The child gets the
message that its sexuality is good, but that it cannot marry its
parents and must first grow to adulthood and find a partner of its
own. Thus, the stage is set for entry into the wider world to learn, to
socialise, to join the peer-group from which the eventual mate will
have to be selected.

Once again, a balance is needed in the parental response between
over- and under-reaction to the child's sexual initiatives. The
combination of infantile sexuality, the oedipal conflict and the
incest taboo provides a powerful motive force towards differentiating from the family (since sex cannot be obtained there) and
learning to cope with the wider society (where sex will ultimately be
available). What is required is an enjoyment by the adult of the
developing child's experimentation with its new-found power to
charm others through its physical attractiveness. But the response
needs to be relaxed and light-hearted; indeed fun – a game that feels
safe despite its excitement.

As in other periods, several related developmental tasks are
being addressed simultaneously, and the achievement of one automatically helps the others. During this third period, the child not
only has to accept that the parents are more powerful, but that they
have a special relationship with each other and enjoy some pleasurable and indeed profoundly exciting activity from which he or she is
excluded. The child has to cope with *jealousy* and *exclusion* from
relationship. Not only does omnipotence suffer a further necessary
reduction; in addition, if this stage is successfully surmounted, the
foundations of the capacity for *sharing*, and so for group membership, are soundly laid.

The child is now well prepared to join the peer-group, a capability
which may have been enhanced by previous experience of coping
with siblings; and the child goes to school. Interest and energy are
transferred increasingly from the earlier biological tasks towards
those of learning and socialisation. The earlier, more open expression of sexuality appears to go underground, though interest
remains active enough, even if confined to discussions or satisfac-

275

tions of curiosity with peers. Males and females divide into separate groups, and even become antagonistic. Teachers and other adults provide new models, additional landmarks on which children can take their bearings to find their own preferred positions and directions. The parents become less important, though they still provide a safe base and refuge.

For the parents, perhaps the main requirement is to let the children go. Mothers who themselves find it hard to separate and differentiate, and have gratified themselves vicariously during the earlier period, make separation difficult for the child. But in normal circumstances, separation is aided by the fact that the mother is glad to be freed of the burdens of the first five years, and is able to resume her separate interests and activities. Almost all studies of marital satisfaction have shown that during the period between the birth of children and the time they go to school, marital satisfaction reaches its lowest ebb, increasing in general thereafter just as it decreased before.

7. Parenting and sexuality in adolescence

The approach of puberty sees a return of the interest in sexual issues which burst into prominence with the hormonal changes at the beginning of adolescence. The child is under biological and social pressures to accept and gratify the emerging sexual needs, and to move away from the primary attachment to the parents and the family towards the loyalties of the peer-group. At the same time, the struggles towards independence alternate with a resurgence of childish dependence, while demands for sexual freedom are counter-balanced by fears and a desire that the parents will set limits within which experimentation can be safely attempted. All being well, the responsibilities of adult sexuality are gradually approached, first by engaging with the opposite sex in the safety of the same-sex group; then pairing off, but in a crowd; then perhaps in small groups or foursomes; finally in couples.

The task of parents is particularly difficult at this stage, for whatever they do will by definition be 'wrong'. They will be seen as too restricting at one moment, uncaring at another; prudish kill-joys when they set limits, neglectful and indifferent when they do not.

Parents who are ill at ease with their own sexuality, or whose sexual relationship is unsatisfactory, will find the task more diffi-cult. They may either become over-restrictive out of anxiety, provoking unnecessary rebellion, or avoid the provision of age-appropriate limits through their need to deny the problem. Such difficulties will be all the greater if the sexual relationship between the parents is unsatisfactory and precarious, since their inhibitions, which may not be insuperable as long as sex is kept in the back-ground as a low-key issue, may be magnified intolerably when they are confronted with the crude directness which can characterise adolescent sexuality.

What is required of the parents at this stage is that they them-selves should have completed their own developmental tasks to an adequate degree. They need to be sufficiently at ease with their own sexuality to enable their adolescent child to be at ease too. The sexual relationship between the parents needs to be satisfying and enjoyable, so that it encounters no threat from the powerful sexuality developing in another member of the family. Instead, they can serve as a positive model to the adolescent that sex, within a loving and responsible relationship, can reach its greatest fulfil-ment. And the parents need to be sufficiently complete in them-selves, as well as satisfied with each other, to contemplate the departure of their offspring from the home without being threatened with pain and loneliness, indeed, to anticipate with pleasure the prospect of freedom from child-rearing tasks.

8. Adulthood and the new family

As the young person reaches 'escape velocity' from the emotional 'gravitational field' of the family, the tasks of gaining acceptance by, and finding a responsible place within, the wider society, become paramount. The individual learns to work, becomes self-supporting, explores the social and physical environment more extensively, and after 'playing the field' to gain more adequate experience of intimate and sexual relationships, is drawn increas-ingly towards a more permanent liaison, culminating in marriage. All these changes require an increasing ability to see oneself as part of a group, to see others as oneself, to accept a certain discipline and self-sacrifice so as to permit the performance of a common task, whether the production of goods in work or collaboration in setting up a home.

The parents, during this time, will be enjoying their new-found freedom, if healthy; or if not, they will be experiencing loneliness and emptiness, behaving as the 'interfering in-laws' of the stock music-hall jokes, and anxiously and impatiently awaiting the arrival of grandchildren.

The arrival of the new-generation couple's first child brings profound changes and new stresses. The wife, who is likely to be working, is obliged to give this up, at least temporarily, and to undergo a total change of lifestyle. Overnight, she loses her former freedom, which may have been greater than she had ever possessed, and must devote most of her attention to serving another individual who makes constant demands for attention by night as well as by day. The husband usually has to continue to work and also to support his wife in this task, while much attention and care she formerly devoted to him is now suddenly transferred to the baby. If he shares more fully in the child-rearing activities, as is common nowadays, the change for him is greater still. The sexual relationship is disrupted for a period, and may be impaired for months or years through fatigue and distractions. The marriage comes under particular stress for all these reasons.

At this stage, and particularly around the time of the birth, the calm supportive presence of the original parents (now the grandparents) provides a crucial input. They have been through it all before, and can reassure by the way they take it in their stride. Through their affection and support, they can help to replace the mutual support which the couple formerly gave to each other, and now must give to the child-rearing task. Other relatives can play similarly supportive rôles, and it is likely that the larger extended families of previous times sustained young parents through this stage more adequately than is commonly possible today.

9. Completing the life cycle

In our description, one cycle is now complete. The original parents, now grandparents, will continue to play an important part in their children's and grandchildren's lives, acting as supports and resources in times of stress and crisis, mediating between the parents and children at times, and providing alternative models. It remains to say something about the later phases of the life cycle. after the children have 'left the nest'.

The beginning of this later stage will tend to coincide with what is often called 'the prime of life'. The powers and achievements of the man will often be at their zenith. The woman, too, will still be vigorous and energetic. If she has maintained and developed her own separate life, identity and interests outside the child-rearing tasks, she can now enjoy a period of unprecedented freedom and achievement. Both partners will normally still be sexually vigorous, and if the relationship has been nourished they may find the sexual relationship more enjoyable at this stage than at any previous time.

As they move beyond this phase towards their sixties, physical strength and energy will diminish, and the most active pursuits will begin to be curtailed. If achievement earlier has been adequate, success and recognition will seem increasingly unimportant. Interest and enjoyment turn increasingly inwards, and the satisfaction of these final years will depend on the extent to which an inner life has been preserved and built up through the earlier years. Simple activities and pleasures become increasingly valued, and life becomes easier as unnecessary complications and meaningless ambitions drop away. To the extent that this change is possible and negotiated successfully, retirement becomes something to look forward to, and brings a new and different phase of enjoyment.

The death of the partner is part of this final phase, followed eventually by the death of the one remaining. To the extent that earlier phases have been successfully surmounted and enjoyed, death will be experienced as a part of life, accepted like the rest.

During this last phase, the caring rôles reverse, the parents taking on a caring and managerial rôle towards the grandparents as the powers of the latter fail, even the grandchildren enjoying helping to look after them. By the time the grandparents die, the parents have already been prepared, therefore, for the new responsibility they undertake as they now become of grandparental age themselves.

This last part of the cycle has been described here in terms of those who manage it well. They will usually be those who have managed earlier phases in the same satisfactory way, so that they have developed satisfactory resources within themselves, and are therefore able to give more willingly, and to demand less. For those who earlier have been deprived and unhappy, looking to each other or to their children to remedy their own deficiencies, the later years are likely to extenuate the feelings of loneliness and misery, so that far from being a support to their children and grandchildren they instead become increasingly demanding and burdensome.

10. What makes for success in the family?

For the process to proceed in a satisfactory, optimal fashion, there should be throughout life a steady decrease in the egocentricity and narcissism of the early infantile stages, counter-balanced by a progressive increase in real skills, interests and internal resources. The meaning and purpose of life must come increasingly to lie in something beyond the individual, ephemeral self, beyond any one other person, and even ultimately beyond the family. For this to occur, not only must interest extend beyond the self to the family, and beyond the family to the wider community, but as we shall see from the Timberlawn Research, some sense of a transcendent value system is needed which can enable the individual to survive even the death of loved ones without destruction of meaning.

It should be clearly emphasised again, perhaps, that this chapter deals throughout with health in the sense of optimal function, in contrast to dysfunction of varying degree which receives adequate coverage in other chapters. Individuals and families conforming to these criteria are of course rare, as Olympic athletes are rare, but we have enough evidence (outlined later) to be confident that these high levels of effective function are approached in a small minority of the population. We will not expect to encounter them in our professional work with dysfunctional families, and we will not expect to raise the level of function of families we treat to this optimal level, not least because, as Beavers (1977) has pointed out, mental health professionals are most unlikely to be functioning at that level themselves (and might not be very good at the job, or might not be motivated to take it up, if they were).

The Experiential Life of the Family

In the two preceding sections, we have looked at the functioning of the family and its individual members. First we considered the family as an interacting system in the present. Secondly, we considered the family as a system developing over time, where newer members are being assisted by older ones to transcend a series of developmental stages (in psychoanalytic terms), or (in behavioural language) at age-appropriate times to acquire a series of behaviour patterns through learning-processes of one kind or another. In both cases, we were viewing the family and its members from outside, from an objective standpoint where the actual behaviour observed would suffice to describe the situation (as those with a behavioural orientation in fact strive to do). If we were confining our studies to central heating systems, steam engines or electronic calculators, these approaches would suffice.

But humans not only go through the motions of interacting and developing, they also achieve something called *experiencing* their lives. They can be 'conscious' (whatever that means) of some aspects of their surroundings and even of themselves and their relations to others. How much this function is shared with other animals we do not know, and humans appear to have additional abilities, almost certainly not shared by animals, of being *aware of their experience*, of being able to be *aware they are conscious*, as well as to be critical and analytic towards it, and to communicate and share that second-order (or as in the case of the present communication between writer and reader, *third*-order) consciousness with other members of the species.

These functions *can* be described in behavioural terms, and a visitor from space studying the human race might have no alternative. But therapists are themselves human, sharing the fact of consciousness and other characteristics of human functioning, so that we are able to *put ourselves in the place of* the different family members to some extent, approaching the problem from inside rather than outside.

It is customary to take these capacities we share for granted, to talk *as if* we do not need to examine or explain them and can safely use them without questioning their nature. This is adequate, when they are functioning effectively, and reflections upon the nature of consciousness can be left to philosophers. But family therapists (and indeed psychotherapists generally) have found their attention drawn particularly to this question because it appears to be precisely in this area of consciousness, communication and control that confusions arise which lead to family systems becoming dysfunctional.

Little or nothing is known, even at the present time, about the *purpose* of consciousness or self-awareness, if by 'purpose' we mean the difference it makes to our functioning, the way we would be likely to operate if it did not exist. In his most recent book Bateson (1979) for example states that:

> ... the fact of image formation remains almost totally mysterious. How it is done, we know not – nor, indeed, for what purpose . . . there is no clear primary reason for using images at all or, indeed, for being *aware* of any part of our mental processes.

Bateson remarks only that

> ... speculation suggests that image formation is perhaps a convenient or economical method of passing information across some sort of interface. Notably, where a person must act in a context between two machines, it is convenient to have the machines feed their information to him or her in image form . . . it will be reasonable to guess that mammals form images because the mental processes of mammals must deal with many interfaces.

Bateson does not elaborate on this, nor is there at present much help to be found, as far as I am aware, from psychological or philosophical writings so far available. We must resort therefore to 'common sense': that is, the writer must speak from what he assumes is common between his own experience and that of his readers. This, as we shall see, is fraught with difficulty, but it is at present the only way to proceed.

1. Consciousness, insight and change

For fifty years or more, it was 'received wisdom' among most of those engaged in psychotherapy that 'insight', that is, consciousness of certain connections between 'symptoms' (limited aspects of present behaviour) and present behaviour in a more general sense (e.g. as shown through 'transference') or with past experiences or memories, was necessary for change in such undesired behaviour patterns to be possible. *Why* consciousness of these connections should produce this effect was never explained very satisfactorily. The rise of behaviourism, and of behaviour modification techniques of treatment, bypassed the whole issue of consciousness and demonstrated that certain types of symptomatic behaviour, at least, could be altered by submitting the patient to new experiences, according to principles elaborated in learning theories. Later still, adherents of communication theory models, particuarly those interested in the pathological and therapeutic effects of 'double-binds', claimed that insight *followed* change, rather than the reverse (Watzlawick, Beavin and Jackson, 1967). Yet others have discovered that 'prescribing the symptom' (instructing people to try to stay the same, or to get worse) can also paradoxically result in relief of symptoms (Selvini-Palazzoli *et al.*, 1978). And if we go beyond orthodox techniques of psychotherapy, we find that encounter groups emphasise the importance of insight and change, while EST (Erhardt Seminars Training) claims similar improvements by getting people to accept that there is no need to change at all. Religious conversion experiences under powerful emotional pressures, or the emptying of the mind of its habitual activities in meditation, or concentration on some impossible question such as a Zen Koan, all appear capable of bringing about changes in habitual functioning which are more or less enduring.

It seems as though heightened consciousness or 'insight' is *in some way* associated with the kind of changes psychotherapists are interested in bringing about, though the connection is clearly less simple than was at first thought.

2. Pathology as the fragmentation of experience

What does seem common to the problems that present to a psychotherapist is a kind of fragmentation of the individual's capacity for experience, whereby he cannot from time to time survey his life as a whole, and is therefore prevented from noting discrepancies which may have arisen between the functioning of different subsystems, which upset the efficiency of the whole organism. Most human behaviour is carried out automatically or semi-automatically, by learned mechanisms which are outside awareness, even if conscious application is necessary to acquire the skills in the first place. When learning to drive a car, for example, we have for some time to give our full attention to the task to the exclusion of everything else, but it would be a disadvantage if driving continued to need the full range of our conscious attention. It is greatly to our advantage that 'lower' centres of the nervous system take over this routine task, leaving our conscious attention free for other purposes (perhaps planning the rest of our day) except when unexpected emergencies alert the higher centres to the need for the maximum available attention.

Group-Analytic Family Therapy

We may reasonably surmise that many subsystems develop integrated, efficient performances of this kind, which will not usually enter conscious awareness *unless something goes wrong* and threatens the organism's well-being or integrity. But if we survey the kinds of situation in which individuals or families complain of symptoms or relationship dysfunctions and seek psychological help, we soon discover that *one common feature of all such situations is a discrepancy or discordance between different parts of the total system concerned.* Some piece of behaviour or experience is labelled a 'symptom' precisely because it does not appear to have meaning and purpose within the functioning of that individual as a whole; indeed, at first sight it appears *dys*functional, interfering with other functions. Similarly, when a family presents complaining of an individual member, the behaviour of that individual at first appears to be disruptive of the functioning of the whole family, and meaningless in terms of the way they are operating as a unit.

Whatever form of therapy is employed, what usually seems to be required is for the therapist to bridge the fragmentation between the deviant individual and the group, or between the deviant subsystem within the individual and the individual as a whole. From a bird's-eye view he makes a deeper sense of the fragmentation and also discovers a more comprehensive organisation in which the deviant subsystem can find a constructive place (once the fragmentation is overcome). Consciousness can then be regarded as something like a 'working party' set up to view the functioning of some large organisation, the various parts of which may be working effectively, but each of which has grown and changed in such a way as to be out of balance and so impairs the functioning of the whole. Once the organisation is brought into balance and is working effectively again, the working party has served its purpose and its energy can be turned to other tasks.

3. The integrative function of consciousness

It is suggested, therefore, that consciousness (in the sense of that self-consciousness to which psychotherapists refer when they use the term 'insight') plays some part in bringing subsystems into more harmonious relationship when some form of imbalance or fragmentation has occurred. As Bateson suggests, such consciousness is not an end in itself, but more a sign that the organism is undergoing some temporary period of self-examination and adjustment. When we are functioning most harmoniously, and are most in tune with our surroundings, we may be intensely aware (in the sense of being alive and responding), but such 'self-consciousness' is at a minimum.

In terms of our present concern, this would imply that healthy families are not, in general, particularly preoccupied with insight, with self-understanding, or with self-consciousness in the sense of a self-absorbed, self-improving stance in relation to themselves and each other. We may expect that they will be open, responsive, spontaneous, alive, and that they will show evidence of a vivid and enjoyable inner world, but this is another matter altogether. We may nevertheless expect that they will have this faculty of self-examination readily available, and that they will not be inhibited in using it should some interruption to their fruitful interaction indicate that something is going wrong. They will be insightful in the sense that they will not hesitate to examine themselves and their relationships openly and objectively, as well as in the sense of having much information already available. But once the problem is resolved we may expect that they will put this capacity for self-examination aside until it is needed again, and get on with their lives. Watching the interaction of healthy families on videotapes, one is struck by the openness, spontaneity and relaxed, alive, enjoyable exchange between the members. One is also struck both by their absence of self-preoccupation or morbid unnecessary introspection, as well as by their willingness to look frankly at themselves when this is made necessary to fulfil a task or because some problem has arisen.

Watching the operation of such healthy families, one is also impressed by the relative absence of persistent, irresolvable conflict, despite the remarkable individuality and difference among the members. Yet conflict and strife seem, much of the time and in most families and social situations, almost as if they are inevitable conditions of human functioning. Freud, among others, certainly took this view of human nature, believing that a constant struggle between the demands of society and the urges of man's animal nature was the price of civilisation.

4. The partialisation of consciousness – another form of fragmentation

There have nevertheless been exceptions to this pessimistic view, stemming from both secular and religious sources. It is interesting how Bateson (1972) links the two so naturally in the following quotation from one of his essays:

> Aldous Huxley used to say that the central problem for humanity is the quest for *grace*. This word he used in what he thought was the sense in which it is used in the New Testament. He explained the word, however, in his own terms. He argued – like Walt Whitman – that the communication and behaviour of animals has a *naïveté*, a simplicity, which man has lost. Man's behaviour is corrupted by deceit – even self-deceit – by purpose, and by self-consciousness. As Aldous saw the matter, man has lost the 'grace' which animals still have. I shall argue that the problem of grace is fundamentally a problem of integration and that what is to be integrated is the diverse parts of the mind – especially those multiple levels of which one extreme is called 'consciousness' and the other the 'unconscious'. For the attainment of grace, the reasons of the heart must be integrated with the reasons of the reason.

In his thirteen-part BBC television series exploring the world's religions, Ronald Eyre (1979) found, despite the diversity of theological views, that the ideas of being *whole*, of being *healthy* and of being *holy* all had similar meanings, in the sense that Bateson has used above.[3]

One real dilemma appears to be this: *all man's achievements, including the capacity to symbolise, the transmission and storage of knowledge through language, the development of science, technology and all that has stemmed from these, depend in fact on man's capacity to fragment, to isolate, to pursue in his thought and imagination ideas and structures which are* not *bound by his senses, and are not just a reflection of the world he experiences before him at a given moment.* He can *abstract* from his experience (Korzybski, 1933) selecting those features of events which interest or attract him, and ignoring others. Having done so, he can play with these as a child plays with bricks, manipulating them and testing out different possible relationships as in logic, mathematics or physics. Then, these experiments with images or abstractions can be tested out and verified or refuted by actual experiment in the real world.

This is the process underlying all scientific discoveries, whereby experiments with inner experience which led to the formula $e=mc^2$ enabled us to harness atomic energy. But the same principle underlies all human behaviour, except that described by the simplest principles of learning theory. Why is the process sometimes helpful and constructive, and what makes it often harmful and productive of inner and outer conflict? The answer has been expressed in many fashions, but is essentially simple. *It seems we are so constructed that our capacity to abstract and isolate parts of our experience readily proceeds past the point where it ceases to be helpful and instead becomes harmful. This point is reached when we focus our attention and interest on the isolated part to an extent where we forget its origin in the larger whole.* We are then no longer aware of the experience we are focussing on as part of a *system*. We cling to the isolated part, which becomes the 'truth', and cease to return to the more profound and complicated source in our total living experience from which this 'truth' derived. Moreover, experience is a flux, the world is in motion, we and others are changing constantly; yet, to employ this process of abstraction, we must take static cross-sections of our experience of constant change.

All 'truth' arrived at by this process must, for both these reasons, be partial, temporary. As long as we remember this, our abstractions help us to deal with, and adapt to, the real world. But as soon as we forget that ideas and abstractions are isolated, frozen elements of an interacting system, we lose touch with the real world (which is the same for all of us and about which we can hope to agree) and begin to live in different incompatible worlds in our heads (over which we can only argue and struggle).

The process can be seen at all levels of human interaction. In the individual, such clinging to a past reality explains the fact of 'transference', where patterns of response appropriate within the family are carried into later social relationships, including marital interaction and the bringing up of children. Even within a family, children may retain inappropriate dependent attitudes towards their parents, and their parents may retain infantilising attitudes towards them, long after both are physically mature. Families as a whole can similarly fail to learn from experience, and instead perpetuate unrealistic images of the family, and of the outside world, over generations. Furthermore, whole societies may become arrested in their development through valuing isolated abstractions above the flux of experience from which they were originally derived, as in the extraordinary interruption for 1,500 years of progress in medicine after the work of Galen.

Is there some crucial factor, open to the possibility of our control, which can influence the use of our vital capacity for abstraction towards that constructive and creative use which remembers the whole system and does not confuse the part with the whole, rather than towards increasing identification with abstractions, uncontrolled imagination, and finally madness? No question is more important for the survival of mankind, and there is already some suggestive evidence from studies of child development and the functioning of healthy families which may help us towards at least a partial answer.

5. The unconscious as a closed internal system

Studies such as those by Bowlby (1967, 1973, 1980) and Winnicott (1958) with human infants, and similar experiments on infant monkeys by Harlow (1966) and others, demonstrate clearly that a certain basic stability, regularity, reliability and consistent support is needed from the mothering figure if the infant is to feel sufficiently secure to venture out away from her into the environment, to explore and begin to cope with change, unfamiliarity, newness. The 'attachment behaviour' described by Bowlby seems essential if the child is to leave the mother and venture increasingly into the strangeness of the surrounding world; the safety of Winnicott's 'holding' situation is vital if the child is similarly to engage in the experimental, spontaneous activity of 'play'.

If this safe situation is not provided, the individual deprived of its security clings to the original mothering figure, or to some substitute for the order and regularity she should have provided, whether in the form of possessions, obsessional activities and routines, recurrent fantasies, or rigid forms of 'thought' or belief that must be protected from correction by external reality for fear they may be changed and lost. The individual's development inevitably becomes arrested. Consciousness loses its integrative power and even in the individual's self-consciousness, there are matters which the person cannot allow himself knowledge of.

Once this situation exists, it is understandable that the individual concerned seeks contact with others who will not disturb it, or who will at least disturb it as little as possible. Stability is maintained at a terrible price. The individual has developed a closed internal system affecting his capacity for consciousness which shuts him off from the experience available to him. People with different views, and above all those who are open to experience, who are constantly learning, growing and revising their ideas, will represent threats to be avoided, and will be seen as aliens if not enemies. It will be safest to keep contact only with family members who share the same rigid beliefs. To the extent that social needs must be met outside the family, friends and acquaintances will be chosen because they hold similar views, rather than for the challenge and stimulation of difference. For the intimacy of marriage (if the individual is able to contemplate this step at all) a partner will be chosen at a similar level of developmental arrest, or in Bowen's (1978) term 'degree of differentiation', who will reinforce rather than undermine the frozen belief system.[4] And children, when they arrive, will be indoctrinated into the pattern and prevented from growing, or at least not helped to grow, beyond it. Thus the pattern can perpetuate itself over generations, as Bowen has pointed out and Fisher and Mendell (1956) have demonstrated experimentally. On this account the unconscious is not a closed internal system but one which is shared by a family or social network.

6. Analogic and symbolic communication

In addition to Bateson, others influenced by his work at the Mental Research Institute at Palo Alto in California (Watzlawick *et al.*, 1978) have emphasised the vital importance of the different modes of communication in relation to these processes. In the passage of Bateson's writings quoted earlier, the most crucial phrase is his suggestion, following Aldous Huxley, '. . . that the communication and behaviour of animals has a *naïveté*, a simplicity, which man has lost. Man's behaviour is corrupted by deceit – even self-deceit . . .' The behaviour of animals, including their simplicity, their completeness, their 'grace', has much to do with their limited capacity for communication, as compared with 'civilised' humankind. Though some higher animals show rudimentary capacities of symbolic communication, animals communicate almost entirely through non-verbal, analogic means. They express their relationships to one another, their feelings and intentions, through actual, though partial and incomplete, expression of them. A threat to attack another member of the species, as in competition between males for available females, is communicated by all the bodily preparations for such an attack (posture, gesture, facial expression, growling etc.) which is demonstrated to be a communication and not an actual attack only by the fact that it is inhibited in its development at a certain stage, and stops short of completion. And if the communication is successful (that is, if it intimidates the competitor without the need for an actual fight) the rival will respond with some bodily signs of submission, sufficient to reduce the threatening behaviour of the opponent. The weaker dog presents the jugular vein to its more powerful rival, whose attacking behaviour then ceases.

Such non-symbolic, analogic communication is *similar in form to what it represents*; it is communicative in that *certain relationships present in the event represented are actually reproduced*. The difference between the real thing and the communication about it is that *a part of the whole is representing the whole*. Even the dance of the honey-bee, indicating to others in which direction nectar may be found, *reproduces* in the pattern of its dance the angle between the direction of the goal and the direction of the sun, and it similarly indicates the distance to be travelled by the speed of its dance, which bear a certain relation to one another. The matter does not quite stop here, and Bateson (1979) has clearly demonstrated how the capacity of some higher mammals to engage in *play* is a vital step towards the kind of experimentation that humans can engage in through use of symbols.

In humans, non-verbal, analogic communication continues to play a vital part. It is the only form of communication possible in the earliest years of the infant's life, and probably remains the most important mode of communication mediating social control in small groups, including families. For example, children may ignore the verbal appeals or expressed threats of punishment by parents over a long period, but their behaviour immediately changes the moment they recognise that the parents 'really mean it', through information conveyed by the non-verbal channel. The parents' glaring eyes, tight lips, flushed faces, harsh voices and tensed bodies are recognised as 'for real' in a way that words may not be, for they *are* real, a part of the developing reality.

The closer humans remain to this non-verbal, analogic mode of communication, then the simpler, more natural and more 'graceful' their social behaviour is likely to be. 'Primitive' tribes, or children and relatively uneducated country people in 'civilised' societies are likely to retain more of the simplicity and grace of animals, since the nature of this form of communication makes self-deceit difficult. But both man's greatest achievements and his greatest vices are consequences, as we have already suggested, of his capacity for the symbolic, digital mode of communications: the capacity to let one thing *stand for* another in a way which is completely arbitrary (though of course *agreed*), where the symbol bears no concrete relationship whatever to what it symbolises; the relationship is a representational one. This ability to use *symbols* (together, of course, with the abstractions or concepts for which we agree they shall stand) enables us to create an infinite variety of inner worlds, differing in any way we wish from the actual one we inhabit. Among other logical expressions underlying this possibility is the word 'not', indicating whether a communication is true or untrue, a communication impossible to make in the non-verbal, analogic mode except by beginning an action and stopping short of completing it (e.g. a threatening fist which does not actually strike) (Watzlawick *et al.*, 1967). 'To be or not to be' is now a question which can be asked, of others or oneself.

However, this development, which makes possible our greatest power, our knowledge, brings with it also the capacity for self-deceit: the ability to create, believe in, live in, a world at variance with the evidence of the senses. Expressed in mythical terms, man has 'eaten of the tree of knowledge of good and evil': he has the possibility, which he did not possess before, of choosing between what is and what is not, of inhabiting an inner world at variance with the facts actually encountered. This new-found power brought with it, inevitably, a loss of that innocence, simplicity and 'grace' that bound us tightly to the evidence of our senses. Now humans could arrest their development at any point they wished, choosing to maintain an inner world which fitted the facts at one stage of development, but which became increasingly inconsistent with later reality. If one wished, one could remain omnipotent, God, co-existent with the whole universe, as if there were no other individual

291

capable of independent action. Alternatively, one could remain a helpless baby to be perpetually looked after, a defiant toddler, or an endlessly competitive child in an oedipal triangle, and so on. However, this is only possible if the individual restricts communication with others to a degree which prevents the discrepancy between the inner and outer worlds from being exposed. Where this discrepancy is at its most extreme, communication may have to be so completely restricted with others that the individual withdraws from all social contact, and is considered 'mad'. Where the discrepancy is less extreme, the individual may ally himself or herself only with those members of the family who support the fantasy, rejecting others; he may choose friends, or a spouse, who do not challenge it; and if there are children, he may train them to behave in ways which reinforce rather than challenge the lack of congruence between the inner and outer world. Thus, families as a whole tend to develop shared systems of fantasy or levels of developmental arrest which they collude to preserve from correction. The collusion may extend to comunities, even nations, as exemplified in the fairy-tale 'The Emperor's New Clothes'.

Nevertheless, the real world cannot be got rid of, and maintaining the fiction must inevitably be a constant struggle. Unless a solution of complete social isolation is chosen, someone, sooner or later, may give the game away. The most complete family collusion will be threatened by the fact that children have to go to school, that parents need to meet others in the course of their work, or that members are forced into social contacts through other external pressures. Even within the family, some may find themselves paying a higher price than others to maintain the fantasy, and be more inclined to rebel or escape. In addition, the threat to the fantasy system does not come only from outside. The actual achievements of each individual, in work, in relationships, in sexual attractiveness, etc., somehow have to be reconciled with the fantasy system.

7. Disordered forms of communication

As a natural result of these constraints, communication, when disordered, becomes extremely complex. Everything an individual says about himself will tend to be influenced by three criteria; or, to put it another way, three simultaneous messages will tend to be contained in every communication:

1. What is said must not contradict too obviously the inner fantasy world.

2. At the same time, it must not be so inconsistent with reality that it will actually be challenged by others.

3. A third message will also be sent (usually non-verbal) exerting emotional pressure on the recipient not to notice any discrepancy between messages 1 and 2, and also not to comment on the inevitable ambiguity and confusion that will have resulted from trying to express two incompatible messages at once.

Needless to say, persons are selected as spouses or friends who will obey the non-verbal command and not challenge the contradictions. Those who do challenge them, including children in the family, will be rejected.

The above complexities in communication, which arise quite naturally from the possibility of clinging to a static inner world at variance with the changing outer world, have been much described under the general term 'double-bind'. However, the explanation given here for this disordered form of communication seems altogether simpler and more understandable than those offered previously. For example, the terrible power struggles, at once immensely destructive though totally denied, seen to characterise the families of schizophrenics by the Milan group (Selvini-Palazzoli *et al.*, 1978), which they attribute to pride or *hubris*, become explicable if each member of the family is in fact seeking to preserve a fantasy that he or she is omnipotent, has no boundaries or limits, is an unchallenged 'Lord of Creation'. The word *hubris*, which indicates a pride which seeks to rival the gods, is absolutely appropriate. If all family members cling to fantasies of God-like omnipotence, the very *presence* of other independent beings challenges this fundamental assumption. And since to compete with them openly is to admit that they exist, even competition with such non-existent beings must be denied.

Where nature produces a poison, she usually also provides an antidote. And so it is with the fragmentation described above which forms the source of so many human ills. Though it is made possible by the unique human capacity for symbolic representation of abstrac-

293

tions from sense experience, by digital as well as analogic communication, our ability to use symbols also enables us to overcome some of these difficulties which symbols themselves make possible. For we can use language to speak about language, and to study disorders of language. Language enables us to step away from reality sufficiently to make independent conceptual thought possible, and so to create science. It also enables us to lose touch with reality and go mad. But by taking a second step, we can stand back from the disorder of language itself, study it and correct it. Should something go wrong with this second-order (meta-level) process, the detachment made possible by conceptual thought enables us to stand back from that in turn, and so to observe and correct our errors, indefinitely.

Research into Differences Between Healthy and Dysfunctional Families

In the preceding pages, we have tried to look at the family from various perspectives as a *system*, and by returning to the simplest first principles we have tried to understand what the concept of *healthy function* would mean in such a system. Let us now turn to a survey of some of the actual research findings available at the time of writing, derived from observation of actual family interaction. Needless to say, in the brief compass possible here, only an outline of the main findings can be given, leaving out many important details which restrict the validity of the results. References are given, however, whereby the reader can explore the subject further.

We might ask first whether healthy functioning is common or rare. No adequate answer exists to this question as regards the family as a system, but we may judge from existing knowledge regarding the mental health of whole populations that truly healthy families are few and far between. For example, the Midtown Manhattan Study (Srole *et al.*, 1962) found 23.4 per cent of a representative sample of the population demonstrating clear psychological dysfunction, and discovered only 18.5 per cent who were definitely well. The results for the Sterling County Study (Leighton *et al.*, 1963), though including a more rural area, found closely similar figures, with 20 per cent clearly dysfunctional and 17 per cent indisputably well. It is important to begin with this kind of information since many existing studies are faulted in that they compare the obviously ill not with the most well, the 'optimal' extreme which forms the main focus of this chapter, but with a measure of 'normality' based more on the statistical average (that is, the *mid-range* group), comprising about 60 per cent of the population in the studies just mentioned, whose mental health was uncertain.

1. Westley and Epstein

Westley and Epstein (1970) examined in detail the families of a group of college students who showed unusual emotional health, and compared these with families of others who were particularly disturbed. The differences observed were checked against a study of a sample of the college population. The main findings were as follows:

1: Regarding the degree of *rôle differentiation between the parents*, the parents of the healthiest children showed a *balance between separateness and overlap* whereby many of the parental functions were shared, but not to a point where there could be confusion between the male and female identities or paternal and maternal rôles and responsibilities. Families where there was greater overlap in the rôles and responsibilities of husband and wife, and less differentiation in the sexual rôles, produced fewer healthy children, often suffering themselves from rôle confusion. The 'traditional', rôle-segregated, male-dominated family, was even worse in its effects, and the degree of ill health in the children was exceeded only in families where the traditional rôles were reversed, with the father performing more than half of the 'traditionally female' household and child-care tasks.

2: Regarding the issue of *power*, the healthiest families were found to be *father-led*. Next most healthy were those which were *father-dominant*, next *egalitarian* and worst *mother-dominant*.

3: In general, it was found that a *high frequency of sexual intercourse*, together with *increasing sexual satisfaction during the course of the marriage*, appeared related with mental health in the children. But this was not always so, and the

295

existence of a *warm, loving and supportive relationship between the couple* appeared even more vital, compensating considerably for emotional ill-health in either husband or wife. Where this was the case, parental pathology appeared to be contained and coped with within the marriage, rather than passed on to the children.

Westley and Epstein were studying individual family members rather than family interaction, but in a comparison of matched pairs of families with or without a schizophrenic child, Mischler and Waxler (1968) found similar features. The more healthy families showed a strong parental coalition, but with authority exerted through negotiation rather than in a rigid, authoritarian way. Communication was clearer and more direct in the more healthy families, and was either rigid and fearfully-controlled, or confusing and disruptive, in the patient-containing families.

2. Stabenau *et al.*

A third research study (Stabenau *et al.*, 1965) has already been summarised in some detail in my previous book, *One Flesh, Separate Persons*. A comparison of families producing children who are either schizophrenic, delinquent or showing neither of these disorders showed many features consistent with other studies mentioned here, and

> . . . in the families with a normal control, affect tended to be appropriate, modulated, positive and warm. Interaction featured considerable autonomy, a coping rather than manipulative or controlling pattern in dealing with the family members, and a goal of mutual understanding and satisfaction. Family organisation was flexible with clear rôle differentiation and expectancy. Empathic awareness with each other's rôle was evidenced, and the father and mother tended to interact in a complementary manner.

3. MacGregor *et al.*

A fourth study, less scientifically rigorous than the others but reporting the treatment of families containing adolescent members who displayed various degrees of disturbance (MacGregor *et al.*, 1964), has been summarised in Figure 4 below.[5] It shows many differences between more healthy and less healthy families, corresponding to those of the other studies. In moving from the description of families of the most disturbed children to families of the least disturbed children, one is struck again by: the importance, for health, of parental cooperation and collaboration in the matter of authority; a clear inter-generational boundary whereby the children cannot disturb this coalition by forming stronger parent–child coalitions themselves; mutual acceptance and understanding; and an ability of the family as a whole to relate to, and accept help from, the larger community. Once again, moving from the families of the most- to the least-disturbed children, one is impressed by the dominant position of the mother, and exclusion of the father in the former; and the position of increasing leadership taken by the father as the degree or level of disturbance decreases.

4. Timberlawn Studies

However, even though these studies show much agreement, none of them examined the actual behaviour and interaction of families which ranged from the most dysfunctional to the extreme of health. A first step in this direction has been taken by the group at the Timberlawn Psychiatric Research Foundation (Lewis *et al.*, 1976). Their research, which reports the first successful attempt to find and examine in depth the personalities, relationships and typical inter-actions found in families at the extremes of health (rather than the mid-range or 'average') is of such crucial theoretical and practical importance that the reader is strongly urged to read the published material of the researchers themselves, either in the book just quoted or in the more popular presentation, omitting much of the detail of the research design (Lewis, 1979).[6] I have attempted to summarise the results in three tables, which have been seen and approved by Lewis, and which should help the reader to grasp their main findings rapidly.

In Figure 5, the spectrum of level of psychological function is divided into three main categories, for the sake of simplicity. It will be seen at once that in moving our attention from the characteristics of the most severely dysfunctional families, through the mid-range group, to the most healthy families, the change is not simply one of degree, nor is it simply a steady increase or lessening of certain features. Instead, in certain respects, progress towards health appears to take place in a step-wise fashion, by stages.

For example, the situation in the most severely dysfunctional

Figure 4. Relationship of Child and Mental Pathology in Galveston Multiple Impact Therapy Study[5]

	SCHIZOID — Infantile functioning (Schizophrenic reaction)	AUTOCRATS — Childish functioning (Near-psychopathic or near-psychotic reaction)	INTIMIDATED YOUTH — Juvenile functioning (Neurotic reaction)	REBELS — Pre-adolescent functioning (Personality disorder)
Classification of children in four groups on basis of degree of arrest				
Degree of arrest in development (author's classification – Erikson's concepts)	Basic trust	Autonomy	Initiative versus guilt	Fear of intimacy and of establishing own identity
Developmental task failed	Oral (depressive position) Capacity for relationship	Anal Acceptance of authority	Phallic Acceptance of sexual role	Genital Pairing, sexual intimacy
Reason for referral	Bizarre, deviant behaviour	Aggressive, destructive, manipulative; refusal to accept limits	Neurotic traits, phobic symptoms, anxiety, psychosomatic symptoms	Rebellious and delinquent behaviour; demand for 'freedom' without responsibility
Group competence of referred patient	No group life	Demands own way, so plays with younger children or acts out destructive impulses for older groups	Desire to be one of group, but cannot fight, hold own; remains on periphery, propitiates others	Seeks to diffuse identity in group; still at gang stage when others are pairing and forming intimate ties to friends of opposite sex
Relation to authority	Authority problems with parents only; leadership and responsibility avoided by all family	Resistance to all authority; all frustration leads to uncontrolled rage	Fear of authority; 'born losers', rebellion expressed only by unconscious passive resistance – learning block	Preoccupied with authority; behaviour designed to provoke firm control from society
Sexual adjustment of referred patient	Autistic response – uninterested in peers	Little differentiation on sexual basis – interaction with others generally exploitative	Fair identification with parent of same sex but generally feels inadequate, fears competition	Ostentatious, bragging over relationships with opposite sex but fears intimacy; still seeks security of same-sex group
Marital relationship of parents	Both spouses unhappy, mistrustful, soon disillusioned and disappointed in each other; father turns outward for satisfaction, mother to child; pattern resembles 'autocrat' but more intense, sicker	Mother dominant, attached to child, excluding father; father accepts exclusion but preserves adequate role in outside world	Both parents intensely competitive for authority and status, jealous of each other's sexual rôle and consequent mutual undermining and quarrels over child-rearing	Incapacity for real intimacy and fearful of sexuality; incestuous competition with the children; father's rôle idealised in unrealistic way

Fathers	Schizoid, inadequate both in home and in outside world, avoiding involvement generally; colludes in exclusion by wife, relieved that her attention switched to child; unstable, unreliable	Detached and colludes in his exclusion like fathers of schizophrenics, but often respected and adequate outside the home, and perceptive and objective about family situation, so able to play more positive rôle if helped through therapy	Dominant façade with underlying feelings of impotence and inadequacy; competitive with wife for maternal rôle, undermining her	Successful, aggressive leaders outside home; placed by wives in superior, idealised position at home yet also undermined, excluded as if regarded as really inadequate; 'good provider'
Mothers	Lonely, narcissistic, seeking recompense for unhappy childhood in marriage and then, when disappointed, by absorption in child; turn away from husbands	Dominant of dependency; denial of dependency; cannot tolerate frustration and treats child as greedy, domineering part of herself; husbands regarded as beneath them, actively excluded; disenchanted when child becomes tyrant	Really need and desire male acceptance because of feelings of inadequacy as women, but defend themselves by aggression, like husbands; resent husband's devaluation and undermine husband's sexual rôle in return	Capable and competent but needy, feel inferior as women; put husbands on pedestal and seek status for themselves through husband's achievement; compete for husband with children
Parental rôle-balance	Father's rôle completely denied in relation to child; father not even potential significant figure	Power struggle with mother left in control of field, father opting out of conflict if potentially adequate if balance changed by therapy	Both parents fighting for supremacy, neither conceding leadership	Father accorded leadership position, even though on 'false' basis, protected against real challenge
Relation to community	Isolated	Mother isolated, father more adequate outside home	Both parents more adequate socially as separate individuals, despite limited ability to function as marital unit	Involved socially, successful in community where there is often considerable investment compared with family interaction
Family response to crisis	First response to exclude child or have him labelled 'hopeless'	Help sought in controlling unmanageable child without other changes in family being necessary	Seek relief of child's symptoms and preservation of marriage	Seek help to contain and cope with problem, without exclusion

Figure 5. Main differences found by Timberlawn Psychiatric Research Foundation Study (Lewis et al., 1976) in the structure and function of families producing mentally healthy, midrange, and severely dysfunctional children.[6]

Level of function of children	Severe dysfunction	Mid-range function	Healthy function
Types of disorder	'Process' (chronic) schizophrenia Psychopathy (Sociopathy)	Reactive psychosis/Behaviour Disorders/Neurosis	No evidence of psychiatric disorder; effective functioning
Power-structure	*chaotic* Parent–child coalition (usually between mother and index patient, father ineffective and excluded)	*structure/rigid* Rigid control, little negotiation. Parents either competing for dominance (behaviour disorders) or dominant-submissive relationship (neuroses).	*structured/flexible* Strong, equal-powered parental coalition, but children consulted and decisions through negotiation. Clear hierarchy with mutual respect
Differentiation	*fusion* Blurred boundaries, unclear identities, shifting rôles. Blaming, scapegoating, evasion of responsibility. Invasiveness	*separateness through distancing* Identities more defined but at cost of emotional distancing, restriction of potential and of spontaneity. Rôle stereotyping, including male/female	*clear identity and intimacy* Identities highly defined and secure, permitting also high levels of closeness and intimacy. High individual responsibility
Communication	Vague, confused, evasive, contradictory. Double-binds. Mystification. Imperviousness	Clearer than in severely dysfunctional, but in rigid, stereotyped way (so often superficially clearer than in healthy) Impervious to new ideas; non-mutual	Open, clear, direct, frank. Lively and spontaneous. Receptive and responsive to new ideas
Relationship	*oppositional* Distrust, expectation of evil (betrayal, desertion) Ambivalent feelings unintegrated, swings between extremes; inconsistency dealt with by denial. Marriage highly unsatisfactory; split by parent/child coalition	*oppositional* Relative distrust; human nature seen as basically evil, needing rigid control of self and others. Repression, suppression. Ambivalence not accepted, dealt with by repression and reaction formation against 'bad' impulses. Lack of marital satisfaction; competing or dominant/submissive roles.	*affiliative* Trust; basic expectation of positive response to positive approach. Warm, caring, mutual regard and responsibility. Ambivalent feelings accepted as normal. Both sides included and integrated. Mutually satisfying, complementary marital roles; sexuality mutually satisfying also

Reality-sense	Reality denied; escape into fantasy satisfactions.	Adequate reality sense to function effectively, but with some distortion and incongruent family 'myths'.	Image of self and family congruent with reality.
Affect	Cyncisim; hostility, sadism; hopelessness and despair	Hostility (behaviour disorders) but without the degree of sadism in severely dysfunctional. Subdued, joyless, restricted (neurotic disturbance)	Warmth, enjoyment; humour, wit. Tenderness, empathy.
Attitude to change, loss	Unable to cope with change and loss. Timeless, repetitive quality, with denial of separation and death, escape into fantasy.	Change and loss faced, but with great pain and difficulty. Separation and death not really worked through; substitutes for lost persons and feelings transferred, instead of internalisation of lost person	Change, growth, separation and death all accepted realistically and losses worked through, due to 1. Strong parental coalition (in relation to older and younger generations). 2. Strong, varied relationships outside family. 3. Transcendent value system.

Figure 6. Main characteristics of 'optimal' families, in order of apparent importance[6]

'Optimal' families could be differentiated from 'adequate' families on all these characteristics except No. 7 (Initiative) to level of statistical significance. Both produced healthy children, but 'adequates' showed many 'mid-range' features.

1. *Affiliative attitude* to human encounter – open, reaching-out, basically trusting (as contrasted with *oppositional* – distrust, withdrawal etc.).

2. *High respect for separateness, individuality*, autonomy, privacy (as contrasted with expectation of agreement, conformity, 'speaking for others').

3. *Open, clear, frank communication* (as contrasted with confusion, evasion, restriction etc.).

4. *Firm parental coalition*, egalitarian with shared power between parents (as contrasted with parental splits and parent/child coalitions).

5. *Control flexible, by negotiation*, within basic parent/child hierarchy (as contrasted with rigid, inflexible control and unchangeable rules).

6. *Highly spontaneous interaction*, with considerable humour and wit – 'three-ring circus, but all under control' (as contrasted with rigid, stereotyped interaction).

7. *High levels of initiative* (as contrasted to passivity).

8. *Uniqueness and difference encouraged* and appreciated – liveliness, strong 'characters' (as contrasted with bland, stereotyped, conformist types).

Figure 7. Differences in marital and sexual function between 'adequate' and 'optimal' families, all producing healthy children[6]

	Adequate	Optimal
RÔLES	Generally traditional gender rôles but in rigid, stereotyped, highly rôle-segregated way	Generally traditional gender rôles but seemingly from choice, with rewarding, mutually pleasurable complementarity and reciprocity
RELATIONSHIP	*Husbands* successful, aggressively work-oriented. More satisfied with lives than wives – distant and providing material but not emotional support	*Both husbands and wives* express mutual pleasure and enjoyment with relationship and life generally. Husbands involved in work but responsive to wife's needs, supportive and emotionally aware
	Wives generally unhappy, needy, lonely, feeling isolated from husbands and overwhelmed by children. Tending to obesity, depression and fatigue. Interests outside home limited	*Wives* feel appreciated, cherished
		Many, active interests outside home, though rôle of mother and wife central and satisfying
SEXUALITY	Regular, generally similar frequency (about twice-weekly). Mostly satisfying to husbands. Wives generally dissatisfied (too much, too little, unpleasurable etc.)	More variable in frequency between couples (several times weekly to twice a month) but highly, mutually pleasurable and satisfying to both partners. Pattern of long-term marital fidelity
LEISURE	Limited involvement of couple with community	More involvement of couple outside the home and family

Both 'adequate' and 'optimal' families shared very high belief and involvement in the idea of the family, and their children's activities families, where there is characteristically a parent/child coalition with the father most often ineffective and excluded, gives way at mid-range function to a rigid structure not only with rigid control of the children by the parents, but also a rigid hierarchy with one spouse dominant over the other. But when we come to the most healthy families, this situation is not simply exaggerated, but radically changed. Structure is present, but is sufficiently secure for the children to be consulted and decisions reached through negotiation, and the parental coalition has become one of equal power.

Similarly, the fusion of the severely dysfunctional family gives way to individuality and separateness in mid-range function but only at the cost of emotional distancing and rôle stereotyping, including rigid differences in sexual rôle. In healthy families this is not taken further, but radically changed. The sense of identity and difference has become so secure that individuals can alternate between intense intimacy, and separateness. A similar transition is seen in regard to communication, where in the mid-range clarity is achieved at the cost of rigidity, while the latter is no longer necessary for healthy families.

As regards relationships, reality sense and affect, the transition is more continuous. The same is true of the attitude to change, loss, separation and death. The Timberlawn Group found that the capacity to deal with these different aspects of change was an especially crucial and reliable feature in differentiating healthy from less healthy families, affecting physical as well as mental health. This one might expect, of course, in the light of our previous discussion, if 'health' is connected with an ability to adapt to the ever changing flux of experience and the challenges posed by the developmental process, by constant change of inner 'models' or 'knowledge' to fit the new information.

Figure 5 presents the findings in broadest outline. But the Timberlawn Researchers also examined in more detail the families producing healthy children, comparing the six families whose function approximated most closely to mid-range function, to six which showed the functioning of the 'healthy' group at its greatest extreme. The former they called 'adequate', the latter 'optimal', and an outline of the findings regarding this comparison is given in Figs. 6 and 7.

Figure 6 needs little explanation and shows that the 'optimal' families could be differentiated from the 'adequate' on seven out of eight criteria, while Fig. 7 shows that there were striking differences between the 'optimal' and 'adequate' families as regards the marital relationships.[7]

Conclusion

It is reassuring to see that many couples showing evidence of considerable degrees of mid-range function can nevertheless produce healthy children by dint of hard work, effort and struggle, even at considerable cost. But it is even more reassuring to see that the greatest health and well-being in family function, like the highest development of all other human skills, appears after the basic knowledge and skills are so well established that they no longer require anxious effort, giving space and time to allow spontaneity, playfulness and enjoyment, reminding one of Bateson's use of the word 'grace'.

Notes

1 This paper was first published in an earlier form in A. Bentovim, G. Gorrell Barnes and A. Cooklin (eds.), *Family Therapy: Complementary Frameworks of Theory and Practice*, 1982.
2 The conception of circular causality offered here takes an account of cybernetics to the limits of what has been described by Hoffman as its 'first generation'. See the editor's introduction, footnote 9. The need for a 'second-generation cybernetics' is pointed to by Skynner, before such terms were current in the literature, in the section entitled 'The Experiential Life of the Family'. Here, and especially on pp. 280–94, he refers to the subjective nature of family life and the relativity of the therapist's position. As is indicated in the editor's introduction, this chapter, like all the others in this section, sets out Skynner's contribution towards this 'second generation cybernetics'. [Ed.]
3 See Skynner's paper on the relationship between secular and spiritual consciousness, 'Psychotherapy and Spiritual Tradition' (appendix reference 27).
4 See Skynner and Cleese, *Families And How To Survive Them* pp. 15–62, where the study of partner choice is the central issue.
5 This table was devised by Skynner using material from the Galveston Multiple Impact Therapy Study, and was first published in *One Flesh, Separate Persons*.

6 Figures 5, 6 and 7 were devised by Skynner using selected material from the Timberlawn Research Foundation Study, described by J. M. Lewis, W. R. Beavers, J. T. Gossett and V. A. Phillips, *No Single Thread: Psychological Health in Family Systems*. This work has been presented in popular fashion in J. M. Lewis, *How's Your Family?*, which omits much of the detail of the research design. See also W. R. Beavers, *Psychotherapy and Growth: A Family Systems Perspective*. Skynner was responsible for the compilation of these tables, and in the process consulted with Lewis who approved their present form. The main text of the study was published in 1976, the same year in which Skynner's *One Flesh, Separate Persons* was published. Lewis and Skynner corresponded about similarities between their research findings and clinical observations at the time of publication of the two books. [Ed.]

7 The family interaction study which provides the essential data on which the Timberlawn Research Study was based was found limited in several important respects in, for example, Gurman's review of Beaver's *Psychotherapy and Growth* in *Family Process*, Vol. 18, **1** (March 1979) pp. 107–109. The most serious flaw is the assumption of a simple causal relationship between family functioning and individual psychological health. This flaw does not extend to the use Skynner makes of this material. He derives clinical hypotheses from it which are tested in treatment and described in chapter 13 below, see pp. 308–316. Skynner's findings have the validity and reliability of a clinician's formulations and he makes no claim to their scientific status beyond this. He was using one of the most reliable family studies of its time to corroborate his own clinical perspectives. It is of significance that the same edition of *Family Process* which carried Gurman's critique of the Timberlawn work also carried the first account of a new generation of family studies which, in making use of multi-variate analysis and multi-axial classification, meets Gurman's criticisms and arrives at findings about the coherence and adaptability of families, which underwrites the views of both Skynner and the Timberlawn Group. See H. Olson, D. Sprenkle, and C. Russell, 'Circumplex Model of Marital and Family Systems', *Family Process*, 18, **1**, 3–21. [Ed.]

13 An Open-Systems, Group-Analytic Approach to Family Therapy

When Gurman and Kniskern were editing *The Handbook of Family Therapy*, so far the most comprehensive and authoritative text, they invited Skynner to write for it the chapter on the psychoanalytic approach. He was reluctant at first, as although he had worked closely with psychoanalysts all his professional life, he was a group analyst and suggested others in his place. Their persistence and their confidence in the group-analytic contribution encouraged Skynner to accept the invitation. He was aware that all contributors would be required to answer an exhaustive list of questions somewhere in their chapters, and welcomed this opportunity to clarify and develop his ideas.

This is indeed borne out, for what follows is his most extensive undertaking, his two previous books excepted. It contains an outline of his basic concepts, principles, methods and techniques, and is built around a detailed and lively individual case study which illustrates most of the theoretical points. It indicates their primary origins in the group-analytic approach but acknowledges the many contributions from psychoanalytic, systems, behavioural and other schools. It also provides a useful section on training, which is the only one in the book.

For those who wish to capture the main points of the group-analytic approach, or who are already familiar with Skynner's work, the three concluding chapters of this book will be of most interest. For these readers, the earlier papers will be of most use in describing Skynner's mode of enquiry, which turns all group situations into opportunities for learning and growth. This open and reflective attitude was the legacy of S. H. Foulkes, and is at the heart of the group-analytic method.

J.R.S.

Introduction: The Group-Analytic Approach

Group analysis is an approach towards psychotherapy particularly (but not only) with family and stranger-groups of various kinds.[1] It originates in the work of S. H. Foulkes (1948, 1964, 1965), a teacher who has been the major influence in the development of my own approach. He worked with groups (in one of which I had my own personal group analysis)[2] as if he understood open-systems concepts (Pines, 1983). However, he failed to communicate this understanding through his writings, because he attempted to formulate it in terms of the Freudian conceptual framework to which he continued to pay formal allegiance but which, as Beavers has pointed out (1977), is inconsistent with open-systems ideas.[3] My own approach derives from this, but is based more explicitly on general systems theory.

In the comprehensive account of my approach offered in this paper, I shall discuss some general theoretical concepts and some of the therapeutic principles. This is followed by a case example which is recounted in detail in a graphic and easily followed way through nine sessions over some months to illustrate my methods. I shall begin with a preliminary account of my views on health and dysfunction in families. With the development of general systems theory, our understanding of personal well-being can be reframed in inter-personal terms to take full account of the familial contribution when considering the pathology of individuals. Dysfunctional families are those in which there is some developmental distortion or delay in the basic processes of family life. I believe that most psychological problems and indeed a wide range of physical problems can be most usefully understood in these terms. Chapter 12 examined these basic family processes.

Here I am concerned with the consequences when something goes wrong with them, and propose a therapeutic approach which is closely derived from an understanding of the family developmental sequence. First I shall set out some of the basic concepts of an open-systems, group-analytic approach, including *family systems, developmental processes, collusive denial, projective systems* and *sexuality* considered as a major factor in differentiation. Applying these basic concepts to clinical experience, a number of therapeutic principles naturally follow, including: *clarifying communication; compensating for developmental deficits; modelling emotions the family are denying and avoiding; promoting differentiation*; and *fostering affiliative attitudes*. The techniques by which these are practically applied draw upon a wide range of possible interventions in the family therapy literature which I have classified (following Beels and Ferber, 1969) into three groups, calling them 'intervention from above', '. . . from below' and '. . . from the side'. Before the illustrative case example, I shall explain how the group-analytic approach, which as will be seen might be called 'intervention by the outsider inside', incorporates something of all these different approaches but differs from them all in important respects.

After the example, and in the section that follows it, 'On Method in Group Analysis and Family Therapy', I shall describe the elements that are most specific in my method.[4] This chapter is concluded with a brief section on training.[5]

Health and Dysfunction in Families

My views on the nature of healthy and unhealthy families are based on clinical and general experience, supplemented and corrected by the research studies we have available at the present time. As already summarised above, I rely particularly upon Westley and Epstein (1970), Mishler and Waxler (1968), MacGregor *et al.* (1964), Stabenau *et al.* (1965), and in particular Lewis *et al.* (1976).[6]

1. Developmental levels in families

Clinical work suggested to me that families can be classified helpfully in terms of their general *developmental level*. If children mature by the family facing them with, and supporting them through, a sequence of social challenges, then failure is likely to be perpetuated over generations unless there is help from outside the family. A mother lacking mothering herself, or a father lacking a firm but kindly fathering experience, will be likely to behave inappropriately when required to play these rôles to which they have not been exposed, and for which they have not internalised an adequate model. Thus, families are seen as suffering from characteristic developmental failures over generations, in similar fashion to the idea of 'fixation' at, or 'regression' to, developmental levels in the Freudian schema.

This *by itself* is not seen as producing problems needing professional help, at least most of the time. To produce a *symptomatic* family there needs to be some stress, in addition, which the family cannot cope with because its limited level of development has not equipped it with necessary models or learning experiences.

Thus, 'pathology' can have two meanings. The first is similar to the psychoanalytic understanding of psychopathology, describing the dynamics of the family system. The second describes the decompensation of that particular system in the face of stress. Needless to say, *the family will be most likely to decompensate when faced with stresses corresponding to the multigenerational family failure in the developmental process.* And by contrast, the more completely the family has coped with the sequence of developmental challenges, the wider the range of responses it will possess and the less likelihood there will be of members breaking down unless confronted with exceptional stresses.

This schema, developed from clinical experience, seems to guide clinical work in a useful manner, and I find this developmental concept the most valuable of all the ideas guiding my practice. The categories to which it naturally leads are also in accordance with research findings on healthy and dysfunctional families.[7]

Figure 5 (p. 300) outlines the Timberlawn findings, while Figs. 6 and 7 (p. 303) attempt to sketch out the results of a more detailed examination of families towards the 'healthy' end of the spectrum. None of these contained dysfunctional children at the time of the study, but there were striking differences between the 'adequate' families, who showed some 'mid-range' functioning and achieved good results by much effort and struggle, and the 'optimal' families, who seemed more effortless, spontaneous and joyful.

It will be seen that the characteristics of the three levels in Fig. 5 correspond in many ways to the three-stage process I have outlined in Fig. 4 (pp. 298–9) with fusion in the first stage, leading through preoccupation with boundaries and identity in the second, and in the third an ability to move easily back and forth from closeness to distance because individual identity is by then firmly established. Similarly, a parent–child coalition (usually between mother and index patient) at the first level leads on to a rigid hierarchy in the second, but develops into a flexible hierarchy in the third level, with sharing of power between the parents and with decisions reached by negotiation among all the family members.

Severely dysfunctional, chaotic, mother-centred families therefore need an activation of the father and more control and structure, even if rigid at first. Mid-range families already possess structure of this kind, and need help in introducing more negotiation and sharing of parental power in their functioning.

One central feature of optimal function noted by the Timberlawn team was an *affiliative* rather than an *oppositional* attitude to others, that is, one based on trust and friendliness which evokes positive responses from others, rather than a distrustful, paranoid stance which evokes the opposite reaction. Another key observation from the research was the close association between healthy function in families and the ability to deal constructively with separation, loss and death. Indeed, this was found to be one of the most crucial distinguishing characteristics between the most healthy and all the less healthy families; difficulty in this area was associated not only with emotional and social dysfunction, but also with physical illness of all kinds.

Healthy families have an accurate perception of reality, so that their projected expectations of the behaviour of others will lead them to predict accurately what others actually do. Moreover, because of the ability to deal with loss so effectively, the old expectations can be discarded easily, enabling members of healthy families to learn readily and grow through the experience of disillusion and disappointment. Because of their secure sense of identity, they will not be vulnerable to the false projected expectations of others, nor will they, having a positive attitude to loss, feel a need to bolster the illusions of others.

When the developmental level is more limited, *diffuseness of boundaries, unclear identity stance, reliance on the satisfactions of fantasy rather than reality, and difficulty in coping with loss, all lead to the development of powerful projective systems that seek to preserve in unchanging form some past state of relationships, real or fantasied, and to manipulate others into behaviour which will confirm this rigidly held view of the world.*

While highly differentiated families are not vulnerable to such manipulative pressure (though they may *deliberately* pretend to conform to it for their own reasons, as where a mental health professional 'humours' the psychotic who claims to be God, or bolsters the weak self-esteem of a deprived family), less differentiated individuals are readily 'invaded' by such projective systems and unwittingly become part of them. In family therapy, this occurs when therapists get 'sucked into the family system' (rather than joining it deliberately and consciously, keeping one foot outside it), or where co-therapists begin to reflect the marital conflict in their own behaviour without insight into what is happening to them. The lower down the scale of differentiation one goes, the less value is placed on separateness, individuality, difference and growth, and the more is placed on sameness, conformity and avoidance of change. The greatest compliments in such undifferentiated families are 'you haven't changed a bit' or 'he's always the same'.

The main difference between 'chaotic' and 'mid-range' families lies in this area. The former try to avoid perception of loss, change or growth altogether, locking all members in a timeless, static, frozen pattern; the latter accept time and change, can move on, but only at the cost of burdening the children with the images and attachments of dead or departed relatives. Children born close to the time when grandparents die are especially likely to experience this emotional burden.

2. The importance of marital choice

It is important at this point to introduce the subject of marital choice.[8] Although social factors and such crucial personal values as mutual sexual attractiveness and shared interests obviously play a part, the mutual 'fit' of the projective systems of the two partners

313

plays an increasing rôle as one examines less and less differentiated families. *Each partner brings to the union expectations and fears corresponding to the level at which some aspect of their developmental process was blocked, and will seek to recreate a situation where the needed experience can be re-encountered and grown through. This is the source of the tremendous potentiality of marriage, and of marital therapy, for growth.* But since both partners will be making similar demands (even if one does so covertly and the other more openly), each wanting the other to function in a perpetually gratifying parental rôle, the situation is fraught with difficulty, since neither can fully perform this rôle simultaneously even if he or she knew how to do so. And, in addition, layers of defensive function protecting against re-encountering the pain originally experienced at the time of the developmental failure are acting in both parties in opposition to the straightforward revelation and gratification of the unmet needs.

This struggle of the two projective systems, both similar in some basic sense, though incompatible in that each is trying to gain control of the other, will destroy the fruitful possibilities of the relationship if one system prevails too completely. The situation may be made more workable if part of the demands can be relieved by off-loading some aspect onto a child of the union, thereby transmitting the 'pathology' and saving the marriage at the cost of the next generation. Or, alternatively, problems may be dealt with by projecting them out into an aspect of the suprasystem, preserving the marriage and family unit from disintegration at the cost of conflict with the environment. For example, some couples avoid marital conflict by projecting a controlling, 'paternal' rôle onto the school, subsequently collaborating to fight the school instead of each other, while the child plays parents off against the school instead of father against mother.

In either case, *therapy requires recognition of the projected parts and bringing them back from whoever presents with the 'complaint', whether the symptomatic child, the suffering school or whatever, into the marriage, where help can be given towards a more constructive resolution.*

3. Symptom formation in families

Many of the concepts outlined above help to explain why symptoms develop in one individual at a particular time, though the details are incompletely worked out. Usually they occur when parents cannot cope with a particular emotion which has been denied and excluded from awareness in a family over generations (Fisher and Mendell, 1956) when its intensity increases to a degree which threatens their defences and so the marriage, and this overload is externalised through the projective system onto one or more other members, who then develop 'symptoms'. The 'sick' member is usually chosen because of some special characteristic (similarity to parent or grandparent, birth at a time of stress, weakness compared with siblings, particular attachment to a parent producing vulnerability to that parent's projected emotions etc.). The individual concerned colludes in the process out of a deep, if unconscious, recognition that he is preserving the parent, the marriage or the family as a whole from disintegration, out of a motive of attachment as well as guilt. *The symptom will often be symbolic of the denied emotion* (fears of broken glass in food, expressing in a disguised way a recognition that the mother's love is mixed with a denied murderous hate), but I believe there are multiple determinants which are imperfectly understood. Many symptoms are 'release' phenomena, due to breakdown of higher level control mechanisms. A 'symptom' in one family ('disobedience', 'violence') may be a virtue in another ('spiritedness', 'toughness').

The so-called 'well' siblings will be found to share the level of differentiation of the family as a whole (though they may be somewhat more differentiated, the index patient somewhat less differentiated, than the parents). *They may be non-symptomatic because they possess more rigid defences and so are more 'sick' than the index patient in the sense of not being as open to the possibility of therapy and growth.* They are usually burdened with other projections which are high in the family hierarchy of values, but which limit their individuality and autonomy – e.g., to be successful for the family, to look after others and neglect their own lives (the latter is a particularly common pattern among mental health professionals).

Severely dysfunctional families also show gender confusion, while mid-range families often demonstrate gender rôle stereotyping. In healthy families children are perceived more accurately and allowed to develop as individuals. They do not have to carry burdens for the parents, who can function adequately without

315

them, and indeed without each other. For healthy families, the pleasures of marriage and family life are a bonus, not an imperative need.

For the healthy family, relationships with the extended family and the outside world are like those between its members, with clear boundaries and the possibility of moving back and forth between close involvement and aloneness. Dysfunctional families tend to be over-dependent on the extended family and vulnerable to disturbance in relatives, or they may maintain a rigid boundary, isolating themselves from relatives or the community (Bowen, 1978; Minuchin, 1974).

4. Forms of intervention and the family life cycle

Barnhill and Longo (1978) have recently reviewed concepts regarding the family life cycle and differences in the form of intervention demanded of the family therapist at each stage. They use a modification of Duvall's (1957) nine-stage schema as a basis. Pincus and Dare (1978) and Dare (1979) supplement these admirably from a more thoroughgoing psychoanalytic object-relations viewpoint. These are all in broad agreement with and complementary to each other, as well as being similar to my own views about the different needs of families during their life cycles described in *One Flesh, Separate Persons*.

Briefly, the first stage is one of mutual encounter, enjoyment, exploration and testing, beginning with the mutual idealisation of courtship. It is followed by struggle and negotiation as real differences and conflicts between values are negotiated during the close contact of early marriage. During this period the partners often make good some of each other's deficits of early nurturance (or fail to meet such needs, if they are excessive, heralding increasing dissatisfaction and bitterness). The arrival of the first child profoundly changes the relationship, for instead of the former mutual nurturance and freedom, both must nurture a helpless and dependent infant, the mother usually taking prime responsibility for the child, the father supporting and nurturing the mother as she does so, but whatever the arrangement, both losing each other's exclusive attention.

The transition of baby to toddler, towards greater rebellion and independence, demands capacities for independence as well as

316

tolerance for separation. In the parents, these are tasks which have to be repeated in greater degree as children begin school and finally when they leave home. Similarly, at the oedipal period, as well as later at the burgeoning of adolescent sexuality and finally with courtship and marriage, the parents re-encounter their own sexual conflicts and inhibitions. Their ability to sustain their own sexual enjoyment as a couple, to develop new interests and turn back towards each other, as well as outwards to the wider social world, will help ensure smooth transitions of these stages for the children and the marriage.

Finally, after departure of children and retirement from employment, the final years can be as rich as any if the partners have both developed their relationship, as well as their individuality as separate persons, throughout the career-building and child-rearing period, avoiding individual or joint impoverishment by excessive investment in any one stage or task. The family and marital therapist can do much, even through simple and brief interventions, to help parents remain aware of the process as a whole, to perceive and cope with the different requirements at each stage, and to maintain a sense of balance and wholeness in their lives.

5. Stages in the parental relationship

The main concepts I have emphasised are the rôle of the father and of a recurrent three-stage dialectical pattern in the process. It begins with the sequence of the Freudian oral/anal/genital stages (or dependency/control/sharing) in childhood, repeated in adolescence and also in early marriage where the couple begins with a period of mutual dependency, next face issues of control, authority and hierarchy when the first child arrives, and, if fortunate, ends with an ability to share power.

A confusion I was unable to resolve in *One Flesh, Separate Persons*, where I concluded from clinical experience that healthy function in families required *both* a clear hierarchy with father accorded the final power decision (a view confirmed by all previous research studies) *and* shared power between the parents, has been corrected by the Timberlawn Research. This demonstrates that both the views expressed in my book are correct but that they apply to families beginning from different levels of differentiation. The severely dysfunctional need the introduction of structure to bring

317

them to mid-range function, while mid-range families may need the already existing structure loosened to bring about more power-sharing and negotiation with children regarding decisions.

The experience of my wife and myself working with couples groups confirms a similar sequence in the family life cycle. Initially, the problem is dominance by the female and passivity in the male, who has to be helped to take control. The females almost invariably express a fundamental wish for this but also use every strategy to maintain control. If the outcome is successful, a period of male dominance and responsibility, reversing the earlier pattern of female dominance, leads finally on to cooperation and sharing of power between them.[9]

Basic Concepts

1. General systems theory

Returning to the comments about group analysis and systems theory made in the introduction, Von Bertalanffy (1968), the main pioneer of general systems theory, helps to explain Foulkes's failure to find an adequate formulation of his methods through psychoanalytic language. He says:

> American psychology in the first half of the twentieth century was dominated by the concept of the reactive organism or, more dramatically, by the model of man as a robot. This conception was common to all major schools of American psychology, classical, and neo-behaviourism, learning and motivation theories, psychoanalysis, cybernetics, the concept of the brain as a computer and so forth.

a. General systems theory and living systems

Miller (1965) has given one of the clearest expositions of general systems theory as it applies to living systems. Like the rest of the universe, from galaxies to sub-atomic particles, living organisms are seen as part of a sequence of larger systems – family, group, community, nation etc. – and composed of a series of ever-smaller subsystems (e.g. organs, tissues, cells etc.). Each system has a measure of independence from the *suprasystem* of which it is a part (e.g. the individual from the family, the family from the community) but only within certain limits beyond which it must comply or suffer. The individuality of each system is maintained by its

318

boundary, a region which contains and protects the parts of the system and where the transfer of information and matter/energy is restricted relative to regions internal and external to it. The communication across this boundary, as well as the coordination of the subsystems within it, is controlled by the *decider subsystem* (e.g. the government of a nation, the parents of a family, Freud's 'censor', etc.). Just as the boundary maintains a degree of autonomy for the system despite a general control by the suprasystem of which it is a part, so feedback loops, adjusting the functioning of the system according to its performance (like a thermostat in a heating system), maintain a general continuity of structure and function despite being 'loose' enough to permit change and growth within permissible limits.

The focus in recent years on the family and its relationship to the individuals within it, as well as to the community and the helping professions outside it, has led to a recognition of the way such concepts can help us remember to visualise the *total* situation and avoid becoming lost in detail.

b. The family therapist at the boundary

To be effective, the family therapist must stand at the boundary *of the family and the community or the* boundary *between the individual and the family, avoiding identification with one or the other side. From this position he can modify communication across the boundary, or the characteristics of the decider subsystem, or the feedback maintaining homeostasis, so as to avoid self-destructive extremes of deviance and rebellion on the one hand or of conformity on the other, seeking to negotiate new compromise solutions which work better for the individual, the family and the community.*[10]

This is perhaps only another way of saying that, *to be effective, a therapist must remain aware of the total system and of his current place in it.* If he does not penetrate the boundary of a family or individual he can have no contact and so no understanding; yet, if he becomes 'lost', identified with the projective system of the individual or the myths or paranoid fantasies of the family, he is as helpless to improve their adaptation as they are themselves. A systems approach does not necessarily involve bringing people into physical proximity, though working with actual groups does indeed have great advantages through the therapeutic potential a well-managed group session can manifest. The essential feature lies in the therapist's awareness and attitude, whereby he never gets completely lost in detail but constantly remembers, with part of his mind, the interconnectedness of the whole – individuals, family and community – thereby straddling the boundaries of all of them. In a systems approach the only *new* system present is in the mind of the therapist, a 'model' of the inter-related system which has been there before him all the time, but which the 'tunnel vision' caused by his theoretical stance has made him neglect.[11]

2. Developmental process

The concepts already outlined would apply to a universe of endless, repetitive process in perpetual motion where, in the long run, nothing changed. But one certain fact about living organisms is that they are programmed to self-destruct and cease existence as separate entities after a limited duration, if not destroyed by the environment earlier. Only the *group* can perpetuate itself, not the individual, though it does so through parts of some of the individuals detaching themselves and beginning the process again.

a. Three levels at which information is organised

This continual reproductive process requires that the information needed to organise the new individual and render it capable of functioning with the relative independence of a system in relation to its environment be programmed into its structure. The basic information is of course provided by the genetic programme. The second source of information is by modification of this basic programme through *direct* interaction with the environment, whereby the responses come to fit the latter more closely through the process we call 'learning'. This second process increases in importance as we ascend the evolutionary ladder, giving a great plasticity to behaviour. Man has the further possibility of transmitting information by *symbolic* communication and storing it in permanent form available to the group independently of the decay and dissolution of the individual systems composing it, permitting thereby an exponential growth in the total store of information available to mankind.

b. The family as an organising agent

The principal source from which each individual receives all three of these inputs, the genetic, the environmental and the symbolic, is the family, which provides all of the genetic programme, much of the second and a good deal of the third. The second and especially the third come increasingly from the school and wider aspects of the social suprasystem after the first five years of the individual's life. The conditions governing the modifiable parts of this transmission process within the matrix of the family are, therefore, of fundamental importance to anyone seeking to have a beneficial effect upon the developmental process or to remedy deficiencies at a later date.

Some avoidable dangers at the genetic level of transmission are prevented by the prohibition of incestuous relationships, which would increase the likelihood of the appearance of disorders controlled by recessive genes.

The second form of transmission, that of non-symbolic learning, requires some awareness in the family therapist of developmental stages through which the child passes, since aid can be given towards mastering the sequence of developmental tasks only if they are presented when his biological growth has reached the right stage, where attainment of preceding tasks has been successfully completed, and where parents and others give the right kind of help and support.

c. The life cycle as an organising agent

1. The first developmental task, occupying the first year or so, demands a transition from the stage where both the self and others are experienced in fragmented form and are not distinguished clearly (the Kleinian 'paranoid-schizoid position' of 'part-objects', 'splitting' and 'projection') to the beginnings of a more integrated existence where the infant distinguishes a boundary between itself and others, becomes aware of and able to cope with the conflict and pain of love and hate experienced simultaneously, and has the first experiences of the caring figure as a *whole* person towards whom concern, rather than wholly selfish demands, can be felt (Klein's 'depressive position' comprising 'whole-object relationships', containment of ambivalence and the beginning of gratitude rather than greed and envy).

During this period the main care-giving figure needs to maintain a consistent, reliable presence and to be sensitively attuned and responsive to the child's needs if the child is to develop a basic trust and confidence in itself and others. The appropriate gratification and support need to be maintained to a lessening degree through later stages, since the awareness of separateness and differentiation of the 'depressive position' brings with it a recognition of being vulnerable, precarious and dependent, necessarily absent from the previous omnipotent undifferentiated state.

Increasing appropriate 'failure' of the care-giver is necessary for differentiation to proceed; too little frustration gives no incentive towards growth and independence; too much too soon can bring a catastrophic sense of inadequacy and depression or, ultimately, a retreat to the illusory safety of fusion and chaos.

2. The second developmental task, requiring the acceptance of a suprasystem which is not there just to gratify, but which demands in return a measure of social conformity, occupies roughly the second and third year, and is played out in the areas of sphincter control (hence the Freudian 'anal' stage), speech and muscular activity – all functions through which the child is developing the possibility of control and choice. This stage requires a setting of firm boundaries whereby new powers and possibilities can be safely tested out within limits requiring that the wider social system be heeded and adapted to. If the mother (or primary care-giving figure) is central in the first stage, the father (or first rival for the original care-giver's attention) is central to the second, so that the traditional family rôles of male and female parent are appropriate to the fulfilment of these developmental tasks.[12]

3. The third developmental task. The fourth and fifth years show an increasing preoccupation with the sexuality of the self and of others, and with the Freudian 'oedipal' romance. It is played out in relation to the *couple* rather than to father or mother alone, and its successful resolution requires that the parental couple has a satisfying marital and sexual relationship which is relatively harmonious and not vulnerable to the child's jealousy and attempts to disrupt it. This makes it possible for the child to have a safe flirtation with the parent of the opposite sex, confirming it to gender-appropriate responses and a feeling of sexual worth. The child also learns to cope with jealousy and exclusion, to witness a balance of true sharing and separateness between the couple and eventually, around the age of six, to see that it cannot mate with the parent. This leads the child to aim, coinciding with the move to school, for substitute satisfactions in the wider social world and the ultimate attainment of a mate of its own.

d. Developmental failures and personality development

In outline failures in the *first* stage are associated, when they occur earlier before paranoid-schizoid functioning is transcended, with schizophrenic or borderline states, and when they occur later, with problems around attachment and separation or depressive and manic-depressive functioning. The *second* stage is associated more with obsessional-compulsive states and other disorders where there is endless preoccupation with control, such as tics, stuttering, soiling and so on. The *third* stage is associated more with hysterical disorders and problems of potency and achievement, both sexual and otherwise.

The relationships with others that the child internalises during this sequence provide 'models' for dealing with its social world. By 'computing' with these recorded data, predictions are made regarding new situations which, in normal circumstances, are constantly revised in the light of increasing actual experience, though in ordinary life we are not usually aware of this as an internal process any more than we are conscious of the cerebral processes mediating our vision. We simply have expectations that people will behave in certain ways in certain circumstances and are surprised and disappointed when they do not. Unless something goes wrong with the process, the expectations are modified through learning so that the predictions are more accurate at the next encounter.

3. Projective systems

This set of learned expectations regarding the social behaviour of others, as well as the expectations others are assumed to have of ourselves, comprises at any given time the projective system of each individual. This is experienced not as something internal being projected outwards, but rather as the way the world is or should be.

From this point of view, the projective systems of individuals showing 'psychopathology' differ in that they have not completed the sequence of developmental tasks outlined above, and instead of

323

moving step-by-step towards social expectations which correspond to the real adult world, they remain burdened with inappropriate expectations, or rather with expectations that may have been appropriate in childhood. Thus, the mentally disordered adult may still expect that mother (and so the world) will always gratify (or will never gratify); that father (and so the world) will always be punitive (or will always be outwitted and defeated); that the parental couple (and so the world, and so also his or her children) cannot tolerate a relationship that excludes others and so cannot experience commitment and full gratification and so on.

Moreover, the person so afflicted has not been able to find the experience to help him complete his developmental tasks from some other source. As the gap widens with age between what he has learned to cope with socially and what society expects of him at each stage, attempts to relate socially become increasingly unsuccessful, frustrating and painful. This leads towards increasing withdrawal from real involvement, and layer upon layer of defensive functioning arise to protect self-esteem and secure alternative gratifications, particularly through fantasy.

Thus, any form of therapy derived from group-analytic principles must *at least* include the provision of a social situation where the patient can develop sufficient trust in the safety of the situation and in the intentions of the therapist to help him find, face and surmount unfinished developmental tasks, for him to stop sheltering behind the defensive system and expose the expectations of self and others he originally learned and never transcended. This is the development of transference in individual therapy, the development of multiple transferential relationships in group psychotherapy, and the opening up of deeper levels of mutual expectation and demand in conjoint marital and family therapy, where the projective systems are already fully developed but hidden and denied.

4. Sexuality

A further complication is introduced by the fact of sexuality whereby, in man as in all more complex forms of life, male and female varieties of the species must combine to create new organisms to replace those that die, and so maintain the species as a group.

From this sexual fusion of the parents comes difference and

separateness, since the fact that children derive half their genetic programming from each parent ensures diversity despite continuance of the basic pattern. Where the child is cared for by two parental figures, psychological diversity is also ensured by the internalisation of parts of the two parental psyches. These form a new combination in the psyche of the child, which will be harmonious if the parental relationship is positive or, alternatively, perpetuate parental struggles in neurotic conflict.

a. The developmental significance of sexuality

Developmentally, sexuality seems central to the formation, growth and differentiation of the family in various ways:

(a) It draws a couple together to create a partnership.

(b) It produces children.

(c) It facilitates bonding of the parental pair, making their relationship *primary* and so, by excluding the children and making parent–child relationships secondary, motivates the children to mature and leave home since their exclusion and consequent jealousy lead them ultimately to reject the parents as hoped-for sexual partners and determine them to have the same pleasure themselves outside the family.

In this way infantile sexuality, oedipal jealousy and the incest taboo combine to facilitate separation and individuation. For this process to function there must clearly be a 'right amount of sex' between parents and children. Too much (overt incest) allows the donkey to eat the carrot, as it were, while too little (parental anxiety over, and so denial of, sexual attraction between parent and child) takes the carrot away altogether. In either case the motivation towards maturation is removed.

For a father to desire his daughter sexually and vice versa (or a mother her son), yet also to keep the boundary and feel the pain that they cannot marry, is also a constant reminder of mortality. By contrast, overt incest and complete denial of oedipal sexuality are partially motivated by denial of the facts of growth, separation and death. Thus, an inability on the part of the parents to deal with loss may lead to excessive sexual involvement between parent and child, or unrealistic denial of its presence; in either case this makes a smooth transition towards enjoyable adult sexuality difficult. Since the choice of mate is strongly influenced by similarities to the parents or siblings, whether at a conscious or unconscious level, and since excessive anxiety surrounding the oedipal romance will thereby be associated with sexuality with the spouse, inhibitions and repressions set up to deal with problematic aspects of the parent–child sexual attraction will lead to avoidance of sexual feelings in the marriage as well. Those who have experienced a pleasurable and safe sexual responsiveness towards and from their parents are, by contrast, free to choose a mate with all the desirable and erotic characteristics of each or both parents, of attractive siblings or other relatives, without confusing this with incest.

b. Sexual differentiation of authority

Lastly, the fact of *two* parents raises additional possible problems and potentialities, since ways have to be found to handle decision-making in the family system. Miller (1965) describes the decider subsystem as 'the essential critical subsystem which controls the entire system, causing its subsystem and components to co-act, without which there is no system', and later, 'if there are multiple parallel deciders, without a hierarchy that has subordinate and superordinate deciders, there is not one system but multiple ones'. Thus, if the family is to exist as an integrated system, as a whole rather than as two fragments, either some hierarchy is essential as between male and female parent (as well as between parents and children) *or* some capacity to share authority in some kind of effective collaboration has to be developed, and the child will internalise whatever solution is found as part of its own inner organisation. We will return to this issue when we come to consider what determines 'normality' and 'abnormality' in family systems.[13]

c. Sexuality in 'atypical' families

All that I have said refers to a 'family' in the usual biological sense of that term as a reproductive unit of human society. But obviously many of these developmental functions can occur in other social units concerned with the upbringing of children, such as families where the children are all adopted, or single-parent families where other relatives or family contacts are used in fact or fantasy to replace the function of the missing parent. I have described in *One*

Flesh, Separate Persons an interesting example of the working out of an unresolved oedipal conflict by a boy in a children's home, where the house-parents were helped to understand the rôles they needed to play. But what I have said does imply that engagement in the functions required by the child-rearing task are vital to the psychological growth of a couple, as individuals as well as in their capacity for relationship. The so-called 'child-free' couple, where that is a deliberate option, risks remaining a 'couple of children'.[14]

General Principles of Therapy in the Group-Analytic Method

1. Clarification and change of structure

This factor must be considered first, because it may be relevant even in the determination of who should be invited to attend the first interview, as well as in persuading them to come and in setting up the structure in the interview room itself. The referral letter or other first contact may, for example, indicate that the father is being excluded or is excluding himself, or that a grandparent living with the family is a crucially powerful influence. *In such situations it is vital to include, or to work towards including, the dominant and the excluded figures when the preliminary arrangements are made by letter, telephone or home visit, if encouragement of communication between key figures is to be possible at all.*

Having brought the key figures together, sometimes it may be enough merely to facilitate communication among them. But even this process will usually involve some change in structure of the established hierarchy and rules of family interaction. The therapist may have to interrupt a parent who speaks for others, draw out a withdrawn and silent member or control (or stimulate the parents to control) a disruptive child who is making constructive discussion impossible. *Such interventions will not only reflect features in the family structure contributing to the dysfunction, but will often tend to change family functioning for the better in the long-term, even if such interventions are made only to improve communications in the interview.*

Interventions may also be aimed more deliberately and systematically at changing the family structure, making this the

327

main feature of the process, as in the work of Minuchin (1974) or Bowen (1978). Inter-generational boundaries may be more clearly drawn, giving parental and sibling subgroups the right to separate lives; an overly dominating mother may be silenced in order to activate a too-passive father, or vice-versa; a referral agency seeking to impose its values on a family inappropriately may be corrected by declining to accept its judgement of the situation. In all such decisions the actual authority of the therapist and of the agency, their place in the hierarchy *vis-à-vis* the family and referrer, will be relevant to success or failure.

2. Clarifying communication

Beyond considering structural issues sufficiently to ensure that the family attend together, often little more will be necessary than to facilitate communication among the members, loosening the boundaries so that a freer exchange is possible, or sometimes establishing clearer boundaries so that privacy is respected and separateness is allowed.

3. Compensating for developmental deficits and teaching new skills

In addition to changing the structure and improving communication, the therapist may note that some abilities have not been acquired in the course of development. The mother may have lacked mothering in her own childhood; the father may have had no father himself and may be unable to take a position of authority; both parents may be unable to share with one another or children may be unable to play. The therapist may in such cases provide the appropriate missing experience, sometimes by formal behavioural techniques, more often by providing a 'model' of nurturance, authority, sharing or playing which the family members can experience and internalise by identification. Such modelling may occur sometimes by conscious demonstration, sometimes automatically through the natural and spontaneous behaviour of the therapist just being the kind of person he or she is. Three simple examples have been given in Chapter 5 above (p. 100). However, I believe one may often be not only teaching new skills during such transactions, but also helping patients reconnect internally with good experiences they have actually received earlier but dissociated themselves from out of anxiety or fear of pain (e.g. fear of acknowledging the good mothering they received because it is connected with the pain of the mother's inadequately mourned death; anxiety over sexual pleasure because it was associated with parental jealousy and rejection). The model provided by the therapist may reassure and support the patient towards reconnection with such vital experiences which appear to be missing but are in fact already internalised, though unavailable because denied.[15]

Teaching new skills gives the family *specific* abilities members lack. But families may also be helped towards learning from experience in a more general way, perhaps by seeing the value of questioning established patterns and by sharing the therapist's pleasure and enjoyment at learning and encountering new experiences.

4. Facilitating differentiation

The above therapeutic mechanisms may involve only slight changes in a family's functioning, sufficient to remove a symptom or change a vicious, descending spiral into an ascending one, even though the new pattern, once achieved, may remain as static as the old. Most types of short-term intervention, particularly behavioural methods, are aimed at limited results of this kind which, in my experience, are all that the majority of patients are seeking if one is dealing equally with the whole range of socio-economic status.

A smaller proportion is, however, interested more in growth and development in a general sense than in relief of discomfort and distress alone, and these more reflective families may welcome longer-term psychotherapy (more often analytic in character) aimed at *facilitating differentiation*. This is perhaps less generally popular because it tends to involve additional suffering, even if temporary, rather than a mere increase of comfort. Couples who venture beyond therapy aimed at the presenting problems alone are likely to encounter periods of increased conflict, painful feelings of loss and aloneness, perhaps actual temporary separation or plans to divorce, sometimes even extra-marital affairs threatening their relationship, which only a detached outsider can recognise as steps towards their differentiation as separate, independent persons, enjoying but no longer simply 'needing' each other.

No effort is made to encourage the first type of family towards the growth orientation characteristic of the second, except to the extent that the achievement of limited goals is impossible without some measure of 'growth' they would otherwise not seek. If anything, my attitude towards deeper exploration than is required for the task is quite discouraging and, unlike many psychoanalytic colleagues who tend to see psychotherapy as a good thing in itself, I tend if anything to push people away from therapy, to make them fight for it and prove their motivation. Nevertheless, the fact that I am *personally* committed to growth and use all situations, including my professional work, for this purpose, may *indirectly* stimulate a growth perspective even when I am overtly discouraging it. Indeed, like other forms of 'modelling' influence, it may have a more profound effect than deliberate attempts to promote the value of insight.

5. Fostering affiliative rather than oppositional attitudes

Persons and families persistently troubled or in trouble tend to show a history of real deprivation, even if superficially 'over-indulged' or 'spoiled'. The deprivation leads to what I call a *philosophy of scarcity*, with expectations that there will not be enough for everyone, that one must hang on tightly to what one possesses, grab as much as one can and defend oneself fiercely against others who are trying to do the same.

In psychotherapy, particularly when it is long-term and aimed at growth and differentiation rather than amelioration of symptoms alone, there occurs in successful cases a quite sudden 'flip' when it becomes recognised that the attitude described above is a self-fulfilling prophecy, and that reality can be totally different if one chooses to view it differently. Patients suddenly begin to operate, when this happens, according to what I call a *philosophy of plenty*, a similarly self-fulfilling prophecy where there is more than enough for everyone and one may as well give everything away since one will get even more back, automatically. Trust replaces distrust. Envy, meanness and angry demand give way to generosity, kindness and giving others room to be, space to move and time to change. The person, marriage or family changes totally overnight.

The Timberlawn Research team found these attitudes to be basic discriminating factors between healthy and unhealthy families. They proposed the useful labels of 'affiliative' and 'oppositional' for these two basic social attitudes, which I have since adopted. The similarity of these ideas to fundamental ethical and moral principles in the main religious systems, and to the sudden 'flip' or 'catastrophe' (Zeeman, 1977) characterising religious conversion, is only too obvious.

The ideas expressed by Boszormenyi-Nagy and Spark (1973) regarding loyalties and obligations among family members need mentioning here. Though I believe these authors have done family therapy a service by reminding us of the need to face and accept responsibility for these issues rather than to avoid them by denial and distancing, truly healthy families do not operate on the basis of 'ledgers' of obligation, 'contracts' or 'giving to get'. In the second state for which I have borrowed the word 'affiliative', everything is given freely without demand or expectation of return, and members are truly free because they are not bargaining or manipulating to get their love returned.

Technique

1. Different modes of approach

Beels and Ferber (1969) describe three principal positions from which the family therapist can intervene and, as they are all used in the method being described here, even if with differing emphases, they need to be mentioned. I refer to these positions as interventions 'from above', 'from the side', and 'from below'.[16]

a. Intervention from above

In this mode, the therapist acts as a 'conductor', a 'super-parent' or grandparental figure, adopting an authoritative, directive rôle and seeking to change the structure and function of the family by active intervention, by giving advice, instruction, praise and criticism, or educating by rôle-playing or deliberately 'modelling' the new behaviour considered more effective. The control may be more open and direct at one extreme, or covert, subtle and manipulative at the other. All behavioural methods clearly come into this category, but such methods will also include those advocated by Minuchin (1974), Bowen (1978) and Satir (1964) among others.

b. Intervention from the side

Another method, labelled 'systems-purists' by Beels and Ferber, also seeks to change the family towards modes of functioning considered more healthy by the therapist, whether the family agrees or not, but does so from a detached position where the therapist's values are not made explicit. Instead, the 'tricks' or 'games' used in the family system to limit communication and to maintain a form of operating giving advantage to the dominant subgroup at the expense of others, or of a scapegoat, are first carefully studied. Once grasped by the therapists, instructions or tasks are devised which will make it impossible for these dysfunctional interactions to continue without their becoming obvious to all concerned.

In this approach the therapists seek to outwit the family at their devious, manipulative modes of control, through using the dishonest forms of interaction characteristic of the family to their ultimate benefit, like a kind of 'psychological judo'. The use of paradox and of 'therapeutic double-binds' is prominent in this type of approach.

Understandably, these methods have been developed most fully in trying to deal with the most severely dysfunctional and devious families, particularly those producing schizophrenics. Some representative clinicians working in this mode are Haley (1976), Watzlawick *et al.* (1967), and Palazzoli *et al.* (1978).

c. Intervention from below

The third approach, exemplified by therapists such as Napier and Whitaker (1978) and Sonne and Lincoln (1965), does not appear to involve any attempt at control. Rather, the therapist appears to *submit* to the control of the family, accepting exposure to and absorption of the family dynamics and so becoming affected by them. The intervention is, therefore, more from the rôle of the 'child', 'patient' or 'scapegoat'.

However, to be effective, the therapist must avoid 'joining' the family system completely, but must maintain some part of his/her personality (unless this function is carried out by the other member of a co-therapy team) outside it and be aware of the effect the family is producing. The therapist's rôle will differ from that of an actual child or patient in retaining the right to *describe* what is being experienced, thereby obliging the family to face the truth about their effect on each other. This method has the advantage that it not only confronts the family members with their pathological functioning but keeps responsibility squarely on them to do something about it. Also, it can produce a vastly more powerful emotional impact when the family perceives that it is actually hurting and harming someone whom they respect and like and whom they see as trying to be positive and helpful to them. It is 'for real'.

Intervention 'from above' or 'from the side' (modes which are increasingly combined today by many therapists) both enable the professional to escape suffering any personal involvement in the family's pathology (unless they outwit him), partly because a position of superiority and control is maintained throughout, and also because the therapist relies on intellectual knowledge and thought to determine his actions, whereby he can keep an inner distance from any emotional reverberations. There is, for instance, much use in both approaches of the word 'strategy', indicating an intellectual, adversarial stance. The word 'systems' is also much used, though by definition neither can be considered truly open-system approaches since the observer is excluded from consideration within the total dynamic. Therapists operating exclusively and predominantly from these positions tend to focus their attention on the family and on their own therapeutic techniques to avoid consideration of their personal dynamics and motivations. They also tend to be 'loners', who do not readily share in co-therapy relationships, in learning experiences with colleagues of equal status, or in other *mutual* interactions. Their students tend to have difficulty in developing independently unless they detach themselves and, as it were, 'leave home'.

Intervention 'from below' can also be carried out from a relatively detached, protected posture using reliance on the intellect, through history-taking and other information-gathering, through emphasis on intellectual formulation of dynamics according to psychoanalytic hypotheses and above all through verbal interpretation. Those with much experience in an individual psychoanalytic approach are more likely to maintain this detached position in their emotional responses to the family, but will be likely to make use of counter-transference responses as an important source of information, even if this is kept under tight intellectual control and is not openly reported to the family or exposed to the constructive criticism of colleagues as information about the *therapist's* residual problems rather than those of the family. Therapists

333

with this background tend also to have difficulty in using systematic manipulative strategies, forceful control or behavioural methods.

2. A group-analytic or open-systems technique

a. General outline

We now have a basis from which to consider the method I favour. The interview begins as a variant of intervention 'from below', but it can make use of intervention 'from above' and 'the side', depending on the circumstances. A main difference from all three approaches so far described is the involvement of the therapist *as a person*, considered as engaging with the family system through a semi-permeable interface permitting mutual exchange of personal information. The therapist and family interact to facilitate a process of growth and development on *both* sides. The family is considered as a subsystem of the extended family, this in turn of the wider relationship network, and next of the class or culture to which it belongs. As much of this broader system as necessary is involved in therapy in each case

The therapist also has a semi-permeable boundary with his professional suprasystem, so that information passes to and fro to inform him of his deficiencies and to correct his blind spots, at the same time enabling other colleagues to benefit from his professional and personal growth in a similar mutual learning process.

There are three systems. The first is the family being treated and their network; the second is the therapist's personal life, his family of origin, family of procreation and other personal relationships; and the third is the therapist's professional life, colleagues, and professional world. They must interact within the person of the therapist in an optimal way if he is to be as effective as possible professionally, and grow and learn from his experience (Figure 8). One consequence of this is that the criteria of 'health', which influence the goals of treatment, are not based on an assumption that the therapist, his colleagues and profession, or his family of origin and family of procreation, or for that matter his own social class or culture, necessarily embody these. Rather, such values will be determined at any time by the best and broadest research available and by mutually corrective experience among therapist, colleagues and others.

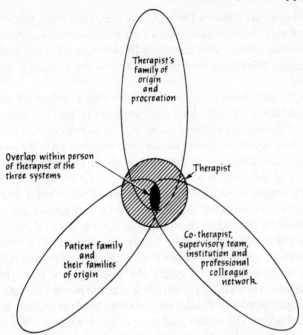

Figure 8. Interaction within the person of the therapist of the three social systems – personal, professional and patient/client family.

It will be seen that this open-systems approach has many features resembling the Timberlawn description of healthy families, as compared with many other methods of a less open and more rigid kind, which often suggest at best mid-range or adequate functioning in their emphasis on rigidity of rôles, of values and of authority structure. These tend to show an imperviousness to new ideas, a lack of the idea of mutuality of influence between therapists and patients, a relative distrust and consequent lack of spontaneity and an oppositional attitude and competitiveness in relation to other schools of thought.

b. Procedure

Coming to *procedure*, one begins with a careful consideration of referral information to determine the group one will try to meet

335

with. At the Woodberry Down Child Guidance Unit, where many of these ideas were worked out, a Referral Committee representing different disciplines met regularly to perform this task, using the principles I have described in Chapter 1 as the *minimum sufficient network*.

Briefly, this means that one tries to bring together the smallest system likely to be capable of autonomous function and change. In terms of Freudian structural ideas, ego, superego and id functions must all be represented. Or, put another way, not only the problem, *but the* motivation *to do something about the problem and the* capacity *to do something about it must all be brought together, if these functions reside in different persons.* Thus, a child who complains of panic attacks or depression *can* be understood and treated separately by individual or stranger-group methods, if old enough to move and cope outside the family system (though I would try routinely, nevertheless, to see the family for a first interview, to gather information and explore the possibility of clarifying the family system as well). By contrast, where the *parents* complain of a behaviour disorder in a child, one must see the family if one is to get the motivation, the power and the symptom together 'geographically'. On the other hand, if the *school* is complaining and the parents seem unconcerned or ineffective, we would usually agree to see the family only at the school (which is suffering, not ourselves or the family), with the headmaster (who has the power) and the class teacher or housemaster (who has the information about the problem) present at the interview. Since it has both the motivation and some power, the school is made responsible for securing the attendance of the family.

Similarly, if the motivation for referral seems to lie in the unrealistic expectations of the referral agency (e.g. a middle-class assumption that working-class children should not be aggressive), or if the family has successfully manipulated the referral agency into an unrealistic acceptance of responsibility, or if several agencies are in conflict with one another, then the referral agent(s) should be included in the interview too.

It will be evident that the first step, in fact, is to educate referral agencies regarding the systems approach, securing their cooperation by demonstrating its effectiveness (and also declining to take over their responsibilities). Gradually, referrers learn that it is helpful to provide some outline of the family structure, including relations or other persons having a powerful influence, so that this may be considered in setting up the first interview. If such information is not available at the start, it may be obtained by letter or telephone from the referral agency; failing this, a brief interview can be arranged with one family member, usually the mother, to secure facts needed to determine the best arrangements.

Though it is valuable to have such information about the family structure and the reason for referral, if too much is discussed at the preliminary interview the family members will often assume that they have performed their part of the therapeutic task and so take a passive rôle, putting responsibility on the therapist to provide answers and advice. Moreover, although it is, in fact, possible to use my methods even if one has received much previous information, it is far more difficult to avoid clinging to the comfort of intellectual understanding of the problem rather than letting oneself be affected by the family dynamics, especially when experience of this approach is limited and there is anxiety that it will fail. In addition, conflicts over confidentiality are far more likely to arise. Ideally, one should have only enough information to set the interview up with the minimum sufficient network adequately established (as far as one can judge this at the beginning of the intervention – one may later see the need to expand it).

The therapist should begin with an open mind, free of expectations which might tend to impose a structure on the information the family provide, so the setting is best kept as simple and unstructured as possible too. Unless there are young children, only a circle of chairs is provided, perhaps with a central table. If young children are present, the circle of chairs is all that is provided at first, to see how the children behave and how the parents manage them when they become restive, but play materials are available, out of sight, to be produced when their limited capacity for sitting still is exceeded (materials readily expressive of fantasy, without needing much supervision, are best; I favour soft, flexible family figures, and paper and crayons). These materials are placed in the centre of the circle (on the table or on the floor), so that the children's play can be observed and linked to the verbal discussion.

The first stage. *The procedure that follows is absolutely simple in its* *outward form, and indeed often rather boring or unexciting, at least at first, to onlookers. The complexity lies in what is evoked in the therapist's inner experience and the difficulty rests in maintaining a quiet, open attentiveness without being pressured into prematurely 'doing something'.* I open by asking about the problem, looking from one to another without catching any one person's gaze in order to indicate that all are free to speak. I listen to what is said, and I try to understand it. That is, I become aware of *not* understanding some aspects and I quite straightforwardly ask questions to clarify these – nothing more. *This position conveys to the family members that it is their task to explain the problem to me, not my task (at the start) to explain anything to them, and this position is maintained despite questions, demands, silences or any other attempt to provoke me into a premature response.*

One has only to maintain an interested, questioning attitude, without hesitating to express puzzlement or bewilderment if one feels it, for the process to continue quite automatically. Usually the power-bearers in the family will begin and do most of the talking, but as one explores the problem one will start to feel the need to invite others to join in, in order to help one understand what is missing in the first account. Sometimes this happens quite naturally, without any particular effort on the part of the therapist beyond interest, curiosity and encouragement to continue. The problem complained of – rebelliousness in a child, for example – may actually begin to occur during the therapy session. Where this is not the case, I find that a few extremely simple principles quickly enable one to draw the whole family into the discussion in a way that is particularly acceptable and arouses no anxiety.

Having started with a clear description of the *problem* as first presented, I invite others to give their views as well, agreeing or disagreeing with the first account. Then I ask questions about the social *context* of the symptomatic behaviour, including its *effects* on others and the *effects of others upon it* – what makes it better or worse and what they do to try to *manage* it. This leads on naturally to explorations of *unexpressed feelings* about the problem as presented and, by asking everyone, including the children, what would most help to improve it, to *exposure of disagreements* and other material about the family dynamics.

This focus on the symptom is reassuring to the family members, since one is beginning with the problem they came about and widening out from this in a way they can readily understand, allaying their fears that one is going to blame some person or subgroup or spring some alarming interpretation upon them. Indeed, one can convey this reassuring message before they arrive by making it clear that therapy is intended to 'help' the therapist through providing information, while also enabling him to 'help' the whole family to 'help' the designated patient through the increased understanding gained. Movement away from this early symptom-focussed stage takes place naturally by steps that everyone can understand, and indeed by steps initiated by the family members as often as not, so that *they* discover the family-systems viewpoint for themselves and begin to look at the symptom in a family context.

During this first stage the responsibility of the therapist is to be as fully *responsive* as possible, simply receiving verbal and non-verbal impressions of the family and avoiding 'closure' towards any explanation, plan or goal too soon. The aim is to be *receptive* to all members of the family, to get to know them *individually* as well as remaining aware of their interaction. The *active* aspect of the therapist's rôle is to maintain this open, wide and clear attention, allowing the information to come in continuously without blocking it by trying to 'understand' it prematurely in an intellectual way or, where glimpses of such 'understanding' do occur, avoiding clinging to these in order that such thoughts will not interfere with the open and formless attentiveness required. This is really a continuation of the way I look from one to another when I open the session, maintaining an awareness of all the individuals present and according value to each one's presence and contribution.

This first stage is always painful for the therapist, in the sense that one has a sense of confusion and chaos, of being overwhelmed by unrelated fragments of information and by feelings of likely failure.

The second stage. The first stage merges into a second (I have noticed no consistent time relation – it may occur on first seeing the family or after twenty minutes), in which I become aware of puzzling emotional responses or fantasies in myself, at first as fragmented and meaningless as the impression made by the family. These gain in clarity and insistence and, though at first appearing to arise 'from nowhere', unrelated to the interview and perhaps personal in origin, they begin to *feel* increasingly as if they are somehow information about the family rather than about oneself alone, even though no rational connection can be made at first. (Of course, such impressions are *also* information about the therapist, in the sense that for one tuning fork to resonate to another, both must be similar, designed to resonate to the same frequency – the therapist is using his human commonality to understand other members of his species.)

This awareness of the effect of the therapist's inner experience is associated with an increasing sense of *conflict*, at first as a vague discomfort, gradually crystallising into an impulse towards some active response, whether a statement, an expression of emotion or movement, which at the same time is somehow felt to be inappropriate and better kept concealed.

Finally, there is a conviction that the response aroused is perhaps exactly what the therapist needs to put into the family system, since one realises on reflecting on the interview that it is exactly what has been missing throughout it – some emotional attitude conspicuous by its absence – and that one is feeling inhibited because one is resonating to the family's taboos on expressing this particular aspect of human nature.

My experience in every case, as far as I can recall, is that this understanding of family problems occurs suddenly, unexpectedly, unpredictably. The period preceding it is *never* experienced as a logical, step-by-step process where one is aiming at, and has a sense of getting steadily closer to, a goal by some systematic, understandable process. Only after the sudden flash of insight, the instant falling into place of the formerly disconnected fragments of information to form an ordered and meaningful whole, does the early period of confusion become suddenly meaningful and understandable.

I have suggested that:

> The explanation must lie in a figure/ground type of phenomenon. *The real family problem is always contained in what is* not *communicated, what is* missing *from the content of the session* [my italics]. To begin with, it therefore cannot be located, and one feels a sense of frustration and inadequacy. Only when a good deal of conscious or 'public' information has been accumulated, providing a 'ground',

can the 'figure' – an empty space in the pattern of facts, what is missing from the facts – be observed against this. And as in visual pattern-recognition problems of this kind, recognition is sudden, even though once seen it appears so obvious that one finds it hard to grasp why one did not observe it earlier. (*One Flesh, Separate Persons*, p. 178.)[17]

The form in which the therapist casts his intervention varies according to understanding, educational level, capacity for reflection and autonomous function, defensiveness and motivation of the family concerned. More intelligent, reflective and insightful families may be best served by an interpretive, explanatory type of feedback, whereby the therapist both provides them with the kind of information they can work out themselves in detail later, and gives them the opportunity to grasp some general principles of exploring family dysfunction they can utilise to tackle future difficulties without professional help. Other families may lack the capacity for reflection and insight, or be deficient in ego-strength or social skills, and the therapist's understanding may be more effective if translated into a more behavioural, educative approach, using advice, task-setting, restructuring, or communication of skills by example and modelling.

But the most powerful intervention, having the most rapid and dramatic effects (hence also the most risky and needing the most careful judgement as to timing) is for the therapist to *act* upon his understanding of the family dynamic, in such a way that the therapist virtually enacts the scapegoat rôle: that is, he voluntarily and consciously personifies the very emotion(s) the family disowns.[18] Viewed in this way, the experience to which the family is subjected is so shocking, so horrifying, that the rapid and dramatic changes which frequently follow are scarcely surprising. It is as if the family members have been fleeing from a monster and finally find refuge in the safety of the therapist's room only to discover, as they begin to feel secure and to trust him, that he turns into the monster himself!

Needless to say, much effort, energy and skill must go into building a relationship of warmth and trust with the family to enable them to tolerate this experience. And this is best done by – indeed follows automatically upon – the earlier period where one seeks to understand, identifies with, and builds a relationship with each separate member of the family. To the extent that this is accomplished, the final phrasing of the intervention will take the needs and fears of *all* members into account, will allow for defences and resistance, as well as revelations and exposure of secrets. The therapist does not become *just* a scapegoat, but rather contains and expresses the collusively denied or repressed emotions, *as well as* representing and expressing the anxieties that led these emotions to be denied and rejected in the first place. By absorbing the projective system of a disturbed family, the therapist suffers from their dilemma himself first, but the solution, if found, is inevitably tailored to that particular family's exact defensive structure. If the therapist succeeds in escaping, he does so by a route that the family can follow.

It will be easier to convey this process and elaborate the details if we take an actual example and study it in some detail. It is, in fact, a family I saw for the second time, just after I began writing the last few pages and with whom I tried in consequence to follow and note my inner experience with a view to describing it more carefully, rather than just using it to treat the family.[19]

Case Example

Session 1

The family telephoned for an appointment on the suggestion of a medical colleague who had since returned to his country of origin. They were middle class and consisted of the parents, Alan, twelve, and Sacha, eight. I had no further information about them. I introduced myself in the waiting room and when they entered my room they sat in the pattern shown in Fig. 9. I reserved my seat by leaving the notes on it so they could choose their positions in relation to me.

Mother, who did most of the talking, explained that the referring psychiatrist had seen them two years earlier for a marital problem. When he left the country they chose not to proceed with his recommendation to contact me as they felt the problem was 'sorted out'. The problem now was Alan, who had been stealing from mother and was not fulfilling his potential at school, where psychotherapy had been recommended. Alan had been attending a well-known clinic for

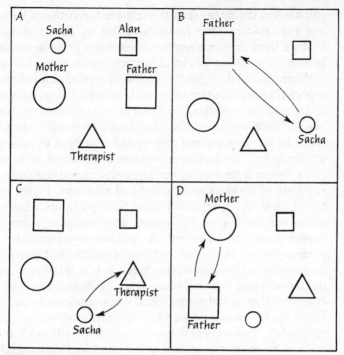

Figure 9. Positions taken up by family members at first and subsequent sessions (persons changing position indicated in latter). See text for details of sequence.

Freudian analysis four times a week for about four months. However, he disliked going, there had been no improvement and he had finally refused to go.

On enquiry Alan said he was unhappy at school, that he often started arguments at home after which he would walk out of the house, and that he had been stealing. Sacha said she had no problem 'except that she could not write stories' which I thought indicated a fear of fantasising. Parents acknowledged but then dismissed the marital problems as no longer important. I thought the children were still anxious about the parental relationship. When Alan volunteered that they had told him a year earlier that they would get divorced, mother

343

emphasised the intensity of the relationship between herself and the children. She rationalised this as due to father's absence from the home and his commitment to his career, but he said the situation was no different when he was at home.

When I asked them for the details of a typical incident, they reported a sequence that began with Alan's stealing, followed by reproof from mother, Alan walking out of the house, both parents' anxieties about him, then finally their relief when he returned late at night and consequent reluctance to exercise any discipline. An argument developed between mother and Alan. He held his own as her aggressive criticism mounted, and both of them looked flushed and animated. Father and Sacha took little part and looked like spectators watching tennis singles. I used this image, queried father's lack of participation and suggested the marital improvement had perhaps meant that Alan had lost a special and powerful position he had possessed in the family before. Mother agreed that he was master of the house when his father was away. I suggested that he had not yet found a new relationship with his father to replace the special relationship he used to enjoy with his mother. This seemed to make some sense to them all; they seemed to enjoy the session and I felt I had established a positive relationship with them. Although he refused to have any further individual psychotherapy, Alan agreed to attend further family sessions.

I can recall no particular feelings during this session, for I was taking things slowly and concentrating on forming a good relationship with them in view of the boy's hostility to the previous therapy.

Session 2

For the preparation of this chapter I had, between the previous session and this one, resolved to study my reactions carefully the next time I saw a family. This was the next family in the appointment book. They entered and sat in the same formation (Fig. 9(A)). Father reported that they had not understood anything from the last discussion but that it had left them all feeling more relaxed and open for a few days. Mother agreed, and then attacked Alan, mainly over his failure to fulfil his potential (and her expectations) in school work, music and exercise. Alan said mother was as bad as he was about not taking exercise and letting herself get fat. Father agreed that Alan and mother were similar in their self-consciousness about their bodies and added that mother had an 'anorexic' problem and over-ate and dieted alternatively. On enquiry he acknowledged that he had lost his own interest in food during childhood and avoided eating between meals. An argument then ensued between the parents in which mother said, 'Why can't you bear people enjoying themselves?'

During this discussion about food I experienced no feelings in me except those of frustration. I became anxious that I might be unable to do anything with this session. I then became aware of a conflict in my own reactions to the mother's vibrant sexuality. At first I tried to prevent my thoughts from proceeding towards the idea of what she would be like in bed. I struggled to keep focussed on the family as a whole, treating my distracted attention as if it were my personal problem and so did not use it.

The aggressive exchange between the parents switched back to the one between mother and Alan. After this sequence had occurred several times, I pointed out how Alan 'drew the fire' on himself when the parents began fighting. Sacha said she was glad Alan stopped the parents fighting in this way.

I continued to be preoccupied about my sexual awareness of the mother, and ashamed of myself for not paying proper attention when they were paying me to do so. Then suddenly I realised that these responses were related in some way to the family problem, though I could not at the time see how.

I now reported these feelings by saying, 'I often find my own feelings during an interview tell me something about the family problem, as if I am tuning in to it. At first I was concerned about feeling nothing, but [to the mother] I have just realised how aware I've been of what an attractive woman you are sexually and [to the father, balancing things up and passing her back to him!] what a lucky man you are to have chosen her.' I added that I had no idea what all this might

345

mean and that I had initially felt embarrassed at my sexual response. But I wondered whether the parents were letting the children jealously interrupt their sexuality as well as their arguments? I suggested that sex was not 'earthed' between the parents but was floating about, getting into the children and into me. The children hotly denied that they were jealous about the parents' sexual relationship, but the parents felt that what I had said made sense. Sacha said, 'I am worried that they do it', but quickly added that she meant the fighting.

As the session ended I felt that no one seemed to like the ideas I was putting forward very much. I felt I had made a mess of the session, had gone too quickly and made them reject me.

Session 3

When the family arrived late for the next session two weeks later, I was anxious they were not coming at all and that my worst fears about the previous session would be confirmed.

After they arrived, there was the familiar attack on Alan by mother, this time for making them late, but it seemed there had been some trouble with a school bus. We were all sitting in the same places. As the argument subsided, mother asked if I remembered saying she was attractive. When I said I did, she replied: 'Well, all the way from here to the station Alan was saying that I wasn't attractive at all, that I had crooked teeth, a big backside [she listed his other criticisms of her]. And as for him [she stabbed a finger at father], he ignored it *completely*. There was a sexual tension that everyone was terrified to admit.'

I experienced relief that the theory was being confirmed. Not only had I, as therapist, experienced the 'missing' emotion and the corresponding fear but, in addition, the family's resistance to it, and their subsequent opening towards acceptance, was following the expected sequence exactly.

Mother recounted how, the day after their last interview, when Alan was looking at a picture of a nude in a newspaper, he began screaming at her when she asked him if he liked it, and he was vehement that he did not. Another battle ensued between Alan and mother, with father and Sacha on the sidelines. Increasingly, I felt the arguments between mother and Alan were expressing, and also avoiding, a kind of sexual engagement. I suggested this, adding that all the sex in the family seemed to be between mother and Alan. Where was the real marriage? Father said he missed his previously good relationship with Alan; he felt he had lost him during the last few years.

I became aware of the seating pattern as a manifestation of the family problem and felt a strong wish to change it by putting father in Sacha's place, and so next to mother, and Alan, but also in between them.

After reporting these feelings and suggesting the change, the new arrangement (Fig. 9(B)) felt better. Father agreed, though he said it made him feel more prominent and therefore uncomfortable. He turned towards Alan and confronted him for the first time. In a warm and quiet, but very firm and authoritative voice, he said that he (father) was quite a jealous and possessive person. He wanted mother for himself and resented the way Alan constantly managed to get her attention. As he finished, mother recalled how when Alan once stole £30, father had not said much and had stood aside. 'Now,' she said, 'he is taking a clear position with Alan for the first time.'

I commented on how, far from being upset, Alan looked pleased with his father's new firmness. As the session ended I was aware that Sacha had been excluded from the whole interaction and I expressed my concern.

Session 4

In the intervening fortnight I described this case at a seminar, at which I said Sacha was still a mystery. A young female student said, with a twinkle in her eye, 'Well, you called her a little sweetie', as if suggesting I had not recognised some sexual attraction. Despite my belief that some measure of sexual attraction between adults and children is beneficial, I found myself embarrassed, as I had been over sexual feelings towards the mother. I wondered whether my embarrassment was an indication that I was now picking up feelings associated with father's unfulfilled oedipal romance with Sacha.

As if in confirmation, Sacha looked lively and bright instead

347

of withdrawn and apathetic. Also, she began by saying she had made a Valentine's Day card for father. Both parents reported that things felt easier and that they were going out more together on their own. Sacha said she fought less frequently with Alan when the parents were absent. Alan next reported that he had felt more energetic and that problems were now solved as soon as they arose because 'all the family try to talk about them right away'.

When father later reproved Alan kindly but firmly, mother joined in the criticism in a more attacking way. I pointed out how she kept breaking up the developing relationship between Alan and father. A discussion followed about Alan spoiling mother's birthday which led to a more intense argument between mother and Alan. He stood his ground firmly and for the first time was able to be quiet and contained, saying he wished to be independent and separate. Father also took a firmer position. But I was again aware of how Sacha was still excluded from the interchange, and said so. She asked for help with inability to stop blinking, a problem which had begun when father returned from a period abroad. Mother said she felt guilty that sometimes she could not bear Sacha's presence and wished she did not exist at all. When the parents again focussed on Alan's spoiling of mother's birthday, I became increasingly aware of mother's own need for mothering, which she was getting vicariously through the children and which they resented. This was confirmed by mother's recollection of how much she had needed and enjoyed Alan's company when she was alone with him before Sacha was born. When he had gone to school, Sacha had replaced him. Father said he could not remember Sacha during this early period.

I again wondered if father had missed out on his oedipal romance with Sacha and vice versa. I had also been strongly aware that Alan was jealous of Sacha having been born.

Session 5
My attention was held throughout the session by a very large and beautiful blue tie the mother was wearing. The family seemed lively and eager when we began. Seating was rearranged twice, with Sacha making two changes in response to

her discontent, beginning with the situation in Fig. 9(A), then as in 9(B) and ending up with 9(C). In the new position, which felt right, the parents were together, I had given mother back to father and was separated from them by the children, who needed my support at losing their previous fusion with the parents.

Mother and father were going abroad soon and so I had agreed to see them only eight days after the previous session. When father expressed anxiety about leaving the children behind, mother said, 'I think he really has great difficulty in leaving the children and being able to be with his wife alone!' Father agreed, saying he would miss the warmth of the home and particularly his relationship with Sacha, which was 'a gift from one day to the other'.

When mother reported that Alan was arguing less with her and drawing fire from father instead, the boy made them argue by comparing them adversely with each other, stimulating rivalry. This stopped when I pointed it out.

Mother expressed her growing sense of differentiation by saying to the children, 'I would like to be able to wash my mind of you . . . what about *my* life?' She realised they had always been able to control her by making her feel guilty about being a bad mother. Although this was expressed forcibly, there was no anger in it. Rather, in a calm way it established a distance between herself and the children.

However, Sacha had once again been left out and her blinking had increased. Noting this, I recounted to the family my recent presentation of their problem as a case example at a seminar. I reported that when I had mentioned my puzzlement about Sacha's rôle to my colleagues, someone had implied that I was denying my sexual attraction to Sacha. I told the family, in an amusing way, how I had felt embarrassed by this – was I flirting with all the females in the family, and if so, what did it mean? This went home to mother, who turned suddenly to Sacha and said with a grin, 'Would you like to take off with father on holiday in my place?' Sacha nodded, grinning too.

The focus turned to father's feelings about Sacha. The normal sexual aspect of the father/daughter relationship did indeed seem to be lacking. It seemed to be based more on father's vicarious infantile gratification. He said, 'I enjoyed my early childhood when I was happy, when I was very small, and I may have tried to relive this through Sacha.' After this happy early period he said he had gone through a time of hostility towards his father. He made a connection between this and Alan's hostility towards him. Sacha's blinking was increasing.

I was feeling increasingly isolated, as if I was being rejected by the family for expressing a view about the normality of sexual feelings between fathers and daughters. Although mother appeared to understand, I felt her basic loyalty had to be to the family's denial. My attention was still caught by mother's prominent tie and I felt impelled to mention it.

When I did so mother grinned and said, 'You mean I am the man in the family?' (Father was wearing a black polo-neck sweater.) It was then revealed that Alan had done up her tie for her. He looked uncomfortable and, in a sudden break-through, mother said she was realising vividly how the sexual pattern between herself and her husband was always dictated by the children. 'We like to make love on Saturday and Sunday, but they barge in whenever they feel like it. There is always some excuse to disturb us and we are fools: we pretend we are doing something quite different when they enter the room. I am longing to get away on holiday so we can make love as often as we like, without worrying about the children.' Father was in agreement but unlike mother and the children, who seemed at ease, he appeared much more embarrassed. He declared to the children, 'Do you want us to have a notice on the door saying "vacant" or "engaged" to tell you what we're doing? Why can't you knock?' I suggested it was difficult if there was not some clear indication such as a locked door. Alan said, 'Why don't you *tell* us what to do? What's the problem about telling us, so we know when to stay away?'

Challenged by mother, father acknowledged his embarrass-ment about sex. He linked it to his own parents' embarrass-ment, but he said he was already relieved by the discussion. He asked the children if either of them minded if he and mother still made love. They seemed accepting, indeed pleased to hear about it, and Alan asked if they were going to have another baby. Mother said they made love simply because it was so enjoyable and I explained, without detail, that people could make love if they wished without needing to make a baby.

The incestuous sexual theme I had introduced earlier, for which I had feared being rejected, now seemed increasingly accepted. Mother, smiling, said to the children, 'I can see it now, goodness knows why I didn't see it before. You two feel the sexual tension between us, you like to smell it, you like to come in and intrude. That's why Sacha is always staying up late and disturbing us and finding excuses. We've never drawn our boundary clearly between you children and ourselves. We've never made it clear.'

Time was up. As they left I found myself chatting with father in a man-to-man way about the forthcoming business trip, as if I were offering the supportive 'homosexual' relationship he had needed but lacked with his father. I was left feeling that all was now well enough between the parents for them to develop the relationship, but that I still needed to help the children to cope with this change.

Session 6

I began the session two weeks later still feeling I had to do something to help the children cope with the loss of their parents who were closer to each other sexually.

Sacha's unusual liveliness, animation and confidence were striking. When we were seated I asked if anyone wished to change places. Mother said she wished to change with father who reluctantly complied (Fig. 9(D)).

Mother began by saying that Sacha, who had been lively, had woken up first and got the rest of the family up, would probably do all the talking. After changing her chair, mother realised she had wanted to put more space between herself and Sacha. She especially resented Sacha's attachment and dependence. Alan said that this was mother's fault, implying that the dependence was mutual. Mother continued that she wished Sacha would fight back instead of denying her hostility. As mother talked, Sacha blinked steadily with a hostile stare

351

which I described as 'stopping the daggers from flying out of her eyes'. Soon we were all again like spectators watching a tennis match, but now it was between mother and Sacha.

I found myself thinking that Sacha could not grow away from mother because father would not accept her oedipal attachment, and expressed this in simple language. Father merely complained that both children stayed up late and interfered with his relationship with his wife. Again I felt that the children were stranded. I had enabled the parents to be comfortable with their sexuality but could not yet see how to help the children cope with the new situation.

When I reported this to them all, Sacha responded by complaining that Alan's anger and teasing prevented a good relationship between them, as if the anger and aggression were a defence against enjoyable sexual feelings.

Still feeling blocked by father's reluctance to acknowledge his side of the oedipal romance with Sacha, I mentioned that I had a beautiful daughter who obviously enjoyed her sexual feeling towards me as much as I did mine towards her. I also said she was skilful at playing off my wife and me against each other and commented that Sacha seemed unable to do this. Mother confirmed this, saying, 'She always failed to pull her father on to her side against me', and 'He was never ready to be her white knight on a charger'.

They all discussed a recent incident where Sacha had gone home to seek father's support when a rough boy had pushed her off a swing. Father had accompanied her back to the playground but had just spoken mildly to the boy, disappointing Sacha, who had screamed afterwards that father was a coward. She now revealed that on returning home to seek father's protection she had become aware that her parents were upstairs making love. Nevertheless, she had intruded despite her feeling that she should not interrupt them, and father had got up and gone with her, leaving mother.

As the discussion continued, it became obvious that the motives for Sacha's interruption were mixed to say the least, and that neither female was at all pleased with the way father dealt with the situation! I became very aware at this point of how Alan and Sacha, like all children, found it difficult to lose the bodily intimacy of babyhood and also to accept exclusion from their parents' intimate sexuality, unless they could find a substitute in their own sexuality.

I said this but acknowledged that I still could not understand it well enough to help them. Mother reported on the 'terrific sexual tension' between the children when they were left alone and said teasingly that they were 'too afraid to have a good time like mum and dad'. This confirmed my earlier awareness that there had been a deficiency of normal sexual feelings of attraction and enjoyment beween the children, which was now beginning to change.

The parents continued to talk in terms of adult sexuality, while the children responded appropriately to each statement as if 'translating' into another language where non-sexual games and play substituted for sex. Sacha said, 'When men and women like each other, they can say they want to be with each other, but children can't.' She seemed to be speaking about intercourse and this led to a relaxed discussion of what it meant. Alan confirmed his knowledge but Sacha was blocked, as if she knew but was denying her knowledge. I explained the details and said it was exciting and enjoyable. The children said they did not wish to do anything like that yet.

The theme changed to complaints about father's inhibitions which limited his forcefulness and potency. Sacha protested to him, as if feeling greatly deprived, 'You never even shout at me, let alone hit me'. When father was again evasive she shouted, 'I'm asking for you to hit me and you keep trying to change the subject'. Finally he acknowledged that he did not want to feel 'sexual overtones coming towards him from Sacha'. Mother teased her, saying she was faithful to her daddy but he did not respond and so she was angry with him.

I was struck by father's fear of violent, animal feelings including sexuality and aggression. Drawing attention to this, I pointed out that father could have been 'a beast' and enjoyed himself three times over in the incident described earlier. He could have finished making love to his wife, smacked Sacha for interrupting and also shouted at the boy who bullied her. Everyone found this hugely amusing. They continued on the theme that father should be the strongest in

353

the family. Mother said that when they all played games together, the children wanted him to win. 'When the father is the strongest in the family,' she continued, 'everything comes back to peace and quiet; there is order, harmony, no wars. But in reality I'm the strongest.' There followed an argument between mother and the children over who was strongest.

Throughout this session I was preoccupied by a filmed interview I had seen at the Institute of Family Therapy where a colleague had interviewed a very similar family. The staff who had watched the film with me seemed as inhibited about discussing sexual, oedipal problems as the therapist had been with the family, though the therapist paid real attention to the children's needs which I particularly admired, since I tended to neglect this aspect myself. I recognised that this was connected with the fact that while I had become relaxed and comfortable about discussing parental sexuality in front of children, I was much more embarrassed at talking about children's sexuality in front of adults.

I experienced a powerful impulse to say something outrageous that established the right of the children to have their emerging sexual needs recognised. I reported this to the family, adding that the fathers in both families seemed (like my own had been) uncomfortable about their potency. I also said that perhaps I, as a child, had also been frightened of my developing sexual potency because of a need to be weaker than my father and to keep him stronger than me, a new understanding that I was brought to by watching the filmed interview. As I was reporting this I had a profound feeling that many things I had not previously understood had fallen into place and become connected.

I said to the family that I had, perhaps, brought myself in more personally than usual because I had been learning something important about myself and my own family of origin. There was no time for further discussion. They left looking quiet and thoughtful and I felt a deep assurance that I had given the children what they needed and that the main work was done.

Final three sessions

After a six-week interval, the family came for three more sessions at intervals of two weeks. The seating remained unchanged except that mother and father changed places with each other twice. At the first of these (session 7), father took an authoritative position for the first time, criticising Alan for lack of effort at school. Alan said the school was too permissive and that he wanted to change to another with more discipline and educational 'stretching' which I personally also thought he needed. The females 'sat this one out', looking relaxed, but when mother tried once to dominate, father told her to 'keep out of it . . . you take too much territory.'

I still felt some lack of connection between Alan and father, and found myself thinking repeatedly that the father's father had failed in his relationship with the father in some way, and that the males in the family were uncomfortable with their homoerotic feelings. I said this, and while father showed discomfort, mother and Sacha agreed, saying the females, by contrast, were getting along famously. I felt myself to be occupying paternal grandfather's rôle, giving the males permission for a more comfortable attitude to their homosexual feelings.

At the next (eighth) session, the father looked much more manly, showing a new quiet firmness, as well as an obviously sexual enjoyment of his wife, moving his chair close and leaning towards her. Both expressed feelings of increasing differentiation, mother saying she 'had her own universe instead of seeing the family as an extension of herself', the father agreeing. The children, rather bored, asked why they were still coming for therapy.

The final (ninth) session began with the parents saying that on the way to the interview they had both found themselves having the same thought – that this would be the last visit. Sadness at parting was expressed, together with pleasure at the changes. Mother reported that Alan had 'changed drastically', was a 'pleasure to be with' and could 'express his pain instead of keeping it inside him'. The changes in Alan and the family were confirmed by other members.

However, Alan was obviously finding the termination more

difficult, showing obvious envy of my rôle which, as I pointed out, made him both deny it ('You only sit there and write') and also want to continue to see me ('We're not perfect, not everything is cleared up, though most things are'). I confronted him with this difficulty in accepting what I had to give him, while I kicked his shoe and punched his arm gently in a friendly fight.

He then expressed more clearly his remaining discomfort in his relationships with girls, where he seemed unable to distinguish real hostility from the aggressiveness and provocation which were really adolescent sexual behaviour. Though I felt he might at some time need and accept some separate therapy, I suggested that he should talk to his father about this first, to see if he could help him.

I had been waiting throughout the treatment for some family history to emerge, and had been surprised that so little had come earlier. Then, in the last ten minutes, mother reported that her mother, who had suffered all her life from 'troubles with her uterus', had telephoned to say she had finally been told by her new doctor that her problem was just that she 'needed a man'. Mother said that her mother obviously felt relieved and released by 'being given permission to have sex' for the first time, but that it would 'cause trouble' with her father, 'who is inhibited'. Mother now said that her parents had never had a fulfilling sex life because of their inhibitions. This was in contrast to the mother's grandfather, who had 'screwed around until he was seventy'.

This discussion of the sexual attitudes of grandparental figures led mother to speak of how physically attractive her husband had recently become. He had begun leading a keep-fit class and she enjoyed seeing how attractive he was to the women attending it. Father laughed and acknowledged he enjoyed it too and was going to 'end up playing for Europe'.

The family left with expressions of warmth and gratitude, as well as sadness. During the seven-year follow-up, all improvements have been not only sustained but extended.

The Key Requirement in the Therapist

The additional information about the parents' families of origin, filled out with genograms in follow-up interviews, supports the view that the same basic pattern or structure is repeated at different levels of organisation, i.e. extended family, family, marital and intra-personal systems. Therapeutic interventions may therefore be based adequately on information obtained from only one of these levels, though the redundancy provided by use of several levels simultaneously will decrease the possibility of important factors being overlooked.

1. Intervening from inside the family

This understanding of the family 'from inside', achieved by opening oneself to the projective system so that one internalises the individuals separately through identification and begins to suffer from the struggle with the family conflict oneself, can be combined with the methods of approach already described and emphasised by other schools of family therapy. To understand 'from inside', one needs to approach 'from below', abandoning a *defensive* use of one's professional rôle and power. Conceptual thought must not be allowed to dominate and obscure the faint emotional responses generated by the family projective system. But the requisite quiet and open attentiveness can eventually be maintained, while thought processes continue to register data and suggest possible explanations in the light of theory. This additional source of understanding of the family 'from outside', reached by routes 'from above' and 'from the side', may be extended and used to explore and initiate change while a deeper emotional interaction is proceeding. Such interventions may be particularly necessary to remove blocks to communication which would prevent the therapist from gaining adequate exposure to the family dynamics. For example, it may be necessary at the start to insist that the father or 'healthy' children attend, despite resistance; to refuse to see parents and children separately until the therapist judges this desirable; to break up communication patterns that exclude or restrict the contributions of some members; or in other ways to use professional authority to change the family structure or the ground rules of the interview.

2. Inside the therapist: a question of consciousness and equilibrium

So far, I have attempted to formulate my experience and behaviour when interviewing a family within the framework of Western psychology, particularly psychoanalysis, group analysis and social learning, even though general-systems theory is, in fact, a return to the more holistic view still preserved in the East. But, to be truthful, I believe these approaches are really inadequate to describe my methods, for I have little doubt that *the key requirement in the therapist is a deep awareness of his own identity which he is able to sustain in the face of overwhelming, if transient, emotional arousal engendered by encounter with profoundly disturbed family systems seeking to externalise their pathology*. This does not mean clinging to a professional rôle, to a particular theory or technique, or even to one's personality in the ordinary, superficial sense (though this is what we are apt to do, and it is what determines our limitations).

If I were to try to express this essential requirement in one sentence, I would say that it entails a more intense consciousness of both one's inner and outer experience, such that reality is completely distinguishable from fantasy, whether the latter originates within oneself or is stimulated in response to the projective (fantasy) systems of others.

Where this heightened consciousness exists, there is no need to cling to anything static (necessarily some sort of fantasy, including rational thought), since reality (necessarily ever-new and changing) is so vivid and fulfilling. *Reality* is *reality and fantasy* is not *reality, in the sense that a menu* is not a *real dinner*.

In this ability to maintain a heightened consciousness of reality, and so to avoid being hypnotised by the fantasies engendered by the projective system of the individuals or family, the therapist is for the family a landmark or beacon by which they can find and orientate themselves. He need, in fact, do nothing but *be* with them, in the sense of maintaining his identity and integrity.

By *being* with them the therapist constantly contradicts their projected expectations, startles them into a new awareness of reality by also dissipating, briefly at least, the fantasy that constantly engulfs and controls them, by showing them how unreal and shadowy it is just as sunshine dissipates a fog and dispels the terrors imagination conjures up to fill its shadows, merely by revealing the quiet countryside. Paradox, 'therapeutic double-binds', koan-like questions, the 'crazy' statements and 'zany' interventions that characterise so much of the work of Carl Whitaker and which I make much use of myself, tasks and suggestions that break up established structures – all have as their common underlying effect (whatever explanation the therapist may use to justify it) the function of *shocking* the family into a level of heightened awareness and so out of their dreams and self-fulfilling negative prophecies.

Western thought, including psychoanalysis and academic psychology, has particularly neglected the issues of intensity of attention and level of consciousness, so central in Eastern approaches.[20] But once this is taken into account, many seemingly diverse techniques readily find an explanation and a place within the concepts put forward here. If consciousness is equated to light, both Freudian and Jungian methods of analysis are akin to searching for objects in a darkened room one by one, striking match after match; the paradoxical and task-setting techniques are akin to setting off a photographic flash bulb, momentarily illuminating the whole room in a vision which it is subsequently difficult to deny one has seen, even if one forgets the details. The various meditative techniques all seek to generate a more powerful and reliable source of light to replace the flickering 'matches' and occasional 'flash bulbs' which comprise our ordinary waking consciousness, thereby illuminating reality and dissipating fantasy just as awakening from ordinary sleep dissipates the reality of sleeping dreams, or at least alters our conviction of their truth.

3. Transitional states and attachment figures

The point of view I am proposing can also embrace and give added meaning to the *attachment* concepts of Bowlby (1967, 1973) and the ideas of Winnicott (1971) regarding the significance of *play* and *transitional objects* in enabling the child to move gradually from the security of the first attachment figure into the wider world. Heard (1978) has recently proposed a most interesting integration of the ideas of these two writers, and though the language she uses makes her proposals at first appear rather complicated, she appears to be suggesting that what both Bowlby and Winnicott have in common is the view that new, experimental behaviour, whether exploring the internal or the external world (both forms of 'play'), can feel safe only within a sufficiently constant, reliable, predictable context (Winnicott's 'held' situation, or the goal of the 'proximity-seeking' behaviour in Bowlby's scheme).

The tendency of severely dysfunctional and mid-range individuals and families to cling to the known, to fear loss and change, to be unable to learn from experience because they order their lives in such a way that projected expectations, based on the internalised models, are never contradicted or threatened with change, for example by choosing a spouse whose inner world will mesh smoothly and confirm past experience; by selecting friends who will not recognise and challenge defences and denials of reality; by embracing political, religious and ethical codes which will avoid new experience which might demand change and growth, can thus be seen as equivalent to proximity-seeking behaviour, a clinging to security because enough safety was not provided in early life to make the excitement of exploration outweigh the corresponding fear. At root, it is a clinging to mother.

Translated into these terms, what I am saying in this chapter is that to use my approach the therapist must simultaneously or at least in rapidly alternating fashion both *maintain a parental, 'holding' rôle keeping the situation constant and safe* and *provide a model of 'play' explore, open up, risk, venture out into the unknown.* To the extent that the therapist cannot do this (be parent *and* child, therapist *and* patient, at once) he will need a co-therapist or colleague-support-system to handle one side of the polarity when he gets stuck in the other. But in whatever way this dual function can be accomplished, the therapist must lead the family members towards the exploratory attitudes they previously turned away from, in a context of safety, support and encouragement.

The approach I favour, therefore, links equally with both the most modern psychoanalytic concepts just described and also with the oldest known form of mental healing, that of Shamanism, and offers a possible mechanism explaining the similar internalisation and partial resolution of the patient's problems described by Jung (1954). The relationship to Shamanism – the need for the therapist's internalisation of the projective system, and the fundamental requirement of an absolute trust in one's own identity and abandonment of all clinging to technique – is expressed most beautifully in the ritual song of a Pacific North West Indian Shaman:

> I know thee. My name is Tom. I want to find thy sickness. I know thy sickness. I will take thy sickness. My name is Tom. I am a strong doctor. If I take thy sickness, thou wilt see thy sickness. My name is Tom. I don't lie. My name is Tom. I don't talk shit. I am a doctor. Many days I haven't eaten. Ten days maybe I haven't eaten. I don't have my tools with me. I don't have my sack with me. My name is Tom. I will take thy sickness now and thou wilt see it. [Rothenberg, 1972.]

On Method in Group Analysis and Family Therapy

Though questions raised about method need to be put and answered, many of them are irrelevant to the practice of my approach, in the sense that a knowledge of knots is irrelevant to the task of cutting the Gordian knot. *What is needed is an understanding of how to keep a sharp edge on one's sword – a wide, deep and still attention.*

1. Assessment and treatment

I hope it will be clear from the description of the method and the example just given that assessment and treatment are fully integrated and that both begin the moment the therapist and family encounter each other.

a. The locus of intervention

Also, assessment and treatment aspects of the interaction are proceeding at a variety of levels, though the balance of these may change in different cases and in the course of therapy. A longer-term treatment is likely to present as an 'individual' problem, to move to examining this as part of a pattern in the nuclear family system and this in turn as a product of unresolved problems in the marital dyad. Exploration of the dyadic relationship will lead on naturally to study of the individual, intra-psychic level and to the beginnings of these individual difficulties in developmental failures in the families of origin. This brings us to the systems level again, either intra-psychically or by bringing the grandparental generation in to the interview, but the object will be to help the differentiation of each member of the couple from these systems from which they sprang, as well as from each other and their children.

361

However, the emphasis may vary. Some 'primitive' families may be best worked with mainly at the level of producing a small structural change in the whole system, sufficient to turn a descending spiral into an ascending one. With others it may be better for all if one individual is helped to differentiate and separate, while the 'treatment' of others is aimed at distancing them from this individual and so avoiding threatening their defences by exposure to more insight and change than they can bear (e.g. by arranging placement of a child in a boarding school).

b. Insight or behavioural orientation

Since the unconscious or unexpressed inner worlds of each person are read mainly through non-verbal communication, and the therapist's understanding is fed back to the family as often by 'modelling' and action as by symbolic communication, it is obviously meaningless to classify the method as either 'behavioural' or 'intra-psychic'; both, like assessment and treatment, are as integrated as inspiration and expiration in breathing.

Because of the desirability to keep the therapist's attention open, clear and free of pre-formed judgement and thoughts, I prefer if possible to avoid tests, questionnaires or other structured devices. I find it hard to imagine any that would not complicate and prolong the process, but if time and cost were not important they could probably be included for research purposes. There is also no reason in principle why the method cannot be used at home, at school or anywhere else, provided the different circumstances are allowed for.

2. Therapeutic goals

It should also be clear that there is a constant concern with clarifying 'goals', though the word is not one I customarily use, either in my work or my writings, because of its associations with the idea of a *therapist making plans or decisions* in order to *do something to or for* a patient or family. But from the moment the family members are encountered they are brought up constantly against the question of what they want, and this is reformulated and clarified over and over again throughout treatment, right to the end.

a. Keeping responsibility in the family

Responsibility is thrown back onto the family at the beginning of each meeting. The therapist's task is to help *clarify* what the family wants, to help expose conflicts and inconsistencies regarding incompatible desires both between and within members, to help them negotiate more generally acceptable compromises, to help them see what stands in the way of their getting what they want and to help them discuss how their wishes might be achieved. It will be evident, too, that I want the answer (or 'goal') to come if possible *from the family,* even if the answer is obvious to me from the moment I meet them. For if all collaborate in achieving a solution, they are more likely to have reached a real joint decision where hidden resistances, which might sabotage the therapist-imposed solution, have already been exposed and allowed for. Moreover, the family will have had the opportunity to learn about *problem-solving in general* (i.e. second-order learning), which they may be able to use without external aid when they meet future problems; such a benefit obviously cannot follow if the therapist does the thinking for them.

b. Ultimate and intermediate goals

Using the method described, a step-by-step process of clarifying a destination and how to get there automatically follows. In this sense there will obviously be intermediate goals (what they think they need when they come) and ultimate goals (the different things they may discover they want by the time they leave), though again I feel this kind of jargon complicates rather then elucidates a simple and obvious process.[21]

It it also often counter-productive for the therapist to formulate plans or goals *explicitly,* since this will enable a resistant, aggressive family to sabotage them. Supervising trainees, I find behaviourally oriented therapists tend to fall into this trap. If, instead, one throws responsibility for decisions and for changing (or for not changing – it is their choice) back onto the family or couple, they can only defeat *themselves,* and the therapist can make it quite clear that the self-defeat is their problem, not his. 'Goals' are established in a language and at a level the particular family can grasp – motoric, conceptual or whatever. The idea of a treatment goal so general as to apply to *all* families would be so broad as to be almost meaning-less. However, 'to clarify the situation' would satisfy me and if that did not satisfy the family I would tell them it is their problem to put the understanding into practice, not mine.

3. Therapy structure: negotiation and control

Essential decisions about therapy structure (whether or not to see the family, whom to invite, how much disturbance they can make) are *absolutely* under the control of the therapist if it comes to the crunch, but despite the therapist's ultimate veto, the structure is as far as posssible negotiated and is used to offer maximum freedom of communication. The family members are encouraged to talk to each other and to do all the work, *but* the therapist will intervene as forcefully and as often as may be necessary. A violent verbal confrontation may, for example, be necessary to establish control or break a defensive pattern. *The therapist both joins the family and remains outside, oscillating between one and the other position in order to pick up the projections and then to reflect on and analyse or act from them.*

The treatment alliance is aimed at by being basically warm, friendly, interested, sympathetic, helpful, humorous and absolutely natural, yet without abrogating responsibility and authority. The therapist also seeks to see the situation through the eyes of each individual in turn.

4. Transference, counter-transference and the therapist's stability

a. Transference

I am here describing the family equivalent of transference in the individual psychoanalytic technique, in terms of systems of projected expectations, more briefly, 'projective systems'. They are recognised by the 'counter-transference' activation of corresponding irrational emotional reactions in the therapist. This is obviously the cornerstone of what is most specific in my method.

b. Counter-transference

This use of counter-transference has never appeared to present a risk to anyone but the therapist, *provided* it is used in the manner described, by the therapist *expressing* his irrational feelings as information the family can either accept as being about themselves, or reject as being about the therapist (rather than as 'interpretations' lobbed into the family like hand grenades from the bunkered safety of 'blank-screen anonymity').

c. Self-disclosure

The degree of self-disclosure required of the therapist is necessarily high, and I see no necessity for any limits to this, provided that it is aimed to be ultimately in the service of the therapeutic task rather than solely for the therapist's benefit, which certainly means the therapist must stay within the limits of what he can cope with emotionally. However, it must be added that, using this approach, crucial breakthroughs in insight and change tend to take place when the therapist feels *at* those limits and even fears he is out of control and is breaking them (the theory underlying the technique explains why this is so and the case example illustrates it only too well).

d. The therapist's stability

This process being central to the method, the therapist's psychological health (together with his objective and open acceptance of his remaining ill-health, which is all part of the same thing) is the most crucial attribute in the therapist. Other important factors are related to this. He must be at ease with himself, able to enjoy himself, relatively satisfied with his life, his marriage, his sexuality and his family (or be able to accept objectively and openly, and to use therapeutically, what he lacks or what cannot be changed).

e. Technical errors and therapeutic damage

There are no *serious* technical errors I have encountered or witnessed in using this method, in the sense of *harming* families.[22] *The commonest errors I have noted are*:

i underestimation of its subtlety

ii attempts to make it into a 'technique', i.e. a set of principles which can be manipulated intellectually without requiring personal involvement and fresh exposure, learning and risk each time. People who want to 'find out how to do it', for example, have not only missed the point completely, but also failed to see that they missed it.

5. Insight, change and technique

Regarding the relationship between 'insight' and 'change', I doubt if anyone can change his habitual behaviour without some change in the way he perceives the world. A fine for speeding not only reduces the average speed of my car but also increases my awareness of the police and my attention to my rear-view mirror. In this unusually *broad* sense, 'insight' and change would go together. But I have not found that an ability to recognise or verbalise such alterations in habitual perception that accompany change is in any way essential to that change, even though it may be necessary to second-order change (the ability independently to continue to change).

a. Interactional and historical insight

In general, interactional insight has appeared more important than historico-genetic insight, but the latter nevertheless often facilitates change because it makes the patients' behaviour both meaningful *and obviously* inappropriate *to present circumstances.* For example, it may for the first time open the real possibility to the patient that he is not just 'naturally' or 'born' miserable or hostile, but that he has developed negative emotional *habits*. Thus, curiously, analytic historico-genetic insight may actually make a person receptive to the idea that change based on relearning is possible and so open him to a behavioural approach. Moreover, relieving guilt, it may also permit more objectivity and ability to face the facts of current behaviour, i.e. increase interactional insight. However, it is also my impression that:

i insight follows change as much as the reverse – they are parts of a cyclic process; and

ii that a combination of historico-genetic and interactional insight is powerful not so much through a process of 'rational understanding' as by making the person aware of the habitual and unvarying nature of his perception and behaviour over long duration and under different circumstances.

This provides a 'shock' of increased awareness through a sudden perception that his usual behaviour, which formerly felt 'natural', suddenly appears ludicrous, totally inappropriate to his present life, 'crazy', and so motivates change.

b. Paradoxical interventions in group-analytic work

'Paradoxical' interventions are particularly relevant to this issue of stimulating a more vivid awareness of contradictions in the patient's thought and behaviour. When disordered, communication becomes extremely complex. As described on pp. 292–4, disordered states are often maintained by double binds, attempts to maintain a fantasy world different from reality in a form which conceals the discrepancy. This is achieved without contradicting either the inner fantasies or the outer realities, and 'hidden commands' are conveyed to others to collude with the self-deception and preserve the discrepancy by helping to disguise it. As described on pp. 196–7, paradoxical therapeutic interventions can be seen not as 'tricks' but as expressions of an essential truth which subtly breaks the 'rule' that fantasy and reality must be kept apart, by relating the two in a seemingly innocent fashion which expresses only the positive aspects. As I shall demonstrate on pp. 393–4, they seem to work because they describe in one statement both the real need and desire for change, and the equally real danger and fear of it. When the essential conflict or contradiction is located by the therapist exposing himself to the projective system (the hidden commands) in the manner described above, the therapeutic intervention can be formulated in paradoxical form as readily as any other. The essential difference in my approach, which combines the group-analytic and the Milan methods, is its systematic and guided use of countertransference information to provide the 'hypothesis' on which paradoxical interventions can be based, rather than leaving this stage of the process unexplained.

c. Technique and skill

'Techniques', in the sense of detached manipulation of the behaviour of others (something you can know how to do before you do it, plans, strategies etc.), are not an important part of my approach and the whole idea is antithetical to it. Nevertheless, most 'techniques' *can* be used at some point in the therapy, if the method described fails, and I have personally learned all I can from other more 'technical' schools of family therapy, using any methods that seem helpful. New *skills* are certainly transmitted as part of therapy, usually more by a gradual 'shaping' and mainly through 'modelling', but didactic methods are used at times, especially with sexual problems.

If one member of the family changes and stays in contact with the rest, then probably all family members change, just as all the solar system is presumably affected by the passage of a comet. But in both cases some changes may be large, others so small as to be immeasurable and irrelevant to practical astronomy, in the one case, or to the handling of the family in the other. The concept of the minimum sufficient network, described earlier in this chapter, is concerned with this issue. The problem of differential motivation has also been addressed. In summary, it is handled as far as possible by constant negotiation and then by addition of separate therapies if the aims of some members go further than others.

6. Duration of therapy

My method is not necessarily time-limited. When the presenting problem is a complaint about a child, the duration tends to vary between a total of one and six sessions, with an average of around three, if one excludes follow-ups. I do not think a time limit would speed this up particularly, and I personally could not cope with an even briefer exposure to a greater number of families without losing my present enjoyment of my work.

Sessions are normally held every three to four weeks, except where more extensive support and supervision are needed, as I have described elsewhere. Bowen (1978) and the Palazzoli group (1978) have found similar advantages to this spacing, which throws responsibility onto the family members and gives them time to digest the experience generated at each interview. The standard length of the session is one hour.

7. Longer-term therapies: couples groups

The above comments apply to cases where the marital relationship is basically positive and such problems as exist can be dealt with indirectly through discussions of the management of the referred patient. Where the therapy leads naturally to uncovering serious dissatisfactions in the marriage, or where a couple present initially with severe marital problems, even short-term therapy is likely to be longer than this, ranging between three and twelve sessions. For more resistant problems of all kinds, particularly where a marriage is reproducing serious difficulties due to powerful unresolved attachments to the families of origin of the couple, we routinely employ couples groups led by my wife and myself as co-therapists, not only for their economy but also for their much greater effectiveness, impact and speed of change, as compared with work with one couple at a time.

Couples groups are particularly effective with those marital partners who employ defensive mutual projective systems which are particularly intense and highly resistant to insight and change, as well as with those couples seeking growth and differentiation as individuals rather than resolution of a specific problem. Couples groups therefore tend to be used by us for both the healthiest and the sickest patients, though naturally the two extremes will not normally be mixed together, but selected for different groups.

Since in both cases the aim is *differentiation* of the individuals rather than change in the marital system alone, with either an improved marriage (in about four out of five cases) or amicable divorce with cooperation over care of the children (in about one in five cases) as equally acceptable alternatives, therapy is much more prolonged than with the short-term 'system-change' interventions. The groups meet weekly with a duration of attendance for successful resolution ranging usually between one and two and a half years (this is about half the time we have found to be needed for similar degrees of individual growth in stranger-groups run along similar lines).

8. Termination of therapy

Termination occurs naturally, usually by some members of the family wondering whether they need to continue coming. This often occurs as the therapist is having similar thoughts, and wondering what else needs to be done. The presenting complaint will have disappeared or diminished to a satisfactory degree, and usually other aspects of functioning will have improved, too.

Termination is ideally a joint decision in this manner, which would be regarded as good/successful. Some families terminate prematurely, i.e. before the presenting problems are solved to the degree thought possible by the therapist, and against advice (such termination is not always appropriately considered bad/unsuccessful, since if the parting is amicable and a good relationship has been

369

established, some such families return and achieve a good/successful result later). Bad/unsuccessful results would be those cases which were not screened out in the first two interviews as unlikely to benefit for one reason or another, and which receive further family interviews without noticeable benefit.

9. Applications of therapy

The methods described here were developed in a wide range of settings from public services to private practice. At the former extreme they have been applied in parts of east and north-east London where I have worked in clinics and hospitals dealing with some of the most severe social problems in the country. At the other extreme they have been applied in private practice with intelligent, well-educated patients, including a proportion of the gifted, rich and famous. A striking feature of these methods is their efficacy in about equal measure right across the social scale.

The wide applicability of this is partly due to the fact that the approach is both highly flexible and compatible with at least some aspects of most other approaches, and partly to the fact that no difficulty has been found in combining it with individual, separate stranger-group or other forms of psychotherapy, medication etc.

10. Combinations of therapy

Such problems as my colleagues and I have encountered in these variations of my approach or combinations of it with other methods have almost always proved to be problems in the therapist rather than in the technique. For example, those accustomed to individual work can sometimes be possessive or jealous over patients. Those with a psychoanalytic background often demand to 'understand' and have access to all available information, rather than to work with the information immediately available in the interview and trust collaborating colleagues to carry out their separate share of the intervention.

a. Borderline and other vulnerable patients

Used in a flexible, highly sensitive way, with respect for defences, the method seems particularly valuable with highly defended, 'borderline' families, since the therapist can 'carry' the pathology in the early stages and take the lead in anxiety-provoking areas, leaving the family members free to follow if they wish or to disown him temporarily if their defences become too threatened. Apart from this, I have found no special indications or contraindications for my approach compared with other family techniques.

b. A family approach for diagnosis and assessment

Regarding comparison with other types of therapy generally, we have also found no contraindication to this family approach for preliminary diagnosis and assessment, even though individual, stranger-group, therapeutic community or other modes of intervention might then be recommended, perhaps with periodic joint family sessions to review progress and integrate the work.

c. Referring on from family work

Separate psychotherapy for spouses or other family members is sometimes recommended when it is vital to establish some measure of separate identity in members whose personalities are very fused, and where they are too threatened to attempt this in each other's company. However, in such cases conjoint sessions can be added beneficially and the combination of treatments may fruitfully lead on to placement in multi-family or couples groups. Separate group or individual treatments of one or more family members may also be indicated when conjoint family or couple therapy has produced as much change as one or more members desire, but others wish to go further in order to explore their inner world more deeply and differentiate themselves more fully from the family system. Such additional separate treatment is more often desired and appropriate when couple therapy has led to agreed separation or divorce, or where family therapy has enabled an adolescent to become disentangled from parents who wish to remain in a state of relative fusion. The separate individual or group psychotherapy is sometimes carried out by myself or my wife, but many are referred to psychoanalyst and psychotherapist colleagues. Where conjoint sessions continue with one of us, it has appeared best to have therapists other than ourselves doing the separate treatment with one or more family members. We have found no difficulty where a good relationship exists with such colleagues, even when they take sides or are overpossessive, since our focus is on the interactions among the family members, or among them and ourselves, and our

371

own responses to the patients' interactions. A combination of four-way interviewing and separate sessions with two co-therapists does, however, seem an especially powerful means of intervention, though, because of its high demand on the therapists' time, we tend to use it only where there is a risk of psychotic decompensation with any therapy less intensive, supportive and coherent.

d. Dealing with specific sexual dysfunction

'Active' methods of treatment of sexual dysfunction, influenced particularly by the combined behavioural/analytic techniques developed by Helen Singer Kaplan (1974), are regularly employed in the course of the conjoint methods described here, with couples who present with relationship or sexual problems or, in the case of family therapy, after the problems displaced into the children have been brought back into the marriage, which then becomes the focus, with the children excluded. In situations where a dynamic understanding is not of great importance, referral might be made to a behaviourist or sex therapist.

Referral to a behaviourist or sex therapist might be made where the initial investigation indicated that the main need was for information, education, training in skills or techniques, or where deficient performance seemed due to cultural attitudes or family prohibitions, relatively uncomplicated by the defences described in the psychoanalytic literature which, through their function of distorting or obliterating the patients' *awareness* of the problem, make re-education impossible until the defence is reduced. In particular, one would avoid referring to a therapist with limited psychodynamic understanding, a patient or couple whose defensive system relied especially on projective mechanisms by which they induced those involved with them to absorb their problem (e.g. the impotent man who relieves his feelings of inadequacy by inducing feelings of incompetence in his therapist), or where the symptoms themselves serve a defensive function (e.g. constant fighting between a couple as a defence against, or disguised gratification of, genital or pregenital intimacy).

e. Medication

Medication would be employed as required to control the more severe depressive states of other emotional reactions interfering with relationship and communication, though this is avoided as far as possible since it generally strengthens defences opposing change.

11. Decisions against therapy

A decision not to recommend any treatment at all is generally made when the family makes impossible demands which do not permit a viable contract (e.g. that a child shall behave well when the parents intend to continue to treat it badly), though even here the door is left open for the family to return should they change their views. Confronting, exploratory approaches are also avoided where a 'borderline' parent is functioning as well as can be expected in the community, though we would ensure that a good support system or 'safety net' existed, or provide this ourselves, in case of future crises and decompensation. Economic considerations, relating the resources of the clinic to the demand upon them, might lead one to avoid therapy in less severe problems if services are already over-burdened by those in more urgent need. But in all these cases, one or two family interviews, which are really a 'trial of treatment', usually provide the most economical and accurate method of screening out those families where intervention should be cautious or minimal, where motivation is inadequate to sustain the effort required to bring about change, or where pathology is too limited to justify intervention, given the resources available.

12. Using co-therapy

Economic conditions influence decisions regarding co-therapy. Following the simple principle that one should not use an expensive or time-consuming procedure where a simpler or less expensive one will do, most treatment is carried out by one therapist. A second therapist is added:

1. Where the system is so chaotic and confusing that one therapist cannot readily cope alone;

2. Where there are gender identity confusions or conflict which make the presence of male and female rôle models or advocates of sufficient advantage;

3. Where important information may be gained by co-therapists

373

absorbing the projective system of a marriage when other methods of understanding have failed;

4. Where the combination of a more experienced and a less experienced therapist has teaching advantages.

Team therapy using the one-way screen is usually reserved for continued learning through peer-group supervision, for research, or for assistance in cases where treatment has become blocked.

In general, either inability to work alone or inability to work with a co-therapist is regarded as an undesirable limitation in the therapist. Co-therapy is regarded as akin to marriage, an advantage if the partners are well matched and work together harmoniously, a disaster if not. Nevertheless, it still provides an opportunity for each therapist to learn and grow.

Conclusion: Training for the Group-Analytic Approach

What follows here is derived from my papers on training and professional motivation which will be published together in due course. Readers are, in the interim, recommended to 'An Open-Systems Approach To Teaching Family Therapy' (appendix reference 31); 'The Large Group in Training' (appendix reference 20), and 'Make Sure To Feed The Goose That Lays The Golden Eggs: A Discussion On The Myth Of Altruism' (appendix reference 42). It is also derived from what colleagues have developed elsewhere and from what I have seen of programmes lacking the open-systems design I believe to be essential. It must be emphasised that this is no more than a résumé of what is elsewhere available in much more detail.

1. Live supervision

The cornerstone of a full 'training', as opposed to an introductory or supportive programme, must be the treatment of actual families under supervision. In view of the vital importance of non-verbal communication, this is best carried out by observation through a one-way screen, where the clearest and broadest impression of the family's non-verbal responses can be obtained or, failing this, by closed-circuit television or videotape. Nevertheless, the quality of the supervision is obviously more important than the 'hardware' and a second-rate supervisor may produce less competent students with the most sophisticated aids than a first-class supervisor using case discussion alone. If I over-emphasise this, it is perhaps because I see so many therapists over-valuing the 'hardware' and hoping that technical 'gimmicks' will somehow substitute for hard-earned understanding, experience and skill.

2. Theories and techniques

Apart from this, I would like to see students exposed to as many theories and techniques as possible, though within a sequence of presentation and of accompanying coordinated discussion which would limit confusion and help them build an approach to suit their individual capacities. The family therapy teaching programmes I initiated within the Institute of Group Analysis, now run within the Institute of Family Therapy, have always had this broadly based character, including psychoanalytic, group-analytic, behavioural, systems, 'action' and psycho-dramatic methods, active techniques of treating sexual dysfunction and so on.

3. The therapist in question: training, like therapy, as shared growth

Whatever technical training is provided, it will be of limited value (though certainly of some value nevertheless) unless the professional is put through experiences which clarify his motivation in taking up his work, put him more deeply in touch with the limitations and deficiencies in himself, his family of origin, his marriage and family of procreation or alternative current personal relationships.

4. The therapist's personality and values

It will be clear that the most essential feature of my approach lies in a very direct, open involvement with patients, where it is taken for granted by the therapist that communication is two-way, that a learning process is set in motion whereby the therapist will change and grow if the patients are to have the best chance of growing too. *The therapist's personality and values, marriage and family life must* actually *be in question every time he engages with the family. He must demonstrate the possibility of facing loss, growth, change and death by the way he functions himself and by the way he changes and learns*

375

from one session to another. This sounds a tall order, but it is more a principle that the therapist should be like a mountain guide who goes ahead and tests the foothold first himself, then helps others up behind him, rather than that he should be like a perfect climber familiar with every detail of the mountain. There is no more problem (and no less!) in teaching from this position than there is in practising from it in therapy, for if the right model is provided by the teacher, it has the same rapid effect on the trainee as modelling by the therapist has on families. This type of rapid (yet apparently relatively enduring) change is worth emphasising, because I believe that the essence of the requisite training experience lies in this kind of modelling, encouraging, supporting interaction. Obviously more can be learned over a longer period, but the crucial aspect of what is needed to teach my approach is totally different from the slow, dogged attempt to accumulate knowledge sequentially through increasing experience, which many family therapists equate with training. The transmission process is not accomplished all at once, of course, but each new understanding is suddenly 'caught' in a flash of illumination, if it is grasped at all.

5. Methods of increasing self-knowledge

Besides helping people to learn about themselves through supervision of their work, where the focus will be more on the personal difficulties which interfere with the task, most methods of increasing self-knowledge are likely to be beneficial unless they are misused in defensive fashion. My experience of students with prior individual or group therapy greatly favours the latter, and though individual therapy may be desirable for trainees with problems over intimacy and separation, rigid classical analysis tends to give trainees a therapeutic experience that appears, more often than not, to make it *more* difficult for them to learn family therapy subsequently. This is because of the excessive preoccupation they develop with intellectual 'understanding' and control of the situation, with focus on detail, with emphasis on therapist passivity and neutrality, with fear of personal exposure, and with a generally rather precious and over-exquisite preoccupation with the importance of the therapist's rôle. I believe that couples groups composed of trainees and their spouses would be better than separate therapy alone, perhaps together with some sessions with the trainees' children as well as their spouses. This we have not done, except 'accidentally' where the trainees sought assistance with marital or family difficulties directly, but Bowen (1978) has attempted it beneficially.

We have, however, made very full use of encouraging trainees in systematic studies of their families of origin, following closely the ideas of Bowen (1978) and Framo (1976). We have found this invaluable, and I would regard it as an indispensable part of any family therapist's training, whatever other form of personal psychotherapy is advocated in addition.

6. Dynamics of staff and student groups

Finally, the constant study and monitoring of the group dynamics of both staff and student groups, particulary the interaction between these and the way in which the professional systems reproduce typical family dynamics (e.g. casting of leaders or subgroups into 'father' and 'mother' rôles, provoking conflict between them etc.), and the feeding back of this information to the staff–student groups, have appeared to me the most powerful learning experience of all, providing both first-hand experience of pathological 'family' dynamics and simultaneous opportunities to learn and move towards more healthy forms of structure and communication. In such studies of the professional system, there is a particular need to focus on (since there is a strong tendency to avoid) issues of loss, separation and death; sexuality; and competition. I have described the application of this method in a number of papers (see appendix references 2, 4, 12, 20).

Another paper (Skynner and Skynner, 1979; appendix reference 31) reports on its use in our introductory teaching programme at the Institute of Family Therapy. Ideally, an expert in group dynamics not involved in the hierarchy of the institution being studied should be brought in for crucial meetings of this kind at least from time to time, acting as 'family therapist' to the 'institutional family'. Difficult though this may appear, it seems to me that senior members of institutions might be able to perform this rôle effectively with institutions other than their own; indeed, the meeting together of different staff groups in conference conditions often has a liberating and facilitating effect of this kind.

Needless to say, the level and extent of self-knowledge needed

377

will depend on the general level of skill required. Simple behavioural methods have the advantage of demanding little of the personality and self-knowledge of the therapist, and are adequate for many cases. Paraprofessionals could use some of the simpler concepts presented here, under supervision, but should obviously not be encouraged to try to work with the projective system in the manner described. Nevertheless, the ideas used here can be extremely valuable in the supervision of paraprofessionals or less highly experienced therapists, if the supervisor makes use of his awareness of the projective process in a manner similar to that described by Caplan (1964), where the supervisor avoids confronting the supervisee with his own psychopathology but uses the supervisee's 'counter-transference' responses to help him understand and identify with the family.

7. Professional motivation: beyond the limitations of the system

Whatever form of personal psychotherapeutic experience is recommended, an open-systems training demands that the trainee's motives for taking up his work be made a constant focus throughout. Since the professional rôles of mental health professionals form a central part of their defensive systems (Skynner, appendix refs. 2, 4 and 20), which maintain a split between 'parental' and 'infantile' aspects of the personality, failure to explore this crucial area adequately must lead to limited self-understanding and a tendency to burden patients and students with infantile aspects of the therapist's or teacher's projective system, restricting the growth of those with whom they work. Also, since the therapy of trainee therapists is inevitably carried out by other mental health professionals sharing a similar defensive system, some collusion in avoiding such exploration is inevitable. *This is one reason why an open-systems attitude to a joint exploration of the group process of training institutes, including the interaction of teachers, students and patients, is so essential. To the extent that its authority is accepted (and only to that extent) the group process provides information which can enable all individuals, including the leadership group, to grow beyond the limitations of their shared defensive system.*

Notes

1 This paper was published in an earlier form in A. Gurman and D. Kniskern (eds.), *Handbook of Family Therapy*, 1981.

2 See chapter 10 above and the chapter introduction.

3 See M. Pines, 'The Contribution of S. H. Foulkes to Group Therapy' in M. Pines (ed.), *The Evolution of Group Analysis*. [Ed.]

4 See chapter 11 above where, in the account of the therapist's identification with the scapegoat in a family, the method begins to take shape. [Ed.]

5 For a more complete account of the group-analytic approach to the training of family therapists, see Skynner's 'An Open-Systems Approach To Teaching Family Therapy' (appendix reference 31). [Ed.]

6 See chapter 12 above and especially tables 1–4 in which the work of Lewis and his colleagues in the Timberlawn Research Foundation Study are set out. [Ed.]

7 See chapter 12 above, footnotes 7 and 8. As these notes above indicate, one of the editors who originally commissioned this paper had, prior to this commission, published his criticisms of problems of method in the Timberlawn work. In their editorial notes to Skynner's paper in the *Handbook of Family Therapy*, Gurman and Kniskern drew attention to the Timberlawn shortcomings, the most serious of which was the assumption in that work that correlation implies causation. This is not a criticism they level against Skynner himself for, using the findings as a practising clinician rather than as a researcher, he measures validity and reliability by different criteria. [Ed.]

8 See the reference to Skynner and Cleese's *Families And How To Survive Them* in the editorial introduction, footnote 8. Skynner worked with Cleese after writing this paper and with him developed the account that follows here into a more extended study of partner choice, a subject which is again referred to in the introduction to chaper 14 below. [Ed.]

9 In the *Handbook of Family Therapy*, Gurman and Kniskern emphasise that Skynner's preceding comments should not be seen as sexist or gender-biased. He is describing a healthy, evolutionary process of change in marital rôles towards a balanced husband–wife power distribution. The stages in the process he describes are based on his experience of normative (but obviously not, to Skynner, desirable) relationship patterns which typify dysfunctional marriages. See notes 12 and 13 below. [Ed.]

10 See chapter 12 above, where Skynner offers a broader account of general systems theory, including other important concepts like those of organisation; control including homeostasis and feedback; and space (structure) and time (process). [Ed.]

11 Gurman and Kniskern point out that general systems theory, whilst it has produced clinically useful principles for family work, does not actually provide therapeutic techniques. There is a wider point to be made here. Theoretical innovators in the field, like Von Bertalanffy, Bateson and more recently Maturana, have not been practising clinicians. Whilst clinical innovators, like Foulkes (as Skynner points out on page 309 above), Jackson, Sullivan and more recently Whitaker and the Milan group, have not articulated a fully developed theory of their own. Skynner's work is arguably most distinctive in providing a bridge between innovators in clinical and theoretical work. [Ed.]

12 The careful wording of this sentence has been chosen to indicate that *at least* as long as the child begins its life within the mother's body and is suckled by her, the biological physical facts determine the mother's rôle as the *primary* attachment figure and the father's rôle as the first intruder into this exclusive dyad, the initial protector of both, guardian of the family boundary, and later a bridge for the child between its initial attachment to the mother and its final independent rôle in the community. Nevertheless, this situation would not necessarily apply with an adopted child, and both nurturant and controlling functions are obviously mediated by both sexes even if in different proportions by different couples. Such evidence as we have suggests that the mental health and effective development of children are best facilitated where there is a balance between clear differentiation of the two parental rôles on the one hand, and overlap and sharing between them on the other (Westley and Epstein, 1970). But as I have discussed in *One Flesh, Separate Persons*, the conflict and uncertainty among present evidence about which male/female maternal/paternal characteristics are biologically determined, which are 'shaped' by differential parental encouragement, and which are accentuated by general imitation of cultural patterns, are such that we must await, and remain open to, further evidence. My own views on this matter have changed so rapidly in recent years that I usually find myself disagreeing with what I write almost before the ink is dry, but the benefit that this changed understanding has brought to me personally, to my marriage and family relationships, and to my professional work has been so great that I believe present social changes herald the possibility of a new and more effective balance between the sexes which will enrich both. *Perhaps our main mistake lies in the very attempt to define these rôles in some stable, permanent way rather than, as in a healthy marriage and family, to remain permanently (and uncomfortably!) open to the developmental experience and expansion of consciousness that these relationships automatically make available to us, if we can bear to accept them.*

380

(As Skynner makes clear here, his views on this subject are open to review and readers can see some important formative stages as he grapples with these issues, in chapter 4, p. 55 and footnote 2; chapter 9, pp. 188–9; and chapter 12, pp. 295–6. [Ed.])

13 See p. 317 for reference to this subject in *One Flesh, Separate Persons*.

14 Skynner is not saying that childlessness necessarily leads to an infantilising relationship between partners, but simply that there is an increased risk of this when there are no children in the marriage. [Ed.]

15 Gurman and Kniskern regard Skynner's point here as 'enormously important and provocative'. Whilst they are inclined to agree with Skynner that even (apparently) limited 'behavioural' changes may produce profound intra-psychic change, they point out that most psychoanalysts would not accept this. For a more extended introduction to these issues in Skynner's work, see the introductions to chapters 11 and 14 and pp. 366 and 395 below. The point made here is at the heart of his work, and the book as a whole describes the development of a paradigm which integrates these different accounts of change. Gurman and Kniskern are confident that some of the claims for this paradigm are an exciting area for new research. See *The Handbook of Family Therapy* p. 54, fn. 8. [Ed.]

16 Beels and Ferber's classification of family therapy technique was the most authoritative and useful for a long time. Hoffman (1981) more recently introduced another classification system which divides techniques into five groups: historical, ecological, structural, strategic and systemic. [Ed.]

17 For more information on pattern recognition and the psychology of figure-ground relations, see chapter 10 and especially footnote 2.

18 See chapter 11 above.

19 The case study that follows is comparable in many respects to the full-length case studies by different family therapists in the memorable collection by P. Papp, *Family Therapy: Full Length Case Studies*. [Ed.]

20 See 'Psychotherapy and Spiritual Tradition' (appendix reference 27).

21 Skynner's claim here is less controversial than might, at first sight, appear. He is not dismissing the importance of goals and outcome criteria that could be of use for purposes of evaluation, or for research of any other kind. In arguing that the partialisation of a problem and the differentiation of goals that are constantly being examined can often distract both therapist and family from the simple and obvious, yet difficult tasks ahead, he is distinguishing his own method from that of, for example, Hayley's problem-solving method. [Ed.]

22 See Gurman and Kniskern, 'Deterioration in Marital and Family Therapy: Empirical, Clinical and Conceptual Issues', *Family Process*, **17** (1978a) 3–20. There they suggest that there are some serious technical errors that can be made in family therapy in general, and some of these errors are especially pertinent in what they call psychoanalytically oriented family therapy. For example, if the therapist 'directly attacks loaded issues and family members' defences very early in treatment (and) does little to structure and guide the opening of therapy or to support family members' (p. 14). [Ed.]

14 What is Effective in Group and Family Therapy: The Self-Renewing Paradigm

This final chapter is the author's Keynote Lecture at the International Congress of Group Psychotherapy in 1984. Here Skynner achieves the comprehensive theory he had set out to find in a paper which is both reflective and provocative, and which has the magisterial quality of what is sometimes referred to as late works.

The dialogue between group analysis and family therapy was opened in Chapter 10 and is here resumed at a higher level after the integration of psychoanalytic and behavioural approaches in Chapter 11; and after the application of the new communications theory to family life in Chapter 12. Skynner brings the threads together looking back on his explorations with families and psychotherapies, and forwards to still-uncharted territory. The crucial ideas that solve the puzzle he had set himself, to complete the picture of how the psychotherapies relate to each other, why their differences exist and how they can be brought together, comes from the study of emotion as 'attitude', postural 'set', non-verbal cues which have the biological function of controlling the behaviour of others.

This was an early interest preceding his psychiatric training and at its end became the subject of his dissertation for the Diploma of Psychological Medicine (appendix reference 1). Whilst training, he had spent time sketching patients as he observed them being interviewed at case conferences, and trying to perceive the links between their emotional state, their posture and their facial expression. This interest is reflected throughout his work, though not discussed in detail in this collection, and is given some attention in

One Flesh, Separate Persons where he recounts the sketching he used to do.

The rôle of such non-verbal communication in marital choice, and in the regulation of behaviour among family members to restrict emotional awareness, had become clear to him for the first time during discussions with his co-author John Cleese while writing their popular book *Families And How To Survive Them*. He realised that these non-verbal signals influence family members to 'toe the line', and they automatically intensify when a member does not heed the warning. Such non-verbal signalling usually takes place below the level of consciousness where family members can maintain the pretence that it is not occurring. But intensification brings postural cues, and the emotions they express, into conscious awareness.

Skynner believes this to be the way in which all effective systemic interventions bring about (experiential) insight, and thereby the possibility of a higher level of integration. Change can occur as a result either of conscious acceptance of the underlying attitudes and motives exposed, which is a result more like a successful analytic interpretation; or in order to minimise this self-exposure which is a result more like a successful strategic intervention.

With these missing pieces of the puzzle, the whole pattern comes together to explain the effectiveness of the methods considered. They are based on a truthful perception of reality, stated in a form that is not experienced as criticism. The same principles underlie successful interventions of both a psychoanalytic and systemic kind. In thus shedding new light on how more accurate perception of reality offers new potential freedoms, this collection concludes at the point from which the next will depart: Skynner's contribution to the field of professional motivation and training.

J.R.S.

Introduction

Before we ask what is effective in group psychotherapy, we must determine how many kinds of group psychotherapy we should be concerned with.[1] The fields of family and marital therapy have shown tremendous growth in the level of professional and public interest, in conceptual clarity and in refinement of techniques, to a point where what we used to call group therapy – the treatment of groups of strangers who have come together at the therapist's suggestion – is almost overshadowed. And within family therapy, the 'systems' communication approach developed on the West Coast of the United States under the leadership of Gregory Bateson (1972) has developed overwhelming influence worldwide as compared with the psychoanalytic approach, pioneered by Nathan Ackerman (1958) on the East Coast, though interestingly the most influential recent advance in systems concepts and techniques has been the responsibility of the group of psychoanalysts in Milan led by Selvini-Palazzoli (Selvini-Palazzoli *et al.*, 1978), an advance which opens the way, as I hope to show in what follows, to a reconciliation of these two previously opposed paradigms.

Moreover, in what we used to call 'group therapy' – that is, stranger-groups – the previously dominant psychoanalytic model has also experienced powerful rivals, though its influence still remains strong. Transactional analysis, encounter groups, EST marathons, psychodrama and its derivatives, and various developments from behavioural methods like social skills training, or the recent work with schizophrenics and their families arrived at by Leff and his colleagues (Leff *et al.*, 1982) in England and by Falloon and his co-workers (Falloon *et al.*, 1982) in the United States, all contribute to a rich but confusing diversity of theoretical models and techniques.

Clearly, the whole field has become too big for any one person to comprehend it all in a satisfactory way. But I think we need to attempt that, makeshift and unsatisfactory though the result is bound to be, and I think we can legitimately *try* to take a bird's-eye view of the whole field, as long as we acknowledge, when we attempt it, the limitations and blind spots most likely to fault our perception. Right at the start, therefore, I need to present my credentials and acknowledge my own limitations by providing a brief note of my own background and experience.

Since I first trained in psychiatry thirty years ago, I have shared a particular interest, with other colleagues like Malcolm Pines, in the group-analytic approach developed by one of our teachers at the Maudsley Hospital, S. H. Foulkes (1948, 1964, 1975). His use of the group process to understand and help the individuals composing it seemed to me to open a way towards a reconciliation of psychoanalytic ideas about the inner world with approaches based on social learning of one kind or another.

If our bird's-eye view is wide enough, trying to span the whole field – however imperfect our detailed vision may become at the necessary altitude – might we perhaps find a simple unifying pattern giving meaning to the whole, a pattern not obvious at closer range where we cannot see the wood for the trees? My impression so far is that this is the case. I have recently had the exciting experience, after I had almost despaired over the increasing and indeed intolerable complexity I first encountered, of finding it giving way to an elegant pattern of simple principles from which the different modalities could be logically derived. My attempt to formulate these principles in a way that is easily conveyed is a task still in progress, but I would like to share some of the conclusions reached so far. Our main requirement is to reconcile and integrate the knowledge we have developed in stranger-group psychotherapy with the principles now well established in family therapy. But family therapy is itself at present divided between two major paradigms – the psychoanalytic on the one side and the various derivatives of 'systems' ideas on the other, and a bridge has to be built here first before we can attempt the major crossing. My own struggle to reconcile these seeming contradictions, going backwards and forwards between conducting stranger-groups and family groups in the course of my daily work, and alternating between group-analytic and systemic interventions in both, trying to live with the confusion all this brought me, has recently borne fruit. Some simple connections between these approaches – so blindingly obvious, once one had glimpsed them, that one wondered why one had not seen them before – unified the two perspectives into a more comprehensive theory than either offered on its own, freeing and enriching the resources available for both types of work. To show that there is no contradiction between them, let me start by outlining some of the fundamental principles common to psychoanalysis and most other dynamic psychotherapies.

Dynamic Theories

First of all, in the theories of dynamic psychotherapy, successful adjustment and mental health are viewed as the result of a child passing through a series of developmental stages, each of which adds to its social competence. Though the details differ slightly as between Freud, Klein, Mahler, Erikson and others, the general principle is that, given a biological readiness, these developmental stages are mastered through the parents (and later others too) presenting certain social challenges to the child and simultaneously supporting it in learning the necessary skills to cope with them. As a result, at each stage the child learns to cope with a different type of emotional constellation (nurturance/trust; authority/obedience–independence; exclusion/jealousy–sharing.

A second principle implicit in these theories, though not always stated, is that if a developmental stage is missed through some social deprivation (e.g. death of a father, lack of siblings), there is a natural tendency to seek out the needed experience at a later date (e.g. to search for father substitutes, or to learn to share with peer groups instead). Although early experience cannot always be made good completely, most early deficiencies tend therefore to be self-correcting unless some complicating factor prevents this occurring.

However, to make good the deficiency, the person concerned must of course be *aware* of it, in the sense of experiencing a feeling of loss, or need, or pain, or failure he would like to be free of, and he must also be prepared to risk revealing this deficiency to others in the course of trying to remedy it. In other words, he must be sufficiently troubled by his problem to be motivated to remedy it. A third principle common to psychodynamic theories is that this process of repair can go wrong if the degree of pain caused by the deficiency, or the shame about it induced by others, or both of these pressures together, are too great to tolerate. In Sullivan's concept, we begin to exercise 'selective inattention' towards some aspects of our experience; we look away quickly, as it were, when we are on the verge of noticing these limitations and the painful feelings associated with them. In psychoanalytic terms, some aspects of ourselves have 'become unconscious'.

Once this has happened, a number of consequences follow. We no longer seek out the missing experience in order to complete our development, but instead we automatically avoid it. As part of this avoidance, we are obliged to choose a marital partner with a developmental failure at a similar level to our own who will collude with us in our avoidance, since otherwise we shall be challenged and exposed. We will also tend to select our friends on a similar basis, and develop a philosophy, a world view, political attitudes and so forth which justify these choices and provide reasons why those who share our defects are superior and those who do not share them are misguided and better avoided. Obviously, children born of such a marriage cannot be helped through the developmental stage at which the parents experienced the key failure because these parents, and to a greater or lesser degree the extended family and that part of the social network over which the parents can exercise choice, have not learned to cope with it either. Like the adults, the children will learn to disguise, avoid and deny the deficiencies.

The situation clearly cannot change without information entering from outside the system, from some person or group which does not join in the collusive denial. The greater the degree of developmental failure, and the greater the anxiety about it, the more the family will tend to operate as a closed system and prevent the needed beneficial exchange with the environment from occurring.

Thus the most troubled marriages and families are the ones least likely to improve 'spontaneously', that is, by the effects of ordinary life encounters.

Communications and Systems Theories

Let us now turn to look at what the 'communications' and 'systems' theorists contribute towards our understanding of this process. Close observation of families has taught us that the denial and avoidance of the family developmental failure, and the painful emotions associated with it, is in fact a highly active process. It involves constant vigilance, mutual monitoring and reinforcement of each other's behaviour by the whole family. This is one reason why I prefer Sullivan's concept of 'selective inattention', since it conveys more clearly this *active* process of avoidance and can more easily be extended from the individual to the family group, rather than the more static image conveyed by the word 'unconscious', though the basic idea is the same. Once the pattern of avoidance is established – and it may go back generations – any move towards more open recognition or expression of the family taboo is discouraged by the family non-verbal signals – frowns, tones of voice, tense postures and so on – which if disregarded are steadily *amplified* until the defaulting member is brought back into line.

However, these patterns of mutual control are learned so early and so deeply that family members are able to read each other's attitudes and expectations from minimal cues. Indeed, though they will be sending and reacting to these cues all the time, they will not usually be aware of them themselves unless they reach a fairly high level of intensity, and an outside observer will at first find it difficult to see them at all. Indeed, even family therapists did not realise that this non-verbal communication system was far more influential in maintaining family collusions than anything said in words, until we became more able to decipher them by using teams of observers, or by repeated viewing of videotape records, or by using 'paradoxical' interventions which provoked the family to amplify the signals.

Once we were able to read the non-verbal communication, it soon became clear that in families suffering from denied developmental failure – in other words, 'pathology' – there was a constant Watergate-type 'cover-up' going on all the time. The so-called

389

'unconscious' is only too visible once the family is seen together and the non-verbal code is broken.

In one way, of course, the image of the Watergate 'cover-up' is grossly misleading, since it implies a collusive deception that is conscious, wilful, deliberate. The truth is that the family members are suffering from the arrangements more than anyone else. They are more or less unaware of what is happening to them, and are usually relieved and grateful to the therapist for releasing them from the prison they have built for themselves, once they are far enough beyond its walls to see how much better life is outside.

In treating *families* we thus find ourselves up against powerful defensive systems designed either to keep us out in case we upset things, or to disarm and neutralise us if we do gain entry. The positive forces for growth and wholeness that characterise all families are often hidden by defensive layers of distrust, suspicion, frustration and anger. But however difficult the journey to reach these positive forces is, we cannot fail to be impressed with the warmth, affection, mutual goodwill and constructive desire for growth, if we get far enough inside to gain families' trust. Between the two positions of being peripheral and at the centre, we usually encounter a very rough passage, at least with more disturbed families. The essential ideas of the psychoanalytic and the 'systems' therapists complement each other beautifully. Psychoanalytic ideas are particularly helpful in understanding the *inner worlds* of family members and the common features of those inner worlds which make up the family's image of itself. The 'systems' ideas are particularly valuable in helping us to understand the *defensive systems* whereby these inner worlds, and the family's self-image, are maintained unchanged against the evidence of experience that contradicts them and which would, if accepted, make them more accurate guides in dealing with the world.

Do these ideas help us to understand why some interventions with families are more effective than others? I think they do. Most people who have tried to transfer to a family setting the kind of interpretations used in individual analytic psychotherapy, or in the therapy of a stranger-group, have found the results disappointing. Any comment implying that something might be wrong, or that the family needs to change, is rather like announcing one's presence and intentions at the front door. It gives the system every chance to raise the alarm and band together to arrange heightened surveillance and camouflage, or to disarm the therapist or if possible to expel him altogether. Straightforward interpretations, even though given in a form which might be effective within the context of an individual psychoanalytic treatment after a long build-up of trust and confidence and of transference feeling, do not take enough account of the defensive power of a family collusion. It is like playing alone against an American football team, who have been training all their lives to bring opponents to the ground and prevent them making any headway towards their goal.

Methods of Family Therapy

There are three different methods that seem *more* effective.

Structural family therapy

One 'systems' approach, the 'structural family therapy' of Minuchin (1974) and his colleagues, is like a carefully planned, sudden, unexpected assault on the family house, disguised as a helpful visit from a friendly neighbourhood delivery man. Once entry is gained by this benign deception, he quickly tidies up the house, cooks nourishing meals for them and generally improves the arrangements so that they discover, before there is time to reorganise and resist, that they are enjoying life much more and want him to stay and continue. Though it is obvious to anyone who knows Minuchin and watches him at work that his consummate skills owe much to his psychoanalytic understanding, particularly his awareness of developmental stages and needs of children, structural family therapy shares with other essentially behavioural methods the aim of getting the family to trust the therapist enough to let him take charge for an experimental period. During this period he gives them an experience of functioning and seeing themselves in a different way. There is usually no direct attempt at providing intellectual insight nor are there explanations of how the problem may have come about in the first place. A kind of 'insight' is involved if the family actually discover, even if they never put the discovery into words, that the new arrangements are more workable and enjoyable than the old. If this were not the case, the changes would not persist in the way they do when the therapist gets the intervention right on developmental grounds.

Strategic family therapy

A second effective method is called 'strategic' or 'systemic' and has been associated particularly with Haley (1971), the Mental Research Institute at Palo Alto (Watzlawick *et al.*, 1967) and the Milan Group (Selvini-Palazzoli *et al.*, 1978). Here also the intentions of the therapists are carefully concealed, those in the room asking innocent, neutral but revealing questions while the others, hidden in their 'stake-out' behind the one-way screen, closely observe the system of non-verbal signals controlling and reinforcing the collusive family denial. Then when enough information has been gathered, some advice, or a task or a ritual, is prescribed for the family which will actually wreck this system and prevent it from operating smoothly. It is often said, by way of explanation, that it is as if a wire is cut in a central heating control circuit, or as if the electrical connections are reversed. But what is not usually said is that if you were able to do this, then instead of the boiler quietly keeping the house warm (when of course no one notices it) it gets either red-hot or stone-cold. You cannot help noticing a red-hot boiler, or a freezing house. By breaking the circuit or changing the rules, the signals become amplified until they are not only visible to others but also uncomfortably obvious to the person sending the signal, who is normally unaware of it. Thus, though some 'systems' theorists have denied the value of insight and claim they bring about change without it, all my experience of using such techniques, and of watching them being used, is that they operate by bringing about increased *awareness*, by *experiential* insight. I have been most convinced when I have been the person on the receiving end of one of these interventions where my habitual non-verbal signals cease to influence the behaviour of another person, despite steady amplification. When this happens, you suddenly feel like a fish thrashing about on the end of a line as the angler no longer adjusts to the fish and lets it run, but instead suddenly draws the line tight.

It is no accident that the most skilful group of practitioners of this approach – the Milan group – were all highly experienced psychoanalysts prior to changing to their present mode of working. This background gives them a marvellous sensitivity to the developmental arrests from which a family typically suffers and to the 'double-think' by which they hide it from themselves. And it gives them a sensitivity for interventions which will simultaneously both obey and expose the family double-bind.

This provides another meaning for the concept of 'double-bind'. As I have said in Chapter 9, above, page 197 and in Chapter 13, page 367, all paradoxes of this kind are attempts to maintain a fantasy world different from reality, by expressing both the family fantasy and the social reality with which it conflicts in a form sufficiently ambiguous to conceal the discrepancy between the two, while at the same time conveying a "command" to others, usually non-verbally, to collude with the self-deception and so preserve the fantasy world against correction. Paradoxical *therapeutic* interventions can then be seen as subtly breaking the rule that fantasy and reality must be kept apart. Instead the two are related in a disguised, seemingly innocent fashion, though emphasising only the positive aspects. Once the couple or family accept the bait, they cannot avoid seeing more than appeared to be implied in the original paradoxical intervention.

Group-analytic family therapy

The third method of effective intervention is the one I call 'group-analytic', which I developed from my understanding of S. H. Foulkes's methods, though it takes them further than he chose to do. In this approach the therapist, having gained the family's confidence, actually takes on a rôle akin to the family scapegoat. The therapist manifests in his behaviour the taboo emotions or anxieties about inadequacy, which the family fear and are avoiding. He picks up the family's non-verbal signals (not necessarily in a conscious way), shares the family's conflict, and leads the way in facing the feared inadequacy. His counter-transference response to the family projective system locates the key family conflict and identifies the denied impulse or missing emotion together with the defensive fear about revealing it.

Contrary to much analytic practice, the therapist discloses this counter-transference response to the family and shares it with them not by attributing it to them but as a strange response in himself which he cannot understand. He thus provides a model of tolerance for a feeling which he thereby gives the family permission to own, if they are ready and willing to do so. The identified patient often protects the family by picking up the family secret like an unexploded 'bomb' and running with it to the mental hospital. Some therapists protect themselves by lobbing the 'bomb' back into the family as an interpretation. With the group-analytic approach the therapist, by defusing the bomb in front of the family, shows them how it can be made safe or even that it may not be a bomb at all. A detailed example of this approach is described in Chapter 13, pp. 342–56.

One vital requirement of both the last two methods, the Milan systemic and the group-analytic, is that impulse and defence – desire for change and fear of change – must both be fully expressed in a single communication. Lately I have taken to combining the two approaches. The therapist's counter-transference response about the missing developmental experience and the family defence against recognising it provides the 'hypothesis', in the Milan group's language. An expression of this in their circular, paradoxical manner acknowledges the two sides of the conflict simultaneously. Once made, this kind of intervention is like a self-steering missile, needing to be made on only one occasion, after which it cannot be shaken off and follows its target like an Exocet. 'Working through' is taken care of automatically, and needs no further attention from the therapist, except to avoid being provoked into interfering with the process. This is one reason the Milan group recommend widely-spaced sessions with monthly intervals, a course I have recommended for more than twenty years.

Group Therapy

If we now change the focus from family therapy to what we more usually call group therapy – the treatment of stranger-groups – are these ideas still helpful to us? I believe that they remain equally illuminating, and that they also help us to understand why so many seemingly different approaches, derived from quite different theoretical principles, nevertheless appear equally effective in the right hands.

1. Selection

If we begin by considering groups where the aim is change and growth, the first vital requirement is that selection of members should be carried out by the therapist, not by the patients themselves. Groups aiming at mutual support and encouragement may indeed resemble families in using group pressures to enforce a common set of values and to preserve the group consensus. This is generally true of self-help associations where the main aim is to enable members to function in the face of disabling symptoms or temporary crises, and where existing defensive systems are respected and strengthened. Some of the 'consciousness-raising' groups, where the problem is seen as outside the membership in other parts of society, may support group norms in a similar way. But one of the most important features of therapy groups aimed at change and growth is that members are chosen by the therapist and other patients have little say in the matter. To the extent that he chooses a reasonably heterogeneous membership, without discriminating too much between those he likes or approves of and those he does not, the members will come from different family backgrounds, and will not share many attitudes and views other than some values and conventions common to the society they live in.

2. The family that haunts the group: the idea of projections and templates

At the start, each person's different family pattern exists only inside his or her head, but each member will bring his family to the group in the form of projections. Projected expectations based on his own typical family experience will emerge, together with the family pattern of non-verbal signals by which he will seek to manipulate other group members into joining in his particular family 'cover-up'. For example, someone from a family where jealousy was denied and avoided may seek to persuade group members to take turns and avoid competition by sharing out time equally. Another member, from a family which denied and avoided dependence by emphasising self-reliance, may instead push the group towards fierce competition. Yalom (1975) says that 'Thus, the family haunts the group . . . (the patient) re-enacts early family scripts in the group and, if therapy is successful, is able to experiment with new behaviour, to break free from the locked family rôle he once occupied' (p. 98). My colleague in the Institute of Group Analysis, Caroline Garland (1982), has suggested that the required corrective emotional experience is precisely that provided by the very simple fact that each member brings a family 'script' which casts other members in transference rôles which they may not be willing to read. Thus in a well-selected group a number of different patterns or templates representing all the members' family systems are laid over one another, without producing a satisfactory fit. Gradually, the family system of each member becomes apparent through the discrepancy between what each person expects of the others, and what actually occurs. The false views of the world that each person picked up in his family become exposed for what they are. They are corrected in this more representative social context, while hidden deficiencies are at the same time made good. For this process to proceed effectively, it is not vital for the patient to talk about his early family background, or even to become aware of the way his present expectations developed. Indeed, a strong interest in such knowledge often represents narcissistic self-preoccupation, or a tendency to excuse behaviour by explaining it, which may be precisely the family pattern which the patient needs to unlearn.

3. Curative factors

For the corrective experience to occur, what is required is not a self-conscious remembering of family experience, but a correction of each person's family pattern of denial and avoidance occurring automatically by people revealing themselves in natural behaviour and receiving honest feedback from others. It will occur if eight of the first nine of Yalom's (1975) criteria for curative factors in group psychotherapy, as judged by patients, are satisfied. That is:

1. Discovering and accepting a previously unknown or unacceptable part of myself.

2. Being able to say what was bothering me instead of holding it in.

3. Other members honestly telling me what they think of me.

4. Learning how to express my feelings.

5. The group's teaching me about the type of impression I make on others.

6. Expressing negative and/or positive feelings towards another member.

7. Existential factors including the assumption of responsibility for one's self.

8. Learning how I come across to others.

9. Seeing that others could reveal embarrassing things and take other risks and benefit from it, helped me to do the same.

It is not essential for even the *therapist* to become aware of the family background, or the details of how these are being corrected by the group interaction. All such knowledge on the part of the therapist can be helpful, though I have grown more sure in recent years that its main value usually lies in the confidence it gives the therapist, to remain more silent and avoid interfering with the process. This operates automatically as long as all the patients try to get the group to do what they want – to operate like their family – and all these separate efforts interfere with each other. During my own group analysis with Foulkes, we all used to complain that he hardly said anything. But I must confess that nowadays, when a group goes really well and I have said nothing except 'Hello' at the beginning, 'It's time to stop' at the end, and perhaps one remark in the middle, preferably a joke, I feel as pleased as NASA Control when the spacecraft lands accurately on the moon with just one small mid-course correction. Perhaps this is the explanation why my own stranger-groups, in contrast to family groups, seem to work so much better when I feel really ill or at least a bit sleepy!

4. The conductor as therapist and group member

Why then is the therapist there at all? The therapist is vitally necessary because this process is inevitably frustrating and painful while it is occurring, and the patients will be able to sustain the exploration only to the extent that there is a high level of trust and confidence in the therapist and in the group. This will be present only to the degree that the therapist has firstly built a good relationship with each member through some kind of individual contact before they attend it, perhaps through a good initial interview; secondly by the support that members continue to feel throughout the group in their experience of his human concern, warmth and understanding for them as separate individuals; and thirdly by his attention to those factors which make for group cohesiveness, thereby ensuring that the group is *basically* a supportive experience too. All these, together with the maintenance of the usual boundaries of time, confidentiality and so on, provide an arena in which it feels safe to open the usual social boundaries and interact in an experimental, playful way, with the aim of learning something new rather than achieving any familiar 'result', and without danger of harmful social consequences beyond the temporary discomfort due to frank feedback from other group members. But we can all only stand so much change at a time, and if we are to avoid being overwhelmed by new and unfamiliar experience we need intervening periods of stability and rest when we close our boundaries while we secure and consolidate our gains, to make ourselves ready for the next 'round'.

This alternation also tends to occur automatically, according to a rhythm characteristic of each group. It is one reason why a very intensive group session is often followed – to our surprise – by a very restrained, 'dull' one. There is a natural tendency to open up and explore after too much stability and dull routine. This alternates with an equally natural tendency to close off and give time to digest the new information and regain balance again. The therapist must respect this inevitable alternation between greater openness and greater closedness, as well as the fact that some patients, more adventurous and impatient, will play a leading rôle in the opening, while others, more cautious and conservative, play an equally necessary part in the closing and reflecting.

The Durkins and their colleagues on the AGPA Task Force on systems theory and group therapy (Durkin, 1981) suggest that the group will be maximally effective if the conductor is willing to take the lead in this opening and closing process *at times*, personally demonstrating his willingness to take the risks he is asking his patients to face, and showing, as he does so, that it is not only less alarming than it appears, but that it also brings rich rewards. These various principles which guide the therapist in establishing a therapeutic climate in the group are far more important, in my experience, than the detailed management of group content over particular issues. This helps to explain why so many different theories and techniques seem to be equally effective, and why differences in effectiveness appear related much more to the experience, attitude and personality of the therapist.

5. Therapeutic principles in managing content

In recent years I have become particularly appreciative of the value of *certain* principles in dealing with content.

a. Verbalising non-verbal material

First, the therapist has to be particularly attentive to the danger of falling under the influence of a patient's family projective system, and being manipulated into joining in an unhelpful repetition of some family dynamic. In our profession we are often vulnerable to depressive patterns, for example, and easily find ourselves paralysed, like other members of the group, as we listen while one patient after another recites a list of woes. We know it is unhelpful to allow this tradition to continue, but also that to lead the way in stopping each Ancient Mariner's Tale may not only be experienced as a rejection by the person speaking, but may lead to a group norm whereby such feelings are concealed rather than examined and outgrown. An effective method, based on the principles described above, accepts and provides empathy for the content of verbal communication but gives greater attention to the *process*, particularly its *non-verbal* components, through which the tale is unfolded in the group. For instance, I might point out that though the rest of the group may *seem* sympathetic, their non-verbal reactions also suggest impatience which is clearly being registered by, and is arousing anxiety in, the speaker. I then suggest that the tale should be interrupted temporarily to explore this less obvious aspect of the interaction. This attempt to verbalise the non-verbal always releases the group from stuck repetitive interchanges. It changes gear and immediately moves to a more productive level of shared interaction. This is, of course, what we usually mean when we speak of an interpretation about 'group process'. The ideas I am describing make the need for, and timing of, such interventions much easier to grasp.

b. Using circular interventions

Secondly, I find that the circular, 'paradoxical' interventions which have been so effective in family therapy are equally useful with stranger-groups. In commenting on any interaction, I now always try to find a way of describing impulse and defence *simultaneously*,

399

without passing even implicit judgement on the behaviour concerned or implying any pressure to change. I also tend to make use of a lot of positive connotation – emphasising only the positive aspect of some interaction – since patients are more willing to look at it and supply the negative aspect themselves, if one merely draws attention to it in this way.

c. *Monitoring group themes*

Thirdly, like all group analysts I find it particularly helpful to monitor the *group themes* as they develop, seeking the connection between these themes and some failed developmental stage with which the group is at that moment preoccupied, though without recognising it. The developmental schemes proposed by different group theorists vary in some respects, but they all seem to be consistent with the simple sequence in child development which begins with the highly dependent infantile relationship in which the mother is all important. This is followed by the toddler struggle for independence and autonomy when rebelliousness and anger are more prominent and the rôle of the father is of particular importance. This leads eventually to a growing interest in the parents' relationship as a couple, the oedipal configuration and a concern with developing equal and mutual relationships of both a sexual and social nature. Closed, time-limited groups tend to recapitulate these stages one after another, while open groups with changing membership repeat the sequence in a circular way, like a continuous cinema programme. Clarification of the group theme in terms of these developmental issues seems in either case to maximise the learning process.

d. *Attentiveness to developmental stages*

In addition to this cognitive input, the therapist's rôle needs to be appropriate to the stage the group is recapitulating. In early stages of therapy, when dependency is to the fore, the therapist must accept some degree of idealisation. He must be more supportive and nurturant, and be relatively *non*-transparent as regards negative feelings and failures. In the second stage, however, more robust responses, more holding firm in issues of control and structure and more frustration are all appropriate. The therapist can speed up the process by being more confrontative and even provocative at times.

In the third stage the therapist needs to be more open, equal, transparent, personal and human. He should be ready to join in the sexual playfulness when it develops, in the sense of enjoying and being amused by it rather than being distant, solemn or forbidding.

Those who have suffered early deprivation may find the interval between once-weekly sessions too painful once they start to regress. We find that some of these patients can be managed in twice-weekly groups, but in our experience the more profoundly deprived may only be accessible if they have individual sessions in addition, or even individual therapy before a group is considered. In addition, the form of therapy has to be adjusted to the prevalent values of the social class to which the patient belongs. Middle-class patients often have more control of their time and more money to spare, so that long-term, open-ended work is practicable. For those on shift-work with little money or time to spare, short-term focussed work with clear goals towards relief of the presenting problem in time-limited group or family therapy (rather than growth and insight generally) has proved much more acceptable.

Conclusion

Finally, the therapist's own needs and aims must be considered seriously too. I believe, like Foulkes, that the therapist who grows and learns through the group experience provides the most effective *model* for the patients, provided the task of looking after the group and the patients remains the primary focus. We then also become steadily more competent professionally, because we reduce the repressions and blind spots that limit our understanding, and can work with an ever-widening range of problems. Most important of all, however, we enjoy our lives more, give more time to our loved ones and our broader interests as human beings, setting our patients *the example* they need and which their own over-anxious, over-concerned parents could not provide. This example is more effective than any amount of knowledge and technique.

Notes
1 Part of this paper was first presented in an earlier form at a Symposium at the American Group Psychotherapy

Association, New York, February 1982. It was published in *The International Journal of Group Psychotherapy*, Vol. 24 (1984) 215–224. In its present form it was given as the Keynote Lecture to the Eighth International Congress of Group Psychotherapy in Mexico City in 1984, and was published in *Group Analysis*, Vol. 19 (1986) 5–24, under the title 'What Is Effective in Group Psychotherapy?'. [Ed.]

Appendix: Robin Skynner's Publications

Papers published in this collection are marked with an asterisk

1. 1957: 'The Relation of Muscle Tension to Awareness of Emotional State'. Dissertation for the Diploma of Psychological Medicine, University of London.
2. 1964: 'Group Analytic Themes In Training And Case Discussion Groups'. *Selected Lectures: VIth International Congress of Psychotherapy*, 1964.
3. 1967: 'Child Guidance From Within: Reactions To New Pressures'. Paper given at the 23rd Child Guidance Inter-Clinic Conference, N.A.M.H. Publications, London.
4. 1968: 'A Family of Family Casework Agencies'. *International Journal of Group Psychotherapy*, **18**, 352–360.
5. *1968: 'The Minimum Sufficient Network'. Paper read to the 2nd Athenian Symposium on Group Techniques, Athens, published in *Social Work Today*, **2**, 9, 28/7/71.
6. *1969: 'A Group-Analytic Approach to Conjoint Family Therapy'. *Journal of Child Psychology and Psychiatry*, **16**, 81, October 1969. Reprinted in *Social Work Today*, 1970, and in S. Walrond-Skinner (ed.), *Developments in Family Therapy*, RKP, 1981.
7. *1969: 'Indications And Contraindications For Conjoint Family Therapy'. *International Journal of Social Psychiatry*, Vol. XV, **4**.
8. 1970: 'An Encounter With Esalen'. *Group Analysis*, International Panel and Correspondence, **3**, 180, 1970.
9. 1971: 'Group Psychotherapy With Adolescent Boys' in *Groups: Annual Review of Residential Child Care Association*, 1970–1.
10. 1972: 'Implications of Recent Work In Conjoint Family Therapy for Group Analytic Theory. *Group Analysis*, **5**, 153.
11. 1973: 'Icelandic Saga'. *Group Analysis*, **6**, 39.
12. 1974: 'An Experiment In Group Consultation With the Staff of a Comprehensive School'. *Group Process*, **6**, 99.

13. 1974:   'Boundaries'. *Social Work Today*, **5**, 290–294.
14. 1974:   'Group Psychotherapy' in V. P. Varma, (ed.), *Psychotherapy Today*, Constable, London.
15. *1974:   'School Phobia: A Reappraisal'. *British Journal of Medical Psychology*, **47**, 1–15.
16. 1975:   'Development of Family Therapy' in W. Finn (ed.), *Family Therapy in Social Work*: FWA Conference Papers.
17. 1975:   'Family Therapy Techniques'. Proceedings of the Tenth Annual Congress, Association for the Psychiatric Study of Adolescents.
18. *1975:   'Marital Problems and Their Treatment'. Proceedings, Royal Society of Medicine, **68**, 405.
19. 1975:   'Some Consequences of Work With Natural Groups'. *Marriage Guidance,* **15**, 319.
20. 1975:   'The Large Group In Training' in L. Kreeger (ed.), *The Large Group: Dynamics and Therapy*, Constable, London.
21. *1976:   'Group Analysis And Family Therapy'. Paper presented to a Scientific Meeting of the Group Analytic Society. Published in M. Pines (ed.), *The Evolution of Group Analysis*, RKP, 1983.
22. 1976:   'Family Therapy'. Precirculated Papers: Conference on the Teaching of Psychotherapy, Association of University Teachers of Psychiatry.
23. 1976:   'Family Techniques in Social Work'. DHSS *Social Work Service*, **10**, 41.
24. 1976:   'Family And Marital Therapy'. Symposium on Psychotherapy, published in *British Journal of Hospital Medicine*, **15**, 224.
25. 1976:   *One Flesh, Separate Persons: Principles of Family and Marital Psychotherapy*, Constable, London.
26. 1976:   'On the Origins of Family Therapy and Developments In Its Practice'. Opening Speech to the Inaugural Meeting of The Association of Family Therapy, Imperial College, London (unpublished).
27. 1976:   'Psychotherapy and Spiritual Tradition' in J. Needleman (ed.), *On The Way to Self-Knowledge*, Knopf, N.Y. Reprinted in J. Welwood (ed.), *Awakening The Heart: East West Approaches to Psychotherapy And The Healing Relationship*, New Science Library, Boulder, and RKP, London, 1983.
28. 1976:   'Towards A Family Approach In A Psychiatric Day Hospital'. *British Journal of Psychiatry*, **129**, 73 (written with Bennett, Fox and Jowell).
29. *1976:   'Sexual Counselling Techniques in General Practice'.

Four papers. *British Journal of Sexual Medicine*, Vol. 3, **6**, 1976; Vol. 4, **1**, 1977; Vol. 4, **2**, 1977; Vol. 4, **3**, 1977.

30. *1978: 'The Physician As Family Therapist' in J. Lewis and G. Usdin (eds.), *Psychiatry in General Medical Practice*, McGraw-Hill, N.Y.

31. 1979: 'An Open-Systems Approach To Teaching Family Therapy'. *Journal of Marital and Family Therapy*, 5, **3**. Reprinted in *Group Analysis*, 8, **1**, 1980.

32. 1979: Foreword to S. Waldrond-Skinner (ed.), *Family and Marital Psychotherapy: A Critical Approach*, RKP, London.

33. *1979: 'Reflections on the Family Therapist as Family Scapegoat'. *Journal of Family Therapy*, **1**, 7.

34. *1980: 'Recent Developments In Marital Therapy'. *Journal of Family Therapy*, **2**, 271.

35. *1981: 'Referral For Psychotherapy'. *British Medical Journal*, Vol. 282, June.

36. *1981: *An Open Systems, Group-Analytic Approach to Family Therapy*, Gurman, A., and Kniskern, D. (eds.), Brunner/Mazel, N.Y..

37. 1982: 'Farewell'. Written for the Maudsley Gazette, Autumn 1982, on retirement from The Bethlem Royal and Maudsley Hospital.

38. 1982: Foreword to D. E. Scharff, *The Sexual Relationship*, RKP, London.

39. 1982: Foreword to R. Whiffen and J. Byng Hall (eds.), *Family Therapy Supervision: Recent Developments in Practice*, Academic Press, London.

40. *1982: 'Frameworks for Viewing the Family as a System' in A. Bentovim, A. Cooklin and J. Gorrell Barnes (eds.), *Family Therapy: Contemporary Frameworks of Theory and Practice*, Academic Press/Grune and Stratton, London and N.Y.

41. 1983: *Families And How To Survive Them*. Written with Cleese, J., Methuen, London.

42. 1983: 'Make Sure To Feed The Goose That Lays The Golden Eggs: A Discussion On The Myth Of Altruism'. *Journal of Psychohistory*, Vol. 10, **3**, pp. 389–395.

43. 1984: 'Institutes And How To Survive Them'. 8th S. H. Foulkes Annual Lecture given at the Institute of Education, London. Published in *Group Analysis* 15, 11/2, 1984.

44. *1984: 'What Is Effective In Group (and Family) Therapy?'. Keynote Lecture, 8th International Congress of Group Psychotherapy, Mexico City. Published in *Group Analysis*, 19, 5–24, 1986.

45. 1985: 'Towards an Integration of Analytic, Behavioural and

Systemic Approaches to Family Therapy'. Paper given at the 8th International Delphic Symposium on Family Therapy, Athens. Published in G. A. Vassilliou and V. G. Vassilliou (eds.), *Family Therapy Evolving*, for the Athenian Institute of Anthropos.

46. 1986: 'The Psychotherapy Teacher – Getting Older: Narrowing Down Or Opening Out?'. Paper given at the 3rd Conference on Teaching Dynamic Psychotherapy, Oxford; Association of University Teachers of Psychiatry. Published in *The Bulletin of the Royal College of Psychiatrists*, Vol. 10, December 1986.

Bibliography

Ables, B. S. and Brandsma, J. M. *Therapy for Couples*, Jossey-Bass, San Francisco, 1977.

Abse, W. 'Trigant Burrow and the Inauguration of Group Analysis in the USA', *Group Analysis*, 12, **3** (1979) 218–229.

    Clinical Notes on Group-Analytic Psychotherapy, John Wright and Sons, Bristol, and Virginia University Press, Charlottesville, 1974.

Ackerman, N. W. 'Toward an Integrative Therapy of the Family', *Am. J. Psychiat.*, **114** (1958) 727–733.

    Psychodynamics of Family Life, Basic Books, New York, 1958.

    'Family Psychotherapy – Theory and Practice', *Am. J. Psychother.*, **20** (1966) 405–414.

    'Family Therapy' in S. Arieti (ed.), *American Handbook of Psychiatry*, Basic Books, New York, 1966.

    Treating the Troubled Family, Basic Books, New York, 1966.

Ackerman, N. W., Beatman, F. L. and Sanford, S. N. (eds.) *Exploring the Base for Family Therapy*, Family Service Ass., New York, 1961.

    Expanding Theory and Practice in Family Therapy, Family Service Ass., New York, 1967.

Ahlin, G. 'Reflections on the Group Matrix', *Group Analysis*, 18, **2** (1985).

Amerongen, S. 'Initial Psychiatric Family Studies', *Am. J. Orthopsychiat.*, **24** (1954) 73–83.

Balint, M. and Balint, E. *Psychotherapeutic Techniques in Medicine*, Tavistock Publications, London, 1961.

Bandura, A. *Principles of Behaviour Modification*, Holt Rinehart, London and New York, 1969.

Bannister, L. and Pincus, L. *Shared Fantasy in Marital Problems: Therapy in a Four-Way Relationship*, Nat. Association of Social Workers, London and Washington, 1965.

Barlow, W. *The Alexander Principle*, Gollancz, London, 1973.

Barnes, E. (ed.) *Psychosocial Nursing*, Tavistock, 1968.

Barnhill, L. R. and Longo, D. 'Fixation and Regression in the Family Life Cycle', *Family Process*, **17** (1978) 469–478.

Bateson, G. *Steps Towards an Ecology of Mind*, Chandler, New York, 1972.

    Mind and Nature, Wildwood House, London, 1979.

Bateson, G., Jackson, D., Haley, J. and Weakland, J. 'Towards a Theory of Schizophrenia', *Behav. Sci.,* **1** (1956) 251–264.

Beavers, W. R. *Psychotherapy and Growth: A Family Systems Perspective,* Brunner/Mazel, New York, 1977.

Beels, C. C. and Ferber, A. 'Family Therapy: A View'; *Family Process,* **8** (1969) 280–332.

Bell, J. E. 'Family Group Therapy', *Publ. Hlth Monogr.,* **64** (1961) U.S. Public Health Service, Washington, D.C.

'Recent Advances in Family Group Therapy', *J. Child. Psychol. Psychiat.,* **3** (1962) 1–15.

'The Family Group Therapist: An Agent of Change', *Int. J. Group Psychother.,* **14** (1964) 72–83.

Belliveau, F. and Richter, L. *Understanding Human Sexual Inadequacy,* Hodder and Stoughton, 1970.

Bennis, W. G. and Shepard, H. A. 'A Theory of Group Development', *Human Relations,* 1956, **9**, 415–437.

Bentovim, A., Gorrell Barnes, G. and Cooklin, A. (eds.) *Family Therapy: Complementary Frameworks of Theory and Practice, Vols 1 and 2,* Academic Press, 1982.

Bion, W. R. *Experiences in Groups,* Tavistock Publications, London, 1961.

Blinder, M. G. '"MCFT": Simultaneous Treatment of Several Families', *Am. J. Psychother.,* **19** (1965) 559–569.

Bloch, D. A. (ed.) *Techniques of Family Therapy: A Primer,* Grune and Stratton, New York, 1973.

Boszormenyi-Nagy, I. and Framo, J. L. (eds.) *Intensive Family Therapy,* Hoeber, New York, 1965.

Boszormenyi-Nagy, I. and Spark, E. *Invisible Loyalties,* Harper and Row, New York, 1973.

Bowen, M. 'A Family Concept of Schizophrenia' in D. Jackson (ed.), *Aetiology of Schizophrenia,* Basic Books, New York, 1960.

'The Use of Family Therapy in Clinical Practice', *Comp. Psychiat.,* **7** (1966) 354.

'Principles and Techniques of Multiple Family Therapy' in J. O. Brandt and O. J. Moynihan (eds.), *Systems Therapy – Selected Papers: Theory, Technique and Research.* Groome Child Guidance Center, Washington, 1971.

Family Therapy in Clinical Practice, Jason Aronson, New York, 1978.

Bowen, M., Dysinger, R. H. and Basamania, B. 'The Role of the Father in Families with a Schizophrenic Patient', *Am. J. Psychiat.,* **115** (1959) 1017–1020.

Bowlby, J. 'The Study and Reduction of Group Tensions in the Family', *Human Relations,* **2** (1949) 123–128.

Attachment and Loss. Vol. I: Attachment, Hogarth Press, London, 1967.

Attachment and Loss. Vol. II: Separation: Anxiety and Anger, Hogarth Press, London, 1973.

Attachment and Loss. Vol. III: Sadness and Depression, Hogarth Press, London, 1980.

Brodey, W. M. 'Some Family Operations and Schizophrenia', *Archs Gen. Psychiat.*, **1** (1959) 379–402.

'Process of Family Change' in N. W. Ackerman, F. L. Beatman and S. N. Sherman (eds.), *Expanding Theory and Practice in Family Therapy*, Family Service Ass., New York, 1967.

Brown, D. and Pedder, J. *Introduction to Psychotherapy: An Outline of Psychodynamic Principles and Practice*, Tavistock, London, 1979.

Brown, G. W. and Rutter, M. 'The Measurement of Family Activities and Relationships', *Human Relations*, **19** (1966) 241–263.

Bruch, N. 'Changing Approaches to the Study of the Family' in I. Cohen (ed.), *Family Structure, Dynamics and Therapy*, Psychiat. Res. Rep. No. 20, Am. Psychiat. Ass., 1966.

Burnham, J. *Family Therapy: First Steps Towards a Systemic Approach*, Tavistock, London, 1986.

Bursten, B. 'Family Dynamics, the Sick Role, and Medical Hospital Admissions', *Family Process*, **4** (1965) 206–216.

Byng-Hall, J. 'Family Myths Used as a Defence in Conjoint Family Therapy', *British Journal of Medical Psychology*, **46** (1973) 239–253.

Campbell, D. and Draper, R. (eds.) *Applications of Systemic Family Therapy: The Milan Approach*, Grune and Stratton, London, 1985.

Caplan, G. *Principles of Preventive Psychiatry*, Tavistock, London, 1964.

Chartham, R. *Advice to Women,* Tandem, 1971.

Sex Manners for Men, New English Library, 1967.

Cheek, F. E. 'The Father of the Schizophrenic', *Archs Gen. Psychiat.*, **13** (1965) 336–345.

Clark, D. H. *Social Therapy in Psychiatry*, Penguin, Harmondsworth, 1974.

Clarke, A. H. 'The Dominant Matriarch Syndrome', *Br. J. Psychiat.*, **113** (1967) 1069–1071.

Cohen, I. M. (ed.) *Family Structure, Dynamics and Therapy*, Psychiat. Res. Rep. No. 20, Am. Psychiat. Ass., Washington D.C., 1964

Colm, H. C. 'Phobias in Children', *Psychoanal. Rev.*, **46** (1959) 65–84.

Comfort, A. *The Joy of Sex*, Quartet, 1972.

Coolidge, J. C., Hahn, P. B. and Peck, A. L. 'School Phobia: Neurotic Crisis or Way of Life', *Am. J. Orthopsychiat.*, **27** (1957) 296–306.

Crawshay-Williams, R. *Russell Remembered*, Oxford University Press, 1970.

Crowe, M. J. 'Behavioural Approaches to Marital and Family
  Problems' in R. Gaind and B. Hudson (eds.), *Current Themes
  in Psychiatry, Vol. I*, Macmillan, London, 1978a.
  'Conjoint Marital Therapy: A Controlled Outcome Study',
  Psychological Medicine, **8** (1978b) 623–636.
  'Conjoint Marital Therapy: Advice or Interpretation?',
  J. Psychosomatic Med., **17** (1973) 309.
Curry, A. E. 'Therapeutic Management of Multiple Family Groups',
  Int. J. Group Psychother., **15** (1965) 90–95.
Cutter, A. V. and Hallowitz, D. 'Different Approaches to Treatment
  of the Child and his Parents', *Am. J. Orthopsychiat.*, **32**
  (1962) 152–158.
Dare, C. 'Psychoanalysis and Systems in Family Therapy', *Journal of
  Family Therapy*, **1** (1979) 137–152.
Davidson, S. 'School Phobia as a Manifestation of Family
  Disturbance', *J. Child Psychol. Pscyhiat.*, **1** (1961) 270–287.
Davis, D. R. 'Interventions into Family Affairs', *Br. J. Psychiat.*, **41**
  (1968) 152–158.
Day, J. and Kwiatkowska, H. Y. 'The Psychiatric Patient and his
  "Well" Sibling', *Bull. Art Ther.*, **2** (1962) 51–66.
Dell, P. 'Understanding Bateson and Maturana: Toward a Biological
  Basis for the Social Sciences', *Journal of Marital and Family
  Therapy*, Vol. 2, **1** (1985) 1–20.
Dicks, H. V. *Marital Tensions*, Routledge and Kegan Paul, London,
  1967. Reissued by Karnac (Maresfield), 1985.
Dollard, J. and Miller, N. E. *Personality and Psychotherapy*, McGraw-
  Hill, New York, 1950.
Dominian, J. 'Marital Pathology', *Proc. Royal Soc. Med.* **67** (1974)
  780.
  Marital Pathology, Darton, Longman and Todd, London, 1980.
Donnelly, J. 'Aspects of the Treatment of Character Disorders', *Archs
  gen. Psychiat.*, **15** (1966) 22–28.
Durrell, V. G. 'Adolescents in Multiple Family Group Therapy in a
  School Setting', *Int. J. Group Psychother.*, **19** (1969) 44–52.
Durkin, H. E. *The Group in Depth*, International Universities Press,
  New York, 1964.
Durkin, J. *Living Groups: Group Psychotherapy and General Systems
  Theory*, Brunner/Mazel, New York, 1981.
Duvall, E. *Family Development*, Lippincott, Chicago, 1957.
Ehrenwald, J. 'Family Diagnosis and Mechanisms of Psychosocial
  Defence', *Family Process*, **2** (1963) 121–131.
Erikson, E. H. *Childhood and Society*, Norton, New York, 1950.
Esterson, A., Cooper, D. G. and Laing, R. D. 'Results of Family-
  Oriented Therapy with Hospitalized Schizophrenics',
  Br. Med. J., **2** (1965) 1462–1465.
Eyre, R. *Ronald Eyre on The Long Search*, Collins, London, 1979.

Ezriel, H. 'A Psychoanalytic Approach to Group Treatment', *Br. J. Med. Psychol.*, 23 (1950) 59–74.

Falloon, I. R. H., Boyd, J. L., McGill, C. W., Razani, J., Moss, H. B. and Gilderman, A. M. 'Family Management in Prevention of Exacerbation of Schizophrenia: A Controlled Study', *New England Journal of Medicine*, **306** (1982) 1437–1440.

Faucett, E. C. 'Multiple-Client Interviewing: A Means of Assessing Family Processes', *Soc. Casework*, **43** (1962) 114–120.

Ferriera, A. J. 'Family Myth and Homeostasis', *Archs Gen. Psychiat.*, **9** (1963) 457–463.

    'Psychosis and Family Myth', *Am. J. Psychother.*, **21** (1967) 186–197.

Fisher, S. and Mendell, D. 'The Communication of Neurotic Patterns Over Two and Three Generations', *Psychiatry*, **19** (1956) 41–46.

Fleck, S. 'Family Dynamics and the Origin of Schizophrenia', *Psychosom. Med.*, **12** (1960) 333–344.

    'Psychiatric Hospitalization as a Family Experience', *Acta psychiat. scand.*, **39** (1963), Supp. 169.

Fleck, S., Cornelison, A. R., Norton, N. and Litz, T. 'The Intrafamilial Environment of the Schizophrenic Patient', *Psychiatry*, **20** (1957) 343–350.

Fordham, M. 'A Child Guidance Approach to Marriage', *Br. J. Med Psychol.*, **26** (1953) 197–203.

    'Technique and Countertransference', *Journal of Analytical Psychology*, **14** (1969.

Foulkes, E. 'The Origins and Development of Group Analysis' in T. Lear (ed.), *Spheres of Group Analysis*, Institute of Group Analysis, 1984.

Foulkes, S. H. *Introduction to Group-Analytic Psychotherapy*, Heinemann, London, 1948. Reissued by Karnac (Maresfield), 1983.

    Therapeutic Group Analysis, Allen & Unwin, London, 1964. Reissued by Karnac (Maresfield) 1984.

    Group-Analytic Psychotherapy: Method and Principles, Gordon and Breach, London, 1975. Reissued by Karnac (Maresfield), 1986.

Foulkes, S. H. and Anthony, E. J. *Group Psychotherapy: The Psychoanalytic Approach*, Penguin, Harmondsworth, 1957. Reissued by Karnac (Maresfield), 1984.

Framo, J. L. 'Family of Origin as a Therapeutic Resource for Adults in Family and Marital Therapy: You Can and Should Go Home Again', *Family Process*, **15** (1976) 193–210.

Friedman, A. S. *et al. Psychotherapy for the Whole Family*, Springer, New York, 1965.

Fromm, E. *The Crisis of Psychoanalysis*, Penguin, Harmondsworth, 1970.

    Beyond the Chains of Illusion, Abacus, London, 1980.

411

Frommer, E. A. 'Treatment of Childhood Depression with Antidepressant Drugs', *Br. med. J.*, **1** (1967) 729–732.

Garland, C. 'Group Analysis: Taking the Non-Problem Seriously', *Group Analysis*, **15** (1982) 4–14.

Gehrke, S. 'Survival Patterns in Family Conjoint Therapy', *Family Process*, **6** (1967) 67–80.

Glasser, P. H. 'Changes in Family Equilibrium During Psychotherapy', *Family Process*, **2** (1963) 245–264.

Glick, I. D. and Kessler, D. R. *Marital and Family Therapy*. Grune and Stratton, London and New York, 1974.

Goldberg, T. B. 'Factors in the Development of School Phobia', *Smith Coll. Stud. Soc. Wk.*, **23** (1953) 227–248.

Gorrell Barnes, G. *Working with Families*, Macmillan, 1984.

Gosling, B. (ed.) *Tavistock Clinic Golden Jubilee Papers*, Tavistock, London, 1973.

Gralnick, A. 'Family Psychotherapy: General and Specific Considerations', *Am. J. Orthopsychiat.*, **32** (1962) 515–526.

Groesbeck, C. J. and Taylor, B. 'The Psychiatrist as Wounded Physician', *American Journal of Psychoanalysis*, **37** (1977) 131–139.

Grotjahn, M. *Psychoanalysis and the Family Neurosis*, Norton, New York, 1960.

Grunebaum, H., Christ, J. and Neiberg, N. A. 'Diagnosis and Treatment-Planning for Couples' in H. Grunebaum and J. Christ (eds.), *Contemporary Marriage: Structure, Dynamics and Therapy*, Little, Brown, Boston, 1975.

Gustafson, J. P. *The Complex Secret of Brief Psychotherapy*, Norton, London, 1986.

Gullerud, E. N. and Harland, V. L. 'Four-way Joint Interviewing in Marital Counselling', *Soc. Casework*, **43** (1963) 532–536.

Gurman, A. S. 'Marital Therapy: Emerging Trends in Research and Practice' in A. S. Gurman and D. G. Rice (eds.), *Couples in Conflict*, Jason Aronson, New York, 1975.

'Contemporary Marital Therapies: A Critique and Comparative Analysis of Psychoanalytic, Behavioural and Systems Theory Approaches' in T. J. Paolino and B. S. McCrady (eds.), *Marriage and Marital Therapy*, Brunner/Mazel, New York, 1978.

Gurman, A. S. and Kniskern, D. P. 'Deterioration in Marital and Family Therapy: Empirical, Clinical and Conceptual Issues', *Family Process*, **17** (1978a) 3–20.

'Behavioural Marriage Therapy: A Psychodynamic-Systems Analysis and Critique', *Family Process*, **17** (1978b) 121–138.

'Research on Marital and Family Therapy' in S. L. Garfield and A. E. Bergin (eds.), *Handbook of Psychotherapy and Behaviour Change: An Empirical Analysis* (2nd edition), John Wiley, New York, 1979.

The Handbook of Family Therapy, Brunner/Mazel, New York, 1981.

Haley, J. *Changing Families*, Grune and Stratton, New York, 1971.
Problem-Solving Therapy, Jossey-Bass, San Francisco, 1976.

Haley, J. and Hoffman, L. *Techniques of Family Therapy*, Basic Books, New York, 1967.

Hallowitz, D., Clement, R. and Cutter, A. 'The Treatment Process with Both Parents Together', *Am. J. Orthopsychiat.*, **27** (1957) 587–607.

Hare, E. H. and Shaw, G. K. 'Mental and Physical Family Health', *Brit. J. Psychiat.*, **111** (1965) 461–471.

Harlow, H. F., Harlow, M. K., Dodsworth, R. O. and Arling, G. L. 'Maternal Behaviour of Rhesus Monkeys Deprived of Mothering and Peer Associations in Infancy', *Proceedings of the American Philosophical Society*, **110** (1966) 58–66.

Hatfield, F. E. S. 'Understanding the Family and Its Illnesses' (unpublished).

Heard, D. H. 'From Object Relations to Attachment Theory: A Basis for Family Therapy', *British Journal of Medical Psychology*, **51** (1978) 67–76.

Henry, J. and Watson, S. 'Family Structure and Psychic Development', *Am. J. Orthopsychiat.*, **21** (1951) 59–73.

Hersov, L. A. 'Persistent Non-Attendance at School', *J. Child Psychol. Psychiat.*, **1** (1960a) 130–136.
'Refusal to Go to School', *J. Child. Psychol. Psychiat.*, **1** (1960b) 137–145.

Hersov, L. and Berg. I, *Out of School: Modern Perspectives in truancy and school refusal*, John Wiley & Son, Chichester, 1980.

Hinshelwood, R. D. and Manning, N. (eds.) *Therapeutic Communities*, Routledge and Kegan Paul, London, 1979.

Hoffman, L. *Foundations of Family Therapy*, Basic Books, 1981.
'Beyond Power and Control: Toward a 'Second Order' Family Systems Therapy', *Family Systems Medicine*, Vol. 3, **4** (1985).

Howells, K. G. 'The Nuclear Family as the Functional Unit in Psychiatry', *J. Ment. Sci.*, **108** (1962) 675–684.
Family Psychiatry, Oliver and Boyd, London, 1963.

Jackson, D. D. 'Differences between "Normal" and "Abnormal" Families' in N. W. Ackerman *et al.* (eds.), *Expanding Theory and Practice in Family Therapy*, Family Service Ass., New York, 1967.

Jackson, D. D. and Weakland, J. H. 'Conjoint Family Therapy', *Psychiatry*, **24** (Suppl.) (1961) S30–45.

Jackson, D. D. and Yalom, I. 'Family Research on the Problem of Ulcerative Colitis', *Archs gen. Psychiat.*, **15** (1966) 410–418.

Jackson, M. and Pines, M. 'The Borderline Personality: Psychodynamics and Treatment', *Neurologica et Psychiatria*, 1986.

Jacobson, N. S. and Margolin, G. *Marital Therapy*, Brunner/Mazel, New York, 1979.

Jay, M. *The Dialectical Imagination*, Heinemann, London, 1973.

Johnson, A. M., Falstein, E. I., Szurek, S. A. and Svendsen, M. 'School Phobia', *Am. J. Orthopsychiat.*, **11** (1941) 702–711.

Jones, M. *Maturation of the Therapeutic Community: An Organic Approach to Health and Mental Health*, Human Sciences Press, New York, 1976.

The Process of Change, Routledge and Kegan Paul, London, 1982.

Jung, C. G. *The Practice of Psychotherapy, Collected Works, Vol. 16*, Routledge and Kegan Paul, 1954.

Kahn, J. H. and Nursten, J. P. 'School Refusal: A Comprehensive View of School Phobia and Other Failures of School Attendance', *Am. J. Orthopsychiat.*, **32** (1962) 707–718.

Kaplan, H. S. *The New Sex Therapy: Active Treatment of Sexual Dysfunctions*, Brunner/Mazel, New York, 1974.

Kellner, R. *Family Ill Health*, Tavistock, London, 1963.

Kennedy, W. A. 'School Phobia: Rapid Treatment of Fifty Cases', *J. Abnorm. Psychol.*, **70** (1965) 285–289.

Klein, M. *The Psychoanalysis of Children*, Hogarth Press, London, 1932.

Korzybski, A. *General Semantics*, Science Press, Pennsylvania, 1933.

Kreeger, L. *The Large Group: Dynamics and Therapy*, Constable, London, 1975.

Kuhn, T. *The Structure of Scientific Revolutions*, University of Chicago Press, 1970.

Laing, R. D. and Esterson, A. *Sanity, Madness and the Family: Vol. 1, Families of Schizophrenics*, Tavistock, London, 1964.

Langsley, D. G. *et al.* 'Family Crisis Therapy: Results and Implications', *Family Process*, **7** (1968) 145–158.

Lao Tzu, L., *Tao Te Ching*, Penguin, 1974.

Lear, T. (ed.) *Spheres of Group Analysis*, Institute of Group Analysis, London 1984.

Leichter, E. and Schulman, G. L. 'The Family Interview as an Integrative Device in Group Therapy with Families', *Int. J. Group Psychother.*, **13** (1963) 335–346.

'Emerging Phenomena in Multi-Family Group Treatment', *Int. J. Group Psychother.*, **18** (1968) 59–69.

Leighton, D., Harding, J. S., Macklin, D. B., Hughes, C. C. and Leighton, A. H. 'Psychiatric Findings of the Stirling County Study', *American Journal of Psychiatry*, **119** (1963) 1021–1026.

Leff, J., Kuipers, L., Berkowitz, R., Eberlein-Vries, R. and Sturgeon, D. 'A Controlled Trial of Social Intervention in the Families of Schizophrenic Patients', *British Journal of Psychiatry*, **141** (1982) 121–134.

Levenson, E. A. 'The Treatment of School Phobia in the Young Adult', *Am. J. Psychother.*, **15** (1961) 539–552.

Leventhal, T. 'Self-Image in School Phobia', *Am. J. Orthopsychiat.*, **34** (1964) 685–695.

Lewis, J. M. *How's Your Family?*, Brunner/Mazel, New York, 1979.

Lewis, J. M., Beavers, W. R., Gossett, J. T. and Phillips, V. A. *No Single Thread: Psychological Health in Family Systems*, Brunner/Mazel, New York, 1976.

Lewis, J. and Usdin, G. (eds.) *Psychiatry in General Medical Practice*, McGraw-Hill, New York, 1978.

Liberman, R. O., Wheeler, E. G., Visser, L. A. J. M. de, Kuehnel, J. and Kuehnel, T. *Handbook of Marital Therapy*, Plenum, New York, 1979.

Lidz, T. *The Family and Human Adaptation: Three Lectures*, Int. Univ. Press, New York, 1963.

Lidz, T., Fleck, S. and Cornelison, A. R. *Schizophrenia and the Family*, Int. Univ. Press, New York, 1966.

Lieberman, S., Haffner, R. J. and Crisp, A. H. 'Teaching Psychotherapy in Mental Hospitals', *British Journal of Psychiatry*, **132** (1978).

Lippman, H. S. 'School Phobia Workshop: Discussion', *Am. J. Orthopsychiat.*, **26** (1957) 776–780.

Lyons, A. 'Therapeutic Intervention in Relation to the Institution of Marriage' in R. Gosling (ed.), *Tavistock Clinic Golden Jubilee Papers*, Tavistock, London, 1973.

McGregor, R., Ritchie, A. M., Serrano, A. C. and Schuster, F. P. *Multiple Impact Therapy with Families*, McGraw-Hill, New York, 1964.

Macklin, E. D. 'Non-Marital Heterosexual Cohabitation', *Marriage and Family Review*, **1** (1978) 1–12.

Mahler, M. S., Pine, F. and Bergman, A. *The Psychological Birth of the Human Infant*, Hutchinson, London, 1975.

Main, T. F. 'Mutual Projection in a Marriage', *Comprehensive Psychiatry*, **7** (1966) 432–441.

'The Ailment' and 'The Hospital as a Therapeutic Institution' in E. Barnes (ed.), *Psychosocial Nursing*, Tavistock, London, 1968.

Malan, D. H. *A Study of Brief Psychotherapy*, Tavistock, London, 1963.

Individual Psychotherapy and the Science of Psychodynamics, Butterworths, London, 1979.

Malmquist, C. P. 'School Phobia: a Problem in Family Neurosis', *J. Child Psychiat.*, **4** (1965) 293–319.

de Mare, P. 'Michael Foulkes and the Northfield Experiment' in M. Pines (ed.), *The Evolution of Group Analysis*, Routledge and Kegan Paul, London, 1983.

Martin, F. 'Some Implications for Individual Psychotherapy from the Theory and Practice of Family Therapy, and Vice Versa', *Br. J. Med. Psycho.*, **50** (1977) 53–64.

415

Martin, F. and Knight, J. 'Joint Interviews as Part of Intake Procedure in a Child Psychiatric Clinic', *J. Child Psychol. Psychiat.*, **3** (1962) 17–27.

Martin, P. A. *A Marital Therapy Manual*, Brunner/Mazel, New York, 1976.

Masters, W. H. and Johnson, V. E., *Human Sexual Inadequacy*, Little, Brown, Boston, 1970.

Maslow, A. H. and Dias-Guerrero, R. 'Adolescence and Juvenile Delinquency in Two Different Cultures' in A. H. Maslow, *The Farther Reaches of Human Nature*, Penguin, London, 1973.

Mendell, D. and Fisher, S. 'A Multi-Generation Approach to Treatment of Psychopathology', *J. Nerv. Ment. Dis.*, **126** (1962) 523–529.

Miller, J. G. 'Living Systems: Basic Concepts', *Behavioural Science*, **10** (1965) 193–245.

Minuchin, S. 'Conflict-Resolution Family Therapy', *Psychiat.*, **28** (1965) 278–286.

    Families and Family Therapy, Harvard Univ. Press, Massachussetts, 1974.

Minuchin, S. *et al.* 'The Study and Treatment of Families that Produce Multiple Acting-Out Boys', *Am. J. Orthopsychiat.*, **34** (1964) 125–133.

Minuchin, S. *et al.*: *Families of the Slums: An Exploration of their Structure and Treatment*, Basic Books, New York, 1967.

Minuchin, S. and Montalvo, B. 'An Approach for Diagnosis of the Low Socio-Economic Family' in I. Cohen (ed.), *Family, Structure, Dynamics and Therapy*, Psychiat. Res. Rep. No. 20, Am. Psychiat. Ass., 1966.

    'Techniques for Working with Disorganized Low Socio-Economic families', *Am. J. Orthopsychiat.*, **37** (1967) 880–887.

Mischler, E. and Waxler, N. *Interaction in Families*, John Wiley, New York, 1968.

Mittelmann, B. 'Simultaneous Treatment of Both Parents and their Child' in G. Chowski and J. L. Despert (eds.), *Specialised Techniques in Psychotherapy*, Basic Books, New York, 1952.

Moreno, J. L. 'Psychodrama', *American Handbook of Psychiatry*, **2**, 1375–1396.

Mowrer, O. H. *Learning Theory and Personality Dynamics*, Ronald Press, New York, 1950.

Nadelson, C. C. and Paolino, T. J. 'Marital Therapy from a Psychoanalytic Perspective' in T. J. Paolino and B. S. McCrady (eds.), *Marriage and Marital Therapy*, Brunner/Mazel, New York, 1978.

Napier, A. Y. and Whitaker, C. A. *The Family Crucible*, Harper and Row, New York, 1978.

Needleman, J. (ed.) *On the Way to Self-Knowledge*, Knopf, New York, 1976.

O'Leary, K. D. and Turkewitz, J. 'Marital Therapy from a Behavioural Perspective' in T. J. Paolino and B. S. McCrady (eds.), *Marriage and Marital Therapy*, Brunner/Mazel, New York, 1978.

Olson, H., Sprenkle, D. and Russell, C. 'Circumplex Model of Marital and Family Systems', *Family Process*, 18, **1** (1979) 3–21.

Paolino, T. J. and McCrady, B. S. (eds.) *Marriage and Marital Therapy*, Brunner/Mazel, New York, 1978.

Papp, P. *Family Therapy: Full Length Case Studies*, Gardner Press, 1977.

Parsloe, P. 'Families Which Do Not Come to Clinics' in *Child Guidance from Within: Reactions to New Pressures*, Proc. 23rd Interclinic Conf. Nat. Ass. of Mental Health, London, 1967.

Patton, J. D. 'Joint Treatment of Adolescent and Mother', *Dis. Nerv. System*, **18** (1957) 220–222.

Paul, N. L. and Paul, B. B. *A Marital Puzzle*, Norton, New York, 1975.

Pincus, L. (ed.) *Marriage: Studies in Emotional Conflict and Growth*, Methuen, London, 1960.

Pincus, L. and Dare, D. *Secrets in the Family*, Faber, London and Boston, 1978.

Pines, M. 'Group Analytic Psychotherapy of the Borderline Patient', *Group Analysis*, 11, **2** (1978).

 'Psychoanalysis and Group Analysis', *Group Analysis*, 11, **1** (1978) 8–20.

 (Ed.) *The Evolution of Group Analysis*, Routledge and Kegan Paul, London, 1983.

 'The Contribution of S. H. Foulkes to Group Analysis in M. Pines (ed.), *The Evolution of Group Analysis, op. cit.*

Powell, M. B. and Monahan, J. 'Reaching the Rejects through Multi-Family Group Therapy', *Int. J. group Psychother.*, **19** (1969) 35–43.

Prince, G. S. 'A Clinical Approach to Parent-Child Interaction', *J. Child Psychol. Psychiat.*, **2** (1961) 169–184.

Radin, S. S. 'Psychodynamic Aspects of School Phobia', *Compr. Psychiat.*, **8** (1967) 119–128.

Rafferty, F. T., Ingraham, B. and McClure, S. M. 'The Disturbed Child at Home', *J. Nerv. Ment. Dis.*, **142** (1966) 127–139.

Rapoport, R. N. *Community as Doctor*, Tavistock, London, 1960.

Roberts, J. P. 'Foulkes's Concept of the Matrix', *Group Analysis*, XV **2** (1982).

Roberts, W. L. 'Working with the Family Group in a Child Guidance Clinic', *Br. J. Psychiat. Soc. Work*, **9** (1968) 175–179.

Robinson, B. 'Family-Based Therapy', *Br. J. Psychiat. Soc. Work*, **9** (1968) 188–192.

Rodriguez, A., Rodriguez, M. and Eisenberg, L. 'The Outcome of School Phobia: A Follow-Up Study Based on 41 Cases', *Am. J. Psychiat.*, **116** (1959) 540–544.

Rosenbaum, P. 'Patient-Family Similarities in Schizophrenia', *Archs gen. Psychiat.*, **5** (1961) 120–126.

Rosenberg, P. and Chilgren, R. 'Sex Education Discussion Groups in a Medical Setting', *Int. J. Gr. Psych.* **23** (1973) 23.

Rothenberg, J. 'The Archaic Song of Dr Tom the Shaman'. Song 99 in H. Roberts and M. Swadesh (eds.), *Songs of the Nootka Indians of Western Vancouver Island: Transactions of the American Philosophical Society, Vol. 45, Part 3*, Doubleday, New York, 1972.

Rutter, M. and Brown, G. W. 'The Reliability and Validity of Measures of Family Life and Relationships in Families Containing a Psychiatric Patient', *Soc. Psychiat.*, **1** (1966) 38–53.

Rutter, M. and Hersov, L. (eds.) *Child and Adolescent Psychiatry: A Modern Approach*, 2nd edn, Blackwells, 1985.

Ryle, A. *Neurosis in the Ordinary Family*, Tavistock, London, 1967.

Ryle, A. and Breen, D. 'A Comparison of Adjusted and Maladjusted Couples Using the Double Dyad Grid', *Br. J. Med. Psychol.* **45** (1972) 375–383.

Sager, C. *et al.* 'The Treatment of Married Couples' in *American Handbook of Psychiatry, Vol. 3*, Basic Books, New York, 1966.

'An Overview of Family Therapy', *Int. J. Group Psychother.*, **18** (1968) 302–312.

Marriage Contracts and Couple Therapy, Brunner/Mazel, New York, 1976.

Sager, C. *et al.* 'Selection and Engagement of Patients in Family Therapy', *Am. J. Orthopsychiat.*, **38** (1968) 715–723.

Satir, V. *Conjoint Family Therapy*, Science and Behaviour Books, Palo Alto, Ca., 1964.

Schaffer, L. *et al.* 'On the Nature and Sources of the Psychiatrist's Experience With the Family of the Schizophrenic', *Psychiatry*, **25** (1962) 32–45.

Scharff, D. E. *The Sexual Relationship*, Routledge and Kegan Paul, London, 1982.

Scheflen, A. E. 'Explaining Communicative Behaviour: Three Points of View' in N. W. Ackerman, F. L. Beatman and S. N. Sherman (eds.), *Expanding Theory and Practice in Family Therapy*, Family Service Ass. of America, New York, 1967.

Scherz, F. H. 'Multiple-Client Interviewing: Treatment Implications', *Soc. Casework*, **43** (1962) 114–120.

de Shazer, S. *Keys to Solution in Brief Psychotherapy*, Norton, New York, 1985.

Selvini-Palazzoli, M., Boscolo, L., Cecchin, G. and Prata, G. *Paradox and Counterparadox*, Jason Aronson, New York, 1978.

Sifneos, P. E. *Short-term Psychotherapy and Emotional Crisis*, Harvard University Press, Cambridge, Mass., 1972.

Slavson, S. R. *Analytic Group Psychotherapy*, Columbia University Press, New York, 1950.

Sluzki, C. E. 'Marital Therapy from a Systems Theory Perspective' in T. J. Paolino and B. S. McCrady (eds.), *Marriage and Marital Therapy*, Brunner/Mazel, New York, 1978.

Sonne, J. C., Speck, R. V. and Jungreis, J. E. 'The Absent-Member Manoeuvre as a Resistance in Family Therapy of Schizophrenia', *Family Process*, 1 (1962) 44–62.

Sonne, J. C. and Lincoln, G. 'Heterosexual Co-therapy Relationship and its Significance in Family Therapy' in S. Friedman, *Psychotherapy for the Whole Family*, Springer, New York, 1965.

Sperling, M. 'The Neurotic Child and his Mother: A. Psychoanalytic Study', *Am. J. Orthopsychiat.*, 21 (1951) 351–364.

Srole, L., Langer, T. S., Michael, S. T., Opler, M. K. and Rennie, T. A. C. *Mental Health in the Metropolis*, McGraw-Hill, New York, 1962.

Stabenau, J. R., Tupin, J., Werner, M. and Pollin, W. A. 'A Comparative Study of Families of Schizophrenics, Delinquents and Normals', *Psychiatry*, 28 (1965) 45–59.

Steinglass, P. 'The Conceptualization of Marriage from a Systems Theory Perspective' in T. J. Paolino and B. S. McCrady (eds.), *Marriage and Marital Therapy*, Brunner/Mazel, New York, 1978.

Sullivan, H. S. *The Interpersonal Theory of Psychiatry*, Norton, London and New York, 1987.

Szasz, T. S. 'The Communication of Distress between Child and Parent', *Br. J. Med. Psychol.*, 32 (1959) 161–170.

Teruel, G. 'Considerations for a Diagnosis in Marital Psychotherapy', *Br. J. Med. Psychol.*, 39 (1966) 231.

Thompson, J. 'Children's Fears in Relation to School Attendance', *Bull. Nat. Ass. School Soc. Workers* (September 1948).

Treacher, A. and Carpenter, J. (eds). *Using Family Therapy*, Blackwells, 1984.

Van Der Kleij, G. 'The Group and its Matrix, *Group Analysis*, 18, 2 (1985).

Varma, V. P. (ed.) *Psychotherapy Today*, Constable, London, 1974.

Vassilliou, G. A. and Vassilliou, V. G. (eds.), *Family Therapy Evolving*, The Athenian Institute of Anthropos, 1985.

Von Bertalanffy, L. 'The Theory of Open Systems in Physics and Biology', *Science*, 111 (1950) 23–29.

General Systems Theory, Braziller, New York, 1968.

Waldfogel, S., Coolidge, J. C. and Hahn, P. B. 'The Development, Meaning and Management of School Phobia', *Am. J. Orthopsychiat.*, 27 (1957) 754–776.

Walrond-Skinner, S. (ed.) *Family and Marital Psychotherapy: A Critical Approach*, Routledge and Kegan Paul, London, 1979.

419

(ed.) *Developments in Family Therapy*, Routledge and Kegan Paul, 1981.

Warren, W. 'Acute Neurotic Breakdown in Children with Refusal to Go To School', *Archs Dis. Childh.*, **18** (1948) 266–272.

Watzlawick, P., Beavin, J. H. and Jackson, D. D. *Pragmatics of Human Communication*, Norton, New York, 1967.

Watzlawick, P., Weakland, J. and Fisch, R. *Change*, Norton, New York, 1972.

Weiss, R. L. 'The Conceptualization of Marriage from a Behavioural Perspective' in T. J. Paolino and B. S. McCrady (eds.), *Marriage and Marital Therapy*, Brunner/Mazel, New York, 1978.

Welwood, J. (ed.) *Awakening the Heart: East-West Approaches to Psychotherapy and the Healing Relationship*, New Science Library, Boulder, and Routledge and Kegan Paul, London, 1983.

Westley, W. A. and Epstein, N. B. *The Silent Majority*, Jossey-Bass, San Francisco, 1969.

Westman, J. C. *et al.* 'Parallel Group Psychotherapy with the Parents of Emotionally Disturbed Children', *Int. J. Group Psychother.*, **13** (1963) 52–59.

Whiffen, R., and Byng-Hall, J. (eds.) *Family Therapy Supervision: Recent Developments in Practice*, Academic Press, London, 1982.

Whitaker, D. S. and Lieberman, M. A. *Psychotherapy through the Group Process*, Atherton Press, New York, 1964.

Whitehead, A. N. and Russell, B. *Principia Mathematica*, Cambridge University Press, 1910.

Will, D. and Wrate, M. *Integrated Family Therapy: A Problem-Centred Psychodynamic Approach*, Tavistock, London, 1985.

Winnicott, D. W. 'Primary Maternal Preoccupation' in *Collected Papers: Through Paediatrics to Psychoanalysis*, Tavistock, London, 1958.

'The Effect of Psychotic Parents on the Emotional Development of the Child', *Br. J. Psychiat. Social Work*, **6** (1961) 13–20.

'Clinical Study of the Effect of a Failure of the Average Expectable Environment on a Child's Mental Functioning', *Int. J. Psychoanal.*, **46** (1965) 81–87.

Therapeutic Consultations in Child Psychiatry, Hogarth Press, London, 1971.

Wolff, A, 'The Psychoanalysis of Groups', *Am. J. Psych.* **3**, 15–16; **4**, 523–558.

Yalom, I. D. *The Theory and Practice of Group Psychotherapy* (2nd edition), Basic Books, New York, 1975.

Zeeman, E. C. 'Catastrophe Theory', *Scientific American*, **236** (1978) 65–83.

Zuk, G. H. 'The Side-Taking Function in Family Therapy', *Am. J. Orthopsychiat.*, **38** (1968) 553–559.

'When the Family Therapist Takes Sides: A Case Report', *Psychother.*, **5** (1968) 24–28.

'Family Therapy: Formulation of a Technique and its Theory', *Int. J. Group Psychother.*, **18** (1968) 42–58.

Zuk, G. H. and Rubinstein, D. 'A Review of Concepts in the Study and Treatment of Families of Schizophrenics' in I. Boszormenyi-Nagy and J. L. Framo (eds.), *Intensive Family Therapy*, Hoeber, New York, 1965.

Author Index

423

Author Index

Author Index

425

Author Index

Subject Index

427

Subject Index

Subject Index

Subject Index